The Image of
Librarians in Cinema,
1917–1999

The Image of Librarians in Cinema, 1917–1999

RAY TEVIS *and* BRENDA TEVIS

McFarland & Company, Inc., Publishers
Jefferson, North Carolina, and London

LIBRARY OF CONGRESS CATALOGUING-IN-PUBLICATION DATA

Tevis, Ray.
The image of librarians in cinema, 1917–1999 / Ray Tevis and Brenda Tevis.
p.   cm.
Includes bibliographical references and index.

ISBN 0-7864-2150-9 (softcover : 50# alkaline paper) ∞

1. Librarians in motion pictures.   2. Libraries in motion pictures.
I. Tevis, Brenda.   II. Title.
PN1995.9.L49T48 2005   791.43'65202—dc22   2004029517

British Library cataloguing data are available

On the cover: Helen Twelvetrees (left) and
Blanche Frederici in *Young Bride* (1932)

Manufactured in the United States of America

McFarland & Company, Inc., Publishers
Box 611, Jefferson, North Carolina 28640
www.mcfarlandpub.com

In memory of grandparents
Raymond and Verna Tevis
who enabled Ray to attend
Saturday and Sunday matinees at the Liberty Theater
in their hometown of Vandalia, Illinois

Acknowledgments

Our sincere thanks to Doris Walker Cox, who has provided encouragement and enthusiastic support for this project continuously since 1978, the first time we discussed the subject of "reel" librarians. Also, our thanks to Norman D. Stephens, who invited Ray to present some of his ideas about librarians in motion pictures at the Library History Round Table session "Images of Librarianship: What Collecting Librariana Can Tell Us About Library History," 1982 American Library Association Conference, in Philadelphia.

In 1981, fourteen library science graduate students at Ball State University—Vicki Addison, Judith Block, Karen Bloom, Debra Fitzpatrick, Joyce Jarrett, John Kihlstrom, Jill Manis, Jane Potee, Sarah Rines, Davonne Rogers, Jane Schmottlach, Janice Stricker, Mara Swanson, and Marcia Winscott—participated in Ray's class "The 'Reel' Librarian." After each showing of eight films dating from 1932's *No Man of Her Own* to 1978's *Foul Play*, students discussed and evaluated the role and image of the librarian in the films. These discussions provided a myriad of ideas and insights that influenced the development of several concepts relating to the stereotypical image of librarians. In addition to these fourteen students, Susan Bayley, Kathleen Dykstra, Elaine Mathews, Jo Ellen Porter, and Teresa Rice completed graduate papers that focused on the image of librarians in motion pictures.

Several individuals provided invaluable assistance on specific tasks: Jennifer Morris assisted with the text of several plays at the New York Public Library for the Performing Arts; Margie Stites and Cathy Chung provided second opinions on several films; and Emalie Wiley, an Arizona licensed cosmetologist, assisted with the identification of all hairstyles.

The authors must thank the staffs at the following libraries for outstanding reference assistance: Margaret Herrick Library, Academy of Motion Picture Arts and Sciences; Archive Research and Study Center, UCLA Film and Television Archives; UCLA Arts Library; USC Warner Bros. Archives; and USC Cinema-Television Library. The authors also extend a special thanks to archivist Ned Comstock at USC's

Cinema-Television Library, whose reference assistance and attention to detail is unequalled, and to Claire at Eddie Brandt's Saturday Matinee in North Hollywood, whose assistance with photographs is greatly appreciated.

Staff members at several Phoenix area libraries provided exemplary service. Especially helpful in locating and obtaining print materials for the authors were Carole Towles and her entire staff at the Interlibrary Loan Center, Phoenix Public Library, and Charlie Smith, Interlibrary Loan, Arizona State Library, Archives and Public Records.

Contents

Preface

As librarians, the authors are keenly aware of the stereotypical image of librarians and the angst it creates. Although it engenders and energizes lively discussions among librarians, the image appears immune to change. It has remained relatively static throughout the twentieth century, and just as the book, for which librarians are caretakers, has remained static in format for centuries, it is unlikely that the image of librarians will undergo any precipitous change.

Our focus is the stereotypical image of twentieth century librarians in motion pictures, primarily in American and British films but also in several Australian and Canadian films that were released theatrically in the United States between 1917 and 1999. Because of the scope of this subject, not every film with a reel librarian is included in our discussion. In addition, the following categories of film are not considered: historical adventure–drama films; adult sexually explicit (erotica) films; prison dramas with inmates or security officers portraying librarians; science fiction and fantasy films (with non–twentieth century reel librarians); made-for-TV films; and direct-to-video films. Films that were presented at film festivals but not subsequently released to theaters are designated as direct-to-video films. In the case of several motion pictures, the theatrical release status could not be ascertained; the authors include in their discussion a minimal number of these films.

In surveying reel librarians, the authors include the total character of the librarian as emphasized in the film—for example, personal attributes, socio-economic conditions, and entanglements with the opposite sex. Critical comments relating to the overall quality of each film are limited; in some instances, the authors refer to the opinions of film critics.

The films of the twentieth century contributed significantly to the development and then to the continuation of the image, primarily because every generation during the century attended movie theaters in great numbers. During every decade, filmmakers provided filmgoers the opportunity to see actors portraying librarians. One reel librarian wearing eyeglasses and sporting a bun hairstyle appeared in a 1921 film; two years later, in 1923, the old age of a librarian—she was 38—was the focus of a film.

The depiction of librarians in sound films began quite ominously. Within the first three minutes of *Forbidden* (1932), two youngsters watching librarian Lulu Smith (Barbara Stanwyck) arrive for work yell at her from across the street, "Old lady foureyes! Old lady foureyes!" This opening salvo in the first sound film to feature a librarian, to a great extent, defines the image of librarians in sound films. The depiction remains intact, but rather than assailing the image in such a verbally abusive manner, filmmakers approach the image with explicit emphasis on visual characteristics—for example, appearing elderly and wearing eyeglasses.

Reel librarians from the 1930s through the 1990s mirrored many of the same fundamental traits, creating and perpetuating a stereotype that filmgoers recognize instantly. Many filmmakers simply used this stereotypical image, which, for all practical purposes, is a convenient commodity that can be projected on screen with minimal effort. However, a small number of filmmakers rejected this image and depicted librarians in a manner that even working librarians applauded.

To delineate the progression of the cinematic depiction of librarians, the authors begin with the silent era and proceed to the twenty-first century. A majority of the films from the silent era are lost, and a great number of the films from the first three decades of sound films, the 1930s to the 1950s, are difficult to locate or are also lost. At some time in the future, many of the films designated as "lost" may be recovered and, consequently, may revise some of our present assumptions. The extant films from these decades, however, provide a sufficient number of reel librarians to discern the attitude of filmmakers toward librarians and their occupation. One problem the authors encountered with these films is the lack of complete cast credits; reel librarians in supporting roles are often not identified. Later in the century, however, filmmakers included everyone in the cast list; oftentimes in these films, the authors could not identify the librarian in the film, even though an actor received credit for the role. The authors detail more extensively the films that feature a reel librarian in a leading role and the films that are most difficult to locate and view—those from the silent era and the 1930s, 1940s, and 1950s. The majority of films, but most certainly not every film, from the last four decades of the twentieth century is available.

1

Reel Librarians in Silent Films, 1917–1928

During the early decades of the twentieth century, American communities were constructing libraries across the country, primarily as a result of the benevolence— more than $45 million—of Andrew Carnegie, to provide residents with books and a place to educate themselves. At the same time, the film industry was constructing theaters (motion picture palaces in large metropolitan areas and small, less ornate movie houses in other cities) and producing motion pictures to placate the insatiable public appetite and demand for entertainment.

As film companies required an inexhaustible supply of stories and ideas for their productions, it was inevitable that librarians, as well as other occupational classes, would appear as screen characters in some of these productions. The process of defining and establishing the characteristics of reel librarians in silent films began in 1917 with *A Wife on Trial* and ended in 1929 with *The Spirit of Youth*. During this thirteen-year period, reel librarians displayed many of the visual characteristics and occupational tasks that film librarians of the sound era would not only duplicate but also greatly exaggerate, creating the stereotypical image that remains widely and easily recognizable.

The first silent film to feature a librarian, *A Wife on Trial* (1917),[1] was based on Margaret Widdemer's best-selling romance novel of 1915, *The Rose-Garden Husband*. Leo Pierson adapted Widdemer's novel for the screen and his storyline parallels Widdemer's novel rather accurately; the aberrations that occur are minor and innocuous. Pierson, in addition to writing the screenplay, appears as Allan Harrington, the male lead in the film. Mignon Anderson[2] stars as librarian Phyllis Narcissa Braithwaite, the film's leading female role.

A Wife on Trial was directed and produced by Ruth Ann Baldwin, one of Hollywood's early feminist writers, directors, and producers. She received a favorable comment for her work on this film from one reviewer: "[Baldwin] is to be congratulated upon the artistic presentation of this story...." He labeled the picture a "cheerful, Pollyanna type" that "will please the average audience immensely."[3]

Phyllis, a 25-year-old children's librarian, works in a public library and receives the respect of the children who enjoy the attention and care that she bestows upon them. They respond by calling her "the teacher with the pretty smile" and "the lib'ry teacher."[4]

On her librarian's salary, Phyllis has few dollars for discretionary spending, but she constantly dreams of a rose garden—a bed of roses similar to what she had while growing up with her parents (now deceased) in New England. A rose garden is now beyond her humble lifestyle. A wealthy elderly couple, Mr. and Mrs. Horace de Guenther (L. M. Wells and Julia Jackson), had met and befriended Phyllis when she began working in the library, several years before she became a children's librarian. She was a frequently invited guest and diner at the de Guenthers'; they were so enthralled by the charm of Phyllis that they invited her to live with them, but she had refused.

One day, Mr. de Guenther enters the Children's Department and invites Phyllis to dinner. During Phyllis' visit to the de Guenthers, they offer her an opportunity to leave the library for money, a rose garden, and a husband. The de Guenthers ask Phyllis to marry and care for Allan Harrington, whose legs are paralyzed, confining him to a wheelchair. Allan's paralysis began after a serious automobile accident for which he was directly responsible and which resulted in the death of his fiancée. The Harrington family is wealthy, and Allan's mother prefers to find someone like Phyllis to marry and care for Allan rather than hire a nurse. This is an urgent matter, as she is elderly, ill, and near death.

Phyllis promises the de Guenthers that she will seriously consider this proposal. Upon returning to the boardinghouse where she lives, Phyllis is accosted by a tenant who lives on the same floor, a "masher" whose obnoxious behavior is more offensive than on earlier encounters. This event, coupled with the advantages of wealth, including the acquisition of the long-dreamed-about rose garden, provides the incentive for Phyllis to accept the proposition. She marries Allan within the week, shortly before his mother dies.

As a librarian, Phyllis' wardrobe is meager but serviceable. Now as Mrs. Harrington, she has the time and funds to obtain a fashionable wardrobe and refresh her appearance; she is an attractive brunette who enjoys her marriage and all of its accoutrements.[5]

Although Allan and Phyllis enter their marriage as a convenience for both—he for the care and she for the rose garden, the couple begin a relationship that ends with love but not without misfortune. Allan enjoys the companionship and comfort that Phyllis extends, but he becomes so jealous when he misinterprets her conversations with one of his college friends, Dr. John Hewitt (uncredited), that he suggests the marriage be annulled. Phyllis agrees but only reluctantly. Before the annulment occurs, however, Phyllis, walking in the early evening, is followed home and attacked at the entry door by her old nemesis, the masher from the boardinghouse. While she is screaming for help, Allan manages to stand and walk a few steps to help his valet Wallis (George C. Pearce) subdue the assailant. Allan realizes that his paralysis is primarily mental, rather than physical, and that he can overcome his self-induced seven-year-long paralytic affliction. The incident reinforces their love and commitment to one another.

A Wife on Trial portrays Phyllis as a poorly paid, hard-working librarian with a work ethic that continues in marriage; she showers her attention upon Allan instead of the children who enjoyed her stories. The decision to leave the library was made quickly; the luxury associated with the marriage was more than she could ever hope to obtain if she remained at the library. Phyllis marries not for the love of a man but for the vision of a better life. Over time, however, the couple develop a love for one another, and the film has an upbeat, happy ending.

Phyllis is the first reel librarian to appear in a sequel film, *The Wishing Ring Man* (1919),[6] which is based on Widdemer's 1917 romance novel with the same title.[7] The storyline occurs approximately seven years later than *A Wife on Trial* and focuses on the romantic complexities between Joy Havenith (Bessie Love) and Dr. John Hewitt (J. Frank Glendon), the college friend of Harrington who appeared as a supporting character in *A Wife on Trial*. The Harringtons, portrayed this time by Dorothy Hagan[8] and Colin Kenney, and their two children are supporting characters. Phyllis' previous occupation as librarian, in all probability, was neither evident nor mentioned in the film.[9]

Two years after Phyllis appeared as the first reel librarian, *A Very Good Young Man* (1919)[10] featured a male library employee as its leading character. The movie, based on Martin Brown's Broadway play with the same title, is a romantic comedy and stars popular actor Bryant Washburn,[11] a handsome, dimpled chinned, 30-year-old leading man who excelled in this genre. Washburn is LeRoy Sylvester,[12] a screen character who, as one reviewer observed, "is too good to be true, so good that even his best girl won't marry him. 'Go out and be naughty,' she says to him, and Bryant starts with results that kept the crowd ... hilarious for an hour."[13]

LeRoy works at a public library and his moral character is above reproach, prompting his girlfriend's mother to argue that men who do not frolic and philander before marriage will certainly do so after marriage. His girlfriend, Ruth Douglas (Helene Chadwick), refuses to marry him because of her mother's objections, telling him that "all good men break out after marriage. Grandfather flirted, father gambles and uncle drinks. I don't trust you; you are too good."[14] If LeRoy is to marry Ruth, he must soil his exemplary moral character in order to eliminate the objections voiced by her mother, his future mother-in-law.

LeRoy progresses through a series of adventures, actually misadventures, to soil his reputation. The plans he devises to corrupt his moral character are simple and straightforward. The implementation of each plan goes awry, leaving LeRoy's angelic reputation intact. One of his plans is to get arrested for gambling. Before going into a gambling hall, he telephones the police, expecting to be arrested when the police raid the establishment. Before the police arrive, however, he wins a great deal of money and the proprietor pays him to leave. Later, when the police finally catch up with LeRoy, they thank him for tipping them off about the location of the gambling hall. This effort is representative of his inability to soil his reputation and his ineptitude in carrying out a simple plan. When LeRoy confesses his failures to Ruth, she agrees to marry him, even though his moral character remains unblemished.

In the Broadway play LeRoy worked at a brass bed factory while in the film he is a librarian. LeRoy's change of occupation is justifiable, especially if the rationale for change was that such an exemplary moral lifestyle is more convincingly portrayed by a librarian.[15]

The first two reel librarians—Phyllis Harrington and LeRoy Sylvester—establish several important characteristics that will continue to be associated with reel librarians. Phyllis portrays a competent and talented children's librarian whose efforts are appreciated by the library's young patrons. LeRoy, however, demonstrates a propensity for ineptitude in non-library situations, a characteristic that both men and women reel librarians will emulate with similar comedic results in future films. Both reel librarians are young and attractive, and both seek marriage. Phyllis establishes a behavioral pattern that becomes a common theme in motion pictures with reel librarians throughout the twentieth century—single woman librarian leaves library employment for love, marriage, or both.

A year later, 1920, the first of two silent film versions of Emerson Hough's 1917 novel about life in a small town, *The Broken Gate*, was released; the second version appeared in early 1927. Both pictures retained the novel's title[16] and reviews indicate that both pictures followed Hough's storyline.

The novel and films narrate the soap opera life of Aurora Lane (Bessie Barriscale in the 1920 release, and Dorothy Phillips in the 1927 release), Spring Valley's milliner who, twenty years earlier, had a son and refused to identify the father. The young boy was sent away immediately; he was never told the name of either his mother or his father. His room, board, schooling, and college expenses were scraped together by his mother and the town's librarian (identified as Julia Delafield and portrayed by Evelyn Selbie[17] in the 1920 release, and identified as Julia Fisher and portrayed by Florence Turner[18] in the 1927 release[19]), who assumed the role of the boy's aunt. After graduating from college, Aurora's son travels to Spring Valley to visit Julia, and during this visit, he learns that Aurora is his mother. The townspeople of Spring Valley are upset about the developing relationship between Aurora and the young man, as the town's residents do not know that they are mother and son. Aurora's son is accused of a murder but escapes prosecution when the village's mentally retarded youngster admits that he committed the murder.

Wid's Daily, commenting on the 1920 film, stated that "Hough's story is such an uninteresting affair" containing "a lot of unpleasant occurrences, many of them implausible and ... lacking in real dramatic strength."[20] *Variety* echoed similar reservations about the 1927 release: "A tiresome picture about the small town lives of small and mean people ... even after it gets into melodramatic speed ... it does not grip.... It will have to be a pretty dumb fan clientele that will take the picture seriously."[21]

Julia is a supporting role in both films; the two actors who portrayed Julia were over 40 years of age. An adaptation of the 1927 screen presentation described Julia's physical appearance and life: "Her face was pale, her chest hollow, her hair scraggy—and besides that she was lame. No man had ever wanted her. She spent her life marking down dates in the back of books and handing them across the counter of the Spring Valley Public Library."[22] Julia, in both films, continues the role of the poorly paid, hard-working reel librarian established in earlier films. She is physically handicapped and treated as contemptuously as Aurora by the residents of Spring Valley. She demonstrates unselfish compassion for Aurora's son, assisting with the finances needed to support him and to send him through college.

In 1921, two years after LeRoy Sylvester appeared on movie screens, another male librarian, but one with a very blemished moral character, appeared in director John Ford's western *The Freeze-Out* (1921).[23] The film stars noted western actor Harry Carey as Ohio, the Stranger, who soon after arriving in Broken Buckle is busily battling the town's entrenched criminal element. His intent is to open a gambling house, but he abandons the project in favor of establishing a school and library in the building. The Stranger selects Bobtail McGuire (J. Farrell MacDonald[24]), Broken Buckle's perennial town drunk, to be librarian. One reviewer was very harsh on the film: "It has no excuse in a picture theatre accustomed to program features of merit.... For a group of actors to participate in a picture that does nothing more than try to imitate some of the early Hart pictures ... invites failure." The same reviewer, however, managed to find and praise one bright spot in the film: "It was MacDonald who romped away with the acting honors as the town drunk. A better screen interpretation of a man saturated with wood hootch hasn't been seen in a long time."[25] Evidently, the most entertaining moments of this picture dealt with the antics of an alcoholic who is elevated to the position of Broken Buckle's librarian by the Stranger, the town's newest resident. Obviously this situation added a comedic touch to the film, and this type of happening—town drunk appointed to a high civic position, most often sheriff[26]— is a familiar scenario of the western film genre.

A month after the appearance of *The Freeze-Out*, director William DeMille's picture, *The Lost Romance* (1921),[27] was released. The film follows the romance of librarian Sylvia Hayes (Lois Wilson[28]). Sylvia receives two proposals of marriage, accepting the proposal of a young physician, Allen Erskine (Conrad Nagel), and rejecting the offer of a young explorer, Mark Sheridan (Jack Holt). Over the next six years, Sylvia and Allen have a child, but slowly the romance of the marriage disappears. When Mark returns from a six-year trip to Africa, he and Sylvia rekindle the spark of their earlier romance and inform Allen of their love. Allen agrees to permit Sylvia to leave him, but Allen's aunt, Elizabeth Erskine (Fontaine La Rue), in an attempt to keep the couple together, arranges for the young boy to disappear for a short period of time. Unaware that the boy is safe, Allen and Sylvia believe their son has been kidnapped and is in danger. Upon the return of their son, Allen and Sylvia recognize that no real threat existed, but having shared moments together while believing their son was in danger, they realize that they are truly in love and their romance is very much alive.

Sylvia appears in one library scene.[29] Standing on a three-step ladder shelving books, she is daydreaming about her vacation which starts the next day. Rather than shelving books, she is listening intently to Elizabeth telling stories to the library's young patrons. While Sylvia listens to Elizabeth's stories, she fails to notice that several adults have formed a line at the library desk, all wanting to exchange books. The library supervisor (Mayme Kelso[30]), alarmed at the number of patrons requiring service, goes for Sylvia, motioning to the patrons that they will be served momentarily. Sylvia, seeing the librarian, begins to shelve books more quickly; she puts one book

The Lost Romance (1921). Mayme Kelso (left) is the librarian-in-charge and Lois Wilson (right) is librarian Sylvia Hayes. Kelso is the first reel librarian to appear in eyeglasses and bun, while Wilson is the first to use a ladder. (Photograph courtesy of Cinema-Television Library, USC.)

upside down on the shelf and corrects her mistake when the librarian tells her to do so. Sylvia steps down from the stool, and the librarian informs her, "Your vacation doesn't begin until tomorrow, Miss Hayes." Sylvia lowers her head and goes to the desk to assist the adults who are awaiting service.

When Elizabeth finishes her stories, she goes to the desk, telling Sylvia, "You've earned a good vacation, my dear. I hope you'll enjoy it." Sylvia admits that she has no money for a vacation, stating that "a vacation with nothing to do isn't very romantic." Elizabeth invites Sylvia to visit her home, where she meets Allen and Mark, both of whom fall in love with her. Sylvia's library career ends when she accepts Allen's proposal of marriage.

Sylvia, as previous reel librarians, is hard working but has little money. She is single, definitely dreaming of romance, and manages to obtain two proposals of marriage at Elizabeth's. An attractive brunette (multi-pincurl bang; finger waves across top, probably a bun at nape), Sylvia wears a long sleeve blouse, sailor collar with bow, and long skirt. The bespectacled supervisor, a brunette (finger waves in front; bun at nape) more than two decades older than Sylvia, dresses modestly, wearing dark clothing with a standing collar. DeMille establishes a precedent in *The Lost Romance* that becomes standard cinematic treatment for two women reel librarians in the same scene—the actress in the leading role is young and attractive, while the second librarian, a supporting actress, is middle-aged and spinsterish in appearance.

Three months later, director Lois Weber's film *The Blot* (1921) opened to mixed reviews. One film historian refers to Weber as "the most important woman director of the silent era."[31] Weber wrote, directed, and produced *The Blot*,[32] one of her many films of the 1920s. Weber's films are thematic, dealing with social issues—birth control, abortion, racial prejudice, capital punishment, and other sensitive and controversial topics. *The Blot* specifically details the inadequacy of salaries for college professors, but its message is applicable to all public service occupations. Phil West (Louis Calhern), a wealthy student, clarifies the title of the film when stating to his father, a college trustee, that "it is a 'blot' on the present day civilization that we expect to engage the finest mental equipment for a less wage than we pay the commonest labor." Phil also confronts his father with the inevitable rhetorical question: "Why are we so niggardly with our teachers?"

The film focuses on the family of a college faculty member, Professor Griggs (Philip Hubbard), whose pitiful salary barely sustains his family. The professor's daughter, Amelia (Claire Windsor[33]), works in the local public library; her salary as a librarian makes no discernible impact on the family's finances.[34]

Amelia, the leading female character, is a striking young brunette (pincurls with finger waves) who wears the same long-sleeve white blouse, V-neckline, in all library scenes, indicating her minimal wardrobe and the stringent finances of the family. A second librarian (uncredited[35]) at the public desk is a middle-aged brunette and, like Amelia, she repeatedly appears in the same dark high-neck long-sleeve blouse. The cinematic pattern of an attractive actress in major role working with nondescript actress in supporting role appears here as well.

Amelia and her coworker are occupied with a variety of tasks while working at the main desk—answering the telephone, checking out books, assisting patrons in

The Blot (1921). Louis Calhern (left, as Phil West), a wealthy college student, visits the public library frequently to talk with Claire Windsor (right front, as Amelia Griggs), a poor librarian with whom he has fallen in love. The actress in the background is not identified.

the stacks, and providing reference service. A large SILENCE sign is prominently displayed at the main desk, but there are no indications that the maintenance of silence is a problem for the librarians. Both women appear extremely competent, undoubtedly the image that Weber wanted to project. Weber uses the library as a public institution where librarians have the opportunity to meet and exchange pleasantries with members of the opposite sex, encounters that may eventually lead to romantic involvement.

Phil is enamored with Amelia and visits the library almost daily to meet and speak with her. As a pretense for these subtle romantic overtures, he claims to be an avid reader, thereby necessitating frequent library visits to return and check out books. During one visit, Phil highly praises the book he is returning; Amelia opens the book and separates the pages that she had deliberately pasted together to determine if he was reading the books. Phil, whose advances are spurned by Amelia, realizes that he has been caught in her trap and remarks, "It's the only way I can get to talk to you. You never have time for a fellow unless it's on business." Weber lightened the overall serious tone of the film by occasionally injecting such humorous touches. Using humor in a library scene is a technique that future screenwriters and directors would expand to heighten romantic tension between women, most often the librarians, and men. Such situations present the opportunity for both comedic physical stunts and sharp, witty verbal exchanges that entertain.

Dejected by Amelia's apparent lack of interest, Phil leaves the library, and an afternoon shower begins as he walks to his automobile. He puts the top on his convertible and then waits for Amelia to leave the library. Working in a cold draft in the library, a result of the doors opening and closing all day, Amelia is feeling ill. When she exits the building, Phil rushes to her and offers to take her home. She initially refuses but relents and joins him. During the ride, Phil notices Amelia's attempt to cover her gloves—they are worn out and open at the fingertips—and that her shoes are extremely worn and lacking proper soles. Weber incorporated these minute visual details, and many others throughout the film, to illustrate the monetary hardships confronting the Griggs family.

The film ends without clearly stating that Amelia will marry Phil and leave her library position, but as the last scene begins to fade, Amelia's facial expression is optimistic as she enters the family home, strongly suggesting that she and Phil will marry.[36] The progression of events—single attractive woman works in a respectable occupation, meets handsome man and falls in love, and as the film ends, she marries and leaves her occupation—becomes a standard narrative for reel librarians, a simple storyline providing innumerable variations and complexities over the decades.

Only 38 (1923)[37] was released two years after The Blot and features a woman librarian, Mrs. Stanley (Lois Wilson[38]). William DeMille directed the film, the second in which he directed Wilson as a reel librarian. Based on A. E. Thomas' Broadway play with the same title,[39] the film parallels the play with some deviations; the major change is the inclusion of academic library scenes in the motion picture. These changes, however, do not affect Thomas' storyline. Lewis F. Levenson stated in reviewing this film, "Every one of William de Mille's pictures stands out like starry diamonds among a mess of rhinestones in the tray of this year's pictures. 'Only 38' is no exception ... it offers ... intelligent entertainment for intelligent and mature movie fans."[40]

Only 38 focuses on 38-year-old Mrs. Stanley whose husband, a clergyman, recently died and whose teenage twins, Robert and Lucy (Robert Agnew and May McAvoy), are just entering Sinclair College. Mrs. Stanley married a minister 23 years her senior when she was 18. She lived a very spartan life as a minister's wife but now desires to jettison the matronly middle-aged image that she has endured since the birth of her children. She begins this transformation by dressing in colorful clothing and by discarding familiar, old, drab household items. She obtains a position at the college library, primarily for the additional money but with the secondary purpose of establishing a life of her own. She meets and falls in love with Charles Giddings (Elliott Dexter), a professor of English literature.

Robert and Lucy, appalled at their mother's actions, reject the transformation and insist that she act her age and maintain the same atmosphere and environment that existed when their father was living. The twins want the mother of their childhood, not a mother who is attempting to reestablish her individualism, which was

Only 38 (1923). Elliott Dexter (as Professor Charles Giddings) meets Lois Wilson (as Mrs. Stanley) in the college library; this chance meeting leads to romance. The actress at the table is not identified. (Photograph courtesy of Cinema-Television Library, USC.)

subjugated during her 20-year marriage, and who is attempting to recapture some of the enjoyment of living that she missed because of an early marriage. Mrs. Stanley is not egocentric; she is willing to abide by the wishes of her children and to forgo her budding relationship with Giddings, as well as anything else that might come between her and the twins. Mrs. Stanley's commitment to her children is evident in her remark, "I'm just beginning to enjoy life—but rather than lose the confidence of my children, I'd give it all up."

Professor Giddings attempts to persuade the twins to give their mother an opportunity to be herself. If Mrs. Stanley reverts back to the mother that the twins desire, her budding romantic involvement with Giddings will end; the professor's self-interest is evident—he does not want to lose the love of Mrs. Stanley. The twins respond negatively to his arguments, but after reflecting on his discussion, they realize that they must support their mother.

This film is about Mrs. Stanley's attempt to recapture at least part of her missed youth, achieve her independence, and realize her potential as an individual. Although Mrs. Stanley is engaged in library work, the emphasis of *Only 38* is her struggle to become an independent woman. Several factors in the film are important to the image of reel librarians. For example, Robert and Lucy believe that their mother is old, failing to realize that "only 38" is an age at which their mother could be vibrant, full of fun and giddiness, intoxicated with love, and looking forward to many years of happiness and love with them and with a new husband. They demonstrate that "only 38" is considered elderly by young people; consequently, Mrs. Stanley and all the other adults at Sinclair College are old. Throughout the twentieth century, the majority of reel librarians, especially those in supporting roles, will be afflicted with this "only 38" characteristic. These reel librarians are portrayed as middle-aged or older, a stigmatization of librarians that begins the first time individuals, when as children, enter a library and encounter an adult librarian, an "only 38" person. In the library, Mrs. Stanley reinforces the "only 38" characteristic; she is a graying brunette (finger waves; jelly roll bun at nape) and wears a long sleeve button-front blouse that has a Dutch collar, with a fob watch pinned at her breast and a dark skirt.

The film also introduces the tall library ladder as a climbing device for reel librarians to reach high shelves in stack areas while assisting patrons.[41] Mrs. Stanley climbs a ladder to locate information for Professor Giddings, and director DeMille handles the scene tastefully. Giddings does not ogle the ankles and calves of Mrs. Stanley. Such activity—males leering at the ankles and calves of women librarians on library ladders—occurs for the first time nine years later in *No Man of Her Own* (1932).

The college library provides respectable employment for a widow with two college students; the library also presents the opportunity for Mrs. Stanley to meet Giddings, resulting in a romantic spark between them. Weber used a similar scenario in *The Blot*—single woman finds romance while working in a library.

The Blot and *Only 38* depict reel librarians who find romance during the course of their employment. Amelia is besieged by Phil's visits to the public library, while Mrs. Stanley welcomes the opportunity to assist Professor Giddings. Neither reel librarian exhibits aggressive behavior in these romantic episodes. These two films, however, develop romantic situations in libraries that involve reel librarians and establish the type of romantic behavior that filmgoers may anticipate from future reel librarians.

The best known silent actress to appear as a reel librarian was Pola Negri[42] in *Lily of the Dust* (1924).[43] The film features Negri as Lily Czepanek, a young, attractive brunette (half-bang; finger waves; spit curls on side) who works in a lending library in a small German village that houses an army garrison. The militia's young officers are attracted to the lovely and charming Lily until the commanding officer, Colonel Mertzbach (Noah Beery), visits the library to uncover the cause of his men's sudden interest in reading. The colonel is attracted to Lily and quickly displaces Lieutenant Prell (Ben Lyon), a young officer who has fallen in love with Lily. The colonel and Lily marry; she leaves the lending library to accept the trimmings associated with his military position and his wealth. They honeymoon in Berlin, where Lily's beauty captures the attention of young men, stirring the colonel to intense jealously. At their honeymoon hotel, the colonel catches Lily and Prell in an embrace in the corridor, resulting in a duel between the two men.

Lily's problem, as one reviewer observed, is "her eyes and fatal beauty. She does not flirt. Men flirt with her, and she, in entertaining them, falls into trouble."[44] Lily demonstrates that women reel librarians can be young and extremely attractive, as do Sylvia in *The Lost Romance* and Amelia in *The Blot*. Lily, as Phyllis in *A Wife on Trial*, is not hesitant about marriage as a means to improve her social and economic position. Lily may not be flirtatious, but she projects a sexual aura and personality that, when coupled with her beautiful eyes, unleashes everyman's flirtatious behavior.

One of the silent era's most noted directors, Rex Ingram, wrote and directed *The Magician* (1926), which includes a brief scene in "The Library of the Arsenal." Oliver Haddo (Paul Wegener), the magician, has just found an ancient formula that he has spent months attempting to locate. The formula outlines "the secret of the creation of human life by magic," which he desperately needs in his endeavors to create life. The magician rips the page from the volume, and as he leaves the library, Haddo stops at the service desk to inform Dr. Porhoet (Firmin Gémier), a physician and rival who disapproves of Haddo's activities, that the formula is not in the volume.

Before the interruption by Haddo, however, Porhoet receives assistance from a middle-aged male librarian (uncredited[45]) with a receding hairline who dresses conservatively—dark jacket over a high, stiff collar white shirt. After retrieving a card from a cabinet behind the desk for Porhoet, the librarian is very animated during his discussion with Porhoet, suggesting that he is providing his best reference service. Another middle-aged librarian (uncredited[46]), a woman wearing a dark dress with a scoop neckline, remains seated behind the desk, turning pages that she is reading or examining. As she picks up the pages and begins shuffling them into order, the scene fades.

The male librarian in this scene is portrayed as helpful and efficient; his coworker is busily attending to desk responsibilities. Both librarians are middle-aged and wear conservative business-like attire. Director Ingram presents reel librarians who are efficiently performing their desk duties.

The last silent film to feature a librarian is director Walter Lang's *The Spirit of Youth* (1929).[47] The film focuses on the adventures of Sailor Jim Kenney (Larry Kent), a fleet boxer who likes village librarian Betty Grant (Dorothy Sebastian[48]). When he goes to sea, Jim promises to write regularly. Four years later, however, Jim becomes middleweight champion and falls in love with a wealthy heiress. In a charity exhibition bout promoted by the heiress, Jim temporarily loses his eyesight during the fight because of resin on the glove of his sparring partner and is knocked out. The heiress deserts him, leaving Grant to pick up the pieces of a once proud man. The love between the librarian and the sailor whom she has always loved is rekindled. After he stages a successful ring comeback, Jim and Betty are reunited.

Sebastian, a former Ziegfeld girl, undoubtedly portrayed Grant as an attractive, young librarian. In addition, Grant maintained the poor economic status of librarians, a characteristic that remained constant throughout the silent era.

The silent picture era ended in the late 1920s, quickly yielding to the demand for sound pictures. The silent era, although brief, featured several reel librarians, including portrayals by such notable actors as Negri, Washburn, and Wilson, as well as by numerous supporting actors. In most cases, these films presented librarians as poorly paid and hard-working individuals; reel librarians were primarily individuals from the ranks of the lower to middle economic stratum, the working class. The only avenue of escape from economic problems for these reel librarians was marriage. Some reel librarians were recipients of romantic overtures, which eventually resulted in opportunities to leave the occupation. In most cases, the women librarians involved in these romantic interludes unhesitatingly abandoned the inadequate remuneration of library employment for love or marriage, a move which definitely improved their economic well-being.

Reel librarians in major roles were single and attractive. Many of these librarians demonstrated a keen intellect, a commitment to providing excellent public service, a talent to excel in various job responsibilities, a moral and social conscience that demanded honesty of them, and the extension of a helping hand to the less fortunate. On occasion, women reel librarians were from homes that provided a degree of intellectualism; for example, Phyllis' father was a minister (*A Wife on Trial*), Amelia's father was a college professor (*The Blot*), and Mrs. Stanley's husband of twenty years was a minister (*Only 38*).

During the silent era, actors and directors portrayed reel librarians in a positive, commendable manner, demonstrating a respect for the occupation. Silent films established not only a multitude of visual characteristics and occupational tasks for reel librarians but also a variety of dramatic, romantic, and comedic situations. The coming era of sound films would utilize and frequently exaggerate all of these characteristics and situations.

2

The Stereotypical Image, 1932–1959

During the twentieth century, reel librarians appeared in more than 200 sound motion pictures, primarily in supporting roles with minimal on-screen time and dialogue, if any. Although this number is minuscule when compared to the total output of films during the century, the impact of these films on the image of librarians is significant. In addition, working librarians also were instrumental in projecting the image of their occupation. Interacting daily with substantial numbers of the general public, working librarians demonstrated visual characteristics and occupational tasks that were easily copied, exaggerated, and caricatured. Aiding in the development of a stereotypical image of librarians was the homogeneous structure of the library occupation itself. Librarians attended academic educational programs that were similar in content, regardless of the geographic location of the institution offering the program. Librarians educated in these programs worked in similar environments—reading rooms, book stacks and shelves, card catalogs, reference and circulation desks—and with similar print and nonprint materials wherever the library was located.

The actual location of the building in which librarians were employed had little impact on their basic tasks. For example, a public librarian in Indiana during the 1970s would have demonstrated occupational responsibilities similar to those of a public librarian in Iowa during the 1950s, two decades earlier. The fact that libraries maintained similar environments and that librarians performed similar tasks created, at least to the casual observation of members of the general public, the appearance of a static occupation and environment. The subtle differences in environment and responsibilities were too far removed for casual observers and library patrons to discern. The apparent stability of this occupation permitted the development of a universally recognizable image of librarians by all generations of the twentieth century.

By emphasizing a minimal number of visual characteristics and occupational tasks that filmgoers observed daily at their local library, actors portraying reel librarians throughout the twentieth century created and formalized an image, a stereotype, of librarians which continues unabated into the twentieth-first century. For their roles as reel librarians, actors simply duplicate the visual characteristics of working librarians. However, the majority of occupational responsibilities of working librarians are acquired through education and experience or on-the-job training, which are impractical courses of action for actors undertaking a role as a reel librarian. Instead, actors simply mimic the actions associated with the occupational assignments of librarians; for example, the actor does not have to shelve a book in its proper place on the shelf, the actor simply places a book anywhere on the shelf. The placement of the book on the shelf by an actor mimics the occupational task of a librarian. These imitative behaviors are occupational tasks that permit filmgoers to easily identify actors as librarians.

Visual Characteristics and Occupational Tasks

Actors use four basic visual characteristics to identify and portray their screen characters as librarians. The characteristics appear so frequently that the identification of screen characters as librarians is simplified by their use. These visual characteristics are:

1. Age. Librarians are depicted as older individuals. The authors designate this as the "only 38" characteristic, a reference to the 1923 film *Only 38* in which a 38-year-old college librarian is considered old by her two college children. The "only 38" characteristic identifies reel librarians who are or appear to be older individuals.

2. Hairstyle. Women librarians display a bun hairstyle, while the equivalency for male librarians is baldness or a receding hairline.

3. Eyeglasses. Librarians wear eyeglasses, frequently removing and putting them on in the library, but seldom wearing them outside the library.

4. Modest clothes. The majority of librarians appearing middle-aged or older dress in modest, conservative clothing. This may be the filmmaker's adherence to his preconceived idea that "only 38" individuals are conservative and, therefore, reluctant to abandon their wardrobes for current fashions. Or, perhaps, a filmmaker's recognition of the financial constraints of working librarians makes the modest clothes of reel librarians a symbol of a sumptuary principle of the occupation that not only promotes but also entrenches the elderly image.

Simultaneous display of these four characteristics by an actor is not required for recognition as a librarian. Of the four basic visual characteristics associated with the majority of actors portraying reel librarians, the most predominant is age; the screen character, man or woman, is an older individual, whether by actual age or by the talents of the makeup artist. The silent film era utilized these same visual characteristics, but reel librarians of the silent period, although extremely poor and humble, were portrayed in a dignified manner; this ended abruptly during the 1930s. With few exceptions, films of the 1930s and the remainder of the twentieth century did not extend such decent treatment to reel librarians.

Actors portraying librarians in sound films released during the 1930s through the 1950s began the process of structuring and formalizing the image of the reel librarian into a stereotype that became a cinematic standard. The reel librarians of these decades not only emphasized the "only 38" characteristic but also eyeglasses, bun hairstyle, and conservative, almost puritanical clothing.

When a young, attractive starlet in a featured role portrays a reel librarian, such as Virginia Mayo in the Technicolor film *Wonder Man* (1945), the beauty of the young actress is not jeopardized by the visual characteristics of the stereotype. In these films, occupational tasks are utilized to sufficiently establish the character's identity as a librarian. The occupational tasks used most frequently by actors are: standing or sitting behind a desk, stamping a book, standing on a ladder, holding or shelving a book, picking up a book from a table, pushing a booktruck, and turning out the lights.

Reel librarians, whether men or women, occasionally demonstrate a one-word occupational vocabulary, first detected by the authors in *The Good Companions* (1933), that is easily recognized as belonging to the province of librarians—"shush." A librarian's insatiable demand for tranquility, for a quiet place, creates the perception that librarians are content with the mundane, ordinary existence that permeates the library and, by inference, their own personal lives. They spit out a "shush" at every minor breach of the library's silence.

This image of librarians, fostered and nurtured throughout the twentieth century by motion pictures, as well as by other media formats, entertained and amused every generation of filmgoers during the century. A precise correlation of this image to every reel librarian is inconsequential because filmgoers easily recognize a reel librarian when only a minimal number of visual characteristics or occupational tasks are displayed. In many films, reel librarians fail to even closely resemble the image. For example, many women who portray reel librarians are extremely attractive, the result of both natural beauty and the makeup artist, parade around in exquisite and expensive clothes, and maintain coiffures that could never be mistaken for buns. When these actresses are in a library and display only one visual characteristic or occupational task, filmgoers recognize them as librarians. These reel images are within the parameters of each filmgoer's own image of a librarian, an image of an "ideal librarian" that is embedded with personal observations of and interactions with working librarians at the filmgoer's local library. This image permits actors a great degree of flexibility and latitude when portraying librarians; the instantaneous recognition of this image by filmgoers and the general public validates and promotes its continuance.

The Formative Films of 1932

Directors and actors unabashedly utilized the visual characteristics and occupational tasks throughout the first decade of sound films. Three films with reel librarians released in 1932—*Forbidden* (January), *Young Bride*[1] (April), and *No Man of Her Own*

(December)—present librarians who embody the stereotypical visual characteristics and perform familiar occupational tasks.

The first film, director Frank Capra's drama *Forbidden*, stars Barbara Stanwyck[2] as Lulu Smith, a public librarian who is as bland and nondescript[3] as her lifestyle and the town in which she works. When Lulu first appears on-screen, she is sauntering down a sidewalk to the library on a beautiful spring morning, as if in a daydream; it is the first time she has been late to work in eight years. She is wearing pince-nez, and two small boys across the street from the library yell, "old lady foureyes, old lady foureyes," and when she glances at them, they run off shouting over their shoulders, "old lady foureyes!" To these youngsters, and filmgoers, Lulu is an "only 38" individual.

A brunette (bun at nape), she dresses modestly—long-sleeve, mid-calf dress, low V-neckline, and ruffled wide collar. When Lulu enters the library, she quietly maneuvers around her desk, replaces the flower on her desk with a fresh one, and sits. Her gray-haired, bespectacled library supervisor, Mr. Wilkinson (Thomas Jefferson[4]), approaches, playfully holds her wrist as if measuring her pulse, and mimics her heartbeat, "Clickety-click, clickety-click, clickety-click, clickety...." Lulu jumps up from her desk, interrupting Wilkinson's attempt at humor, and shouts, "I wish I owned this library! ... I'd get an axe and smash it to a million pieces, then I'd set fire to the whole town, and play a ukulele while it burned!" She sits down as suddenly as she had jumped up, pulls her bank book from her desk, and reveals a balance of $1,242.68.[5] The scene shifts immediately to Lulu in the bank withdrawing all of her money, then to a cruise ship on its way to Havana. Lulu's abroad, a new woman.

Capra's Lulu Smith illustrates the cinematic dichotomy between a woman who is a librarian and a woman who is not. When Lulu jettisoned her eight-year-long occupation in brash anticipation that the future would be different, would be brighter, would permit her to participate fully in springtime, she no longer is a librarian, a circumstance that permits a transformation from commonplace to beautiful. As a librarian, Lulu possesses visual characteristics of the stereotype—"only 38" and wears pince-nez, a homely woman. She conforms to the image because she is a librarian. Even the low V-neckline of her dress does not deflect from Lulu's matronly image, although such a neckline permits more exposure than one would reasonably expect from an "only 38" librarian. Lulu's youth and beauty are submerged by her occupation, a restraining factor that is unleashed when she hastily departs the library for the Havana-bound cruise ship.

Lulu's coworkers are men, a factor further inhibiting any display of Lulu's attractiveness. Although both her supervisor Wilkinson and coworker Phil (uncredited[6]), who is younger than Wilkinson but in the "only 38" category, display the visual characteristics of reel librarians by appearing in business dress—dark jackets and ties—there is no woman reel librarian to assume the visual characteristics other than Lulu. Most often when a starlet or established star portrays a librarian, at least one woman coworker in a supporting role appears in the library scene and exhibits the unflattering visual characteristics. This permits the principal actress to maintain her beautiful screen persona; she becomes a reel librarian by occupational tasks and by interacting and associating with supporting actors who project the stereotype.

Capra's film emphasizes one visual characteristic of reel librarians—eyeglasses.

Wilkinson wears wire-rimmed frames, while Lulu dons pince-nez. The director initiates a cinematic emphasis on the appearance of librarians, as evidenced by the inclusion of a scene at the beginning of the film when two youngsters call Lulu "old lady foureyes." This image of a visually unflattering reel librarian is a distinct modification of the reserved, respectful portrayal of librarians in the majority of silent films.

The second film of 1932 with reel librarians, *Young Bride*, is a modest, unpretentious 75-minute film containing four library scenes totaling more than 18 percent of the film. As with *Forbidden*, the film focuses on a young librarian. Helen Twelvetrees,[7] the film's star, portrays Allie Smith, a young, attractive and very poor children's librarian who yearns for a storybook romance and dreams of faraway places, the very things that Lulu in *Forbidden* so desperately craved. In addition to Allie, there are two other women reel librarians in important supporting roles—Margaret Gordon (Blanche Frederici[8]), library supervisor, and Daisy (Polly Walters[9]), coworker and friend of Allie. Both Allie and Daisy are blondes (collar length with finger waves) and dress similarly in the first library scene—long sleeve, belted dark dresses with large white collars. The large white collar is a dominant feature of the modest clothing of reel librarians in early sound films. Allie and Daisy are permitted the luxury of being young and attractive, while Gordon, an "only 38" brunette (horseshoe finger wave with bun), dresses modestly and conservatively. Gordon assumes the visual characteristics of reel librarians, as do two other reel librarians who appear very briefly onscreen in minor supporting roles.

Allie's dreams of romance and faraway places begin to crumble after she marries Charlie Riggs (Eric Linden), a tenement loudmouthed bantam rooster, with a matching strut, who brags about his big business projects and deals (pure braggadocio). Charlie quickly tires of Allie and her boardinghouse single room, where they live, and when Allie becomes pregnant, the couple's relationship deteriorates. After Allie and Charlie argue in the library, she realizes that the marriage has bottomed, lamenting, "It's all over now, there's nothing left." Depressed about what the future may hold for her, Allie deserts her romantic viewpoint and optimism. Confronting her belief in white knights, faraway places, and romance, she denigrates the role of books in the learning process of children: "What good does it do to bring those children up believing in all this bunk. Peter Pan. Goldilocks. Happy ending. Lies! Lies! Lies!" Allie is facing a major set of crises—pregnancy, financial insecurity, and a disgruntled husband threatening to leave her, but she does not have a savings account, as did Lulu, to begin a new adventure. Continuing bravely on is not the choice that Allie selects, as she slips into a drugstore to purchase a bottle of poison on her way home.

The third film, *No Man of Her Own*, stars Clark Gable as handsome, big-city gambler Jerry "Babe" Stewart, and Carole Lombard[10] as Connie Randall, small-town librarian who lives at home with her parents and younger brother. Connie works at the Glendale Public Library with Mattie (Lillian Harmer[11]). Connie and Mattie are reminiscent of Allie and Gordon in *Young Bride*. Connie, as Allie, is young and attractive, untouched by the visual characteristics of the stereotypical image, while Mattie and Gordon in supporting roles appear mandated to demonstrate the "only 38" characteristic and as many of the remaining characteristics as possible. Connie's blonde hair is neatly styled (collar length; soft, loose curls); Mattie's dark hair is pulled back into a bun at her nape. In the library, Connie and Mattie appear in conservative clothing; both wear dark dresses with large white collars—Mattie's fits snugly around her neck, while Connie's has a low V-neckline. Neither of the two women wears eyeglasses.

Connie is dissatisfied with Glendale and views the city as a hopeless situation for a young woman; she is patient, facing the future is not as disturbing for her as it was for Lulu and Allie. Connie summarizes the lack of life and excitement for a young woman in Glendale in her exclamation: "I have a steady date every night. My bed! That's Glendale! Rah, rah, rah!" Babe, in essence, is the perennial sweet-talking traveling salesman looking for an amorous adventure but who is not quite ready to settle down. Connie, however, is the superior of Babe, both in intellect and in psychological machinations. Her future with Babe is determined by a coin toss. As Babe tosses a coin in the air, he proclaims, "Heads we do, tails we...." Connie interrupts to complete the game of chance with terms more advantageous to her, "Get married!" They marry and head for New York City, where Babe continues his card-sharking ways. Although Babe is Mr. Right for Connie, rescuing a small-town girl from a life tottering between boredom and humdrum, he fails to realize until the end of the film that he is madly in love with her, so much in love that he accepts a 90-day prison term in order to mollify the police for his misdeeds and to begin anew with Connie.

The foregoing three films of 1932 present varying images of librarians, all according to discernible patterns. The stereotypical image of librarians is primarily reserved for supporting actors. A young or established principal star does not appear in unflattering attire or makeup, unless she is the only woman librarian in the film. Of the ten librarians in these films, eight are women, two are men. Women have always held the greatest number of positions in this occupation, a continuing, fundamental truth; the dominance of women in roles of reel librarians is a reflection of the gender makeup of the occupation.

Two of the three principal reel librarians in these films—Lulu and Allie—demonstrate a dissatisfaction with their occupation; Connie's displeasure is with Glendale, and continuing to live there is a fate that she is determined to avert. Lulu and Connie grab the proverbial brass ring and quit—Lulu simply withdrew her money from a bank and took a cruise to Havana, while Connie married a gambler and moved to New York City. Leaving the occupation, however, does not ensure happiness.

Lulu had a lifelong tumultuous affair, including a daughter out of wedlock, with a politician, a married district attorney named Bob Grover (Adolph Menjou) whom she meet on the Havana cruise and who could never muster the courage to divorce his wife and marry Lulu. Grover and his wife adopt Lulu's young child, who never learns that Lulu is her mother. Lulu marries a newspaperman, Grover's archenemy, who discovers that Grover is the child's father. Lulu's husband threatens to expose Grover as the father of her child on the evening he is winning the gubernatorial election. Lulu finds a revolver, shoots her husband, and burns the damning evidence. She is imprisoned but pardoned by Governor Grover, who is ill and dying. At film's end, Lulu is at Grover's bedside when he dies; walking away, Lulu tosses into a trash can the governor's hastily written death-bed will granting one-half of his estate to her and acknowledging that she is the mother of his daughter. Although Lulu professes to be happy with Grover, this could not have been the life she envisioned when she left the library with her bankbook.

Connie and Allie enjoy happier endings. Babe is back from prison and going straight and the couple appear to be happy as they rekindle their marriage, beginning a new relationship without the fear of police intervention. Allie, the only one of the three living in poverty and without a results-oriented husband or suitor, remains in the tenements. Charlie returns to Allie's boardinghouse room, just in time to stop her from drinking poison, and begs her to forgive him. Allie sums up their problems, "You, kidding yourself that you could swing big business around. Me, kidding myself that, that life was like a story with a happy ending." Realizing the futility of their dreams, they pull together to begin a marriage without illusion.[12]

Allie and Gordon (*Young Bride*) and Connie and Mattie (*No Man of Her Own*) demonstrate a strong camaraderie among librarians. Gordon is more than a supervisor to Allie; in fact, their relationship resembles that of a mother and daughter. She visits Allie at the boardinghouse, discussing library work and providing maternal advice. The purpose of one evening visit is to assist Allie "with ... reference papers," but Allie had already completed the task. Gordon stays for tea and displays a sincere concern for Allie, stating that she is "alone too much" and "should find some nice young people to go about with." She wants Allie to be happy and encourages her to mingle with people her own age. Allie insists she isn't lonely for people but "places I've never been to.... Faraway places. Rangoon, Mandalay.... And ... somebody to be there with you. Somebody you can be proud of and look up to. You don't know who. I guess all girls are that way when they're my age. Just crazyheaded." Gordon sums up her condition in one inquisitive word, "Romantic?" "Terribly," responds Allie.

In another evening visit to Allie, Gordon enters the room when Allie fails to answer the door; she finds Charlie and Allie in an embrace on the floor. Gordon, visibly unsettled by the situation, informs Charlie that she is "Allie's oldest friend" and that "if you have the decency to go, Allie will make whatever explanations are necessary." During the ensuing conversation, Charlie states that he doesn't have to go because they are getting married. Gordon is not disappointed with Allie's choice of Charlie as a husband; her primary interest is Allie's well-being and happiness.

Gordon, in one scene, demonstrates that she is a stern supervisor—she discharges Daisy. Only minutes after firing Daisy, Gordon joins Allie and Charlie at the front desk and demonstrates her understanding of the machinations of young people in love and her sense of humor. It is Charlie's first visit to the library and he wants to ask Allie for a date. Verbally stifled by the presence of Gordon, he writes a note and hands it to Allie. The note underscores the unflattering image of "only 38" librarians: "How about lunch? Drug store across street. We can talk some more without old frozen face horning in." He leaves, and Allie asks permission to go to lunch, which Gordon approves. Shortly after Allie leaves the desk, Gordon picks up the note, and as she reads it, a shocked expression appears on her face but it slowly fades into a big smile and laugh.

The conversations between Connie and Mattie display more of an older sister–younger sister relationship than that of a mother and daughter, even though Mattie

Young Bride (1932). Helen Twelvetrees (left) is children's librarian Allie Smith and Blanche Frederici (right) is library supervisor Margaret Gordon, who offers sympathy and support as Allie struggles with her personal problems. Note the large white collars.

is old enough to be Connie's mother. They exhibit a propensity to talk about men, a conversational topic perhaps not expected from librarians. During the film's only library scene, the topic of discussion is Babe, as he is seemingly exasperating Connie in an attempt to obtain a date. After a trying excursion into the library stacks with Babe, Connie returns to the main desk, exclaiming, as if she were displeased at Babe's overtures, "And he asked me to go out with him!" She then quickly questions Mattie, "Is he looking?" Mattie is very perceptive, "You do want to go out with him, don't you?" and urges her to go. Connie is more reserved, insisting that women have to "play hard to get" with men like Babe. Mattie, however, upholds conventional honesty: "That's not the way I treat my young men. I've always been frank and above board." Connie, in a manner approving Mattie's treatment of men, responds, "You're such a nice person, Mattie." Connie, explaining the makeup of men like Babe to Mattie, maintains that "the girl who lands him will have to say no and put an anchor on him." Although Mattie demonstrates an elegant feminine charm and wisdom in her conversations with Connie, she still lives in Glendale, a future Connie fears.

Despite the dismal, dark atmosphere of the tenement surroundings that permeate *Young Bride*, Allie and Daisy provide filmgoers with occasional bits of humor. Daisy delivers her first humorous line in the first library scene. When her boyfriend Pete (Cliff Edwards) discovers that Daisy has not obtained a date for Charlie, he suggests that Allie "looks hot." "Yeah," Daisy responds, "hot like a Frigidaire." Daisy then asks Allie about going on a date with Charlie; she refuses the invitation, "Blind date. No, thanks." Daisy, however, is very quick to correct Allie's apprehension, "Aw, this guy Pete's got ain't blind." Daisy is a cinematic blonde—she demonstrates not only all of the physical characteristics associated with young, attractive blondes but also their rumored greatest deficiency—impoverished intellect. Daisy utters another inane response later in the film while partying with Pete and another couple. When the young woman, a past girlfriend and dancing partner of Charlie's, remarks that she will get even with Charlie, the man replies, "Baloney." Daisy, stretched out on a bed, suddenly perks up and blurts out, "Do we have any left?" A similar type of response occurs in the second library scene when Daisy, still mildly inebriated from the previous night's carousing and with Gordon eavesdropping, recounts the evening's debauchery. Allie, in a critical tone, insists that she "shouldn't go around like that." Daisy maintains unhesitatingly that "I'm not going around, it's, it's this room. Make it stop!" On occasion, Daisy is the recipient of unflattering terms that Pete and others use to identify her. At dinner, Pete asks Daisy, "What'll you have, Unconscious?" When Charlie arrives a few moments later, he greets Daisy with "Hello, Dizzy." Daisy is not perturbed by these terms; she is a partygoer whose major objective is fun. She does not take her library position as seriously as she does her hunt for excitement, nor does she appear to care about working in a library. After being fired by Gordon, Daisy remarks on her way out, "I should worry. I never liked books anyway." Daisy projects many uncomplimentary images of librarians:

• She is the epitome of a scatterbrained blonde, a librarian whose intellect is suspect;

• she is a partygoer, a librarian whose major concern is having a good time, even if the party is less than wholesome;

No Man of Her Own (1932). Lillian Harmer (left) is Mattie and Carole Lombard (right) is Connie Randall, librarians at the Glendale Public Library. Note the large white collars. (Photograph courtesy of the Academy of Motion Picture Arts and Sciences.)

- she is inebriated at work in the library, a librarian who demonstrates the boldness to relate her carousing adventures to a coworker while her supervisor is listening; and

- she is a librarian who does not care a whit about either her job or books.

On several occasions, Allie reveals by her statements that she lives a very cloistered life. At the Chop Suey restaurant, she looks at the menu and remarks, "Well, I don't know what this all means, but it looks exciting." She asks, "Now, what's that?" and Pete responds, "That's bird nest zoup," emphasizing the "z." Allie continues to inquire, "What kind of bird?" "Cuckoo," he replies and orders it for her. Her questions about the menu's items are partially explained later when she mentions that she had "never been to a chop suey place before." After Charlie joins them, he is fascinated by a tune the orchestra is playing, "Listen to that guy playing the sax, it's my favorite piece." "What is it?" Allie asks. "'Whispering,'" he answers. The only rationale that could possibly justify Allie's ignorance of "bird's nest soup" or her failure to recognize a popular tune of the 1920s is that she is a librarian who lives a sheltered existence.

Although Allie is lonely, longing for a storybook romance and faraway places, her inability to see through Charlie is inexplicable. Only one of the film's young female characters, a librarian (uncredited[13]), snubs Charlie. This occurs during one of his visits to the library. This librarian, an attractive brunette (bun at nape), is arranging a display, and Charlie stops and stands several feet behind her while she works. When she finishes, she turns around; surprised to see Charlie, she stops momentarily to look him over, down to his shoes and up to his head. She then pushes her eyeglasses up with her left hand, tilts her head up in the air, and walks away.

Every perceptive filmgoer undoubtedly recognizes Charlie as a braggart without substance the first time he appears on screen. When he joins Pete, Daisy, and Allie at the Chop Suey restaurant, he immediately begins his threadbare lines on Allie, and she is fascinated by them. One of his first lines—"Say, you ought to be in the movies with that face"—sparks a humorous response from Allie: "Sure, I'd make a swell target for custard pies." Allie is quick to recognize Charlie's lines and calls him on them, but she is unable to ignore them, especially when they evoke images of faraway places. When he mentions Calcutta, Allie wants to know if he's really been there. "Sure, I've been all over. Calcutta, Rangoon, Mandalay, but I never met a girl like you before." Moments later, he remarks that "only once did I see blue like you got in your eyes and that was on the China Sea one morning after a typhoon." Allie enters a pensive state when he talks about such places. On their first date—a night boat trip on the Hudson River, he conjures up a similar image when Allie asks, "Gee, did you ever see such a moon?" He promptly answers, "Yeah, once off Madagascar, but I didn't have a swell looking gal like you along." Allie immediately rejects such a trite line, "Suppose you get a new line for me, I sort of thought we'd be different?" Charlie manages a compromise: "I'll never say anything to you that I've said to another girl, or if I do there'll be a big difference.... I'll mean it!" Charlie's sincerity is irrelevant because Allie wants desperately to believe him and does.

No Man of Her Own and *Young Bride* demonstrate the spectrum of occupational tasks of librarians that can be utilized by directors and actors. *No Man of Her Own* contained the first library ladder comedic scene in sound films, providing Babe the opportunity to ogle Connie's ankle and calf. In response to Babe's request for a book on a high shelf, Connie climbs up a ladder, trying to locate the book he wants. When Babe responds negatively to every title she identifies, Connie stretches out a little more to read the title of the next book down the shelf, exposing a little more calf and ankle. She finally turns around, catches Babe ogling, and shouts, "Are you showing me a grand time, mister? Or, are you showing me a grand time!" She scampers down the ladder and heads for the library desk. It would not be until one of the last films of the twentieth century with a reel librarian, *The Mummy* (1999), that a comedic ladder scene would equal the humor of this Gable-Lombard scene. The four library scenes of *Young Bride* reveal the greatest variety of tasks from which an actor or director can select to identify a reel librarian. These include pushing a booktruck, picking up books from desks, explaining a library display to children, presenting a children's storyhour, shelving books, standing and working at the main desk, organizing a book rack display, stamping dates in books and checking out books to patrons, answering patron inquires (reference service or reader's advisory), and working with or filing in a card file tray.

Cinematic depictions of librarians depend upon visual characteristics or occupational tasks for easy recognition, but filmgoers determine whether or not to accept a reel librarian as the parallel of one of their local working librarians. When reel librarians emulate the same quality of service that the filmgoer's local librarians provide, they are discernible as the equivalent of working librarians. However, it is evident in the majority of films with reel librarians that the primary intent of directors and actors is not to emulate the quality of services provided by the filmgoer's local library. Excluding scenes from these three films that are designed primarily for comedy purposes, only *Young Bride* provides scenes that parallel the services of working librarians.

Allie, a children's librarian, enjoys working with children, as demonstrated in two scenes occurring in the Children's Room. In the first, Allie is identifying and explaining the objects and characters that are part of a table display to three of the eight young visitors. When the closing bell rings, she strolls to her desk with a young girl and boy; walking between them, with hands on their shoulders, she reminds them, "Now, don't forget storyhour next Thursday." The young girl replies, "We won't!" The boy, however, is not as enthusiastic: "You won't get me in here for any cockeyed storyhour!" As the well-mannered children leave, they give Allie a "Good night, Miss Smith." The children, polite and inquisitive, enjoy Allie and the Children's Room. In the second scene, Allie is conducting a storyhour about the birth of Christ for approximately six children; they are very attentive to the details of the story, prompting one young girl to ask about the "cows and chickens." The children beg for another story, but Allie declines, telling them that she is ill. Allie provides competent services to these children and has a very good rapport with them. They interact freely with her, displaying no hesitancy to ask questions or to come to her aid. Allie's portrayal of a children's librarian, in these specific instances, is representative of the quality of service provided by working librarians.

The library scene in *Forbidden* does not show the librarians providing services or performing occupational tasks. In *No Man of Her Own*, the primary emphasis on providing services is Connie's search for a book that might interest Babe. The problem is that Babe's only curiosity in the library is Connie; there is not a book in the building that would interest him. This restricts the scene to humor, as the hunt for a book is bogus. Clearly evident in Glendale's library is Connie and Mattie's apparent lack of concern for the orderliness of library materials. They are not meticulous caretakers of books; quite the contrary, some library materials appear purposely neglected. Two overhead views of the stack area of the library reveal books and rolled-up documents lying in disarray on the top of every shelving range. As the shelving ranges are not full, appearing only about 60 percent filled, the books on top could be integrated easily into proper shelving order. In addition, too many books are lying down on shelves in all ranges for this to be other than the normal situation.

The directors and actors of these three films of 1932 began the process of formalizing the stereotypical image of reel librarians in sound films. In addition to the visual characteristics and occupational tasks, the films depict librarians as women with problems similar to those confronted by every woman—boyfriends, pregnancy, children out of wedlock, financial insecurity, and husbands of dubious quality. Single women librarians use the library as a "cocoon," a safe haven, a respectable place of employment, until they marry or boredom propels them elsewhere. Such storylines indicate the variety of film genres in which librarians can be utilized in supporting roles and, on occasion, leading roles. The utilization of these characteristics and tasks by succeeding filmmakers and actors will engender the stereotypical image of librarians.

Ascendancy of the Image, 1933–1959

Directors and actors during the 1930s unabashedly utilized the visual characteristics and occupational tasks for screen characters appearing as reel librarians in supporting roles. One of the first films appearing after 1932 with a librarian (uncredited; Hugh E. Wright[14]) in the cast is *The Good Companions*, a British film released in the United States in 1933. *The Good Companions* contains a brief library scene in which a librarian utters for the first time the most famous and infamous word in a librarian's lexicon—"shush."[15]

Susie Dean (Jessie Matthews) visits a public library to locate the address of a physician. As she glances through a book, Susie asks the librarian in a loud voice, "How far is Dingley?" The librarian responds with a "shush" and shakes his finger at her. Moments later, he adds, "About 50 miles." When Susie goes to the desk for additional assistance, director Victor Saville maintains the position of the camera behind the librarian, as he did in the earlier question-shush-answer exchange. With the camera behind the librarian, filmgoers can only see the back of the librarian's head and a portion of his left cheek when he moves. In this less than 40-second library scene, Saville does not permit an "only 38" librarian in a dark suit wearing eyeglasses to share screen time with the film's star, Jessie Matthews.

A year later, First National Pictures' *Gentlemen Are Born* (1934) follows the attempts of four recent college graduates to obtain jobs and establish careers during the Depression era. A girlfriend of one graduate, Trudy Talbot (Jean Muir), answers an advertisement for a roommate placed by Susan Merrill (Ann Dvorak[16]), a public librarian. During their initial meeting, Susan identifies her occupation, "I work in the public library. That's why I don't keep any books around, but you may if you like." They become roommates, and Susan eventually meets the four young men. She volunteers to attend the "second-string" fights with Bob Bailey (Franchot Tone), remarking, "After Monday at the library, it will be a pleasure to see somebody beat up, all bloody." The fight card includes a match with Smudge Casey (Dick Foran), one of the graduates and the college's football star, who is battered, bloodied, and KO'd by a more experienced fighter. Smudge, unable to secure a football coaching position or any type of employment, took the fight to earn $10. They invite Smudge to Sunday morning breakfast, beginning a Smudge-Susan romance that results in marriage. Smudge occasionally finds temporary work, but Susan's library position provides the necessities for the couple until she is dismissed. As the financial condition of the couple deteriorates, Smudge takes a watch to a pawnshop but the pawnbroker mistakenly believes Smudge is reaching for a gun in his pocket and immediately holds up his arms. Smudge asks for $10 and runs out of the store. A policeman pursues Smudge, shooting and killing him. Susan then moves back to her hometown of Des Moines.

Susan, a brunette (multi-pincurl bang; side finger waves; pincurl flip at nape), wears modest clothes throughout the film; most of her outfits have large, white, wide collars. In the library scene, she wears a dark dress with a large white collar and narrow white bow tie. Her "only 38" library supervisor, Miss Graham (uncredited; Virginia Howell[17]), a brunette (pulled back close to head; bun at nape) with a touch of graying, wears a dark dress with large, white, wide lapels. Both present the same basic appearance in dress, but each has a slight variation on the design. When Susan reports to Graham's office for a meeting, her supervisor is wearing pince-nez and reading a book at her desk. She informs Susan that she has heard some "gossip" and that it is her "duty to know the character of the girls working" at the library. During a brief question-and-answer exchange, Graham discovers that Susan is married and rebukes the young librarian, "If you are married, you certainly cannot expect to keep your position. Why did you hide that from me? You knew the rule." Susan pleads to retain her position, as it provides the only source of income for her and Smudge, but Graham's response is accusatory, "You have been depriving some other girl with no means of outside support from obtaining a position here." In conclusion, Graham comments, "I will thank you not to use the library for future references."

Gentlemen Are Born and *Young Bride* (1932) illustrate the contrasting manner in which library supervisors in Depression-era New York City handle subordinates. As a supervisor, Graham does not display a friendly relationship, personal or administrative, with Susan; Graham's personality is contrary to that of supervisor Gordon in *Young Bride*. While Gordon takes a personal interest in the affairs of Allie, wanting to assist Allie succeed and achieve happiness, Graham appears completely detached from and uninterested in Susan as a person or employee, demanding Susan leave the library according to the "rule." Graham is not concerned about the quality of Susan's work; the only point of contention is Susan's marital status. The "rule," which is not explained but is implicit, restricts employment at the library to single women.

A second contrasting image of library supervisors, also evident in *Gentlemen Are Born*, is undoubtedly the result of the film's budget rather than purposeful intent. Graham sits at her desk and reads books, while Gordon, only two years earlier, worked in the library's reading room, where her desk was located, and assisted patrons. Graham's library office required only a few pieces of basic library furniture—a desk surrounded by several book shelves—to create the illusion of a library setting. This minimalist approach successfully projects a library office, especially with a bespectacled "only 38" librarian reading a book while seated at the desk. Future films use minimalist sets to create the appearance of a library.

Gentlemen Are Born, while relating the difficulties of young people during the Depression era, presents its characters in sets and surroundings that are in stark contrast to Allie's spartan boardinghouse room in *Young Bride*. Although both films are set in New York City during the Depression, Susan's Manhattan apartment, where several scenes occur, is large and bright with nice furniture. The apartment has a

1930s modern kitchen with seemingly new appliances, and at least one large, nicely furnished bedroom; the dining-living area accommodates a dining table that seats eight. The contrast of economic conditions between Allie and Susan is perplexing and is inexplicable in terms of salary. The salaries of Susan and Allie, both working in public libraries, could not have been so out of kilter, so outlandishly dissimilar, to permit Susan to live in a nice apartment and to force Allie to live in the tenements. The young men in *Gentlemen Are Born* are college graduates, perhaps explaining why they appear in better surroundings than the tenement-bound young men and women in *Young Bride*. A more logical explanation for this disparity, however, may be that by 1934 many filmgoers preferred films that offered, if not pure escapism, a plausible, upscale image more optimistic than their own impoverished environment.

Reel librarians, as demonstrated by Susan and her predecessors of 1932, make imprudent decisions in the selection of mates—Bob Grover (*Forbidden*), a married attorney who cannot confront his wife about a divorce; Charlie Riggs (*Young Bride*), a tenement braggart without substance; Babe Stewart (*No Man of Her Own*), a professional cardsharp seeking a safe retreat from police; and Smudge Casey, an athletic jock and unemployable college graduate. The first three are self-centered, creating economic hardships and psychological problems for their partners. Smudge, a dynamo on the football field, exhibits a subdued, passive personality off the field; the inability of Smudge to find employment and, thereby, to manifest his masculinity as the couple's prime moneymaker demoralizes him, extinguishing his self-confidence. The four men are transparent; filmgoers who saw one, or all four, of these films could see their imperfections and shortcomings and may have even wondered if their local working librarians suffered from the same myopic conditions that afflicted these four reel librarians.

The activities of several passengers aboard an ocean liner is the focus of *The Captain Hates the Sea* (1934). One passenger is Schulte (Victor McLaglen), a private investigator attempting to recover $250,000 in Trans-Pacific Company bonds; another passenger is Janet Grayson (Helen Vinson[18]) who is identified as a librarian, but as the plot unfolds, Janet's occupation appears a pretense to conceal her illegal activity. She is in possession of the Trans-Pacific bonds, holding them for her partner-in-crime, Danny Checkett (Fred Keating), who joins the ship after it leaves port; the two bond thieves pretend to be strangers. When Schulte and Danny are with the head steward, Danny asks the steward about "the danger signal"—Janet. The steward comments that she is "from Boston. Works in the library there. Must do it to pass her time away because it's a cinch she has a bundle of dough." He adds that his knowledge about Janet comes from people who tell him "things." Danny gives $10 to the steward to secure a seat next to Janet at dinner. Even though Schulte has a rap sheet on Janet (real name, Blanche Ditworthy, aka Michigan Red), he becomes romantically involved with her during the cruise. Danny makes two references to her alleged occupation during the film. First, in response to a remark from Janet while they are together on the dance floor, Danny quips, "Tut, tut, Miss Grayson, and what would the trustees of the good old Boston library say to such language?" The second comment occurs in Janet's cabin; when she comes out of the bedroom in a nightgown, Danny exclaims, "Ah, pretty hot, Babe, for a library dame." These statements are spoken in jest, indicating in all probability that Danny is cognizant that the other passengers not only mistakenly believe she is a librarian but also are definitely unaware of her past criminal behavior.

Appearing as an attractive brunette (finger waves; soft curls at sides and back) in black-and-white, Janet is undoubtedly a redhead, as her alias implies. Janet dresses fashionably throughout the film, displaying none of the visual characteristics of the stereotypical image. Whether or not Janet is a librarian (and the authors believe that she is not), her occupation is inconsequential to the storyline.

Clark Gable appears in *Cain and Mabel* (1936), his second film containing a library scene; this time, however, he is not pursuing the librarian. Gable is Larry Cain, heavyweight boxing champion, and Marion Davies is Mabel O'Dare, broadway musical star; they fall in love and use the public library as their tryst to plan their elopement. As they sit together, Larry holds up an oversized book, *Ichthyology*, to hide their kiss from public view. They are interrupted immediately by a librarian (uncredited; Lillian Lawrence[19]) who stares at them in a very stern, disapproving manner. She continues to stare at them as she slowly walks around the table at which they are seated and picks up books. This prompts the couple to leave the table and hurry into a book stack aisle, searching for privacy. As they kiss in the aisle, another librarian (uncredited; Harry C. Bradley[20]), whom they fail to notice standing on the higher rungs of a tall library ladder, accidentally drops a book, almost hitting them. Larry picks up the book, *Care and Feeding of the Baby*; looks up at the librarian, and exclaims, "Hey, aren't you rushing things a little?" He hands it to the librarian and they leave.

Both Lawrence and Bradley reinforce the stereotypical image. They are "only 38"; Lawrence's hair, which is turning gray, is styled in a bun, while Bradley's gray hairline is receding, and both wear eyeglasses. Lawrence is dressed in a patterned long sleeve blouse and matching skirt. A decidedly bookish touch is added to her outfit by the use of black sleevelets to cover the arms of her blouse. Bradley, smiling impishly as he stands on the ladder bungling books in an attempt to shelve them, is dressed conservatively in dark suit and tie, complying precisely with the stereotypical image.

Reel librarians in supporting roles are instrumental in keeping the stereotypical image in front of filmgoers, but motion pictures with reel librarians in major roles must appear in movie theaters, at least intermittently, to maintain a stable and enduring stereotypical image. Reel librarians in these films must appear in library scenes that clearly not only establish their status as librarians but also sustain or bolster the visual characteristics and occupational tasks of the image. Two such films with reel librarians in leading roles were released in 1937—*Sea Devils* and *Navy Blues*, five years after the first appearance of librarians in leading roles.

Sea Devils, an adulatory film on the Coast Guard, stars Victor McLaglen as Chief Petty Officer William "Medals" Malone and Preston Foster as Seaman Mike O'Shay and focuses on their trials and tribulations. Their relationship resembles that of the well-known army duo—Captain Flagg and Sergeant Quirt. Mike likes Medals' daughter, Doris (Ida Lupino[21]), and Medals hates Mike. Within five minutes after arriving at his new assignment, Mike manages to meet and kiss Doris, a young, attractive librarian. Mike follows her to the public library, where he attempts to impress her, but Doris

Sea Devils (1937). Doris Malone (Ida Lupino) stares disapprovingly at Mike O'Shay (Preston Foster) as he pinches the cheek of Miss McGonigle (Fern Emmett). Note the white collars of both librarians and McGonigle's pince-nez and bun hairstyle. (Photograph courtesy of the Academy of Motion Picture Arts and Sciences.)

is able to squash his advances with ease. Picking up a Shakespeare book, Mike reads a quote from Shakespeare, remarking, "They should have broken his arm at the shoulder before he learned to write." Doris, knowing just what to recommend for him, asks her coworker, Miss McGonigle (Fern Emmett[22]), to show Mike the picture books in the Children's Department. McGonigle demonstrates a degree of consternation about this, but Mike refuses the offer, extending a rhetorical invitation to McGonigle: "You must come over and see my picture book sometime." He leaves the library, and McGonigle, showing her modicum of wisdom about men, looks at Doris and asks, in apparent seriousness, "Do you think I ought to go?"

Doris and McGonigle mirror the appearances of Connie and Mattie in *No Man of Her Own* (1932). Doris, a brunette (bob with pincurls around face), wears a black skirt, and a black jacket with a white front vertical panel and white front collar and black bow. McGonigle is the stereotype—"only 38," pince-nez, dark hair pulled back into a bun at the nape, and a dark long-sleeve dress with a small white collar and dark bow. McGonigle reveals a lack of common sense, which reinforces the dimension that Daisy (*Young Bride*, 1932) first introduced to the stereotypical image. McGonigle's statements, as Daisy's five years earlier, compel filmgoers to suspect her wisdom, her intellect.

McGonigle and Mattie, by their roles as supporting characters, emulate the stereotype, but the importance and the relationship of their characters to the leading female role is markedly different: Mattie plays a mature, matronly advisor to Connie, while McGonigle plays comedic sidekick to Doris. McGonigle's activities mimic any one of a number of comic sidekicks who played second fiddle to the B-western cowboy stars of the 1930s, 1940s, and early 1950s. In a second library scene, McConigle reinforces her role as comic sidekick. When Mike speaks loudly in the reading room, Doris simply points to a large SILENCE sign on the wall, missing a perfect opportunity to utter a "shush." She begins shelving books under a library ladder, as Mike recites several lines of Shakespeare to her, remarking this time that "he's a great writer, that guy." Telling Doris that he is "completely daft over" her, Mike puts his hand on a ladder rung and leans in to kiss Doris, only to have McGonigle step on his hand as she descends from the top of the ladder. He jumps back, screaming "Oh!" McGonigle, waiting until she reaches the floor, exclaims, "Oh, I beg your pardon!"

The screenwriters of this film, Frank Wead, John Twist, P. J. Wolfson, and director Benjamin Stoloff, initiated a new function for the stereotype. Writers and directors now can employ this screen character for more than enhancing the beauty of the film's star; they can utilize the character to perform attention-grabbing comic antics.

Released a month after *Sea Devils*, *Navy Blues* renders such a visual and verbal assault on librarians that the motion picture effectively released the film industry from continuing any semblance of decent and respectful cinematic depictions of librarians. When the stars of the film are introduced by picture and name in the opening credits, Mary Brian[23] is first shown as an "only 38" woman with a bewildered look on her face, and wearing a dark, wide-rimmed hat, eyeglasses, a dark coat and gloves. Brian then lowers her head and reappears as a youthful, attractive brunette, wearing a fashionable hat and V-neckline dress with a patterned mock vest. The contrast between Brian's two appearances—elderly bewildered matron to young vibrant woman—in these opening credits is important in defining the film's attitude toward librarians. Even though filmgoers at this point are not aware that she is a librarian, the unflattering opening appearance has all the traits of the stereotypical image. More importantly, in this film the sailors continually lambaste its librarian, demonstrating outright disrespect for women librarians.

Navy Blues is about the fortunes of sailor Rusty (Dick Purcell), a lady-killer whose ego irritates and exasperates his three cohorts—Chips (Joe Sawyer), Gateleg (Horace MacMahon), and Biff (Warren Hymer). Biff is a simple boxer, not too smart but very personable. He serves as Rusty's sidekick, and as all sidekicks, he is always in a state of befuddlement and blurts out what he knows when silence is the preferred course of action. The trio, at Chips' suggestion, present a challenge that Rusty's ego cannot turn down. They put up $25 against Rusty washing their outfits and shining their shoes for a month that he cannot take a woman—of their choosing—on a date to their favorite barrelhouse, Crow's Nest Café. Chips has already informed his two friends that he knows just the girl—"I saw a dame in a public liberry [Chip's enunciation] once. I just ducked in there out of the rain.... Well, I took one gander at this dame and then ran right out again, rain or no rain.... A bowwow."

They drive Rusty to the library, and when he asks about the woman, Chips replies, "She's got on a pair of glasses as thick as cookies. You know the type." The three sailors break out in laughter as Rusty enters the building. Doris Kimbell (Mary Brian), the librarian, is behind the main desk, and Rusty immediately recognizes her. She is a brunette (side finger waves with bun at nape) with eyeglasses, and wears a dark long-sleeve blouse, a high, stiff ruffle collar with a string bow, and a long skirt. Doris appears to be middle-aged, a dowdy spinster; she matches Chips' description.

Rusty attempts to engage her in a conversation at the desk, but she quickly dismisses his overtures. He selects a reference book at random, asks her to notify him at closing time, and sits at a table. Doris soon approaches a nearby stack area and uses a three-rung stepladder to shelve some books. As she stands on the second rung, Rusty glances at her ankle, at her complete figure; he then frowns and closes the book. This ladder scene is a feeble reenactment of the Lombard-Gable scene in *No Man of Her Own* five years earlier. Gable, however, is enthusiastic about Lombard's calf and ankle, while Rusty is grimacing at the thought of obtaining a date with this homely librarian. Near closing time, Doris' beau, Julian Everett (Edward Woods), enters and offers to walk her home. Rusty exits the building accompanying Julian and Doris. The three sailors are still in front of the library, and Biff, looking at Doris, remarks, "It must be Thanksgiving or something. She's all made up like a pilgrim." Gateleg rejoins, "It'll take a brave man to wheel that museum piece into the Crow's Nest." The trio stare at Rusty as he walks away with the couple.

When Doris, Julian, and Rusty arrive at Doris' home, Rusty enters the house; this upsets Doris' aunt, Beulah Wayne (Lucille Gleason), who approves of Julian. Rusty engages Doris' uncle Andrew (Chester Clute), a high school mathematics teacher, in a glib conversation about algebra, eliciting an invitation from Andrew to return the next day. Rusty returns the following day and takes Doris to the beach. She projects the stereotypical image for the trip to the beach—eyeglasses, dark dress, small white collar and bow, black hat with feather, and a bun. While sitting on the rocks at the beach, Rusty manages to remove her glasses, remarking, "Say, what a difference." Doris admits that she can see without them, and as she turns to enjoy a view of the scenery without them, he sneaks a kiss, then drops her glasses, breaking them. He invites her to a dance on Wednesday, suggesting that she "take a good look in the mirror without your glasses.... Get yourself a permanent wave.... And then put on a dress that's got ... you know. And ... take off those shoes." She retorts the shoes are sensible. "That's the trouble with them," Rusty responds. Julian suddenly appears, remarking, "Why, I scarcely know you without your glasses." He invites Doris to a concert on Wednesday, but she is going dancing with Rusty.

Beulah forbids Doris to go with Rusty on Wednesday but permits her to go with Julian, and as Doris and Julian leave the house, Rusty intercepts them. Doris confronts him about having lied to her aunt and uncle, but Rusty cunningly leads her into believing that he's in naval intelligence—"I had to [lie to you].... Men in my branch of the service take an oath.... Well, there's secrets in the Navy and men assigned to guard those secrets. Now do you understand?" Doris, excited about the danger involved with intelligence service, agrees to accompany him to the Crow's Nest Café, where she believes he is going to a perilous meeting. Doris has completely transformed her image—new hairstyle and cute hat, a modern knee-length dress, V-neckline. At the café, Chips and Gateleg refuse to believe the attractive woman with Rusty is Doris. "He's trying to run in a ringer on us," Chips maintains. Rusty leaves Doris momentarily to speak with "his men"; Chips insists that they will "pay off on the librarian and nobody else," while Gateleg asks about her glasses. When Rusty rejoins Doris, Julian enters; Rusty takes his glasses and tells Doris to put them on so that she will not be recognized as they leave. When Chips and Gateleg see her in glasses, they realize she is the librarian. It is the last time she wears eyeglasses in the film.

Several days later when Rusty and Doris, again fashionably dressed, are on a dinner date, he attempts to explain his deceptions. Before Rusty can finish his apologies, Biff arrives and recommends that Doris receive a part of the bet for going along with it. Doris storms out of the restaurant with Rusty in pursuit. They take a taxi to her home and, on the stairs to the house, he tries to explain, severely wounding her feelings by saying, "Sure I made that bet. Why else would I have bothered with a freak like you." "A freak!" Doris shouts at him. Rusty continues tactlessly, "Well that's what you were. I changed you over from a crow, a bookworm, made you into a girl that can take her pick of anything." They exchange recriminations; Rusty tells her to go back to Julian, "He's just your speed," as she closes the door in his face.

As Rusty leaves the house, a German espionage group kidnaps him, believing that he is in naval intelligence. When he refuses to answer questions, several gang members go to the library and kidnap Doris, assuming that she may have the information they need. Seeing Rusty when she enters the hideout, Doris immediately blames him, but other gang members soon arrive with her uncle in custody. The Germans receive an order to assassinate a baron arriving at a nearby airport, and Julian, a member of the Nazi gang, remains to guard the prisoners. Rusty overpowers Julian, and with Doris and Andrew, rushes to the airport, foiling the assassination plot. Rusty receives a promotion to the rank of warrant officer. As they celebrate the happy ending, Rusty and Doris express their love for one another and plan to wed as soon as they can obtain a license.

The sailor-inspired epithets—"bowwow," "pilgrim," "museum piece," "freak," "crow," and "bookworm"—about Doris buttress the visual characteristics of the stereotypical image. Rusty uses terms just as derogatory as his trio of friends to describe her. Doris is the stereotype until she falls in love with Rusty. From that point, she sports a modern hairstyle (pincurls and finger waves); discards her eyeglasses, and wears distinctive, modern clothing.

Navy Blues is one of Republic Pictures Corporation's 69 releases during 1937.[24] Republic primarily produced low-budget ("B") features—films with low-grade production values—and *Navy Blues* is one of them. *Variety* called *Navy Blues* "An all-around weakie, and ... story is, at best, incredible, and likely to be snickered at."[25] In addition to being a mediocre film, *Navy Blues* is an extremely insensitive assault on librarians. Not all cinematic depictions of librarians in preceding motion pictures are commendatory toward the occupation, but none is more outlandish in its derision of librarians. *Navy Blues* provides several moments of laughter for filmgoers, but these instances are at the expense of the reel librarian. Although filmgoers were unaware that Brian is a librarian during the opening credits, the quartet of sailors use "bow-wow" to refer to a librarian in less than four minutes after Brian's opening picture. Furthermore, in less than three minutes after that descriptor is used, a library scene with Brian dressed similarly to her opening picture occurs. Filmgoers of 1937, regardless of their level of sophistication, could not have misinterpreted such an implied association.

Louise Campbell[26] stars as Nora Langdon, a young, attractive librarian in 1938's *Scandal Street*. Nora is going to work in the Midburg Public Library, where she is "organizing another state library,"[27] while her fiancé, Joe McKnight (Lew Ayres), an engineer, is on assignment in South America. In the film's opening scene, Nora and Joe in a restaurant, she wears eyeglasses but removes them within thirty-five seconds. In the next scene, Nora and Joe in the back seat of a taxi, she talks about her library job but does not wear glasses. By wearing eyeglasses in the first scene, Nora prepares filmgoers for the revelation that she is a librarian in the second scene.

Scandal Street has only one brief library scene, less than 50 seconds, about midway through the film. In the library, Nora, a bespectacled brunette (multi-pincurl bang; pageboy, with sides braided back), wears conservative clothes—a dark long sleeve blouse, plain neckline, with leg-of-mutton sleeves, and a dark, straight skirt. She assists Austin Brown (Roscoe Karns) with a question on postal law, without success, and offers to look for information the next time she goes to the city. He asks her to purchase a book for him when she goes and gives her some money, telling her to get something for herself with the remainder—"maybe another bottle of that enticing perfume you use." Nora mentions that it is lunch time, and Austin offers to drive her downtown. She grabs a fur-collar coat off the chair at a nearby table and leaves with him. This one scene visually confirms Nora's status as a librarian.

Although Nora's coat is undoubtedly expensive, she maintains the frugal lifestyle of reel librarians—renting a room, with board, in the Smiths' home, "a refined family, in [an] exclusive neighborhood" on Peachtree Drive. Nora dresses fashionably in this film, often in outfits with large white collars. Her use of eyeglasses is limited—watching home movies and reading; in other scenes, she is without them. In a kitchen scene, she is preparing a dessert while reading the recipe and asks the boyfriend of the Smiths' oldest daughter to remove her glasses, as her hands are "all gooey." He does, remarking, "Hey, with those cheaters off, you don't look any older than the kids I go around with at school."

The focus of the film is the gossip that develops around Nora and Austin, who is developing a "secret" mail order nylon business with James Wilson (Porter Hall). Austin occasionally offers Nora a ride to the library, speaks to her about his business, and takes "candid camera" pictures of her legs for his promotional brochures. He makes subtle passes, but Nora repels them.

The women of Peachtree Drive believe this attractively dressed librarian to be a challenge to their status quo and are quick to spread innuendos about this visible but meaningless relationship. Nora's youthful beauty, coupled with the fact that she is seen publicly with Austin, prompt the women of Peachtree Drive to believe that she is a flirt, leading Austin astray. The "candid camera" pictures also attest to the fact that Nora is a flirt; otherwise, there is no rationale for a librarian's legs to be photographed. One evening, Nora visits Austin's house to retrieve a pair of glasses that she left there. Nora spots Austin on the floor and rushes to him, only to discover that he is dead. As Nora is bending over the body, Austin's wife returns home. Nora is arrested for murder; the women of Peachtree Drive arrive at the only conclusion their gossip and slander support—Nora murdered Austin. The case against Nora is overwhelming, based on the district attorney's interviews with the women of Peachtree Drive. The women enjoy repeating the gossip and slander they created among themselves to the district attorney; they make a concerted effort to implicate Nora. Joe returns from South America the day after the murder, and Willy Murphy (eleven-year-old Virginia Weidler), who likes Nora, manages to convince Joe that Austin's partner is the murderer. The district attorney permits Joe to question Wilson; the partner makes a verbal faux pas, then confesses his guilt.

With Nora's innocence established, the women of Peachtree Drive quickly inform her they always believed in her innocence. Nora, seemingly appreciative of their faith in her, informs them they will be receiving a little book in remembrance. The women of Peachtree Avenue express their happiness at receiving such a gift, until she announces its title—*How to Be a Hypocrite.*

Reel librarians do not appear in major leading roles again until 1945—*Adventure* and *Wonder Man.* Librarians continue to appear in supporting roles from 1938 to 1945, including such popular and classic films as *The Philadelphia Story* (1940), Orson Welles' *Citizen Kane* (1941), *The Human Comedy* (1943), and Alfred Hitchcock's *Shadow of a Doubt* (1943). A lesser-known murder mystery, *Quiet Please, Murder* (1942), uses a public library as its primary setting. The stereotypical image is dominant in supporting roles and, whenever possible, involved in some type of comical activity.

Start Cheering (1938), a college musical comedy, contains a brief library scene that highlights the talents of Jimmy Durante. The story is about Ted Crosley (Charles Starrett), a Hollywood star who plays college football heroes in movies but quits his movie career with Empire Pictures to attend Midland College. Ted desires to attend college without fanfare and does not reveal his identity.[28] The activities of his manager, Sam Lewis (Walter Connolly), and Sam's assistant, Willie Gumbatz (Durante), however, create disturbances on campus that are designed to get Ted expelled so that he will return to movies. They have an ultimatum from the head of Empire Pictures to get Ted back to work for the studio or forfeit all future business with Empire Pictures.

While walking on campus, Willie passes the library and decides to get a book. In the library, Willie meets a bespectacled librarian (Arthur Hoyt[29]) at the reference desk. The librarian adheres to all of the visual characteristics—"only 38," balding, dark suit, and glasses. He poses questions for Willie to answer, giving the incomparable Durante ample opportunity to display his talents. Two illustrative examples are representative of the comedic verbal exchanges between the librarian and Willie. First, as the librarian attempts to fill out a membership card for Willie, he asks Willie if he knows any responsible people. Willie responds, "Put down Judge Higgins ... he's responsible for my spending four years in jail." Second, when Willie asks for a book, he cannot remember its title but believes it begins with a "z." "Just a minute," responds the librarian; Willie, shaking his head and waving his arms, rejoins, "No, that ain't it." Hoyt portrays the college librarian to stereotypical perfection. He is perplexed at all of Willie's responses, and he displays the appropriate degree of exasperation and consternation to indicate that Willie has disturbed his staid occupational duties.

Confessions of a Nazi Spy and Mr. Moto in Danger Island, both released in 1939, include brief library scenes. In Confessions of a Nazi Spy, the scene occurs in the New York Public Library, where Kurt Schneider (Francis Lederer), an American spying for Nazi Germany, is looking for information. A young male librarian (uncredited[30]), located at a desk in the reading room, points Kurt to the material he is seeking. Although the librarian wears a dark suit, this brief exposure—less than 15 seconds—relies solely on occupational tasks to identify the screen character as a librarian. Without dialogue and the basic visual characteristics, other than a dark suit, the actor simply pantomimes the actions of a librarian to establish his credibility.

Peter Lorre is Mr. Moto, the popular Japanese detective, in Mr. Moto in Danger Island, a murder mystery involving the smuggling of South American diamonds through Puerto Rico. During his investigation, Moto, accompanied by Twister McGurk (Warren Hymer), who plays the role of bodyguard and comic sidekick, visits the San Juan Public Library to obtain the titles of items checked out by a murdered U.S. investigator. An "only 38" brunette (braided bun at nape), the librarian (uncredited; Renie Riano[31]) is very talkative and unhesitatingly gives Moto the titles of the items but not until after lamenting the fact that the books were never returned: "We haven't any other copies, and it's most annoying. If people would only realize the true value of books, and not take them away from the library, other people come...." At this point, Moto manages to cut off her discourse. She later gives Moto the directions to a swamp that is mentioned in one of the books, and as Moto and McGurk leave, the sidekick pulls out a cigar and starts to light it at the desk. The librarian stares him down; he extinguishes the match, muttering to the librarian, "Oh, read any good books lately, sister?" He tips his hat and hustles out of the library.

Motion pictures released during the 1940s, on the whole, base the recognition of reel librarians on the stereotypical image. In the majority of films released during the 1940s in which reel librarians appeared, they were in supporting roles, on-screen for brief time periods.

The first release of the 1940s with a reel librarian, Strike Up the Band (1940) stars the young singing and dancing duo of Judy Garland and Mickey Rooney in one of their teenage musical comedies. Garland[32] is Mary Holden, a young, attractive, and fashionably attired teenager, and, for one brief library scene and one song, a librarian. The library scene occurs just after Mary is jilted by Jimmy Connors (Rooney) for Barbara Morgan (June Preisser). The library creates the proper melancholy, desolate atmosphere for Mary to sing "(I Ain't Got) Nobody." The library is an excellent setting for a ballad, especially one with lyrics lamenting loneliness. This is the first motion picture in which the authors detected a library being used for a musical number. Garland's role as a librarian is limited to this scene and is inconsequential to the storyline.

In The Philadelphia Story (1940), journalist Macaulay Connor (James Stewart) visits a public library to research some local biography and history. Macaulay meets a librarian (uncredited; Hilda Plowright[33]), evidently a Quaker as suggested by her usage of "thee" and "thou," who momentarily stops shelving books in order to provide assistance. She wears a front pleated dress with small lace collar and has a low fishtail bun. As he walks around the library, Macaulay meets Tracy Lord (Katharine Hepburn) at a library table reading his book. As they chat, their voices elevate, and the librarian twice gives them a "shush" as she walks by the table. Actress Plowright projects the stereotypical image and adds one new dimension to the stereotype in American films— the "shush" for silence. Although the "shush" was used seven years earlier in *The Good Companions*, Plowright is the first American reel librarian the authors detected using the term; succeeding reel librarians added the "shush" to their vocabulary almost immediately.

From 1932 through 1940, the film industry's repeated use of visual characteristics and occupational tasks to identify reel librarians created a well-defined stereotypical image. That a vigorous image is firmly established and exists in films is corroborated by one scene in *Maisie Was a Lady*, a January 1941 release. Playboy Bob Rawlston (Lew Ayres) is responsible for Maisie (Ann Sothern) losing her job and is directed by a judge to provide employment for Maisie for two months. Bob, driving Maisie to the family's estate, suggests that she could work there. When Maisie questions him about the type of work she might do, he responds, "Well, we have quite a few books." Maisie, smiling, counters his suggestion, "Ah, c'mon now, do I look like a librarian?" Bob laughingly remarks, "Maybe you're right." For Maisie to know that she does not "look like a librarian," an image, a stereotype, for comparison is necessary. Bob also is cognizant of such an image, as he agrees with her analysis. Maisie convincingly demonstrates in these early scenes that she is not associated with the stereotype. She is an attractive blonde (collar length ringlet curls) whose youthful appearance belies the fact that Sothern was 34 in 1941. Maisie wears a short sleeve dress—sweetheart neckline with a bow, matching bows on sleeve cuffs and three rows of ruffles on the bottom of the dress. Her accessories include a dark picture hat decorated with flowers inside the brim and on top; ankle strap, open toe black pumps; multiple costume jewelry bracelets on both wrists; and long earrings. Maisie's quick rejection of working with books is in harmony with her personality, as looking "like a librarian" would imperil her individuality.

John Wayne stars as Lynn Hollister, a young attorney attempting to solve the murder of a friend, in *A Man Betrayed* (1941). The film has a one-minute library scene, with a librarian (Minerva Urecal[34]) displaying all of the visual characteristics of the stereotype—"only 38," eyeglasses, a dark long sleeve dress with cuff and neckline lace, and a bun at her nape. She is at the main desk, assisting Morris Slade (Harold Huber), an insider of the corrupt political party in power. When Morris leaves the desk, he walks by Lynn, who is doing legal research, pats him on the back, and says, "Hi ya sucker!" in a loud voice. The librarian responds immediately with a loud "shush" from the desk, halfway across the library. Shortly after Morris leaves, Lynn jumps up with a book in hand, screaming "Yea ho!" and runs out of the library as the librarian waves her arms, shouting, "You can't take books out of here." Republic Pictures, the studio responsible for *Navy Blues*, continues to promote the stereotype in this film.

In addition, the studio further advances the use of "shush," a negatively-charged connotative word that was introduced into the lexicon of American reel librarians only three months earlier. Its use by librarians in supporting roles, as in *The Philadelphia Story* and *A Man Betrayed*, reinforces the stereotypical image and continues the unflattering cinematic depiction of librarians. Associating the stereotypical image with the most obnoxious word in the occupation's lexicon reinforces the stability, the inalterability, of the image.

In May 1941 Orson Welles' masterpiece, *Citizen Kane*, appeared in American theaters. The film includes two brief library scenes (separated by an enactment of a text being read), which occur in the Thatcher Memorial Library of Philadelphia. Jerry Thompson (William Alland) visits the library in his search for the meaning or relevancy of Kane's last word, "Rosebud." The library's interior is inhospitable, menacingly imposing with its marble tile floors, walls, and matching large columns extending upward to its high ceiling. The library lacks any degree of warmth and comfort. Miss Anderson (Georgia Backus[35]) sits behind a desk, informing Thompson of the restrictions regarding the use of Thatcher's memoirs. She is abrupt and curt with him, and she does not respond to his remarks, repeatedly breaking into his statements to continue her litany of rules and regulations. Anderson leads him to a large steel door that opens into a large room with a single table and single chair. The only light in the room is provided by a skylight that directs a bright ray onto the table. An armed guard brings the manuscript to the table, and Anderson informs Jerry that he is to confine his reading to the chapter dealing with Kane. "Pages eighty-three to one forty-two," she remarks as she exits the room, leaving Jerry and the guard in the room. The sound of the heavy steel door echoes loudly as she closes it, imprisoning Jerry for his allotted time.

As Jerry reads the manuscript, the words slowly dissolve into a visual enactment of what he is reading. Anderson returns promptly at 4:30 and, with a grin, speaks to the guard, "It is 4:30, isn't it?" They appear to be happy that it is closing time. She informs Jerry that he has "enjoyed a very rare privilege" and then inquires, rather perfunctorily, "Did you find what you were looking for?" His response is an emphatic "No." He stands and gazes at the enormous framed painting of Thatcher hanging near the door and then asks Anderson if she is Rosebud. He immediately turns away and exclaims, "Goodbye, and thanks for the use of the hall." Anderson, dismayed by his question, takes off her glasses as he leaves.

In the script, authors Welles and Herman J. Mankiewicz describe Anderson as "an elderly, mannish spinster"[36] and Backus, as Anderson, faithfully projects this image. She wears a dark suit, white shirt, and tie. Her hair is short, combed straight back with a part in the middle; her wire-rimmed eyeglasses complement the manly appearance. Because she appears to enjoy reciting rules and regulations, providing minimal assistance, and smiling when announcing closing time, Anderson is a reel librarian whose personality is as inhospitable as the library in which she works.

The action in Warner Bros.' *This Was Paris* (1942) occurs in 1940 Paris, shortly before the German occupation. A newspaper reporter for the *Sidney-Chronicle*, Paris Office, Butch (Ben Lyon), is working on a fifth column story but is having difficulty verifying facts. Butch has one very important journalistic asset—he never forgets faces;

unfortunately, he is plagued with a major liability—he never remembers names. After meeting Van Der Stuyl (Robert Morley), Butch believes that he works for Nazi Germany and to uncover some information about Van Der Stuyl, the correspondent visits the newspaper's library.

The scene opens with Butch sitting atop a tall ladder, tossing documents out of folders onto the floor. The newspaper's librarian, Watson (Miles Malleson[37]), complains that Butch is "undoing the work of years." Watson insists, "You should put your request through me.... I can find the information you need." Butch, however, maintains the librarian couldn't find his "Aunt Fanny," and as he slides down the ladder, the reporter accidentally crunches Watson's fingers, causing Watson to scream. Butch then blames the librarian for the mishap, "You pushed me," and Watson, shaking his fingers in pain, comments that he will inform the managing editor immediately. Visibly upset about the mess, Watson continues to complain, "Look at my library. Look at it. For years I've keep these files, like my own children ... you come in like a bull in a china shop!" Butch, in a threatening manner, grabs Watson's coat lapel and screams, "Listen, you dried up little squirt. Germans in Paris, get that! Fifth column activity. Nazi spy recognized by our own correspondent. Get that word, recognize. And you talk about your files. Phooey!"

At this point, the managing editor enters and admonishes Watson, "How dare you keep this place in such filthy condition." Watson mumbles in response, but the editor points at the mess, "Tidy it up. Tidy it up. I'll talk to you later." The editor and Butch argue about his fifth column story; the editor, disbelieving what Butch has uncovered, finally tells Butch to "go and get drunk." As Butch leaves, the angry editor walks to Watson's desk, tosses documents into the air, and exclaims, "About this shambles. Would you like to clear it up? Or, shall I do it for you!" As the editor leaves, Watson removes his eyeglasses and covers his face with his hand.

This scene is primarily a comedy sketch, with Watson playing the buffoon. He becomes the pathetic individual to whom events happen, events he can neither combat nor control. As the scene begins, Watson attempts to exert a degree of authority but is immediately overrun by Butch. Watson never regains his composure. Watson's humiliation occurs quickly—Butch crunches his fingers, a comedic device used five years earlier in *Sea Devils*. Watson, an "only 38" librarian, dresses conservatively—dark suit, white shirt, and tie; his eyeglasses are propped on his forehead and occasionally fall down, only to be pushed back up.

For filmgoers, the humor may have been most entertaining when directed at Watson's occupation. Watson's occupational talent for locating information is discredited by Butch—"You couldn't even find your Aunt Fanny." Watson's request of Butch to maintain the orderliness of the library is ignored; the reporter cannot be curbed in his quest for information. Watson's cry for Butch to stop his devastation of the newspaper's library file system is the equivalent of a public librarian's "shush" for silence. Watson's ability to maintain an orderly library is then questioned by the managing editor, who blames the librarian for the rampant disorder of materials. During this scene, Butch further denigrates the librarian when he resorts to personal name-calling, labeling Watson a "dried up little squirt." Filmgoers undoubtedly laughed at Watson's consternation and ineptitude, at a bewildered librarian deficient in coping skills. Watson is a librarian, an occupation that thrives on orderliness, standing in the midst of disarray.

The primary setting of 20th Century–Fox's 1942 murder mystery *Quiet Please, Murder* is a public library located on K Street in Washington, D.C. The film opens in the public library with a rare book thief and forger, Fleg (George Sanders), admiring *The Richard Burbage Edition of Shakespeare's Hamlet* and discussing its value with a library guard. As the guard walks away, Fleg shoots him and steals the book. Fleg makes copies of originals and sells them to buyers who know that the book they are buying is stolen but believe they are buying the original, not a forgery.

More than 48 minutes of this 70-minute film occur in the library, and five reel librarians—four women and one man—weave in and out of the story as the plot unravels and Fleg and his gang are apprehended. Three of the women librarians are elderly and one is very young and attractive, continuing the cinematic pattern of enhancing the beauty of the youngest librarian by surrounding her with coworkers who are substantially older and who dress conservatively. The male librarian not only is older and conservatively dressed but also the on-duty supervisor.

The plot is so convoluted that its progression is extremely difficult to follow. As one reviewer remarked, "If it were vaguely possible to determine just who is chasing whom and who gets caught there might be a little more reason for all this snooping and shooting in the dark. But the whole thing is oddly bewildering; the plot is as thick as a stew."[38] The complexity of the plot accelerates when Martin Cleaver (Sidney Blackmer), a collector for the Nazi party, purchases a forgery and then demands the return of his money when he discovers he has been swindled. Fleg's dishonest and belligerent associate, Myra Blandy (Gail Patrick), refuses to return the $20,000 purchase price[39] and places the blame on Fleg. When Hal McByrne (Richard Denning), a private detective investigating the sale of a forgery to a New Yorker, visits Blandy, he reveals that he has traced a forgery to her. Sensing that McByrne likes her, Blandy agrees to dine with him. After he leaves, she devises a plan to eliminate McByrne, satisfy Cleaver's desire to eliminate Fleg, and keep the money. She informs Cleaver that Fleg, whom he has not meet, will pick up a book at the library at 8 P.M., using the name McByrne. After dinner, Blandy stops the taxi at the library and asks McByrne to pick up a book for her. Cleaver and his henchmen are in the library waiting for McByrne, believing he is Fleg. The real Fleg, however, is also in the library posing as a Lt. Craven of the Homicide Department; he is planning to steal some additional rare books.

The inevitable mix-up of identities results in the murder of Cleaver by a member of Fleg's gang who believes Cleaver is McByrne. After the murder occurs, Fleg (as Lt. Craven) takes command of the library and seemingly telephones police headquarters for assistance; he actually telephones his gang who are waiting for his call. The gang, some dressed as police officers, arrive and close the library, keeping everybody inside. McByrne figures out the identity problems and succeeds in getting the real police to the library, but only after several misguided attempts. When the real police arrive, Fleg and his gang are apprehended and Blandy is murdered by one of Cleaver's henchmen shortly after she leaves the library.

Librarians appear in the film as soon as McByrne walks into the library. Miss

Philbert (uncredited; Fern Emmett[40]), an "only 38" librarian, is busy checking out books at the Information Desk. She wears a dark long-sleeve dress with a large white collar and black bow tie, and has a bun at her nape. Librarian Kay Ryan (Lynne Roberts[41]), a youthful, attractive brunette (sides pulled back into shoulder length ringlet curls; soft curls on top), shouts a greeting at McByrne as he enters the lobby, mistaking him for her boyfriend. Kay is attired in a light suit with a white revers collar; the suit coat has a white V-neckline front. As she and McByrne walk to the Information Desk, he asks, "Say, Where's the Information Desk?" Kay, displaying a keen, but not abrasive, sense of humor, responds, "Why, its always been right here!" He asks about a book for Blandy and converses with Kay about her job:

McByrne: How long have you been in this racket?
Kay: About a year.
McByrne: Like it?
Kay: Most of the time.
McByrne: Gee, how do you stand the quiet in here?
Kay: I'm hardened to it.

McByrne turns around, looks into the lobby and reading room, and leans back against the desk, while Kay turns to look for Blandy's book on the shelves behind the desk. Philbert returns to the desk as McByrne continues to talk. "You know, you ought to be in pictures, Beautiful," he declares as he turns around, only to discover he is facing and speaking to Philbert. She looks dumbfounded, and he quickly adds, "I'm not kidding." Cleaver approaches McByrne, believing he is Fleg, and they go into a library room to discuss the forgery; the cat-and-mouse game of identities begins.

Two librarians with administrative responsibilities appear frequently during the ensuing 40-minute sequence in the library. Edmund Walpole (uncredited; Byron Foulger[42]), head of the Reference Room, is a mustachioed man of small stature with a nervous personality; he wears a dark vested suit, white shirt, dark tie, and wire rim eyeglasses. Miss Oval (uncredited; Margaret Brayton[43]), a brunette (bob with soft curls), works in the manuscripts room and is attired in a dark suit. Very concerned about protecting the library's rare items, Walpole and Oval remove several important books from the manuscripts vault and a Jefferson manuscript from a display case and give them to Fleg (as Lt. Craven) for police protection. As Fleg examines the Jefferson manuscript, McByrne manages to place the other books on a booktruck which is taken away by a library staff member. Blandy, now in the library, manages without being observed to purloin and hide the books in the stacks. When Fleg's gang notices the books are missing, they begin scouring for them, while McByrne, in addition to searching for the books, is trying to alert the real police.

As they hunt for the books, McByrne and Kay engage in several conversations. On one occasion, McByrne remarks that there are many books in the stacks; Kay responds, "two miles of books." Impressed, McByrne asks if they could get lost in the stacks; Kay, smiling, bounces back quickly, "You might." Kay explains the Dewey Decimal classification system to him as they walk through the stacks; he appears to understand its overall design and principles and, later, uses the information gleaned from this brief informative lecture to find the missing books. McByrne, never tiring of making passes at Kay, continues to flirt with her, "You ever try using all of that con-centration on something that wears pants and smokes a cigar?" Kay smiles at his per-sistence but insists she is happy with her boyfriend. McByrne counters, "I wish I'd met you before noon today."

"Why?"

"Then I wouldn't have already fallen for somebody else [Blandy]," he replies.

Kay enjoys McByrne's humor but has no romantic interest in him. He appears to go through these futile overtures to appease his ego, as he realizes that she is very happy in her present relationship and plans to marry her boyfriend. He provides an opportunity, however, for a reel librarian, as well as filmgoers, to smile at his attempts.

During the frantic search for the missing books, the library is notified of an impending air raid alert. When the sirens begin, Walpole, the building's air raid war-den, anxiously orders Oval and Miss Hartwig (uncredited; Mae Marsh[44]), to get every-one into the basement shelter. Walpole is shouting, "Please walk, don't run," as he hurriedly dashes to the Information Desk to get his helmet and turn off the lights. Hartwig wears a dark suit and white blouse, and sports a bun. "Don't be nervous. Our shelter is bombproof," Hartwig informs the crowd as she, Oval, and the library guards corral everybody into the shelter. When Walpole receives a suspicious all clear signal from McByrne, he wants to call his warden to verify the signal. Oval, however, is so upset by the murder and blackout that she begins switching on the lights, as Walpole shouts, "Miss Oval! Miss Oval! You're disobeying my orders!" Oval's dis-obedience, however, compels the police to rush to the library to determine the cause of the violation of the black out, and as soon as the police enter the building, they arrest Fleg and his gang.

The librarians in *Quiet Please, Murder* are competent and handle their responsi-bilities efficiently. Kay has a larger role than the other reel librarians and, as in ear-lier movies, she is younger than her coworkers—by at least two decades. Her attire is more fashionable and brighter than the dark, conservative clothes worn by the oth-ers. Kay is knowledgeable of her occupation, as evidenced by her explanation of the Dewey system, and she has adjusted to McByrne's presumed "quiet" condition of the library. Kay is friendly, personable; she appears to enjoy McByrne's company, listens to his overtures and just smiles. She never verbally rebuffs him. When pursued by one of Fleg's henchmen in the stacks, she displays the intelligence to remove her shoes, thereby eliminating the sound of her footsteps and making it difficult for the henchman to find her in the dark.

Walpole displays many of the same characteristics as Wilkinson in *Forbidden* (1932)—elderly, eyeglasses, conservatively dressed in a dark suit with a vest. Supple-menting Walpole's "only 38" characteristic is a receding hairline that is making significant strides toward baldness. He is visibly nervous and anxious, displaying a personality trait not exhibited by earlier reel librarians. The anxiety-laden Walpole, especially during the air raid, becomes a comic figure, demonstrating his knowledge of the situation but carrying out his responsibilities in a very humorous manner. In addition to being head of Reference and air raid warden, he has a wide range of administrative responsibilities in this film, including the authority to offer a reward of $5,000 for the missing books.

The actors portraying librarians in *Quiet Please, Murder* project the same basic characteristics as the actors in the films of the 1930s and early 1940s. The director, John Larkin, also wrote the screenplay; the majority of his work in films was as a writer, primarily of mysteries. His reliance on previous film images of librarians is evident. One image, Emmett's portrayal of Miss Philbert, is almost an exact visual copy of Emmett's Miss McGonigle in *Sea Devils* (1937), but without pince-nez. Larkin uses librarians for the lighter moments in the film—the banter between Kay and McByrne, Philbert's reaction to McByrne's comment about being in pictures, and Walpole's nervous antics throughout the film. Although Larkin depicts librarians as capable workers, he emphasizes the basic traits of the stereotype, as well as using them for humor.

Six motion pictures released in 1943—*Shadow of a Doubt, The Human Comedy, The Seventh Victim, Flesh and Fantasy, Whispering Footsteps,* and *Mystery Broadcast*—have screen characters who are easily identifiable as librarians. The reel librarians in these films have supporting roles with minimal screen exposure.

The reel librarian in Alfred Hitchcock's *Shadow of a Doubt* (1943) is on-screen for less than 30 seconds. Charlie Newton (Teresa Wright) rushes to the public library to check a newspaper but arrives several minutes after closing time. The librarian, Miss Cochran (uncredited; Eily Malyon[45]), is turning off the lights, and Charlie knocks on the door until the librarian responds. Although clearly reluctant to permit Charlie to enter, the librarian states that "if I make one exception, I'll have to make a thousand" and after giving Charlie a brief lecture about using the library during its regular hours, she permits Charlie to look at the newspapers for three minutes.

An "only 38" librarian, she is attired in a dark long sleeve wrap-around dress, V-neckline, with contrasting light lapels; her hair is gray and pulled up into a bun on her crown. The librarian's defense of library hours further promotes the stereotypical image by showing librarians to be dogmatic about rules. Such inflexibility reinforces the mundane, ordinary existence of librarians. The fact, however, is that she permits Charlie to use the library after hours in violation of library rules. Later in the film, Jack Graham (MacDonald Carey) in a discussion with Charlie remarks that Charlie's sister "wants to marry a librarian ... so she'll always have plenty of books around to read." Charlie breaks out in laughter at the remark as Jack smiles. This remark conjures up the image of librarians as bookworms and, consequently, results in laughter. These brief scenes promote the stereotypical image.

The Human Comedy (1943) contains a library scene in which a librarian (uncredited; Adeline De Walt Reynolds[46]) appears on-screen for about 50 seconds. Two youngsters, Lionel (Darryl Hickman) and Ulysses Macauley (Jack Jenkins) visit the public library to return a book. The two boys walk up and down the aisles of the bookshelves, admiring the books—Lionel points out several books, "There's a red one," "There's a green one," while Ulysses, the younger of the two, points towards an unabridged dictionary on a stand and says, "There's a big one." As they continue walking, the librarian, standing on a tall ladder, notices them and asks, "What are you boys looking for?" She descends the ladder, and questions the boys in a stern manner but mellows very quickly when she discovers that neither boy can read but both enjoy looking at books. "One day when you learn to read, you'll find there's a great deal to be said for the inside of books." She smiles brightly, adding, "I've been reading for 70 years; it hasn't been nearly long enough. Now run along and look at the books." Reynolds is wearing a long sleeve blouse, black bow, and long dark skirt; she has gray hair (horseshoe waves; bun at crown). No filmgoer can mistake Reynolds' stereotypical image.

Producer Val Lewton and director Mark Robson are the creative team responsible for *The Seventh Victim* (1943). This horror film completely overwhelmed one critic who wrote that "we have no more notion of what 'The Seventh Victim' ... is about than if we had watched the same picture run backward and upside down."[47] *The Seventh Victim* contains a 50-second library scene in which the librarian makes one of the most culpable errors of judgment that a librarian can make—disregarding the confidentiality of a patron's library records.

Jason Hoag (Erford Gage) visits a public library to find out what books two people have been reading. He compliments the librarian, Miss Gottschalk (uncredited; Sarah Selby[48]), "You have such lovely hands ... so slim and capable," as her fingers flip through a patron library card tray. She informs Jason that it is against the rules to give out information about patrons but then asks why he needs the information. He intends to give his friends some books and wants to know what books they have been reading. When Jason asks to see the books, Gottschalk plays his game, flirting and teasing back with a smile on her face, "Why Mr. Hoag, most of these books are on the closed shelf. You'll have to get permission." The ease with which Jason charmed Gottschalk into providing this information, coupled with her flagrant disregard of the library's rules on patron confidentiality, is alarming. Filmgoers observed a reel librarian being easily manipulated by a member of the opposite sex with a simple compliment. The extent to which filmgoers believe Gottschalk's behavior is transferable to working librarians depends upon whether they believe that reel librarians accurately reflect the ethics of working librarians. Gottschalk, a single "only 38" reel librarian, dresses conservatively and sports a modified Gibson, jelly rolled around the circumference of her head and flat at the crown.

Flesh and Fantasy is a trilogy of stories; the second story occurs in London and contains a brief library scene. Marshall Tyler (Edward G. Robinson) visits a library to obtain information on poisons. As he leaves, the bespectacled librarian (uncredited; Ian Wolfe[49]), with back to the camera, asks a most appropriate question, "Did you find what you were looking for, Mr. Tyler?" Photographed primarily in shadows, the librarian is an elderly man in a dark suit; his right profile appears only momentarily. As did Jessie Matthews in *The Good Companions* (1933), Robinson shares very little of the limelight with the reel librarian.

Two murder mysteries from Republic Pictures, *Whispering Footsteps* and *Mystery Broadcast*, have librarians in supporting roles. *Whispering Footsteps* focuses on Marcus "Mark" Borne (John Hubbard), a resident of Ma Murphy's (Mary Gordon) boardinghouse in Medallion, Ohio. When Mark returns from a vacation near Cambridge, Indiana, where a college student was murdered, a special investigator begins to tail him because he resembles the description of the murderer. The boardinghouse's residents begin to suspect Mark, especially after he is questioned by the investigator and cannot provide alibis for the times that other murders occurred. When a woman living next door to the boardinghouse is murdered, the residents are extremely suspicious of Mark.

Shortly after the film begins, the residents are breakfasting at the boardinghouse. One of the boardinghouse residents is an "only 38" librarian, Sally Lukens (Marie Blake[50]), who works at the Medallion Public Library. Ma Murphy shows Sally a bracelet that Mark gave her upon his return; the librarian, seemingly perturbed, responds, "Of course, Mrs. Murphy, I can't wear jewelry in the library. It gets in my way when I'm marking the books." Sally may not wear bracelets, but she wears large earrings, necklaces, and rings.

Later, while in the city at lunchtime, Mark notices an investigator following him and darts into the public library. As he stands near the desk and watches the investigator, Sally, preparing to leave for lunch, greets Mark, "Why, Marcus Aurelius Borne! At last you've condescended to visit my dull little sanctum." She asks Mark to join her, but all he wants is a book, any book. He takes one from the desk and hands it to Sally who, hoping to lunch with Mark, responds, "You can take the book now, and the card will be ready for you when we come back from lunch." Mark states that he will get the card later and exits the library. Sally, displeased with missing a luncheon with Mark, turns and looks at the librarian (uncredited[51]) behind the desk, who is smiling; the smile evaporates quickly as Sally stares. She has an innocent crush on Mark, but he is oblivious to the fact. She is always polite to Mark at breakfast, and he occasionally offers a compliment, "Well, what lovely earrings." Sally appears in two additional very short library scenes, each no more than ten seconds in length, and in various other scenes at the boardinghouse.

Sally is a very talkative individual, as illustrated by her chattering at Ma Murphy's breakfast table; she enjoys gossip. She also has a morbid curiosity about the details of murders. When one of the boarders reads the newspaper account of one murder, Sally encourages him, "What about the murder? Read some of the gory details." On the occasion of another murder, she asks the boarder, "Where did it happen? What town?" When told the name of the town, she smiles, "Only 90 miles from here. Well, go on, what else?" Sally's facial expressions indicate that she welcomes and enjoys this type of news: it is radically different from the sterile environment of her "dull little sanctum." This type of behavior is reminiscent of librarian Susan Merrill (*Gentlemen Are Born*, 1934), who welcomed the excitement of the boxing ring after a day at the library.

A brunette (finger waves, soft curls at nape), Sally wears modest clothes, indicating a low to moderate income, which is in accord with her lodging at a boardinghouse. She fancies costume jewelry, always wearing several pieces quite conspicuously. Although Sally is comfortable in her library position, she projects the image of a single woman who is interested in a male companion, preferring a husband to a lifetime of work in a library.

The second librarian, a young brunette (bun on top of head; accessorized with a wide bow) wearing a short sleeve checkered blouse, open collar, is stamping books at the desk when Mark enters the library. Although she smiles when Mark leaves the library without Sally, this librarian is quick to put on a stern business face when Sally glances at her. The Medallion Public Library is an institution with a serious-minded supervisor.

In *Mystery Broadcast*, Jan Cornell (Ruth Terry), a radio mystery show host, announces that on her next show she will identify the murderer of Lenore Fenwicke, whose death is an unsolved crime of 1931. After the show at a local restaurant, Jan unexpectedly meets her radio rival, Michael Jerome (Frank Albertson), who hosts a mystery show on the air at the same time. While dining, Jan receives a telephone call from Mida Kent (Alice Fleming), one of her show's cast members. Michael volunteers to take Jan to Mida's apartment where they find her dead; she has been murdered. Jan telephones a newspaper reporter about the murder of Mida; the reporter informs the police and rushes to the apartment.

After being questioned at police headquarters, Jan and Michael accompany the reporter to *The Chronicle* to research the murder of Lenore Fenwicke. Arriving at the building shortly after 3:00 A.M., Jan and Michael go to *The Chronicle*'s morgue to locate clipping files and old newspapers. The person in charge of the morgue—the Library and Index Department—is Mr. Crunch (Francis Pierlot[52]), who suddenly appears while Jan and Michael are going through vertical files. He informs the surprised couple that the reporter "hadn't any right to send you down here without my permission. I'm in charge of this morgue." Crunch, although a little brash when first encountering them, provides the appropriate guidance and information for them to research the murder. As Jan reads through the newspapers and Michael sleeps on them, Crunch sits at his desk, laughing as he reads a book, *The Pitchfork Murders*. He mutters, "Oh, excuse me. This story is so amusing." Crunch appears several other times throughout the film. His contribution to the case is important, as he has the one item, a photograph, that identifies the murderer. Realizing the danger he may be facing, Crunch telephones Jan and leaves the photograph in the morgue where she finds it in time to identify the murderer on her radio show.

Crunch is a bespectacled, balding, "only 38" individual who dresses conservatively (vested suit and tie). He typifies the stereotype, as all visual characteristics are evident. To further solidify his status as a librarian, he reads on the job and maintains that he is "in charge" of the Library and Index Department.

Reel librarians of the foregoing six films of 1943 display the visual characteristics of the stereotype. The stereotypical image is extremely important when actors appear on-screen for only a few seconds as librarians. Actors and directors must use these seconds to convince filmgoers that the character is a librarian using visual characteristics and occupational tasks. In addition, standard occupational colloquialisms of working librarians—"shush," "did you find what you were looking for," "if I make one exception, I'll have to make a thousand"—spoken by reel librarians strengthen the cast member's identity as a librarian. Gottschalk in *The Seventh Victim* is an unprincipled librarian; even though her indiscretion may be interpreted as a minor infraction of the rules, she knowingly violates one of the basic principles of her occupation.

One top grossing film of 1944, *Lady in the Dark*, contains a brief library scene. The Technicolor film stars Ginger Rogers as Liza Elliott who, in a flashback of her high school days, recalls meeting the most handsome boy in her class, Ben (Rand Brooks), in the library on the evening of a big dance. Ben, having broken up with his girlfriend, plans to skip the dance, while Liza never attends such functions. The two begin a conversation, and the librarian, Ms. Black (Mary MacLaren[53]), attempts to quiet them by shushing, tapping a pencil on the desk for silence, and finally by uttering a stern, "Please." Liza and Ben decide to go to the dance together, and as the two teenagers rush out of the library, Black is momentarily visible. An "only 38" individual, she is attired in a dark dress.

Weird Woman (1944), one of Universal Pictures' Inner Sanctum Mystery entries, stars one of the best-known actors in "B" horror and mystery genre films of the 1940s, Lon Chaney, Jr. The story focuses on Norman Reed (Chaney), a professor of ethnology at Monroe College; Paula Reed (Anne Gwynne), his wife; and their problems with antagonist Ilona Carr (Evelyn Ankers[54]), the college's librarian.

Ilona expected to become Mrs. Reed when Norman returned from a research trip to "the islands," but is distressed and embarrassed when he arrives back on campus with Paula, his new bride. Ilona, angered by Norman's rejection, begins a campaign to destroy the newlyweds. She convinces Evelyn Sawtelle (Elizabeth Russell), wife of Professor Millard Sawtelle (Ralph Morgan), that Paula, with her "witchcraft and island magic," is a "witch wife" and will prevent her husband from being appointed chair of the Sociology Department, a position for which Millard and Norman are candidates. Millard's new book has just been published, and Ilona informs the professor that Norman will soon disclose the book is plagiarized from a student's thesis. According to Ilona, Norman plans to disgrace Millard in order to obtain the vacant chairmanship. It is Ilona, however, who discovered Millard's plagiarism; Norman is unaware of Millard's misuse of the student's paper. Millard commits suicide rather than face academic disgrace, and Ilona assures Evelyn that Paula and Norman are responsible for her husband's suicide. Ilona also manages to arouse the ire and jealousy of the boyfriend of Norman's student worker; the irate young man decides to shoot Norman, but the plan goes awry. As he struggles with Norman, the young man is wounded when the pistol discharges and he dies several days later in a hospital.

When Norman finally deduces that Ilona is the scheming troublemaker, he develops a plan, with assistance from Evelyn, to expose Ilona. Fearing a prediction of the evildoer's death that Evelyn supposedly received from Millard in a dream, Ilona admits her guilt. When she realizes that she has been tricked into a confession, Ilona bolts out a second story window and, as she runs across a lattice cover, the wood breaks and Ilona falls, only to have the vines wrap around her neck, hanging her at the precise time of the prediction.

Ilona, an attractive young blonde (ringlet curl bang; pompadour front; bun at nape) is stylishly clothed in dresses, modish suits, and formal evening attire throughout the film. She fails to project visual characteristics of the stereotype; the costume jewelry that she wears in most scenes is as outlandish as that worn by Maisie in *Maisie Was a Lady* (1941). Three scenes occur in the library and Ilona's office, which opens into the library. As in *Gentlemen Are Born* (1934), the sets are minimal. Visible in the library are a small study table with two chairs; two walls of built-in shelving with books; a tall ladder; a dictionary stand with an unabridged dictionary; and on a third wall, a large world map hanging above a small display table with books. The door to Ilona's office is next to the wall map; the office contains a desk and chair, one visitor's chair, three vertical file drawers, a hat rack, a vase stand with plant, and a small four-shelf glass enclosed bookcase. Ilona's office appears to be almost as large as the library, which is drastically inadequate for any college but, for cinematic purposes, establishes the illusion of a library.

Earlier librarians worked toward improving their own positions in life. The sheer mean-spirited, calculating, and jealousy-driven personality of Ilona is unique to reel librarians. Ilona directs her energies toward ruining the lives of Norman and Paula; her passion to destroy Norman is an unrelenting obsession. To ensure Norman's downfall, she designs and executes a dastardly plan. She repeatedly lies to Evelyn and to Millard, resulting in the professor's suicide. She gleefully utters innuendoes and insinuations about Norman to the boyfriend of his student worker, resulting in the death of the young man. Ilona demonstrates that deceit can be masterfully exercised by reel librarians. Filmgoers undoubtedly believed that Ilona's misdeeds justified her death, a fitting end to an evildoer.

A supporting character in *Destiny* (1944), Betty (Grace McDonald[55]), identifies herself as a librarian but the film does not contain a library scene. Betty is driving her convertible coupe late at night on a lonely mountainous road and picks up hitchhiker Cliff Banks (Alan Curtis), an ex-convict being pursued by the police for a bank robbery. Betty is a personable, young, talkative brunette (multi-pincurl bang; sides pulled back; soft curls at nape) who displays no fear of Banks after listening to a radio announcement describing him. He puts his hand in his jacket, pointing a pistol at her. She makes a remark about the "heater," prompting Banks to ask, "Where did you get that heater stuff?" "Oh, I read a couple of books," she responds, identifying herself as "the librarian at Bentley Springs." He convinces Betty that he is the "fall guy," which is true, and she hides him from a motorcycle patrolman who stops her car. Minutes later, however, he directs Betty to turn off the highway and drive on a country road. She stops the car at his request; he takes the ignition key and walks away, leaving Betty stranded in the countryside.

Betty's occupation is not important to the storyline of *Destiny*. Betty, evidently to convince filmgoers that she is in a position to know about a "heater," declares that she is a "reader" and a "librarian." Her attire—a light jacket, narrow dark lapels, a white blouse, V-neckline, and large sparkling earrings—is not typical reel librarian attire. Filmgoers could not have deduced Betty's occupation based on her personality and attire, which contradict the visual characteristics.

The repetition of the stereotypical image is commonplace in motion pictures during 1933–1944, especially if the library scene is of short duration and the reel librarian appears on-screen for only seconds.

The popular and critically well-received motion picture *A Tree Grows in Brooklyn*, based on Betty Smith's popular novel with the same title, is the first picture released in 1945 with a reel librarian. The story is about a family living in the tenements of Brooklyn. The film's focus is Francie Nolan (Peggy Ann Garner), the young daughter of Katie Nolan (Dorothy McGuire), a mother constantly struggling against poverty. Francie visits the public library to return a book and to check out a new one—Richard Burton's *The Anatomy of Melancholy*. Surprised by Francie's choice of this book, the librarian (uncredited; Lillian Bronson[56]) questions her about it. Francie responds that she is reading her way through the library and Burton's book is the next one on her list. Francie, in an almost defiant manner, tells the librarian, "I want to read clear through the alphabet. I want to know everything in the world." The librarian offers her another book, *When Knighthood Was in Flower*, to read "just for fun," adding, "It's Saturday. I'll have a headache thinking about you wrestling with *The Anatomy of Melancholy* all weekend." Francie agrees to take the book, leaving the library with a happy smile on her face.

The librarian, a youthful-looking "only 38" brunette (bun at crown), wears a striped, long sleeve blouse with long, narrow necktie in a Windsor knot, similar to a man's necktie. She unnerves Francie when she asks about the choice of Burton's tome but changes her approach when Francie explains her reasons for selecting *The Anatomy of Melancholy*. By suggesting a second book "just for fun," the librarian is able to regain Francie's trust, as evidenced by Francie's smile when she leaves the desk. Although the stereotypical image is identifiable, director Elia Kazan and actress Bronson present a reel librarian who mirrors the type of encounter that filmgoers expect from and experience with working librarians.

Although *Lady in the Dark* (1944) is the first Technicolor motion picture to include a librarian in its cast, the role of the librarian is very inconsequential; she appears on-screen for only a few seconds. Filmgoers enjoyed their first reel librarian in a leading role in Technicolor in Samuel Goldwyn's *Wonder Man* (1945), a Danny Kaye vehicle featuring lovely Virginia Mayo[57] as librarian Ellen Shavley. A stunningly attractive, young blonde (shoulder length soft curls), Ellen works in a small, busy public library where silence is paramount. Large SILENCE signs are prominently displayed on walls, Quiet Please signs on library tables, and the "shush" is the preferred method of enforcement.

The first library scene occurs within the first ten minutes of the film. Ellen is in a glass-enclosed study room assisting a patron, Mrs. Leland Hume (Natalie Schafer), quite obviously without success. When Ellen exits the room, she walks to Edwin Dingle (Kaye), a scholar who uses the library daily, leans over his shoulder, and whispers, "I'll go off the deep end any minute if that woman doesn't...." Exasperated with Hume, Ellen is content to let the patron struggle alone. Edwin and Ellen continue whispering, and the glances exchanged between the two reveal that she is romantically interested in him, while he is embarrassed and visibly uncomfortable. Hume exits the study room, complaining in a very loud voice to Ellen—"young woman," as she calls her. Trying to placate Hume, Ellen responds, "Madam, I've been doing my best." Edwin interrupts their discussion and quotes from memory the information Hume is seeking. Hume looks at Edwin, who is writing notes with both hands, and shouts, "Oh good Heavens! He writes with both hands!" Other patrons "shush" at Hume, point to Quiet Please signs, and utter "Please" in a plea for silence. Hume, taking affront at this reaction by other patrons, responds loudly to all of them, "Don't 'shush' me, this is a public library. I pay my taxes." Ellen takes Hume aside, informing her that Edwin studies in the library "every day from 9 to 6" and is "writing a book called 'The Outline of Human Knowledge.'" Impressed, Hume invites Edwin to entertain at one of her literary teas. Thoroughly disgusted with Hume's loud outbursts, the other patrons, making as much noise as possible, slam their books shut and walk out of the library. Edwin declines the invitation, stating he has "ochlophobia, a morbid fear of crowds, especially women." Unsuccessful, and not wanting her friends exposed to this terrible affliction, as well as herself, Hume rushes out of the library.

Wonder Man (1945). Milquetoast Edwin Dingle (Danny Kaye) and librarian Ellen Shavley (Virginia Mayo) on rolling library ladders, just seconds before he falls and brings down several shelves of books. (Photograph courtesy of the Academy of Motion Picture Arts and Sciences.)

Alone in the library with Edwin, Ellen apologizes, "I'm sorry I let her bother you, it was my fault." He assures her that the incident was handled properly. Ellen rejoins, "I can't imagine how you ever controlled your temper. You should have spit in her eye!" She promises he will not be disturbed when he returns, adding coyly, "Do you think you'll be coming back tomorrow?" Edwin will be back, because he likes the library and "loves the smell of leather bindings." Ellen, disappointed at his response, walks away; he follows immediately, asking her to have dinner with him "sometime around the first of next month." The delay, he explains, has "to do with my allowance." Not to be denied an immediate dinner date, Ellen invites him to her apartment, "I've got millions of canned things." Edwin accepts, and she asks with a flirtatious smile if there is a cure for ochlophobia. He responds, "Oh, yes, decidedly," then sheepishly, "decidedly."

In this library scene, Ellen dresses conservatively in a long black dress with a large white collar and yellow bow. Her occupational tasks include providing reference assistance and, equally important, maintaining decorum, with a strong emphasis on silence. Ellen's inability to locate the answer to Hume's question is understandable—librarians cannot be experts in all subject areas. Ellen's exasperation with Hume is obvious in her remark to Edwin, "You should have spit in her eye;" a latent desire of Ellen's that she would never realize. She is conspicuously attracted to Edwin, coupling her suggestive verbal comments with body language that even a milquetoast like Edwin could understand. The ultimate advance is asking him to her apartment.

Preparing dinner at her apartment, Ellen praises Edwin's intellect endlessly while denigrating her own. "If I had any mind at all, I'd be a brazen hussy," she says. The comment, uttered primarily to elicit a laugh and ease the tension between them, works. However, the self-analysis is evident—she does not consider herself smart. Ellen's cooking skills also fail her; the soufflé falls. They decide to have frankfurters, and Edwin goes out for potato salad; however, he is sidetracked to Brooklyn to meet the ghost of his murdered twin brother, Buzzy Bellew, who is able to enter and take over Edwin's body. This begins Edwin's dual-role comedic murder-mystery adventure.

When free of the ghost of Buzzy, at least momentarily the next day, Edwin returns to the library to explain his predicament to Ellen. The library is filled with patrons and very quiet. Ellen again is dressed conservatively—grey skirt, light blouse, bow tie, and a dark jacket. She is shelving books, climbing up a rolling ladder to access the top shelves. Edwin, upon entering the library, leaps over a waist-high barrier rail, walks to the shelves, and begs Ellen to listen. She refuses, and he climbs a second ladder, rolls it next to her ladder, and attempts to explain. Ellen's attempts to quiet Edwin are unsuccessful; she becomes as loud and vociferous as he as they climb up and down the ladders. The facial expressions of the patrons exhibit their total exasperation with the situation and noise. After climbing up and down several times and rolling the ladder back and forth in an effort to be near Ellen, Edwin falls off the ladder. He lands on the floor and the top shelf and its books tumble down on him. The scene fades and resumes with Edwin pacing in front of the library building. As Ellen emerges, Edwin runs to speak with her; she responds harshly, "You've got a nerve hanging around here, you just got me fired!" He tries to describe the events of the previous night, but she doesn't believe him, cutting off his attempt by suggesting that he's "nutty as a fruitcake, first thing you know two men in uniform will be coming to carry you off." At this point, a police car arrives, two policemen grab Edwin by the arms, put him in the car, and drive away. Ellen, somewhat shocked, mutters, "Only yesterday he was just a nice, sweet ordinary genius." The ensuing action permits Kaye, as Edwin, to demonstrate an array of his many talents, as he runs and hides from the villains.

As the film ends, Edwin and Ellen marry, and in their bedroom on their honeymoon, Ellen quotes an insipid statistic about Niagara Falls. Edwin quickly responds, "You know, Honey, what you need is to get away from those musty old books."

Ellen's appearance and dress do not reflect the visual characteristics of the stereotype; however, occupational tasks identify her as a librarian—answering questions, standing on a ladder, and shelving books. Ellen's romantic interest in Edwin is so obvious that her behavior clearly demonstrates that she is more interested in Edwin than in a career as a librarian. She reveals that single librarians act as other single individuals, especially in matters relating to the opposite sex. Ellen displays more ingenuity in her attempts to lasso Edwin than she does in her efforts to maintain silence in the library. She cannot handle unruly patrons; consequently, after two consecutive days of unacceptable noise levels, she loses her position. Unfortunately, the library only provided Ellen with respectable employment rather than with a rewarding career.

During the 1940s the number of films utilizing Technicolor increased, permitting actors and directors to present reel librarians in vivid, colorful apparel. Ellen's attire in *Wonder Man* demonstrates that traditional black-and-white clothing is not mandatory for reel librarians. Actors portraying librarians may have worn colorful costumes during the filming of a motion picture released in black-and-white, but onscreen their costumes appear as black, white, and varying shades of gray. To continue presenting reel librarians as they appeared in black-and-white films affords filmmakers and actors a comfort level—the absolute certainty that filmgoers will recognize the stereotype. To change such an entrenched and fundamental visual characteristic—dark, modest, conservative clothing—is a challenge that many filmmakers may have been reluctant to undertake.

Clark Gable returned to motion pictures after World War II in *Adventure* (1945), the third film in which Gable appears in a library scene. *Adventure* contains one of the most entertaining reference encounters in twentieth century cinema. Harry Patterson (Gable), an irreverent, boisterous, smart-mouthed boatswain in the merchant marine, takes Mudgin (Thomas Mitchell), a member of his crew, into a public library to seek assistance for Mudgin's despair. He broke his solemn promises to God—to avoid bad women, hard liquor, knife fights, and to give the church all of his money—promises Mudgin made on a lifeboat while awaiting rescue. After breaking his promises to God on the first day back in San Francisco, Mudgin believes that he has lost his soul. Now, Mudgin faces a moral dilemma—how can he, a sinner, regain his soul?

The 1940s library reading room, quiet by signage and "shushing," becomes a stage for Harry to display his irreverence and boisterousness, the nightmare of every librarian. As librarian Emily Sears (Greer Garson[58]) and Mudgin discuss his "soul" problem so that she can locate materials for him, Harry voices loud quips, antagonizing Emily and library patrons. The materials selected for Mudgin are read aloud by Harry, eliciting a chorus of "shushes" from surrounding patrons. Mudgin does not like the content of the materials, and Emily suggests he might like to talk with a local clergyman or a psychiatrist. Mudgin refuses and thanks her profusely for helping. He retreats from the reference room, hoping that Harry also will leave.

Harry stays and proceeds to engage Emily in a bitter conversation that reveals his disillusionment with learning and education and his reliance upon "it," which sends Emily into a recital about the definitions of "it," only to interrupt herself to tell Harry that he cannot smoke in the library. At this point Helen Melohn (Joan Blondell), Emily's roommate, strolls down the hallway toward the reading room to meet Emily for dinner. She catches Harry's eye; he immediately perks up and starts a lively conversation with her, stating emphatically that she does not belong "in this graveyard." After a "shush" by Emily and a loud whistle response by Harry, Emily

Adventure (1945). Librarian Emily Sears (Greer Garson) copes with the boisterous antics of merchant marine boatswain Harry Patterson (Clark Gable); it is love at first sight, almost. Note the eyeglasses in Emily's right hand.

grabs Helen's hand and rushes her through the door to a back room. As they hustle out of the reference area, Emily exclaims that she has to get her hat and get out of the library before she gets fired. Emily's statement explicitly identifies the maintenance of decorum and silence as major responsibilities of the on-duty librarian; she is aware that failure to maintain such order may result in a reprimand.

The repartee between Harry and Emily is witty and amusing, with Emily demonstrating that she has the intellect to meet and beat the merchant marine quipster at his own game. For instance, she responds to Harry's smart remark about the location of the tree of knowledge in the library by suggesting that he try the bar down the street. In the development of the story line, this is the first encounter of opposites, and as every filmgoer knows, opposites attract.

Emily projects many aspects of the stereotypical image. She wears glasses, but takes them off and puts them on at random; she doesn't need them to shelve books, but puts them on to write and place notes in books at the library desk. She struggles to maintain decorum in the reference room, which is disrupted repeatedly by Harry. "Shushing" is one of her methods to enforce silence, but its usage is futile on a boatswain whose respect for silence is nonexistent. Emily demonstrates a respect for silence and order—whispering in the reading room, telling Harry to cut out the nonsense or she will "call a guard," and asking Harry and Mudgin to whisper. The reference interview conducted by Emily and the assistance she provides Mudgin are exceptional; this reference transaction could not have been improved significantly.

Emily is an attractive blonde (half bang; collar length with side and back curls) and conservative dresser—long dark skirt, long-sleeve white blouse, dark vest, and large polka-dot bow. In comparison, Helen is wearing a similar long dark skirt, but a tight-fitting polka-dot blouse, V-neckline, and a saucy hat. Helen is precisely the woman to grab the attention of a merchant marine, but not his heart—that is Emily's magic.

Harry waits on the steps of the library for Emily and Helen to exit, and when they appear, he begs them to have dinner with him. Helen convinces a doubting Emily that it is a good idea, and they are off to a dinner club. Helen and Harry are a dance couple, with Helen hanging all over him. The notable verbal interplay at the dinner club, however, is between Harry and Emily, with Helen frequently and unknowingly serving as the pass-through intermediary. Harry characterizes Emily as a "mild girl," and when his rambunctious merchant marine crew appears, he remarks to Emily, "I want you to meet some friends of mine, nice and mild, right down your alley." Emily, thoroughly disgusted, does a personality about-face, turns on the feminine charm for Harry's crew, creates a fracas among the crew members that results in a free-for-all fight, and then knocks down Harry with a plate to the back of the head. A new woman has emerged from the ranks of librarians, but as she concludes, "If that's life, I'll take the library."

The next day Harry imposes upon Emily and Helen to take him with them to Emily's farm in the country. After dinner, Emily and Harry become engaged in a heated confrontation about "it." Harry defines "it" as "excitement that don't die," and in his combative style, confesses his attraction to Emily,

> If I say the sea is the only road that leads to it, it's because the sea sounds like it. She does the talking, you do the listening. And if I picked on you to talk to, it was because of the ocean in your eyes that done it. I never saw it in no eyes before.... I'm sick to death of you.

The initial belligerence between the two is replaced by love. Emily discards the restraints of the library and they run off to Reno and marry. Emily's personality radically changes from that displayed in the library. She becomes vibrant; the library becomes a memory. Three days later, however, Harry leaves Emily to return to the sea.

Although *Adventure* contains only one library scene, the library is mentioned several times during casual conversations, as is the fact that Emily is a librarian. While in Reno assisting Emily with a divorce, Helen explains Emily's pre–Harry personality and state of mind to two women, also waiting on divorces, remarking that Emily "was a happy librarian" before meeting Harry. Emily immediately interrupts Helen, retorting to the contrary that she "worked in a morgue. You should have seen the dead rise up when that sailor came in. Even Gabriel's horn couldn't pipe him down."

The library atmosphere, far from being idyllic, was more of a tomb rather than a life for Emily. Later in the film, she comments to Harry, "I was alone for a long while." The library appears to provide a comfortable work environment for Emily, but she transforms its status to that of a "morgue," at the same time that she is transformed from a single woman to a bride, three-day wife, pregnant divorcée, and soon-to-be single mother. Such remarks denigrate libraries and librarians; a librarian calling a library a "morgue" does not elevate the status of libraries or promote a favorable image of librarians. The library, in retrospect, served as a safe harbor of employment for Emily until she matured and blossomed into a woman of the world.

Emily's dedication to public service is commendable, her intellect is obvious, and she manifests the ability to handle problems while providing assistance to patrons. Outside of the library, however, her decision-making ability is questionable—she steals chickens from a farmer, falls for the rhetoric of a merchant marine boatswain, and then on a whim ventures off to Reno and marries the boatswain. Emily projects a personality radically different from that displayed by Harry's so-called "mild girl" librarian. She is a strong, feminine character, nevertheless, and one who is willing to confront the frivolous and flirtatious personality of the man she loves with staid indifference in order to gain his love and devotion as the story ends.

In director Howard Hawks' mystery *The Big Sleep* (1946), Phillip Marlowe (Humphrey Bogart) visits the Hollywood Public Library to obtain some information on a rare book. After taking several notes from a reference book, he returns the book to the main desk and encounters a young, attractive librarian (Carole Douglas[59]). She asks him one of the occupation's standard questions, "Did you find what you wanted?" "Yes, thanks," he responds, and the librarian in a patent attempt to engage Marlowe in conversation remarks, "You know, you don't look like a man who would be interested in first editions." Marlowe shows little interest in her eagerness, as he nonchalantly replies, "Well, I collect blondes in bottles, too," and walks away with a subtle smile on his face. Douglas' dress is indicative of the stereotype—black with a large white collar and three-quarter length sleeves. Her long blonde hair is neatly rolled into a large bun at her nape, and she is wearing wire-rimmed glasses. The librarian's conversation with Marlowe belies her appearance but reinforces the sexual overtone situations that occur frequently with reel librarians. A second librarian[60] is at the desk; she is a brunette (large bun at nape) and wears a light suit. During Marlowe's conversation at the desk, this second librarian checks out books to patrons; she is in the center background with her back to the camera, with Marlowe on the left and the blonde librarian (Douglas) on the right. The background status of the second librarian emphasizes the beauty of the blonde librarian.

Director Frank Capra, whose 1932 *Forbidden* presents the prototype—Barbara Stanwyck as Lulu Smith—for the stereotypical image of reel librarians, reveals in *It's a Wonderful Life* (1946) that during the intervening 14 years he perfected the essence of the stereotype. In this film, George Bailey (James Stewart) is given the opportunity to visit and to see how his hometown would have evolved without him. He rushes to find his wife, Mary (Donna Reed[61]), who without George is an "old maid" and works at the public library. As Mary leaves the library, she is wearing wire-framed eyeglasses, dressed in a dark conservative suit and buttoned blouse with a narrow black neck band, and has a bun hairstyle, which is quite visible under the brim of her fedora. Mary, as she walks slowly away from the library and directly toward the camera, projects the fully developed, mature stereotype, complete with all the visual characteristics. When George approaches her, she becomes frightened and runs for safety into a nearby crowded shop where she faints as George shouts that she is his wife.

The impact of Capra's *It's a Wonderful Life* in maintaining and perpetuating the stereotype is monumental, especially since the advent of television and its unrelenting programming demand for motion pictures. *It's a Wonderful Life* is one of only a small number of films with reel librarians released during the 1930s and 1940s that continues to appear repeatedly on network, cable, and satellite television; perhaps no other film released during the 1930s and 1940s, with or without a reel librarian, has been televised more frequently on so many channels during the December holiday season. The image of Donna Reed's character, "old-maid" librarian Mary Bailey, makes an indelible visual impression on viewers. Mary Bailey is a very crafty cinematic depiction of librarians. Visually she reinforces the negative characteristics of the stereotype, but as a woman, Mary poses a dichotomy that is a devastating indictment of the image of librarians. When married to George, Mary is vibrant, a very capable woman, the quintessence of womanhood; without George, she is an impoverished woman, a meek, mild librarian, the failure of womanhood.[62] The popularity of *It's a Wonderful Life* assures its disquieting image of librarians will continue to be seen annually on television by millions of viewers. Eradicating the stereotypical image of Mary Bailey, if possible, shall challenge the intellect of working librarians for generations.

One writer identifies *Margie* (1946), a modest film directed by Henry King about the many problems of teenagers in their senior year of high school during 1928–29, as "the best high school movie."[63] A Technicolor film, *Margie* stars Jeanne Crain as Margie MacDuff, a senior at Central High; Glenn Langan as Professor Ralph Fontayne, the young French teacher who has all the high school girls in a daze (including Margie); and Lynn Bari[64] in a supporting role as the school's librarian, Miss Isabelle Palmer.

Early in the film, Margie hurriedly dashes into the school library to fix her falling bloomers, the first of many bloomer elastic mishaps. Palmer, an attractive brunette (pompadour front; hair pulled back at nape) wearing a pink blouse, long pointed collar, and reddish necktie, greets Margie and informs her that she has the books for the debate. Margie, more interested in bloomers than books, maintains she has some additional research to do and heads for the stacks. Fontayne soon enters the library and says, "So this is where you hang out." Palmer responds immediately, "every other day from three to five." She asks about his first day of class, and he remarks, "Standing room only. I've never heard of a high school with such a passion to acquire French." "Mostly girls, I imagine," she states, giving him a flirtatious smile and blinking of the eyes. She informs him that his "ears should be burnt to a crisp ... all the girls think you're just 'too darling' for words." A little embarrassed, he tells her to "cut it out," adding as he looks around, "It's quite a nice library you have here." Fontayne inquires about a library card as he walks toward the stack area, and she replies, "Oh no, my dear, we trust the faculty."

Fontayne discovers Margie fixing her bloomers when he pulls a book from the shelf and peers into the next aisle. They meet at the end of the aisle and exchange

Margie (1946). Professor Ralph Fontayne (Glenn Langan), Central High School's new, young, handsome French teacher, visits the library and meets school librarian Miss Isabelle Palmer (Lynn Bari) and senior student Margie MacDuff (Jeanne Crain).

some pleasantries; Palmer then arrives to introduce Fontayne to Margie. After Fontayne leaves, Margie informs Palmer that she doesn't enjoy being introduced as a "debater and younger than other people." Palmer insists, however, that "he'll appreciate you being so smart," and quickly questions Margie. "Don't you think he's cute?" Margie, responding with her biggest lie of the day, "I don't know. I don't generally notice how teachers look."

Although this is Fontayne's first day at school, he and Palmer exchange banter that is indicative of good friends. Several days later when Fontayne joins Palmer for lunch in the school cafeteria, all the young girls swoon as he enters. One boy asks his girlfriend, "Are you still mooning over a French teacher? ... he's got a yen for Miss Palmer, just watch them." His girlfriend glances at the couple and comments, "Well, I don't see what he sees in her. She's old. She must be twenty-five at least." Palmer ribs Fontayne about the "flutter of all the little girls' hearts" when he enters a room and then coyly asks in a youthful voice, "Oh, Mr. Fontayne, what's the French for 'I adore you?'" To which he replies, "How would you like ... a punch in the nose." This conversation reveals the two are good friends, and one remark by Fontayne—"There are times when I regret that I took your suggestion to join the faculty here"—indicates they evidently knew one another before he accepted a teaching position at Central High. The two staff members appear to be a "couple," as suggested by the girl's boyfriend. Palmer continues to be a snappy dresser in this scene, wearing a dark green suit and multicolored large bow.

On the afternoon of the high school debate, Palmer and Fontayne meet in front of a message board after a faculty meeting. Whispering, Palmer asks if he is driving her home, but he "has promised to hear the rest of the debate." She informs him that "high school debates are pretty dull," but he manages to avoid a flat rejection of her offer by countering, "See you, later?" She smiles and utters, "Maybe," as she turns to leave the building, wrapped in a fur coat and wearing a outsized beret.

Fontayne takes Palmer to the prom, and when they pass Margie and her date, her father, Mr. MacDuff (Hobart Cavanaugh), remarks to Margie that Palmer is "very attractive." Margie replies back, "She's well preserved for her age." Palmer wears an exquisite blue evening dress with wide shoulder straps. When she and Fontayne go on the dance floor for a waltz, the football coach cuts in and is unreserved in showering Palmer with a compliment, "You look very beautiful tonight, Miss Palmer."

Palmer's appearance and dress do not emulate the stereotypical image. She engages in several of the basic occupational tasks of librarians to authenticate her status as librarian. Palmer is not elderly—she has many years to go before reaching "only 38." The intransigent reasoning of the high school students reinforces their belief that if one is not young, one is, therefore, old. Filmgoers undoubtedly smiled at the high school students' assessment of her age. The underlying encompassing belief—librarians are old—continues to assail filmgoers, if not by reel librarians who are visibly "only 38," then by screen characters whose dialogue repeats the elderly accusation, which may or may not be true. In the case of Miss Palmer in *Margie*, the accusation is blatantly false.

In 1947, Republic Pictures gave Dale Evans a brief respite from western genre films to appear in a murder mystery, *The Trespasser*. Evans received top billing but a minor role, as the story is about Stephanie "Stevie" Carson (Janet Martin[65]), a recent graduate of Westfield College who obtains a job in the Research Library at the *Evening Gazette*. She and Dee Dee (Adele Mara[66]), who also works in the library, are supervised by Danny Butler (Warren Douglas[67]), a womanizer. The library is very large; it contains several office desks with ample surrounding free space and a back-to-back arrangement of file cabinets, floor to ceiling, with rolling ladders for easy access. When Stevie reports to work, Danny, standing on a ladder as he works in the files, informs Stevie, "I expect people who work for me to be on their toes. I demand, well, I think you got what I demand." As Danny turns his back on her and climbs up the ladder, Stevie puts her purse down, grabs the ladder, and pushes it forcefully to the end of its rail; the abrupt stop causes Danny to go somersaulting off the ladder, landing on his back on Dee Dee's desk. Understanding one another, Stevie and Danny become friends but continue to quarrel throughout the film. One of Stevie's first assignments is filing folders in the higher cabinets, requiring the use of ladders. Danny props his feet on his desktop and ogles her ankles. When she complains and asks why she is always in the "roof gardens," he replies, "two very good reasons." She understands the meaning of his statement, and her co-worker Dee Dee comments, "I used to put on the floor show till you came along." Stevie gives Dee Dee the folders, remarking "now you can put it on again." She informs Danny that "from now on ... I'll keep my feet on the ground."

During one of her errands for Danny, Stevie briefly inspects a rare book that she is delivering to the newspaper editor and suspects that it is a forgery, basing her skepticism upon information she had gleaned from a bibliology course at Westfield. During the ensuing action, the newspaper's literary editor dies in an automobile crash. The police suspect that the driver of the automobile, the newspaper's associate editor, purposely crashed the automobile to kill the literary editor. The two librarians work together to prove the rare book is a forgery and to establish the innocence of the associate editor. After the film's typical Republic action finale of fistfights and a shootout, Stevie suggests to Danny, "Let's kiss and be friends," and Danny, somewhat hesitant, responds, "What's life without friends." They embrace and kiss. The give-and-take of these two undoubtedly led many filmgoers to anticipate a romantic entanglement; there is an occasional perfunctory kiss but not a serious romance.

Stevie, a college graduate, is an attractive brunette (finger waves on sides with shoulder length, loose curls) and dresses fashionably. She is not only intelligent but also independent. Although Stevie engages in many tasks, she refuses to play the acquiescent role of a girl Friday; when the literary editor calls, "Oh, girl," and "young lady," she responds, "My name is Stevie Carson. In the future please remember that." Dee Dee, slightly younger than Stevie, is an alluring blonde (finger waves on sides with shoulder length loose curls); she also dresses fashionably. This is one of the few instances in which a leading actress and a supporting actress—both reel librarians—sport the same hairstyle. Dee Dee's appearances are limited to library scenes. When Danny somersaults off the rolling ladder onto her desk, she kisses him before he realizes what has happened. She obviously likes Danny, but he never displays any interest in her. Danny wears suits and ties, as do all of the *Evening Gazette*'s management team. He is a working supervisor; he is frequently on the ladders filing in the cabinets. With Stevie, he stresses work rules, most often demanding that she be at work on time, but never takes any disciplinary action. When he threatens to fire both women, Stevie negates his threat by explaining that he is frequently away from work, the same accusation he gave for firing her, while with Dee Dee, the threat was more in jest. As other male reel librarians, Danny continues the tradition of being a bumbler. For instance, when the newspaper editor goes to the airport for an out-of-state meeting, Danny and the editor's secretary use the editor's office for a tryst. The editor, however, does not go on the trip, and returns to his office, finding Danny and his secretary in an embrace.

These three cast members are easily recognized as librarians even though they engage in a minimal number of occupational tasks. In the library, they are frequently on one of the rolling ladders filing in the cabinets, but they also scissor materials for filing and answer the telephone.

Good News (1947), Metro-Goldwyn-Mayer's Technicolor college musical comedy with reel librarian Connie Lane (June Allyson[68]), is about the romantic machinations

Good News (1947). Librarian Connie Lane (June Allyson), a student working her way through college, assists star football player, popular big-man-on-campus, and wealthy student Tommy Marlowe (Peter Lawford). Note the white collar.

of Tommy Marlowe (Peter Lawford), Tait College's star football player and popular big-man-on-campus who is rejected by his latest female interest, Pat McClellan (Patricia Marshall). He visits the college library to find the definition of *incorrigible*, a French word that she called him.

In the first library scene, Connie, a student and assistant librarian, is seated at a desk by the card catalog handing books to a student, remarking, "I think these have what you're looking for, Jim." He thanks her, and as he leaves the library, Tommy comes wandering in and looks around, as if it were his first time in the library. Seeing Tommy, Connie remarks, "Why, Mr. Marlowe, what on earth are you doing here? ... This is scarcely the favorite hangout for the football team." Unwilling to admit he is not a serious student, he replies with a lie, "I don't know what you mean. I've often been in here doing research, you know." "Not in the past three years you haven't," she retorts. As Connie carries two large stacks of books in her arms to her desk, he admits lying to her but does not offer to assist her. When he finds out that she is a student, he asks, "Why do you want to work here for?" "Oh, it helps pay my tuition. It's something called working your way through college." "Oh, I'm sorry," he replies, realizing that she is not as wealthy as he and the majority of students at Tait. Tommy asks about the definition of *incorrigible*, and Connie, a language major, tells him the meaning. Although disheartened that the definition is precisely what he expected, Tommy remarks that he needs to learn French to impress Pat. He then asks for the name of the best French teacher on campus. It is Professor Kennyon, but Connie informs him the professor "hates football players." "I've never flunked a subject yet," he responds. Showing confidence in his academic ability, he adds, "I bet it's easy. C'mon, throw me a few words." "Oh, don't be silly, it's closing time," Connie replies, but he insists. They break out into a song, "The French Lesson," and she manages to shelve several books while they sing. After the song, they exchange childhood reminisces about reading as they walk out onto the portico. Tommy remarks, "You know, when I walked in here a few minutes ago ... I was feeling kind of sorry for you."

"Why?"

"Oh, I don't know, having to work your way through school, missing a lot of good times, not having the best things in life." Connie replies that she has them; everybody has them, she maintains, as she sings "The Best Things in Life are Free." After the song, Tommy and Connie kiss. Tommy, exuberant about his French lesson, can hardly wait to show off his French to Pat. "That'll put a dent in her," he tells Connie. Upset by his complete denial of their romantic moment, Connie angrily replies, "Why don't you just hit her over the head with a hockey stick," and rushes back into the library.

Connie is an attractive blonde (half bang; collar length pageboy; popularly known as the June Allyson hairstyle), fashionably dressed in a polka dot dress with a white collar, matching cuffs, and narrow tie. She is a librarian, not by appearance, but by maintaining that she is the assistant librarian and by working in the library. Another factor supporting her status as assistant librarian is her financial situation. It is evident that the majority of Tait College students are from prosperous families, and Tommy expresses sorrow for Connie's failure to have the "best things." Even though Connie insists the best things are free, the tuition at Tait College is not, requiring her to work in the library.

The film's second library scene occurs on the afternoon of the opening football game; Connie watches the game from an open window, jumping up and down and shouting for Tommy. An "only 38" woman (uncredited[69]), undoubtedly Connie's library supervisor, attired in a grey dress, white collar and bow, with an armful of books, walks by Connie and taps on her shoulder. Connie quickly leaves the window and walks down an aisle smiling. The supervisor possesses the visual characteristics of the stereotypical image. This contrast of librarians continues the basic cinematic treatment of leading (youthful) and supporting (elderly) roles that was established in silent films.

Connie, as many alluring reel librarians, attracts a handsome man—Tommy, the college's star athlete whose family is wealthy. The romance has a tenuous beginning, as Tommy believes that he is in love with Pat. With a whimsical beau like Tommy, Connie encounters many disappointments—the most difficult to accept graciously concerns the prom. When Pat refuses to attend the prom with Tommy, he asks Connie, who accepts. When he wins the football game, Pat changes her mind, and Tommy dumps Connie at the last minute. When Tommy telephones, Connie is wearing a fashionable lacy blue prom dress. Connie's roommate looks at her and remarks, "You sure don't look like a librarian." The comment, similar to Maisie's remark in *Maisie Was a Lady* (1941), reinforces the stereotypical image, the underlying fundamental implication is that librarians have a recognizable "look." When a screen character utters "You don't look like a librarian," the implicit suggestion is that a librarian looks just the opposite. Consequently, librarians with the "look" are not beautiful women who dress fashionably. In *Good News*, the statement also implies that prom dances are not the domain of librarians. The repetition of the "look" statement in motion pictures further advances the image utilized in films by writers, directors, and actors. When filmgoers instantaneously recognize actors as librarians by their appearance, the stereotypical image is well-established.

So Well Remembered (1947), a British film based on James Hilton's best-selling novel of the same title, chronicles the life and career of George Boswell (John Mills) from 1919 to the end of World War II. George, a newspaper editor and councilman in the Borough of Browdley, defends the nomination of Olivia Channing (Martha Scott[70]) by the Library Committee for the position of assistant librarian. Most council members demand the withdrawal of her name because of the community's animosity toward her father, the owner of Channing Mills, who served almost two decades in prison for gambling "with the life savings of a trusting, simple people" during a reorganization of the company. George maintains that the misdeeds of Olivia's father are not relevant for determining her qualifications "for giving out books at the library." He further adds, "Unless, of course, you consider it our duty here to punish young women for choosing to be born in families with more money than marbles." George is questioned about his relationship with Olivia, replying that he has seen but not met her. He argues that she is "better qualified"; her "schooling has included several years in France, Switzerland, and America." George's position is upheld; Olivia's nomination stands, and she is eventually selected. This council meeting provides a brief glimpse into the hiring process of librarians and emphasizes the importance of educational preparation of candidates for library positions. George bases his argument on one specific qualification—education.

Olivia visits George at his office later the same day to thank him for defending her nomination. She is subsequently appointed assistant librarian but soon has a problem with a library patron. Walking near the library, George hears a commotion and goes into the library to investigate. He asks Chief Librarian Mr. Teasdale (Roddy Hughes[71]) for details. Teasdale, a portly man, is visibly upset by the incident; he is very nervous and continually mops his brow. Teasdale maintains that he "can't go through another hour of this sort. My heart won't stand it."

The incident occurred while Olivia was working at the desk. Confronted by a patron who screamed at her about her father, Olivia's responses only infuriated him more and he continued screaming until Olivia picked up a book and, according to Teasdale, "squashed it squarely in his face." The chief librarian concludes, "I'm afraid she'll have to go." When George asks about her, Teasdale replies that "she fled into the shelves weeping." George finds Olivia in the shelves, only to discover that she is upset because she and her father are broke and the bank is taking over the family home. She had hoped that they could maintain the home by paying the bank out of her library salary. George, expressing incredulity at her plan, remarks, "Out of 15 shillings a week." He smiles and offers to take her home.

Chief Librarian Teasdale resembles the stereotypical image—an "only 38" individual with a receding hairline. He dresses conservatively—dark vested suit, high white collar and bow tie. Teasdale, very nervous and upset about Olivia's participation in the outburst, immediately concludes that "she'll have to go." The decorum of the library is his top priority; this is such an important standard to maintain that he does not elicit Olivia's explanation of the confrontation before announcing his solution to George. In this scene, Olivia, a brunette (multi-pincurl bang; curly ponytail at nape accessorized with large bow), is dressed in a long, dark skirt and long sleeve sweater over a Peter Pan collar. Olivia's identification as a reel librarian is substantiated by having been nominated for the position of assistant librarian and by appearing in the library's stacks. This is the only library scene in the film; libraries or librarians are not mentioned again.

Walking Olivia home after the library incident, George finds the courage to propose. They marry, but Olivia is not the kind, unpretentious woman he believes her to be. Rather, she is egocentric, an aggressive social climber who pushes him to pursue a seat in Parliament, to forego his interest in local social and humanitarian causes, and to associate and align himself with the wealthy instead of the underprivileged. Although the marriage appears to be happy, Olivia is discouraged and angry with George when he withdraws from the race for Parliament. Shortly after his withdrawal from the election, their son dies of diphtheria; Olivia disliked the public health clinic so intensely that she refused to wait in line to get an injection for their son. Olivia divorces George, concluding that he lacks the drive to be a financial and political success. The trappings associated with such success are necessary for her way of life, for her happiness. Olivia leaves Browdley, but returns at the beginning of the war to reopen the mill. She remains a principal character in the story but demonstrates the opposite values of George. She lacks compassion for the underprivileged and the mill-workers, as he continues to struggle against "poverty and injustice." Olivia, as the majority of women reel librarians who marry, leaves the library, assuming the role of full-time wife and, with the passage of time, mother. The library was not part of Olivia's plan for her family—social status and wealth are seldom associated with individuals who work in libraries.

A film noir release of 1947, The Web, contains a 45-second scene in the Index Department of the New York Star. Attorney Bob Regan (Edmond O'Brien), the film's leading character, visits the Index Department to research newspaper items on a five-year-old case. When the scene opens, the librarian (Robin Raymond[72]) is standing on a ladder, retrieving a large bound volume of newspapers from one of the top shelves for Regan, who is reading newspapers at the only table in the room. She drops the volume on the table, remarking, "Well, here's all we got on the Kroner case." He looks at the spine of the volume, pushes it aside, and states "No, this won't help." As she busily brushes her blouse and skirt in an attempt to get rid of the dirt and dust from the volume, she suggests that he "try one of the other papers." She then picks up a cold drink cup from the top of a vertical file, stirs and sips its contents. Regan asks if Nolan, one of the reporters on the case, is still with the newspaper. "James Timothy Nolan on a newspaper," she responds. "Did you read that famous bestseller, *Whither Away Mankind?*" She informs him that Nolan wrote the bestseller and "these days, he lives and insults people at the Barclay Towers." Regan hustles out of the office, stopping briefly at the door to remark, "Oh. Thanks for the help."

The librarian is a young, attractive brunette (shoulder length, soft wavy curls) attired in a dark blouse, V-neckline, and light skirt. She is talkative, exhibiting some subtle cattiness when discussing Nolan. As with Crunch four years earlier in *Mystery Broadcast*, filmgoers may have encountered difficulty recognizing this supporting character as a librarian. The Index Department does not resemble a typical library. It is a small room, appearing no larger than 15 by 25 feet, and there are few shelves and books. In addition, the librarian walks around the small library with a drink cup in her hand, an activity prohibited in a typical library.

Apartment for Peggy (1948), a Technicolor romantic comedy about World War II veterans, their wives, and the problems they encounter while attending college, contains a brief reference to a librarian. Retired Professor Henry Barnes (Edmund Gwenn) lectures about philosophy to a group of young veterans' wives, all of whom are jittery about their marriages because they are unable to converse with their husbands about intellectual topics. Delighted by their enthusiasm and response, Professor Barnes offers his personal library for their use, doubting the college library can meet their requests for philosophy books. Peggy (Jeanne Crain[73]), who, with her husband Jason (William Holden) is living in the professor's attic, volunteers to be his "librarian." In the next scene, Peggy is busy checking out books at the professor's home. Jason reads aloud the author and title and she writes it down. Peggy, surrounded by books and checking them out, appears to be a librarian; many filmgoers undoubtedly believed that she was, even though she demonstrates none of the visual characteristics of reel librarians. She checks out books, one easily recognizable occupational task. Peggy, an attractive brunette (shoulder length, soft waves), matches the image of many previous reel librarians in leading roles. She engages in banter with Jason that parallels the type of verbal exchanges in which reel librarians have participated since *No Man of Her Own* (1932).

The last film of the 1940s with a reel librarian, *Special Agent* (1949), follows railroad agent Johnny Douglas (William Eythe) as he investigates an armed railway robbery that resulted in the murder of four employees and the theft of $100,000. His search for information includes a trip to a library that the criminals visited before the robbery. The librarian, Miss Tannahill[74] (uncredited[75]), embodies the characteristics of the stereotype, excluding eyeglasses. She is an "only 38" brunette (knot bun at nape) and wears a dark two piece suit. Tannahill vividly remembers the two men about whom Douglas is inquiring. She was extremely upset that they had scratched the floor with their shoes, remarking as she points to the floor, "Just look at that. Isn't that an outrage, Mr. Douglas? To think anyone would have so little consideration for public property." She was busy assisting other patrons when they scratched the floor. "If only I could have gotten my hands on them," she adds. When Douglas informs her that they are murderers, she becomes visibly nervous but is able to give him some details. She finally remarks, "Oh, my. To think I came that near death. Oh, my, my. I got a notion to resign, if it wasn't for my sister, and my invalid mother, I do declare...." Douglas interrupts her wandering conversation, thanks her for the information, and makes a speedy exit.

Tannahill, a responsible public servant, is dismayed that people would deface public property and is upset that she did not have the opportunity to confront them. When told they are murderers, however, Tannahill's instinct for self-preservation dominates; she is ready to resign her position, believing that she may be in danger. Only the welfare of her sister and invalid mother, whom she evidently supports, keeps her working in such a dangerous place. Astute filmgoers undoubtedly smiled at her predicament—working in a heretofore very safe environment, a public library, she now works in a place that murderers visit; the safety and sanctuary of the library is an illusion. Tannahill's self-induced dilemma—quit for personal safety or remain to support her sister and mother—is disturbing, but she is dependent upon a librarian's salary for life's basic necessities. The reticence to leave also indicates that librarians are uneasy about change. Tannahill is a minor supporting character, a role that relies heavily on the stereotype; she also provides a touch of comic relief with her nervous consternation and garrulous chatter.

Shortly before the decade of the 1940s ended, working librarians whose indignation was not upended in 1941 by Ann Sothern's piercing remark in *Maisie Was a Lady*—"Ah, c'mon now, do I look like a librarian?"—were challenged again, this time by two articles published in the August 1949 issue of *Magazine Digest*.

The first article, "Morons Can Be Millionaires,"[76] highlighted several research studies, including one conducted by Bernardine G. Schmidt "of 254 boys and girls between the ages of 12 and 14, all classified as feebleminded on the basis of clinical intelligence tests. Their IQs ranged between 27 and 69." Schmidt followed this group "through a five-year, post-school period," which revealed that "slightly more than 27 per cent completed a four-year high school course." The article identifies the skilled and unskilled jobs that many of these individuals were able to obtain, stating that "some of the sub-normal subjects ... worked as beauty operators, as private music and dancing teachers, *reference librarians* [emphasis by authors]; one qualified as [a] graduate nurse." This statement not only raises questions about the intellectual and philosophical foundations of librarianship but also appears to debunk the necessity of academic educational preparation as a requisite for librarians.

The second article, "Morgues of Culture,"[77] identifies lack of funding as a major problem for libraries and librarians. The writer of this article notes that a study of groups of women revealed that "only social workers showed less interest in male association" than librarians but that librarians "displayed the lowest interest in people." The inability of libraries to attract greater numbers of users is a reflection of the personality of librarians: "The psychology of spinster librarians is the psychology of library salesmanship; it is too self-effacing, too withdrawn from the people it serves." The writer tempers his statements by concluding, "In all fairness to most librarians, their salaries (sometimes as low as $1,300 a year and rarely above $2,500) scarcely encourage them to work any harder than they have to. Nor do such salaries encourage many to become librarians." Libraries require individuals, according to the author, "who feel that they are the guardians of the public interest—not of their own private libraries."

A librarian at General Electric Company, Samuel Sass,[78] brought the foregoing two articles to the attention of librarians and the library world in a brief item, "Definition of 'Librarian' Too Loosely Applied," that was published in *Library Journal*,[79] one of the major periodicals that circulates among librarians. Sass summarizes the articles and suggests that librarians require a precise definition of reference librarian, asking, "Is it anybody who works in a reference library, whether he pastes book pockets or dusts shelves or sweep floors?" Sass, in posing an answer, points out that the general public believes "*everybody* who does any work at all in a library is a librarian" and asserts that the "loose definition of 'librarian' is to a large extent responsible for the poor salaries." Sass contends that librarians "will have made a great step forward when that misconception has been eliminated from peoples [sic] thinking."

For librarians to achieve this "great step forward," a metamorphosis of their image in American society, including their stereotypical image in motion pictures, would have to occur. The film industry, a commercial venture over which librarians are powerless, however, continued to dictate the image of reel librarians. At mid-century, it was evident that the stereotypical image of librarians was entrenched in motion pictures and imbedded in the culture of the general public and that working librarians were cognizant of this stereotype and of their image problems.

Universal-International released two motion pictures in 1950—*I Was a Shoplifter* and *Peggy*—with reel librarians in the cast of characters. Not surprisingly, *I Was a Shoplifter* is a crime drama about shoplifting and features Scott Brady as Jeff Andrews, an undercover operator who is pursuing a shoplifting gang, and Mona Freeman[80] in the leading female role as shoplifter Faye Burton, an attractive 22-year-old librarian suffering from kleptomania. Faye, whose father is a judge, is detained by department store detectives for shoplifting and released after promising not to shoplift again and signing a confession.

While working at the library desk, Faye is approached by Ina Perdue (Andrea King), one of the leaders of a shoplifting gang. Ina asks if the book *Kleptomania* that she pushes toward Faye is "interesting." Faye informs her that it is a reference book and cannot be taken from the library. Ina suggests that Faye "must have taken it home a few nights." During their conversation, Ina mentions Faye's confession, adding that confessions are "bad things to be leaving around." Faye agrees, stating that she will "pay almost anything" to retrieve her confession. Ina requests that they talk somewhere "away from this tomb" at 8 P.M., but Faye is reluctant to meet her. Ina then remarks, "Any time after that I may be on the phone calling some newspaper friends of mine." Hearing this, Faye agrees to the meeting. Ina picks up *Kleptomania*, remarking, "I'll read up on your case a little," as she leaves the library with the book.

At home that evening, Faye's Aunt Clara (uncredited; Nana Bryant) forbids her to leave the house: "Library business at night. How can you expect me to believe that?" The two women engage in a lively conversation, with Faye defending not only her right to go out as she pleases but also her library position. Clara labels her irresponsible and attacks her job, "Taking that silly job instead of going abroad with your

I Was a Shoplifter (1950). Andrea King (left) is Ina Perdue, a member of a shoplifting gang, and Mona Freeman (right) is librarian Faye Burton, a kleptomaniac whom the gang is attempting to recruit. Note the white collar.

father." Faye defends her library employment. "The job at the library might be silly to you, but it's the only thing I've ever gotten completely on my own," she says. As Faye gathers her things to leave the room, Clara delivers an ultimatum, "You step out of this house tonight and I'll see that you leave that silly job." Faye, rather than retreating, challenges Aunt Clara, "Then we will have it out.... Nobody's taking the library away from me. At least not without a real fight!" Clara attempts to moderate the language and convince Faye to stay home, but when it is apparent that Faye is going out, Clara remarks, "There's a man behind this, isn't there?" "I wish it were that!" Faye exclaims as she hurries out of the house.

At the meeting with the shoplifting gang, Faye is shown a copy of her confession and is offered the opportunity to obtain the original, providing she shoplifts for the gang. She accepts this arrangement, and Ina teaches her several shoplifting techniques. The gang sends Faye to San Diego, where she becomes so despondent that she attempts suicide. Just as Allie Smith in *Young Bride* (1932) did, Faye selects suicide as the solution to her problems. This method of resolution appears to be the preferred choice of action for reel librarians who are confronting a personal crisis of major proportions. Just as Charlie Riggs saves Allie in *Young Bride*, Jeff rescues Faye before she drowns in the ocean. Jeff informs her that he works for the sheriff's office and asks her to work for the gang so that authorities can arrest its members. The plan goes awry, however, and the gang escapes, taking Faye with them to Mexico, where Jeff and the police arrest the gang and liberate Faye. As with many of the young, attractive women reel librarians, she falls in love. Jeff gives her a diamond ring as the film ends.

The library provides Faye, a judge's daughter, with respectable employment. Having obtained the position on her own merits, she is very proud to be a librarian and does not hesitate to defend her employment against Aunt Clara's fulminations about the "silly" job. Faye's criminal behavior is the result of kleptomania, a neurotic impulse she has difficulty repressing. Given the choice of continuing her shoplifting activities or being exposed as a shoplifter, which would embarrass and humiliate her family, she joins the gang but redeems herself by assisting Jeff.

Throughout the film, Faye, a brunette (bob; hair flipped at nape and sides) appears in modest, conservative clothing. This is the only visual characteristic of reel librarians that Faye displays. During the library scene, she works behind a circulation desk, an occupational task that easily identifies her as a librarian. After checking out a book, *Gulliver's Travels*, to a young boy, she remarks as she slides the book across the desk to him, "There you are Jimmy. I think you'll like this." Her interaction with Jimmy, whom she called by his first name, indicates that she is a friendly, competent librarian. She is knowledgeable of library rules and enforces them—she informs Ina that reference books cannot be removed from the library.

Peggy, Universal International's second release of 1950 with a reel librarian, is a Technicolor collegiate comedy starring Charles Coburn as Professor Brookfield and Diana Lynn as his daughter, Peggy Brookfield. Long-time competent supporting actress Ellen Corby[81] is Mrs. Privet, the librarian. A review in *Variety* notes that the "script spreads a lot of chuckles over the footage," adding later that "completing the comedy of errors for laughs is ... Ellen Corby, a librarian."[82] Again, the reel librarian in a supporting role serves a comedic purpose.

Katie Did It (1951) is a light romantic comedy and Universal International's third motion picture within two years with a reel librarian in the cast, the second with the reel librarian in the leading female role. Ann Blyth[83] stars as young, attractive librarian Katherine Standish, a descendent of the founder of Wakely, Massachusetts. The town's residents, including Katie, continue to follow "the rigid Puritan laws that were laid down by their ancestral forefathers" and "the one characteristic that must always prevail is modesty." Katie lives with her aunt, Priscilla Wakely (Elizabeth Patterson), the town's matriarch and vigilant surveyor of morals, and Priscilla's brother, her uncle, Nathaniel B. Wakely VI (Cecil Kellaway), whose career as a New York attorney was abruptly curtailed when his gallivanting escapades appeared in the press. Although Nathaniel is controlled by Priscilla, he is still a rebel in spirit and enjoys a clandestine drink and occasional adventure. The antithesis to the puritanical mores of Wakely is artist Peter Van Arden (Mark Stevens), whose brief vacation to Wakely sets in motion a series of events that results in Katie breaking the two-century-old dictum of modesty.

Katie's troubles with Peter begin on the morning she passes the White Horse

Inn on her walk to the library; she stops briefly to exchange pleasantries with the inn's owner. Standing atop a tall stepladder and painting a new sign for the inn, Peter accidentally drops his paint brush, which falls on and ruins Katie's hat. Infuriated at the loss of her hat and at Peter, who is painting the sign in exchange for 12 bottles of ale, Katie suggests that he must have been paid in advance. In preceding films, librarians in their own bailiwicks, the library, are always on the ladder. In this film there is a touch of irony, a sarcastic twist of events, as the librarian, no longer within the safe confines of a library, is under the ladder, becoming the unintentional target of a falling object.

The inn's owner informs Peter that Katie is the "niece of Priscilla Wakely, who runs this town," and, instead of apologizing, Peter should "get the first train out of town." Peter, however, visits the library. Katie is on a library ladder retrieving a book for Steven (Jimmy Hunt), a youngster whom she is determined to wean from comic books. Before climbing the ladder, a modest Katie asks Steven to turn his head. Peter approaches the ladder, and while ogling her calves and ankles, he whistles. Appalled by the wolf whistle, Katie begins scolding Steven before turning around to see Peter's smiling face. Katie ignores him and tells Steven that "this is the type of literature a young man should read." Steven dishearteningly responds, "*The Story of King Arthur.* Sounds awful dull." Peter chips in, "It is dull." Hearing this remark, Katie immediate acknowledges his presence. "Is there something I can do for you?" The question prompts a very brief Abbott-Costello inspired exchange between the two:

PETER: Is this a library?
KATIE: Obviously.
PETER: You do lend books?
KATIE: Naturally.

Katie asks Peter to look around the library, as she advises Steven that *The Story of King Arthur* is "one of the best American novels ever written, very interesting." Standing with Steven at the desk, Peter voices a critical comment, "Corny." Katie maintains the novel "is a literary classic filled with fine wholesome characters" and assures Steven it will be "just as exciting as your comic books." Peter volunteers to tell Steven about the story to pique the boy's interest. Katie has no objection, but Peter's interpretation of *King Arthur* is too ribald for the modest librarian. According to Peter, King Arthur and his group of men sat at a round table eating and drinking, with occasional excursions into the countryside to beat up defenseless strangers, and while Arthur and his men were on these expeditions, Arthur's wife and best friend at Camelot were.... At this point, Katie objects, "Now just a minute," and walks over to take the book from Peter. Steven, however, is now very interested, "Go on mister. It sounds super!" At this point, Peter reveals his primary purpose for visiting the library is to apologize, and he gives Katie a new hat to replace the one he damaged earlier. As Peter leaves, Katie is trying on her new hat and Steven is reading *King Arthur*, exclaiming, "This guy Sir Lancelot is dynamite!"

Later, Peter and Nathaniel meet at the White Horse Inn, and Nathaniel accepts Peter's invitation to accompany him to look at some horses and then go on to the racetrack. During the trip, Nathaniel makes a bet with Peter's bookie, mistakenly bet-

Katie Did It (1951). In the Wakely Public Library (left to right): Librarian (actor not identified); artist Peter Van Arden (Mark Stevens); comic book reader Steven (Jimmy Hunt); and librarian Katherine Standish (Ann Blyth).

ting $500 instead of $5 on a horse to win. The horse places, and Nathaniel is $500 in debt to a bookie who collects from his "customers." When Nathaniel informs Katie of his problem, she decides to visit a New York music company that has expressed an interest in publishing some of her musical compositions. Hoping to obtain at least $500 to pay Nathaniel's debt, Katie journeys to New York by train, only to be joined on the trip by Peter. He sits next to her, and Katie complains to the conductor who demands that Peter move. Peter then convinces the conductor that Katie is his wife and he is taking her to see a doctor about her mental condition. During the trip, Peter suggests that she pose for him—"I'll pay you well," but she refuses to pose for "one of those pictures." A commercial artist, Peter paints scantily dressed models for calendars and advertisements. As every filmgoer undoubtedly anticipated, the inevitable happens to Katie in New York—the music company rejects her compositions, compelling her to earn the $500 by posing five days for Peter at $100 a day. Shortly before Katie arrives at Peter's apartment on the day that she is leaving for Wakely, his sister and nephew appear for an unannounced stay. When Katie enters the apartment, Peter's nephew is there; as soon as she discovers the youngster's name is Peter Van Arden, she assumes that he is Peter's son and leaves immediately. Peter rushes after her, but this time the train conductor believes Katie and removes Peter from the train.

In Wakely, Katie is besieged by telephone calls and inundated with flowers from Peter. She refuses to accept his telephone calls and permits the delivery boy to give the flowers to his girlfriend. Returning to Wakely from a fishing trip with her uncle and a friend, the trio notices a large highway billboard with her picture on it. They stop; Katie utters, "How could he do this to me?" Nathaniel responds, "Van Arden.... Why you could sue him for every penny he's got. I'll start proceedings immediately." Katie admits she posed for the picture, remarking that they needed money. Nathaniel quickly deduces that the $500 to pay off his debt came from posing, not her musical compositions. The three begin a nightly "smear campaign" to paint the billboards so that Katie's image cannot be recognized, but the police catch them and they spend a night in jail. The Wakely gossip is exuberant, and "Katie Did," the two words on the billboard, become the most frequently used words of Wakely's gossip vocabulary. Katie leaves her library position, telling her library coworker, "I guess librarians and scandal just don't mix ... least not in Wakely."

Katie agrees to marry the banker's son, but Peter appears and explains about his nephew. Priscilla urges Peter to leave, proclaiming, "This scandal will ruin Katherine's reputation beyond repair." Peter, however, is prepared to fight for Katie. An amateur historian, he has uncovered a "spicy bit of information" about Wakely. Its founder was a self-appointed minister, not a real minister; consequently, the legitimization of the second generation of Wakely townspeople is questionable. Peter informs the residents that he will forget this historical fact, "but if at any time you nice people ... decide ... to gossip about the future Mrs. Van Arden, well, you understand, I'm sure." They marry, and as they drive out of Wakely, Katie sees the Monticello Motel, and blissfully remarks, "It's such a long drive to Niagara Falls." Peter turns into the motel.

Katie, a brunette (pompadour front; sides pulled back with curls at nape), dresses modestly throughout the film, excepting the modeling scenes at Peter's studio and a brief scene in a rural pond early in the film. In the first and longest of three library scenes, she wears a light-color dress, small white collar and dark bow. She demonstrates her readers' advisory skill with Steven during her attempt to keep the young reader away from comic books. She recommends *The Story of King Arthur* as an interesting alternative. The basic occupational tasks are evident and, in addition, she supervises a bespectacled "only 38" gray-haired male coworker (uncredited[84]), who wears a visor. He dresses very conservatively—dark suit, white shirt, dark tie—in all three library scenes. These two librarians reflect the modesty dictum of Wakely.

Assailed by gossip, Katie voluntarily leaves her library position. Although she has fallen in love with Peter, Katie finally decides that the proper step is to marry the banker's son, a sophomoric action that a librarian might undertake if, indeed, her private lifestyle contradicts the mores of the community. In the end, however, Peter quiets the gossip of the townspeople, reestablishes her character and reputation, and then marries her. This approach—the attraction of opposites—is used frequently by filmmakers in all types of film genres. When a reel librarian is involved, the result is predictable—the librarian marries her antagonist and leaves the library. Katie's closing remark as they drive by the motel, "It's such a long drive to Niagara Falls," reveals that she is a woman, no longer a librarian.

A lighthearted comedy dealing with mandatory retirement, *As Young As You Feel* (1951), is about the struggles of John R. Hodges (Monty Woolley) to regain his position at Acme Printing Services, a subsidiary of Consolidated Motors. Released from his position because he has reached the mandatory retirement age of 65, John decides to contact the president of Consolidated Motors to challenge the "absurd policy." The personnel department at Acme Printing Services, however, does not know and is unable to ascertain the name of the president of the parent company. To find this information, John visits a library. The 20-second library scene opens with a librarian (uncredited; Carol Savage[85]) standing on a ladder and flipping through the pages of an oversized reference book. A young, attractive blonde (finger waves; flipped in back), the librarian wears a light-color dress, large pointed collar, and small flat bow pinned with costume jewelry. She scampers down the ladder, enthusiastically exclaiming, "Here it is. I found it!" After she identifies the president, John praises her reference skills, "Congratulations, Miss. Whether you are aware of it or not, you have just solved one of the great mysteries of the age." As he leaves, a puzzled look comes over the librarian's face as she attempts to comprehend his remark. Although two occupational tasks identify Savage's character as a librarian, the actress and director Harmon Jones portray this librarian as an enthusiastic, cheerful, willing-to-help reference provider.

Clifton Webb makes his third appearance as the urbane Lynn Belvedere in *Mr. Belvedere Rings the Bell* (1951). Requiring a Tibetan stamp for one of his schemes, Belvedere visits a public library for the express purpose of obtaining (by theft) a Tibetan stamp. Belvedere and his associate Emmett (Zero Mostel) briefly encounter an "only 38" librarian (uncredited; Dorothy Neumann[86]) whose only dialogue, delivered as the camera focuses on the stamps, is "These are the Tibet stamps." The stamps are in an open display case, and as soon as the librarian delivers her line, she leaves, and Belvedere removes a stamp from the collection. The librarian, a brunette (bun at crown), wears a long-sleeve patterned dress with a V-neckline and a narrow lace collar. The clothes, hairstyle, makeup, and mild, unassuming personality of this actress, who is on-screen for less than ten seconds, exhibit, unquestionably, an attempt to replicate the visual characteristics of the stereotypical image.

A sprightly Technicolor musical comedy set in the late 1920s, *Has Anybody Seen My Gal?* (1952) bills Rock Hudson (Dan, a young drug store soda jerk) and Piper Laurie (Millicent Blaisdell, daughter of the owner of the drug store) as its stars. The film's story, however, is about Samuel Fulton (Charles Coburn), a wealthy, elderly character who, before leaving his entire estate to the Blaisdell family, arranges for an anonymous gift of $100,000 to the family to test their stability. *Has Anybody Seen My Gal?* contains one library scene, less than a minute long, in the Hilverton Public Library.

As Millicent rushes into the library to meet Dan, she passes a male librarian (uncredited[87]) in dark suit and tie, who acknowledges her entrance with a nod of his head. Seated behind a desk in the foreground, he appears only momentarily on-screen. A second librarian (uncredited[88]), with an armful of books, climbs a ladder to shelve them. Millicent informs Dan that her mother-mandated romance with another boy is over, and Dan, so happy to hear about the breakup, jumps up and shouts "Yippee!"

Millicent and Dan are standing only a few feet from a large SILENCE sign hanging from the ceiling, and the second librarian appears immediately at the table, uttering "Shush! Quiet! Don't you know this is a library!" Dan utters a meek "Sorry." The librarian then returns to a booktruck for more books to shelve, and as Dan turns to leave with Millicent, he walks into the booktruck, overturning it, causing the books to spill onto the floor. He manages another meek "Sorry" as they rush out of the building.

This second librarian, a brunette (front and sides brushed back with curls at nape), is attired in a long-sleeve black dress with a scoop neckline, and wears pince-nez, which she removes when she talks. She exhibits the basic visual characteristics and occupational tasks of the stereotypical image. This scene is designed specifically for laughs. Using the reel librarian for comedy purposes occurs frequently in films and is an effective stratagem for filmmakers whose scripts are in need of a brief comedy scene or a quick laugh. The continual vilification of librarians in such comedic scenes as the foregoing not only solidifies the image but also promotes its continuation in comedy scenes.

Richard Widmark stars as three-time loser Skip McCoy in director Samuel Fuller's film noir thriller, *Pickup on South Street* (1953). Skip, a pickpocket, manages to lift the purse of Candy (Jean Peters) during a subway ride. The purse contains top-secret plans on microfilm that the Russians are attempting to obtain. When Skip realizes that the microfilm may be valuable, he visits the New York Public Library to use a microfilm reader. Walking into the microfilm room, Skip passes a counter-height desk where two librarians (both uncredited) are working. The first, a bespectacled individual[89] attired in a dress shirt and tie, is busy assisting a patron; the second,[90] a much younger man, wears a suit and tie. A third librarian (uncredited; Jay Loftin[91]) greets Skip with "May I help you?" Skip requests "the *New York Times* for January 5, 1947." The librarian hands him a form, "Fill this out please," and the scene immediately cuts to Skip using a microfilm reader. Loftin, a Black American, is attired in a dress shirt and tie, and appears to be the youngest of the three; he is the first Black American the authors detected portraying a reel librarian.

George Pal's popular science fiction thriller in Technicolor, *The War of the Worlds* (1953), stars Gene Barry as Dr. Clayton Forrester, a professor at Pacific Institute of Science and Technology, and Ann Robinson[92] as Sylvia Van Buren, a young, attractive library science teacher at the University of Southern California.[93] When Sylvia, a redhead (full bang; sides pulled back with curls at nape, accessorized with large barrette), first appears on screen, she is dressed casually, but fashionably, wearing a sienna-colored, ribbed yoke turtleneck sweater and a light brown skirt.

During their first meeting, Sylvia praises the talents of Dr. Forrester: "He's top man in astro and nuclear physics. He knows all about meteors." She fails, however, to recognize Clayton, explaining her knowledge about him by stating that she "did a thesis on modern scientists" working for her master's degree. Clayton asks, "Did it do you any good?" Without hesitation Sylvia responds, "Why, sure, I got it." When Clayton reveals his identity, she gushes in an apologetic tone, "Ohhhh, oh, you certainly don't look like yourself in that getup [denims, open collar shirt, and windbreaker] Dr. Forrester, but I'm happy to meet you anyway." The romance begins immediately, and the story emphasizes the emotional and feminine (for example, screaming at appropriate scary junctures and preparing breakfast) aspects of Sylvia rather than her intellect. A woman with some educational preparation to partner with Clayton is essential in order to make the romance believable. Sylvia, therefore, possesses all of the necessary academic attributes—master's degree, knowledge of modern scientists, and a faculty position at USC. Sylvia's self-proclaimed statement that she is "a library science teacher" is the only reference in the film to indicate that she is a librarian. Sylvia's occupation is not pertinent to the storyline.

Rosalind Russell[94] portrays Kim Halliday in *The Girl Rush* (1955), a Technicolor musical comedy. Within the first six minutes of the picture, Kim appears behind the Information Desk at the Providence Historical Museum, Early American Wing, a position she has held for "three months, three days." Kim demonstrates little interest in her position but provides efficient reference service. She receives a telephone inquiry and responds, "I have that information right here for you." Grabbing a notepad from her desk, she rapid-fires the answer to the caller, concluding the conversation with, "Sorry, I couldn't tell you that when you were here. It was right on the tip of my tongue." Kim's Aunt Clara (Marion Lorne), also a museum employee, comes into the room, suggesting that Mr. Henderson might visit them to show his slides from Martha's Vineyard. Kim is not enthusiastic about a possible visit. "No, no he isn't very handsome, is he?" Aunt Clara muses. After Kim insists that is not the reason, Clara defines what Kim expects in a man, "No, you want to be swept off your feet. A dashing young man. Colorful, romantic, high-spirited." They both smile at such an image. The four o'clock bell rings, and Aunt Clara rushes off to her lecture as a group of visitors begin marching through the room. Kim turns on a radio in the top desk drawer, tunes in a horse race, and urges on her horse, "C'mon, Morning Star!" Listening intently to the race, she fails to hear the telephone ringing. Several people pass through the room, including the administrator, who shouts, "Miss Halliday. Your phone is ringing." The call is from Las Vegas, informing her that she has inherited half interest in a Las Vegas hotel. She and Aunt Clara are soon on an airline flight to Las Vegas, and Providence is a city of the past. Kim's hotel partner arranges for them to stay at the Flamingo, and Kim mistakenly believes she owns half of the Flamingo, leading to numerous comedic mishaps and adventures, as her inheritance is an old run-down building that once was a hotel.

Kim is an "only 38" brunette (bob; full bang; pincurls at sides) who dresses colorfully and fashionably. Kim exhibits many occupational tasks of reel librarians; in addition, she sits at a desk that is surrounded by books. She displays a lack of interest in her position and dreams of the perfect suitor, as have many previous reel librarians. The lure of adventure in Las Vegas, coupled with a half-interest in a hotel, propels Kim to leave Providence immediately. Although the future is unknown, she believes the prospects outweigh the security of her "three months, three days" position.

Twentieth Century–Fox's Technicolor crime drama *Violent Saturday* (1955) is about a bank holdup in Bradenville, a small fictional town in Arizona. The cast includes a purse-snatching librarian, Elsie Braden (Sylvia Sidney[95]), who makes three appearances during the film.

As three holdup men assemble at a hotel, preparing and finalizing their plan to rob the local bank, the story focuses briefly on several of the town's residents, examining their imperfections. One of these residents is Elsie, a librarian at the Bradenville Public Library.[96] When Harper (Stephen McNally), leader of the holdup trio, visits the public library to examine a map of Bradenville, he observes the activities of the two librarians. Elsie and a second librarian, Dorothy (uncredited; Joyce Newhard[97]), are seated at a counter-height main desk at the back of the library; Dorothy is checking in books and filing in a card file, while Elsie is reading her personal mail. Elsie is visibly agitated by a note from the bank:

> Unless the past due installment and interest are paid before closing time this Saturday, we will be compelled to execute an assignment against your wages at the library.

After reading the bank's warning, Elsie leaves the desk to pick up books from library tables. She is stopped by a woman wearing a fur neckpiece who says, "Do you have anything on bird habits, Elsie? I have to give a talk to the Ladies Aid next week." Elsie points to the other side of the library, and responds, "In the file index under Ornithology." As the patron walks away, Elsie resumes her task and notices an unattended purse at a nearby table. She picks up a book, hides the purse behind it, and drops them into the rolling book bin. Pushing the book bin past the main desk, she informs Dorothy that she will "be back in a few minutes." Elsie goes to the confines of a non-public area to examine her spoil.

Both Dorothy and Elsie are "only 38" librarians and dress conservatively. Dorothy, whose reddish hair is pulled into a bun at her nape, wears a green dress with a pointed collar; Elsie, a brunette (short bouffant layered cut, brushed back at front and sides), wears a blue dress with a small white collar and matching wrist cuffs. Elsie and Dorothy project the visual characteristics of reel librarians and they are busily engaged in mimicking the occupational tasks of reel librarians. Shush is evidently seldom uttered by either of these two librarians; the library is relatively small and the patrons are well behaved. In addition, there is a large, framed QUIET PLEASE sign posted on the wall behind the main desk that is visible throughout the library.

Elsie's second appearance in the film occurs when she attempts to make an unobserved late-night trip to an alleyway behind a hotel to throw the purloined purse into a trash can. In the alleyway, however, is Harry Reeves (Tommy Noonan), the bank manager who wrote the demanding note to Elsie. Harry is Bradenville's Peeping Tom, and under the guise of walking his dog, he goes to the alleyway to watch a nurse undress in her hotel room. Hearing Elsie approaching, Harry hides in the shadows, and when Elsie tosses the purse into a trash can, his dog barks. Harry emerges from the shadows and walks toward Elsie. He lifts the trash can cover, removes the purse, and confronts Elsie, "You stole this, didn't you?" The two argue briefly, and as Harry mentions the police, his eyes drift to the hotel room where the nurse is undressing. He stops talking and stares at the window, giving Elsie the opportunity to prepare her defense. "I just dare you to go to the police.... While your wife's at home asleep, you sneak out and watch that girl undress." As Harry interjects an ineffectual "No," Elsie continues, "You're disgusting!" She throws the purse back into the trash can, telling Harry, "There you are Mr. Peeping Tom. I just dare you to go to the police." Elsie walks away, and Harry continues to watch the nurse's window until the light goes out and then he leaves. Knowing the foibles of one another, Elsie and Harry exit the alley-way with the understanding that the incident never occurred.

When Elsie enters the bank to pay her overdue obligation, she goes to Harry's desk, informing him that she has received many "annoying letters about an overdue payment." She suggests that he personally take the money and close her account. Too busy to be interrupted, he asks her to go to one of the teller windows. Elsie tells the bank cashier, "I want a receipt marked 'Paid in Full,'" as the bank robbers enter. Harper announces, "Everybody stay where you are. This is a holdup." The trio corrals the bank's customers to one side of the bank and waits for the time safe to open. One of the robbers, Dill (Lee Marvin), grabs the money out of Elsie's hand. She strug-gles with him, maintaining, "That's my money. Give it to me." He shoves her against the teller's window as Harper shouts, "Leave her alone." When the safe opens, they collect the money and make their getaway.

Elsie Braden is the first reel librarian to commit a crime[98] while working in the library. Stealing money from a library patron is a despicable act, even more so when it is the librarian who is the thief. As the film does not detail Elsie's finances or indi-cate the type of debt, the most obvious inference is that her salary is inadequate. She appears to live a frugal, rather than extravagant, lifestyle.

Violent Saturday is the first film to depict a librarian whose moral values are cor-rupt—not only the instance of stealing but also the *quid pro quo* arrangement with the town's Peeping Tom. Elsie's actions during the bank robbery illustrate her self-delu-sional state of mind. Having stolen the money from a library patron, she demands that Dill, the bank robber who pulls the money out of her hand, give the money back to her—"That's my money. Give it to me." Elsie has rationalized her theft. She now assumes the money is her money and considers Dill's theft of her money offensive, grappling with him until realizing the futility of the situation.

Elsie's moral character is not of the same stature as earlier reel librarians. Amelia in *The Blot* (1921), for example, mistakenly believes that her mother stole a neighbor's chicken and attempts to pay the neighbor for the chicken as soon as she receives her meager paycheck. In *Violent Saturday*, screenwriter Sydney Boehm and director Richard Fleischer create one of the most unsympathetic reel librarians in twentieth century cinema.

An entry in the Bowery Boys series, *Fighting Trouble* (1956), stars Huntz Hall as Horace Debussy "Sach" Jones and Stanley Clements as Stanislaus "Duke" Coveleskie. In this "B" movie, Sach and Duke visit the *New York Blade* Library, photographic files unit, to locate a picture of a gangster. They stop in a hallway in front of a Dutch door, top half open; Duke holds up his arm in a plea for attention and blurts out, "Miss?" A young, attractive librarian (uncredited[99]) comes to the door. "Yes. What can I do for you gentlemen?" Duke tells her what they need, and she replies, "Wait, I'll check the files." Sach, eyeing the young librarian as she turns around, mutters under his breath, "And, I'll do some checking also!" As she turns from the door, she faces the camera and displays a big smile as she takes four steps to reach the file, which has sev-eral books shelved on it. She opens a vertical file folder drawer and begins flipping through folders as the scene fades out.

This librarian, a blonde (angel wing bang; bun at nape), wears a black dress with a V-neckline. With minimal expense on this set, the studio managed to project the impression that this was a library. The sign on the door, a card catalog near the door, Sach and Duke asking for specific photographs, the reel librarian searching through folders, and books on top of cabinets provide the aura of a library. The actress displays several visual characteristics and is not only efficient but also attractive. Even Sach, as evidenced by the remark he utters when the librarian turns away from the door, manages to appreciate her beauty.

The Man Who Never Was (1956), filmed in DeLuxe Color and set in England during World War II, is based on Ewen Montagu's book of the same title. The film recounts the development of Montagu's successful plan to give the Third Reich false information about a forthcoming invasion of the continent. The plan requires creating a fictitious military persona (Major William Martin) for a cadaver that is intentionally dropped into the sea off the coast of Spain. Montagu anticipates that the Germans will be able to obtain and examine the contents of an attaché case attached to the wrist of Major Martin and, hopefully, will believe the contents and divert troops away from the actual invasion site. Clifton Webb portrays Montagu in this suspenseful film, and Gloria Grahame[100] portrays Lucy Sherwood, a librarian who is very instrumental in convincing a German agent that Major Martin existed, thereby verifying the accuracy of the top-secret documents in the attaché case.

Lucy and Pam (Josephine Griffin), Montagu's office assistant, share an apartment, where Pam often meets Lucy's boyfriends; Lucy's current beau is Joe, a Royal Air Force flier. Pam, believing that Lucy is too serious about Joe, warns her not to fall in love. Lucy responds, "Who? Me? Lucy, the languishing librarian, not a chance. If ever I fall in love, it will be with a guy who goes out at 9 to a nice safe office and comes back at 6. Not one of these flyers—here today and gone tomorrow." But the denial cannot hide the fact that she is in love with Joe. In this scene, Lucy, a redhead (shoulder length soft curls), wears a long sleeve sweater, large multicolor neck scarf, and black capri pants. Both Lucy and Pam are very attractive young women. Pam's makeup is very soft, enhancing her beauty; Lucy's makeup appears harsh throughout the film, as if deliberately overdone, detracting from her beauty. *Variety* noted that "there is something very much amiss with her makeup in this picture."[101]

On the day that Joe gives Lucy an engagement ring, Pam is struggling to compose a love letter to put in Major Martin's personal belongings. Lucy, disappointed that Joe is going on another mission, dictates a very emotional, poignant letter to Pam; the letter reveals Lucy's emotions about her relationship with Joe, and is exactly the type of letter that will authenticate Martin's persona and that of his nonexistent girlfriend. Pam signs the letter "Lucy," and after an office discussion about including a photograph of a young woman, Montagu asks Pam to obtain a photograph of Lucy. Major Martin is deposited off the Spanish coastline, and the Germans, as expected, obtain copies of the contents of the attaché case and Martin's personal belongings. A Nazi agent is dispatched to London to verify the facts relating to Martin's personal activities and life, including his girlfriend Lucy.

While working in the American Library, Lucy receives a telephone call from one of Joe's friends, informing her that Joe has been killed. She is so overwhelmed with grief that after she hangs up the telephone, she walks out of the library. That same afternoon, the Nazi agent visits Pam and Lucy's apartment; when no one answers the door, he waits in the stairwell until Pam arrives. Pam knows that he is a German agent as soon as he asks about Martin and Lucy. As he prepares to leave the apartment, Lucy arrives, totally distraught about Joe's death. When the agent asks her about Martin, she begins a sobbing discourse about losing a loved one. Impressed by the sincerity of her grief, the agent believes mistakenly that she is distraught about Martin. When he returns to his apartment, he immediately transmits a message suggesting that Martin may be genuine if he transmits a second message in an hour,[102] which he does, causing the German army to deploy forces away from the invasion site.

Lucy's one scene in the library utilizes several of the visual characteristics and occupational tasks of reel librarians. She sits behind a desk, stamps books, and wears large, oversized eyeglasses, which she uses only in this scene, removing them before responding to her telephone call. She dresses very similarly in all of her scenes, basically white tops and black pants or skirts. Lucy closely approximates the image of reel librarians.

Lucy's occupation is not important to the storyline, but Pam, as an assistant to Montagu, requires a roommate of similar or comparable occupational status. Pam is rational, very sedate, and extremely sensible about waiting out the war to find a boyfriend. Lucy, on the other hand, is emotional and enjoys male companionship, remarking, "I don't know how you keep away from these boys, Pam." Lucy is a librarian looking for love, and in wartime London, she appears to have successfully attracted several young men.

A second library employee (uncredited[103]) who answers the telephone before handing it to Lucy is evidently her supervisor, as she remarks to Lucy in a tone nearing anger, "It's for you, and you really must get them to ring up out of work, you know." A graying brunette (finger wave; loose curls at sides and back), the librarian is "only 38" and dresses modestly—a charcoal grey suit and red blouse.

One of the few films released during the twentieth century that deals primarily with a library topic, censorship, is *Storm Center* (1956). The frenzy associated with the cold war and McCarthyism in post–World War II America is captured by screenwriters Elick Moll and Daniel Taradash, who also directed the film. *Storm Center* attempts to recreate the accusatory climate of the McCarthy era by focusing on the issue of censorship, the removal of a book from a public library.[104] In *Storm Center*, members of the voter-elected city council ask librarian Alicia Hull (Bette Davis[105]) to remove one book, *The Communist Dream*,[106] from the library's collection. Alicia initially agrees, but when she changes her mind and puts the book back on the shelves, the furor begins.

Alicia is a respected, long-time resident of the city; she enjoys the children who visit the library, addressing many of them by their first names, and exchanges friendly greetings with adults. When invited to attend a luncheon meeting of the council, Alicia assumes the discussion will be about the children's addition to the library. The council members immediately approve a motion to build the children's addition, much to Alicia's astonishment, but then move on to one of their problems—the removal of a book that residents are complaining about. A *quid pro quo* is proposed;

The Man Who Never Was (1956). Gloria Grahame, busy stamping books, is librarian Lucy Sherwood. Although Grahame wears eyeglasses in the library in the film, she has removed them for this publicity photograph.

they voted to construct the children's addition for her, and now Alicia is to remove this book from the library for them. She reluctantly agrees, and rather than permitting the book to be thrown "out with the rest of the garbage" at the restaurant, she offers to take the book back to the library, informing the council members, "I'll dispose of it some way. I don't quite know how. You see, I've never been forced to remove a book from the library before."

As Alicia ponders the fate of *The Communist Dream* at the library, she poses a rhetorical question to her assistant, Martha Lockridge (Kim Hunter[107]), "How do you get rid of a book?" Alicia concludes, "That's my problem." After Martha rushes out of the library to meet her date, Paul Duncan (Brian Keith), the youngest council member and the council's most vociferous critic of the book, Alicia realizes that she cannot destroy the book and returns it to the collection.

Alicia then informs one of the council members that she has decided to retain the book. When Paul is notified of Alicia's action, he tells Martha about the events of the day. Martha is surprised that Alicia agreed to remove the book; she "is set in some of her ideas ... civil liberties, censorship, intellectual freedom." Paul listens intently; drifting into a reflective mode while assimilating this information. Realizing that he has been inattentive, Paul apologizes, remarking, "You gave me a thought."

In the next scene, Alicia is meeting with the council to defend her decision to retain the book. In this give-and-take discussion, council members indicate that they are responding to the community's desire to remove the book, while Alicia upholds the right of ideas to be in the public library, even such unpopular ideas as those expressed in *The Communist Dream*. Paul suddenly changes the discussion, focusing attention on Alicia's activities; he identifies several Communist-front organizations in which Alicia was a member. Paul sums up his argument by suggesting to Alicia, and the other council members, that "you were easy prey for a lot of high sounding slogans ... you were duped once you could very well be again." One council member who is aligned with Paul rhetorically remarks, "Do you realize what could happen if this got out?" Alicia, realizing the attitude of the council, summarizes the council's position and her position: "You have the power to remove the book from the library and you have the power to remove me. If you do one, you have to do the other."

Alicia is fired from her library position. Although a longtime resident, she rapidly loses support within the community, as she becomes labeled a Communist sympathizer. Children now avoid her; on one occasion, several youngsters refuse to attend a movie matinee with her, even though she offers to pay. On the night a public meeting is held to garner support for Alicia, the evening newspaper publishes an article on the council's reasons for firing Alicia, quoting a council member who stated that "Mrs. Hull admitted membership in numerous Communist-front organizations." Only twenty people attend the meeting, and support for Alicia is practically nonexistent. Some citizens fear that they will be called "Reds" for supporting her. Seeing the futility of organizing community support for her cause, Alicia tells the group to forget about supporting her. "I've left the library, and, I believe, we should let it rest at that," she says. Although a few citizens object to Alicia's refusal to fight for her library position and cause, the majority are happy to maintain their position and prestige within the community without exposing themselves as supporters of a Communist sympa-

Storm Center (1956). Bette Davis (left) is librarian Alicia Hull and Kim Hunter (right) is her assistant, Martha Lockridge.

thizer. The consensus is expressed by one attendee as he hustles out of the building, "Everything considered, I think you've made a wise decision, Mrs. Hull."

Martha succeeds Alicia as city librarian and visits Alicia to discuss the problems that she is having with Freddie Slater (Kevin Coughlin), a young boy who adored Alicia before the scandal occurred. A well-behaved and avid book reader before Alicia's firing, he is now a troublemaker. In her attempt to get advice about handling Freddie, however, Martha receives a very cool reception from Alicia, "I don't do a lot of things I used to do, and not by choice. I should think you and Mr. Duncan would have suspected that." At this point, Martha suddenly realizes that Alicia blames not only Paul but her too. Trying to apologize for the problems Alicia has encountered, even to the extent of maintaining that Paul was only one member of the council, Martha is cut short by Alicia. She asks, "Do you mind if I am not concerned about making you and Mr. Duncan feel better?"

At a country club party, Martha recognizes, perhaps for the first time, that Paul is a politician. Bantering with a state office holder whom he is thinking about challenging for office, Paul remarks, "Remember, I have an issue, you haven't." The state politician replies, "You mean, you once got a librarian fired." The ensuing discussion includes comments, both positive and negative, about Alicia. Martha is alarmed at Paul's statements and responds, "Paul, you aren't really serious about any of this." She is beginning to question Paul's involvement with Alicia's dismissal. She believed that the firing of Alicia was a move by all council members, but the conversation among the politicians indicates that it was spearheaded by Paul.

When construction on the children's wing begins, a large public ceremony is held. Freddie, by winning a library contest, has the privilege of reading the titles of the ten best books that will be placed in the cornerstone. Alicia, at the urging of Judge Robert Ellerbe (Paul Kelly), Alicia's most loyal supporter on the council, attends the outdoor ceremony with the judge. Their entrance immediately creates loud whispering through-out the crowd. As they walk to the speakers' stand, Freddie becomes so distraught that he cannot finish reading the list of titles. Ellerbe is given the privilege of turn-ing the first shovel for the groundbreaking, but defers to Alicia, telling the crowd, "There is only one person who should have this honor, Alicia Hull." His remarks draw the applause of only three members of the large crowd. As Alicia begins to shovel, she turns to Freddie, "How about helping an old friend?" Freddie, in a state of frustration, shouts, "You're not my friend. You're not anybody's friend. They kicked you out. You don't belong here.... You're not the librarian anymore. You're a Com-munist. A Communist...." During this outrage, one woman in the crowd stands up and encourages Freddie to continue, shouting, "You're right son. Tell her! Tell her! Tell her again!" Alicia responds by slapping and shaking Freddie, who turns and runs away. Alicia buries her face in her hands; the ceremony disintegrates; the crowd leaves.

Later that evening as Martha and Paul walk to a council meeting, Paul fails to understand his fiancée's comments about the problem with Alicia. Martha states the issue very simply: "A stubborn woman was fired. Your council blew itself up with civic virtue. City got something to buzz about. I got a better job. You got a platform." Paul responds that she makes "it sound like a grabbag." Martha retorts, "What do you think it was, patriotism?" Paul leaves Martha for the council meeting, where the members are in an uproar about the day's events. The judge wants to issue a public apology and reinstate Alicia, while Paul insists that in the fight against Communism, some innocent people will "get hurt." As the council wrangles with words, a confused and frustrated Freddie starts a fire in the library. The blazing building is quickly sur-rounded by residents who have rushed to see the fire, including Alicia, Martha, and the council members. Paul attempts to comfort Martha, but she retorts, "Just don't get it, do you? ... I don't want to be engaged to a rising young politician. I'd rather crawl into a hole somewhere."

As the flames continue to engulf the library, Alicia acknowledges that she shares part of the blame when she says, "I didn't fight back." The mayor then asks her to help rebuild the library, and Alicia responds, "I'm going to help rebuild this library, and if anybody ever again tries to remove a book from it, he'll have to do it over my dead body."

Storm Center reinforces the visual characteristics of reel librarians. When Alicia, a brunette (bob, with horseshoe finger waves), first appears on screen, she is wearing a modest dark suit and molded black half-hat. Martha first appears in a multicolor-stripe blouse with an open convertible collar accentuated by a large-bead choker necklace. Martha, also a brunette, sports a flipped-up bob with a half-bang. Both librarians wear very similar conservative clothing throughout the film; even in the country club scene, Martha wears a modest sleeveless black dress, with the same (or similar) necklace that she wore in her first library scene.

Alicia and Martha demonstrate a very limited number of occupational tasks while in the library, but Alicia's ability as a librarian is established within the first two minutes of the film when Martha asks about a book that she cannot locate for a patron. "Oh," Alicia responds with little hesitation, "look under Architecture, Modern. 724.9, I believe."

Alicia is very adept at serving young patrons. She suggests to Freddie that he read *Stories from the Bible* instead of continuing to read about monsters, but Freddie is too enthralled with monsters to switch genres. Alicia's communication skills with Freddie's father, George Slater (Joe Mantell), however, are suspect. She requires a better understanding of the problem, as well as compassion for the father, than she demonstrates. Upset about his son's interest in books instead of sports, George visits the library to confront Alicia about his son's incessant reading. She suggests, in a lecturing manner, that Freddie is "different" and that George should "value that difference." She continues to press her point by stating, "We put far too much stress on conformity in this country. The ball park isn't the only place a person can be a hero. Some people lead exciting lives locked in a laboratory ... or, even in a library." Alicia's comments are patronizing and presented rather smugly, further tormenting and alienating Freddie's father, as evidenced by his body language.

As city librarian, Alicia is cognizant of bureaucratic politics. When Judge Ellerbe visits the library to find *The Communist Dream*, she solicits his support for a new children's addition. She personally checks out the book and proffers a librarian's point of view to the judge: "It's not exactly light summer reading.... I hope you enjoy it more than I did." Martha's occupational skills, other than carrying books, are less visible. She becomes city librarian upon Alicia's dismissal; being Paul's girlfriend undoubtedly was considered an asset by council members. As city librarian, she quickly discerns Freddie's change in personality and her own inability to handle the young boy. She turns to Alicia for help but is hastily rebuffed. She breaks her engagement to Paul at film's end, realizing that they are incompatible. Martha cannot accommodate the philosophy of a rising young politician who, in his exuberance to rid the community of its red menace, can so nonchalantly dismiss the consequences of his actions: "Sure some innocent people are going to get hurt. Well, that's too bad." Martha's reluctance to see Paul as an egocentric politician is similar to Allie's failure to see Charlie as a tenement braggart in *Young Bride* (1932).

The absence of a close relationship between Alicia and Martha is atypical for reel librarians. Their relationship is never developed in the film, and after being fired, Alicia displays a great degree of hostility toward Martha. In previous films, relationships between reel librarians are supportive, resembling a mother-daughter relationship. In these motion pictures, the leading role is the daughter while the supporting role is the mother. Alicia in *Storm Center*, however, is almost a generation older than Martha, a reversal of the relationship portrayed in other films. Both Alicia and Martha project passive personalities, acquiescing to events and permitting events to control them, a *que sera, sera* attitude; it is not until the end of the film that they corral the courage to effect change.

A third librarian, Susie (uncredited; Alice Smith[108]), appears twice in the film but is not involved in the storyline. She is a young blonde (full bang; ponytail at crown) and works at the circulation desk. Of the three, Susie wears the most modish outfits, undoubtedly because of her youth.

In 1957, two color films with reel librarians—*Interlude* and *Desk Set*—were released within weeks of one another. Both films abandoned the traditional visual character-istics of the stereotypical image, replacing the dark hued clothes of past reel librari-ans with colorful, contemporary costumes and jettisoning the bun for stylish coiffures. After utilizing the stereotypical image for more than two decades, filmmakers could now examine in *Desk Set* a dramatic change of image—an image that emphasizes the youth and vibrancy of librarians rather than the attributes of being "only 38" and dowdy; an image that stresses the efficiency and competency of librarians rather than the "shushes" and the shelving of books; and an image that permits librarians to par-ticipate in cinematic humor rather than being the humor. However, as films released after 1957 illustrate, the traditional stereotypical image of librarians is so basically entrenched in the psyche of filmmakers that any change to the image will occur slowly, if at all.

June Allyson[109] portrays a librarian for the second time in *Interlude* (1957), a melo-dramatic romance filmed in Technicolor. Allyson stars as Helen Banning, who falls in love with Tonio Fischer (Rossano Brazzi), a distinguished pianist and conductor. Tonio is married, however, and his beautiful wife, Reni (Marianne Cook), suffers from mental illness. As Helen enjoys and suffers in her love affair with Tonio, she is pursued by a very patient and understanding American cardiologist working in a Munich university hospital, Morley Dwyer (Keith Andes), who loves her and wants to take her back to the states. Near the end of the story, Helen rescues Reni from an estate pond, an attempted suicide, instead of permitting Reni to die. Although Reni's death would have eliminated the one obstacle prohibiting Helen and Tonio's happi-ness, Helen realizes that her love for Tonio will neither permit her to standby idly as Reni drowns nor to disrupt Reni's overwhelming need for Tonio. With this revela-tion and the firm belief that a relationship with Tonio "is impossible," Helen asks Morley to take her back home to America as the film ends.

Helen and librarian Gertrude Kirk (Frances Bergen[110]) work in the library at Amerika Haus, an information center in Munich. Helen, a blonde (June Allyson hair-style), and Gertrude, a redhead (shoulder length page), are attractive, mature women; they are stylishly coiffured and dress in colorful, modern clothing. There are two brief library scenes in *Interlude*. In the first scene, several occupational tasks are displayed. Helen, picking up books from desks, informs an elderly patron reading at a desk that "we close at 5." The patron looks at the wall clock, announces, "It is four minutes to 5," and continues reading. Gertrude arrives moments later at the main desk and attempts to warn Helen about European men—they "act differently" than American men. Helen responds by assuring Gertrude that "there's nothing to worry about. Really nothing." In the second scene, Gertrude is busy putting books on a booktruck in the reading room, and Helen arrives shortly after the scene begins. The fact that Helen and Gertrude are librarians is not pertinent to the development of the storyline. The story features one twist of events that is most unusual for a reel librarian— Helen's rescue of Reni from an estate pool. In previous motion pictures with reel librarians, the cast member attempting suicide is the librarian.

The Spencer Tracy–Katharine Hepburn romantic comedy *Desk Set* (1957),[111] filmed in DeLuxe Color, was released shortly after *Interlude*. Tracy is Richard Sumner, a methods engineer and inventor of the Electronmagnetic Memory and Research Arithmetical Calculator (EMARAC), who is hired by the Federal Broadcasting Company (FBC) to determine the feasibility of installing EMARAC in the company's Reference Department. Hepburn[112] is Bunny Watson, head of the Reference Department, who supervises an outstanding staff that relies on memory and print materials for obtaining information. The storyline is a familiar love triangle: Richard meets Bunny, who is in love, at least superficially, with Mike Cutler (Gig Young), the company administrator responsible for the Reference Department. Richard and Bunny develop a friendly but subtle adversarial relationship, and at film's end, Richard and Bunny fall in love as Mike quietly and unnoticeably walks out of the Reference Department, leaving the couple alone with EMARAC.

Early in the film, the president of FBC, Mr. Azae (Nicholas Joy), informs Richard that he must not tell the "girls in research" what he is doing; Azae does not want them to know "about this big thing that's coming up. It's vital that it be kept a secret." The girls are Peg Costello (Joan Blondell[113]), Sylvia Blair (Dina Merrill[114]), and Ruthie Saylor (Sue Randall[115]), and with Bunny, they are a formidable reference staff, providing answers to a variety of questions covering every subject matter. Of the four librarians, only Bunny's educational preparation is revealed; she is a college graduate, with a library course at Columbia. She was going "to take a Ph.D., but ... ran out of money." Approximately 70 of the film's 102 minutes occur in the Reference Department, and the competency of the staff is demonstrated repeatedly throughout the film, as they answer numerous telephone inquiries. Although each librarian is a generalist, they have subject specialties—Peg, for instance, is the "baseball expert." They are a cohesive team and exhibit a great degree of camaraderie; although personal money is tight, Bunny brokers the loans (mostly from her purse) so they have spending money until payday. Each librarian has a keen sense of humor. When Richard is standing on the balcony reeling in his measuring tape after determining the distance from the balcony to the first floor, Sylvia asks "Catch anything?" Just moments later when he asks Sylvia to hold the tape for him, she responds, "35, 24, 35." Richard bounces back with, "Oh, and very nice too," indicating that he understands their humor. Even Mike displays a sense of humor. He often checks on the department, primarily to see Bunny. After chatting with her on one occasion, he remarks to the staff as he leaves, "Bye, girls. Always a pleasure seeing your freshly scrubbed, smiling faces. Remember our motto: Be on time, do your work, be down in the bar at 5:30."

Although humor is a key ingredient in the atmosphere of the library, when rumors about the purpose of Richard's work reach the Reference Department, staff members become apprehensive about losing their jobs. The installation of EMARAC in payroll resulted in a 50 percent reduction in staff in that department. Although

Desk Set (1957). The "girls in research" are (left to right): Dina Merrill as Sylvia Blair; Katharine Hepburn as Bunny Watson (her hair in a bun), head of the Reference Department; Joan Blondell as Peg Costello; and Sue Randall as Ruthie Saylor. The "girls" present one of the more positive cinematic depictions of librarians in twentieth century films.

Bunny assures Peg that a machine cannot replace them, the staff is pessimistic about the future. The Reference Department's Christmas party, however, is loud and jovial, due in part to the imbibing of champagne and the staff belief that it is their last convivial occasion. The party reaches its zenith when Richard offers to take them all to the Plaza for drinks. As Richard opens the door for them to leave, Miss Warriner (Neva Patterson) from his lab enters. He immediately suggests that she come back after Christmas, but she begins talking about moving the furniture for the installation of EMARAC on Monday. The staff is aghast at her pronouncement—their first notice of the impending change; Warriner seemingly validates the rumors that they will soon be terminated when she later adds, "According to Mr. Sumner's figures, it will save in this department alone 6,240 man-hours a year." The group's holiday spirit is dashed, as is the group's esteem for Richard. Attempting to reignite the holiday spark, he continues, "Now, why don't we all go over to the Plaza and have that drink we were ... uh...." Bunny stops him with "Why don't you and Miss EMARAC go over and hoist a few?" Richard, realizing the futility of the situation, ushers his employee out the door.

Pausing at the door to attempt a reconciliation, he utters, "Look, uh...." Bunny responds before he can say anything else, "And a very merry Christmas to you, too."

Two weeks later, EMARAC is operational. Staff members, busy assisting Warriner prepare EMARAC for its debut, are very somber as they await their imminent dismissal. Peg reveals their depression in her reply to Ruthie's concern about the late delivery of paychecks, "There's probably something extra in it, like a pink slip."

Later the same day, Azae gives a tour of the building to the "boys" and requests Richard to give a brief overview of the capabilities of EMARAC. When Richard asks for a question to test EMARAC, Bunny offers a question that required three weeks for her staff to research the answer: "How much damage is done annually to the American forest by the spruce budworm?" FBC's president then asks Bunny if she remembers the answer; she does, "$138,464,359, and some cents." Emmy, as Richard affectionately calls the machine on occasion, prints out the answer—$138,464,359.12. The touring "boys" are impressed by the quickness and accuracy of EMARAC. Turning to Bunny, Richard asks how much staff time it took to find the answer. Acting nonchalantly and with a quick snap of her fingers, as if it were an easy question, she responds, "Forty-five minutes." Richard, emphasizing the efficiency of EMARAC, remarks, "Well, even at that, you can see that this one operation alone saved your department 44 minutes." Azae is impressed with the increased efficiency and leads the group to payroll, where another of Richard's EMARAC machines is installed.

As soon as the tour group exits the library, paychecks arrive. Each staff member stares at her pay envelope, each anticipating termination. Bunny breaks the silence, "Oh, who's afraid. C'mon, all together." All four have pink slips, and Bunny, attempting to lighten the impact of the bad news, comments, "Not only that, but they took out for Blue Cross again this week." They now turn their attention to finding some boxes and helping Bunny pack her office items—she has eleven years of accumulation.

As staff members scurry about gathering personal items in preparation for leaving, Warriner handles the telephone inquiries, revealing for the first time a complete absence of reference skills. When Richard returns from the tour, she asks for help; he, in turn, asks, "Where is everybody?" Bunny replies, "Here we are, Mr. Sumner," as the four staff members with pink slips stand idly by and watch the developing fiasco. When it becomes apparent to Bunny that their clients will be receiving inaccurate information, she puts her staff to work to demonstrate that they can be as effective as EMARAC in answering questions. Upset and in a state of confusion, Warriner makes a mistake with EMARAC, and its console begins to smolder, the lights on the display flash off and on, and its bells and whistles sound. She begins screaming and crying, while Richard wants to know the "stupid mistake" she made so that he can fix the problem. Crying and screaming in anger that the staff sabotages her work and creates an atmosphere of hate and suspicion, she blames Bunny for the problems, maintains that Richard is just as bad as the reference staff, and runs out of the department.

As Richard and Bunny reset EMARAC, the department courier arrives with mail for Richard. The telephone rings, prompting him to ask why they refuse to answer the telephone, and Bunny responds, "We don't work here anymore." "I don't understand," he remarks, adding inquisitively, "What did you do?" Opening the envelope, he finds a pink slip, exclaiming, "I don't even work here!" Realizing the staff has been fired, he rushes to telephone the president. "Azae, you broke a promise to me. You know everybody down here in research has been fired?" Azae, waving his pink slip in the air, shouts into the telephone, "The whole darn building's been fired. That crazy fool machine of yours in payroll went berserk this morning and gave everybody a pink slip." Richard exclaims, "That's impossible, that just couldn't happen." Richard informs the reference staff of the mistake, assuring them that they are still employed, that the workload will be increasing, and that the company will be adding "a few more girls. I just hope they're as good as all you are." The staff is ecstatic, and Richard's popularity soars among staff members in the Reference Department.

Bunny, Peg, Sylvia, and Ruthie make a distinct break with the image of librarians in previous films, especially in clothes; they wear very colorful, fashionable ensembles. Being smartly dressed is important to the staff, as indicated by Ruthie in the first six minutes of the film. Answering the telephone, Ruthie responds to a caller, "Oh, yes," and then lowering her voice, continues, "I called earlier about that little black velvet strapless you had in the window.... But, I saw an identical one for $10 less in a store downtown." All of the "girls in research" are stylishly coiffured women: Peg, a blonde, has a pixie style bob with a full bang; Sylvia, a blonde, has a page with a half bang and both sides held back with combs; Ruthie, a brunette, has a bob with a flip in back; and Bunny, a redhead, sports an attractive bun with pincurls on the top and side—the only hairstyle that even closely approximates the visual characteristic. Costume designer Charles Le Maire either failed to examine or purposely ignored the costumes of past reel librarians. His costumes enhance the beauty of these four, as does the makeup artistry of Ben Nye.

Bunny and Peg are "only 38" but project images and personalities radically different from previous "only 38" librarians. They sing, they dance, and they drink champagne in the library—conduct unbecoming for preceding "only 38" reel librarians who were deliberately portrayed as sedate; as elderly by costume, makeup, and age; and as autocratic interpreters of library rules, often illustrated by the commanding "shush" for silence.

Because the Reference Department is a special library, the research unit of a large corporation, the governing rules are established by the company and do not parallel the restrictive rules for behavior and conduct of tax-supported libraries; for example, municipal public libraries and state university libraries. The department is not silent; in fact, the opposite is true, and until EMARAC arrived, smoking was permitted. Although the department does not resemble the traditional library of previous motion pictures and its staff does not resemble previous reel librarians, the "girls in research" exhibit most of the occupational tasks that identify reel librarians—answering telephones, finding answers to inquiries, sitting behind desks, and working in book stacks. That they are librarians is indisputable. That they are creating a new image of reel librarians is indisputable. That this new image will be acknowledged by and reflected in the post–1957 work of actors, writers, and directors is very problematical.

It is remarkable that in 1957 two motion pictures—Desk Set and Interlude—depict all reel librarians as strikingly attractive, fashionably clothed, and stylishly coiffured. Each film relies heavily on occupational tasks to validate the cast members as librarians. More importantly, the storylines of *Desk Set* and *Interlude* emphasize that Bunny and Helen are indeed women and, as women, crave and seek male attention. No filmgoer can conclude that the lives of Bunny and Helen reflect or mirror the silent and stoic atmosphere within the popular Carnegie libraries during this era of the twentieth century.

The five remaining films of the decade with reel librarians—*Curse of the Demon* (1957), *Hot Spell* (1958), *The FBI Story* (1959), *Web of Evidence* (1959), and *The Crimson Kimono* (1959)—rely heavily on the stereotypical image. In the case of actress Vera Miles, who portrays an attractive reel librarian in both *The FBI Story* and *Web of Evidence*, the role of the reel librarian is principally for romantic purposes.

Curse of the Demon, one of the many B-horror films of the 1950s, contains a scene in the British Museum. Dana Andrews stars as Dr. John Holden, a prominent psychologist whose London host, Professor Harrington, is found dead the morning that John arrives. In researching the circumstances surrounding Harrington's death, John visits the British Museum. While in the library, he is assisted by an "only 38," balding, portly male librarian (John Salew[116]), who is very helpful. The librarian takes notes as he speaks with John, and when he informs John that one of the books "is not available," John inquires about the meaning of that phrase. "It should be in our restricted section. The only known existing copy. Over four hundred years old, you know," the librarian responds, adding that "it seems to be missing. Most peculiar. I'm having it checked." The librarian assures John that he will "trace it." The librarian's service is impeccable—he is polite, articulate, knowledgeable of materials, and willing to trace a lost book. On-screen for only 45 seconds, the librarian demonstrates an excellent work ethic. He wears a dark suit, white shirt, and dark tie. Though he adheres to most of the stereotypical visual characteristics, he, quite surprisingly, does not wear eyeglasses.

A male librarian also appears in *Hot Spell*, a drama about the disintegration of a southern family mothered by Alma Duval (Shirley Booth) and fathered by Jack Duval (Anthony Quinn). For Jack's birthday, Alma buys presents for her children (all young adults) to give to Jack. As she bounces across the city to give these presents to her three children, Alma visits the library where her youngest son, Billy (Clint Kimbrough[117]) works. She rushes into the library, passes a counter-height main desk where an "only 38" librarian (uncredited; Elsie Weller[118]) is busy writing on a notepad. The librarian, a brunette (bun at crown), is attired in a short-sleeve blouse and ribbon bow tie. The librarian has no dialogue but glances briefly at Alma as she dashes by to see her son. "Billy! Billy!" Alma shouts as she waves at him, walking through the large reading room and disturbing all of the patrons. Billy rushes to her and begs for silence, "Do you want to get me fired, or something?" They go into an aisle in the book stacks, and Alma, looking around at the books, states, "What a lovely place to work. It's so peaceful." Billy maintains he has to "get back to his books," as he attempts to curtail Alma's visit. A determined mother, Alma explains her plans for Jack's birthday in her very strong and somewhat loud voice. An elderly bespectacled man, walking down a perpendicular aisle, utters a loud "Shush!" at them when he reaches the intersection of the aisles.[119] Alma quickly finishes informing Billy what she expects of him and rushes off to visit her daughter.

Filmgoers easily recognize Billy as a librarian; he works in a library, pushes a rolling book bin around the book stack area, and talks about books. He is a sensitive youth searching for identity. When his father runs away with an 18-year-old girl, Billy reacts by enlisting in the Air Force. On the whole, reel librarians leave library positions for love or marriage. Billy's motivation to leave family and library was not only to avoid participating in the family's further disintegration, but also in anticipation of becoming independent, his own man.

Vera Miles[120] portrays a reel librarian in two 1959 releases—*The FBI Story* and *Web of Evidence*. Miles is librarian Lucy Ballard, girlfriend of FBI agent John Michael "Chip" Hardesty (James Stewart), in *The FBI Story* (Technicolor), a laudatory history of the Federal Bureau of Investigation. The historical narrative begins in 1924 when the Knoxville agents are instructed to attend a meeting in Washington to meet the bureau's new director. After receiving this news, Chip visits the library, responding to a telephone call from Lucy. An attractive blonde (angel wing bang; bun at nape), Lucy is working with another librarian (uncredited[121]) at the main desk in the center of the public library when Chip enters. He returns two books, which Lucy immediately stamps. He asks for another book, and Lucy responds, "Well, if we do [have it], it'll be in the mystery section. I'll show you." The two are very coy to hide their relationship during this conversation; neither their behavior nor words indicate a couple in love. Once they arrive in a secluded nook in the mystery section, they embrace and kiss. "Jim, darling," Lucy remarks, "not every day. Somebody's going to notice. Nobody can read books quite that fast." During their conversation in the alcove, Chip remarks, "It's not very romantic kissing somebody right in the middle of the murder section." Lucy asks if he has a better suggestion, and his response is, "I think we ought to get married." The wordplay suddenly loses its frivolity, becoming very serious. Lucy's one demand is that he quit the bureau and enter private law practice. She wants him to "do something important;" rather than exist in a job where he occasionally receives "a pat on the back from some political appointee." As they discuss the future of their relationship, he realizes that a life with Lucy means a life outside the bureau and, consequently, acquiesces to her demand. "I think I'd give up anything to marry you, Lucy. I really would," he says. The couple embrace and kiss again; Lucy then rushes back to her work place and Chip wanders about the book stacks. This is the film's only library scene.

Lucy's involvement with the library ends at the altar. Although she occasionally styles her hair in a bun, Lucy becomes the dedicated wife of Chip and is the loving and caring mother of their three children, traveling extensively and living uncomplainingly in dirt towns, urban areas, and farm country. Except for one brief episode, Lucy resembles the picture-perfect wife and mother that evolved on television programs during the late 1950s and early 1960s.

In the only library scene, Lucy's coworker is stationed at the main desk; she is an "only 38" brunette (bun at nape), wears a sequined dress that has a V-neckline infilled with white fabric to match the large lace collar, and eyeglasses. Director Mervyn LeRoy and cinematographer Joseph Biroc are almost successful in blocking this coworker from the view of filmgoers. When the camera is in front of the desk, Chip is positioned in front of the coworker, and when the camera is on the patron's right side of the desk, Lucy is in front of the coworker; both camera angles essentially block the coworker from view. She is visible briefly when Chip enters the library and when Lucy takes him to the mystery section.

LeRoy continues the cinematic practice of surrounding a star in the library with an older supporting actor, increasing the attractiveness and beauty of the star. Using camera positions to minimize the presence of supporting actors when the star is in the same shot is not a new technique. In *The Good Companions* (1933), the camera is behind the supporting actor, and in *Flesh and Fantasy* (1943), the supporting actor is in shadows. A second librarian is required in this scene so that Lucy can accompany Chip to the mystery section.

In her second appearance as a reel librarian in 1959, Miles portrays Lena Anderson in *Web of Evidence*. She co-stars with Van Johnson as Paul Mathry, an American who travels to Liverpool to research his family's history, discovering that his father was not a war hero and was not killed in World War I, as his mother insisted during her lifetime, but is an imprisoned murderer. Paul enlists the assistance of Lena in his struggle to prove his father's innocence and to free his wrongly convicted father from prison. Lena assists Paul during this crusade and the two fall in love.

A film noir, *The Crimson Kimono* (1959) focuses on a murder investigation and the tensions of an interracial romance. Detective Sergeant Charlie Bancroft (Glenn Corbett) and Detective Joe Kojaku (James Shigeta), who are assigned to investigate the murder of a burlesque dancer, are pursuing investigative leads when they visit the Los Angeles Public Library and meet with the city librarian (uncredited; Stafford Repp[122]). After they show the librarian a drawing of a suspect, the librarian states the drawing resembles Paul Sand (Neyle Morrow[123]), a library specialist whose expertise is Asia. He maintains that Paul could not be the individual they are pursuing, "You suspect Paul?" Laughing, he continues, "Believe me, officers, when you meet him you'll see why it's ridiculous." The librarian telephones to ask Paul to come to his office, and after listening intently, he remarks to the two police officers, "This is a fantastic coincidence. Paul Sand just resigned without explanation." The scene ends with this pronouncement.

The city librarian dresses conservatively, has a receding hairline, the balding characteristic, and puffs and holds onto a cigar during the scene. Because this individual is not identified as a librarian, filmgoers may not have realized his occupation. It is evident, however, from the city librarian's conversation with the two police officers that he is Paul's supervisor and that Paul is a librarian. Paul, however, does not appear in a library scene. Although he dresses conservatively in a dark suit and necktie, only the most discerning of filmgoers would recognize that he is a reel librarian.

Conclusion

The visual characteristics and occupational tasks of reel librarians in silent films are the fundamental idiosyncratic traits used during the first three decades of the sound era to develop a stable, recognizable stereotypical image of reel librarians, a stereotype easily transferable to working librarians. The first words addressed to a reel librarian in the sound era were ominous for the occupation and its stereotypical image: "old lady foureyes." A large majority of reel librarians were women, many of whom were attractive, single women working in a respectable, but poorly paid, occupation while waiting patiently for the Galahad of their dreams to whisk them away from their self-imposed purgatorial environment. Although a Galahad appeared for several reel librarians, he often failed to meet their expectations.

The majority of motion pictures with reel librarians during these three decades were filmed in black-and-white, a factor reinforcing the "Pilgrim" appearance of librarians, as corroborated by a cast member's remark about the reel librarian in *Navy Blues* (1937): "It must be Thanksgiving or something. She's all made up like a pilgrim." With the continuing and expanding use of color in films, the attire of reel librarians could change from black and white to outstanding colorful and modern clothing. Reel librarians appearing in brief supporting roles in color films, however, retained the basic visual characteristics. Modest clothes are available in fabrics of various colors; the many variations of base hue colors—plum, cobalt, olive and similar dark variations—can serve as a substitute for black and retain the essence of the stereotypical image. In 1957, Allyson and Bergen in *Interlude* and Hepburn, Blondell, Merrill, and Randall in *Desk Set* challenged the visual characteristics, the stereotypical image, of preceding reel librarians.

The utilization of reel librarians for comedic purposes was widespread in films released during this thirty-year period. Reel librarians commit humiliating mishaps for the enjoyment of filmgoers, but, on the whole, they seldom participate in physical pratfalls. The humor and enjoyment often results from the banter between a reel librarian and a suitor. In the majority of these instances, the intellect of the reel librarian is obviously superior to that of the suitor. Clark Gable, a suitor of two reel librarians, for instance, fell unceremoniously twice to the intellect and psychological machinations of reel librarians—first, to Carole Lombard in *No Man of Her Own* (1932) and, thirteen years later, to Greer Garson in *Adventure* (1945).

The studio system of filmmaking dominates this thirty-year period, but change was evolving quickly in the 1950s. A new era of filmmaking was beginning, and filmmakers had the opportunity to discard the stereotypical image of reel librarians and to embrace the "girls in research" persona for reel librarians. A filmmaker's creativity may effect change in the stereotypical image created over the past three decades, or his lack of creativity, his reticence to change, may embed the stereotype even deeper into the psyche of popular culture. Unfortunately, early films of the 1960s indicate that many filmmakers chose the latter approach.

3

Continuance of the Stereotype, 1960–1979

To adhere to court-imposed rulings regarding the distribution of motion pictures and to meet the challenge of television, the American film industry changed rapidly and radically during the late 1940s and the 1950s. The studio system disintegrated and, shortly after mid-century, the production of "B" films waned. Each motion picture became an independent production and, consequently, had to demonstrate its profitability without artificial underpinnings. Movie theater attendance was in decline, and by 1971, the average weekly attendance plunged to a low of 15.8 million.[1] Attendance numbers, however, rebounded quickly and improved significantly throughout the remainder of the decade. The era of double feature programs, a staple of the past, rapidly disappeared, as did the concept of continuous showings—the option of a filmgoer to enter the theater at any time to see a movie and to stay until he desired to leave. Black and white film quickly lost its dominance, as color film became the choice of most filmmakers. Many excellent films, however, continued to be released in black and white. The majority of the films with reel librarians during the 1960s and the remainder of the century were in color. This permitted a more colorful wardrobe for reel librarians, but the conservative nature of clothes worn by reel librarians was unchanged. Reel librarians in supporting roles continued to dress in the more conservative dark value variations and dull intensity variations of base colors. These librarians possessed the visual characteristics and engaged in the occupational tasks that reel librarians have demonstrated on-screen since 1921.

The basic structural changes in the film industry primarily affected methodologies relating to the production and distribution of motion pictures. The creativity of writers and directors, however, were not dramatically affected by these changes, nor would one expect them to be. During the 1960s and 1970s, there were no significant changes in the cinematic depiction of librarians, as the stereotypical image continued to prevail in motion pictures. The image, which can be duplicated easily and with minimal effort, remains an effective cinematic tool for screenwriters, directors, and actors. Although *Desk Set* presented an impressive challenge to the stereotypical image in 1957, most filmmakers continued to rely on the established stereotype for their cast of characters.

Five films released in the 1960s are noteworthy because of the impact reel librarians had on the story line. Four had reel librarians in major roles: *Only Two Can Play* (1962, b/w[2]), *The Music Man* (1962), *You're A Big Boy Now* (1966), and *Goodbye, Columbus* (1969), and one had a reel librarian in a supporting role, *My Side of the Mountain* (1969). Some of these librarians are presented in a flattering manner; some are presented in a most unflattering manner. In all cases, however, the reel librarians are entertaining, and in several cases, they are charming.

Peter Sellers[3] delighted filmgoers as librarian John Lewis of the Aberdarcy (Wales) Public Library in *Only Two Can Play*. John suffers from the male crisis popularly known as the seven-year-itch, a problem that afflicts many male film characters. As a librarian, unfortunately, John's finances are meager; he is married with two small children and lives in "three rooms and half a bathroom." John, dissatisfied with his perceived destitution and hopeless home situation, attempts to indulge his "itch," but his boundless ineptitude prevents any semblance of success.

John's predicament is identified in the opening library scene. When an attractive young brunette saunters into the library, the camera shifts to John, who peers through bookshelves at the woman—he appears to be looking through bars of a jail cell; the library is his prison. Approaching John, she asks, "Have you *Conditioned Reflexes?*" The book is out, but not John's reflexes. To place the book on hold for her, he obtains her name and telephone number. As she walks out of the library, John stares at her every step; looking at her telephone number, he shakes his head in a negative manner, as if to discard the fantasies within his mind. He turns, grabs a handful of books and heads for the stacks. While shelving, he drops *Sex, Sin, and Sanctity*, and bending down to retrieve the book, he observes two lovely legs in the next aisle. When he stands up, a pretty brunette smiles at him through the shelves. She walks to the end of the aisle, passes John, and struts out of the library, with John eyeing every swivel of her hips. He looks at the book he just picked up; its title is now *Is Sex Necessary?* He tosses the book onto a shelf, walks to the library desk, and buries his face in his hands as a quotation from Ralph Waldo Emerson appears on-screen: "It is not observed that librarians are wiser men than others."

In the next scene, John, lying awake in bed early in the morning, muses about "the well-known biological fact" that some men "need more than the normal outlet for our creative urges." His musings lead to the inevitable male dilemma, defined by John as "doing something and regrettin' it or not doing something and waking up in a state like this every morning." A typical morning for John is noisy and mundane—his daughter knocks on his head in an effort to get him out of bed, he shares the bathroom with another apartment building dweller, and his wife Jean (Virginia Maskell) insists that he apply for the sub-librarian position, as the "extra 150 a year would make all the difference." In addition, the young girl with a bountiful bust on the first floor leaves her apartment door open while putting on a sweater, just as John walks by on his way to the bus stop. On the crowded double-

Only Two Can Play (1961). Peter Sellers is John Lewis, a librarian at the Aberdarcy (Wales) Public Library whose "creative urges" engender numerous and humorous escapades.

decker bus, John is squeezed in next to a buxom blonde, and when John exits the bus with Ieuan Jenkins (Kenneth Griffith[4]), a fellow librarian, and the blonde, she gives John an enticing look. As he walks with Ieuan, John poses a serious question, "Do you ever ... think about other things, you know ... things like women?" Ieuan, completely baffled, responds, "Women?" Frustrated by his colleague's lack of understanding, John ends the conversation. Ieuan then goes into a pharmacy and John follows the bouncing blonde to her place of employment, standing outside the door wondering whether or not he should go in, which he doesn't, or on to the library, which he does.

John's frustration only intensifies at the library. An early patron, Mr. Hyman (Graham Stark), returns his three-week overdue book, asking excitingly, "You got any more books like that?" John comments, "Well not exactly like that, Mr. Hyman, no. Not quite so many egg stains." As Hyman converses with John at the desk, Mrs. Elizabeth Gruffydd-Williams (Mai Zetterling), an attractive, seductive, and influential woman and wife of the chair of the Library Committee, enters the library and is assisted by Miss Jones (uncredited[5]). John leaves Hyman at the desk to offer his assistance and says to the other librarian, "Well, Miss Jones, if you'd like to deal with that gentleman over there, I'll attend to this." Elizabeth is looking for illustrations of costumes in medieval Wales for a production of the local D'Arcy Players, and as they talk, she realizes that John, in addition to being a librarian, is "The Mr. Lewis," the *Aberdarcy Chronicle*'s local drama critic. He takes her on a stroll through the stacks looking for books, remarking that "most of the good stuff is out at the moment." Although they look at several books, John finally takes her to Ieuan—"he's the expert around here on all things Welsh."

As Elizabeth leaves the library, she suggests that both librarians attend one of her "literary parties one of these days." They soon receive invitations, but plans are interrupted when Ieuan's wife becomes ill and cannot baby-sit for John and Jean. Liz then sends her current paramour to baby-sit. Gareth Proberty (Richard Attenborough), one of John's old friends and antagonists and now a locally renowned playwright, also attends the party. When they meet, Gareth gibes John, "How are you, Lewis? Still peddling trash to the masses?" John's response indicates the depth of their unrestrained disdain: "Yes, that's right, yes. How about you? Still writing it?" They continue their mutual disrespectful bickering until Elizabeth's husband Vernon (Raymond Huntley) joins them. Gareth informs Vernon that they are having a problem with costumes: "Poor Elizabeth ... has been trying for the last month to persuade Mr. Lewis' public library to disgorge some books which could help us, but, of course, without any success at all." John's rebuttal: "Perhaps if we knew what you wanted, we might be able to do something about it. You see, it's rather difficult to get hold of a book when you don't know the title or the author. Isn't it?" When Gareth leaves, Vernon remarks, "I suppose being a poet entitles him to be a bit different from us chaps, don't you think?" John, speaking as the local drama critic, responds, "I suppose I should agree with you, sir." Speaking personally, however, he believes that Gareth is "a puffed up, undersized, four-eyed little twit."

Elizabeth manages to pair off with John in a room and they discuss the sublibrarian position until his "creative urges" propel them into an embrace. The romance is on, and Elizabeth, now in pursuit of John, contrives successfully to arrange a tryst. She manages to get John to her home while Vernon is away, but as soon as they jump into bed, Vernon returns home with guests. John gets away, but only after bumbling and stumbling, quite humorously, through various inventive ploys to exit the house. The tryst was a disaster and only intensified John's frustration. Elizabeth quickly devises a rather ingenious second tryst. On the opening evening of Gareth's play, she entices John to leave with her rather than sitting through the play. They drive out into the countryside, park the car in a pasture, and are soon in a passionate embrace. Elizabeth suddenly screams; the cows in the pasture are sticking their heads into the car. As John attempts to restart the car, all the wrong buttons are pushed or pulled, creating so much noise that the farmer rushes out of his house with a shotgun and begins shooting as they speed out of the pasture. When they get back to town, John writes his review and drops it off at the newspaper office, his regular routine.

Next morning at breakfast with Jean and the children, he discovers the misfortune that can befall a husband with "creative urges":

JEAN: I see you gave the play a good notice.
JOHN: Yes. Well I thought I wouldn't be too unkind.
JEAN: Very noble of you in the circumstances.
JOHN: What circumstances?

Jean then shows him the front-page headline: "Theatre Catches Fire During Performance."

On the day of interviews for the position of sub-librarian, four candidates—a nervous lot, all expecting the worst—meet in the lavatory. Kennedy (uncredited[6]) parks on the toilet, unable to get any distance from the stool. The eldest candidate, a graying Mr. Beynon (David Davies[7]), is the first to be interviewed. He enjoys being first, suggesting "first impressions stick.... I'll set the standard." But when he returns from the interview, he just shakes his head and leaves quickly. The remaining three are now confronting runaway fear. When John faces the committee, one of the questions is about the percentage of books that should be Welsh. "Supplied as asked for," is John's response, but when a committee member insists that the Welsh population is large, John counters by stating, "Well, I'll take your word for that, sir. It's just that I very seldom get asked for books in Welsh, except by, uh, foreigners." The woman on the committee asks her question through the chairman: "What would be your attitude if a member of the opposite sex came into the library and asked for *Lady Chatterly's Lover?*" John fails to respond, sitting silently until the chairman asks if he understands the question. "Yes, sir," John replies, "and I think I could be relied upon to know my duty." The woman, pleased by the answer, smiles and thanks the chairman, adding, "That's all I wanted to know."

After the interview, John joins Elizabeth for drinks, declaring that he "muffed" the interview. She states that he got the job—"It was all fixed ages ago. The interview was just a formality." Vernon, she states, "is well trained, too." She has a weekend tryst worked out for them and suggests he buy a better-fitting suit. John looks over to the bar where Bill, her current paramour, is dutifully obtaining drinks for them. He realizes what his fate will be in a short time—a lapdog. He informs Elizabeth that he is neither taking the job nor continuing their romantic affair. "The price is too high. Goodbye, Liz."

John rushes home to Jean, only to find his wife entertaining Gareth, whom he chases out of the apartment. Realizing the value of his love for Jean, John leaves the Aberdarcy Public Library, hoping such a move will reinforce and strengthen their marriage. In the next scene, John and Jean are the operators of a traveling library (bookmobile), which is parked in the countryside. John, revealing some degree of improvement, manages to thwart the overtures of an attractive brunette. Proud of the way he handled the situation, John maintains that he is "improving." Jean, however, insists that he's "got a long way to go." They embrace and kiss, and then begin the "long drive home."

As a librarian, John demonstrates a minimal number of library skills; it is evident, however, that he could function competently as a librarian. His occupational intellect is not in question, but he projects an uncaring, lackadaisical image, the result of his affliction. John's crisis—the male need for "more than the normal outlet for ... creative urges"—is the essence of *Only Two Can Play*. John's trysts with Elizabeth are not carried out with the debonair precision of an accomplished paramour. Rather, his escapades with Elizabeth demonstrate a total incompetence in such affairs. His impossible dream of amorous adventures is victimized by his own hilarious clumsiness. John's bungling behavior is believable, especially coming from a librarian whose staid work mirrors his home life. John's ineptness is reminiscent of Bryant Washburn's portrayal of LeRoy Sylvester in *A Very Good Young Man* (1919) more than forty years earlier. Their motivations, however, are greatly different: LeRoy is attempting to tarnish his outstanding moral record in order to marry the woman he loves, while John is attempting to circumvent his commitment to the woman he married and loves in an effort to satisfy his sexual craving. Neither is successful.

John and Ieuan dress conservatively—John in a suit with leather elbow patches and a tie, and Ieuan in a dark sports coat, slacks, and tie. For Elizabeth's literary party, John puts on a tuxedo for which he is waiting "to come back into fashion." John's wardrobe is limited and appears to hang on him rather than fit him, which prompts Elizabeth to suggest that he purchase a better-fitting suit. Miss Jones appears more fashionably attired than John and Ieuan, as would every woman. A young, attractive brunette (shoulder length, soft curls), Miss Jones wears a patterned flare skirt and dark pullover sweater. Jones' occupational tasks include shelving books, working at the desk, and assisting patrons. Two other librarians, Beynon and Kennedy, who appear for interviews for the sub-librarian position, are "only 38" individuals and dress conservatively.

John needs, as do the other three applicants, the higher paying sub-librarian position. His present salary provides only the basic essentials for his family, explaining his wife's remark that the "extra 150 would make all the difference." One minor humorous act by John also reveals his financial condition—he takes cigarettes from a coffee table at Elizabeth's home and puts them in his empty cigarette pack. John's marginal economic existence engenders a serious questioning of his choice of an occupation. Although well-educated, John at one point inquisitively remarks, "Why did I bother to cram to pass the exams, to take degrees. Where did it get me? I'd be much better off as a road sweeper! There's no doubt about it. I would be, I would be far better off as a road sweeper." John, however, stays with his occupation, a course of action not taken by many other reel librarians.

Only Two Can Play presents an unflattering image of male reel librarians. However, the impact of the humor of John's mishaps is intensified by the fact that he is a librarian. Filmgoers do not expect suave, debonair playboys to come from the ranks of librarians, and as John demonstrates, emphatically and repeatedly, librarians are not of the same stature as Casanova in matters of amour. John, as the majority of male reel librarians, never rises above the level of a comic figure—the male reel librarian who becomes preposterously dysfunctional when interacting with the opposite sex.

Meredith Willson's musical comedy *The Music Man* (1962) reached movie theaters in June 1962, making the transition from successful Broadway play to successful motion picture. The popularity of the play enabled filmgoers to know the songs, romance, and story line of *The Music Man* long before they entered a movie theater. The film stars Robert Preston, reprising his Broadway role as Professor Harold Hill, a traveling pitchman intent on bilking the residents of River City, Iowa, of their cash under the guise of starting a boys' band. Hill has developed a devious near-perfect scam—he promotes the many virtues of a band, selling musical instruments and uniforms to unsuspecting parents who have high expectations of their sons' musical talent. When the instruments and uniforms arrive, he collects the cash and absconds without teaching the boys to play their new instruments. Shirley Jones[8] co-stars as Marian Paroo, the best-known reel librarian in twentieth century cinema—Marian the Librarian. In addition to being River City's librarian, Marian also teaches piano. She is highly suspicious of the professed talents and education of Professor Hill. A conflict between professor, who cannot "read a note of music," and librarian, whose goal is "improving River City's cultural level," is inevitable.

Harold, the essence of the perennial traveling sales (con) man, maintains that "maiden lady librarians who give piano [lessons] are a specialty of mine," but he discovers quickly during his first encounter with Marian that she is a formidable antagonist. Marian is an intelligent young woman, quite capable of holding her own with a traveling pitchman such as Harold. On his first effort to converse with her as she walks home from the library, Marian easily dismisses his worn-out cavalier attempts at conversation, and as she climbs the stairs to her home, Harold tries one more time, "I'll only be in town a short while." Marian's caustic response, as she enters the house, is "Good!"

A charismatic individual, Harold exudes charm—he persuades Marian's mother to purchase an instrument for Winthrop (Ron Howard), Marian's younger brother, and almost sells an instrument to the mayor who, at the last moment, realizes that he doesn't have a son. When the instruments and costumes arrive, the money is collected, the last train is about to depart, and the professor is exposed as a fraud, Harold cannot leave River City—he has fallen in love with Marian. As he explains to Winthrop, "For the first time in my life, I got my foot caught in the door." In the end, it is the charm of Marian that prevails, capturing the heart of Harold and preventing him from scampering off with the money, even though the townspeople are preparing to tar and feather him. Harold stays, confronts an angry group of residents, and with Marian's urging, directs the boys' band, which has labored two weeks with the professor's "think system" of musical instruction. The band, to the professor's disbelief, receives overwhelmingly enthusiastic accolades; all, of course, from the parents of the boys. The boys' band is a success.

In the first library scene in *The Music Man*, Marian defends a classic piece of literature. Eulalie Mackechnie Shinn (Hermione Gingold), the mayor's wife, returns the *Rubaiyat of Omar Khayyam*, complaining that it is unsuitable for her teenage daughter and insisting that the work is "dirty Persian poetry." Marian maintains that the book is a "classic," but Eulalie counters, "It's a smutty book, like most of the others you keep here." Marian suggests that Eulalie's daughter should be reading classics rather than Elinor Glyn.[9] Eulalie, totally unaware of author Glyn, responds, "What Elinor Glyn reads is her mother's problem. Just you keep your dirty books away from my daughter." She bobs her head to conclude the conversation and leaves the library. This encounter reflects the conflicting opinions of Marian, who promotes the classics, and the social ladies of River City, who decry the classics as smut.

The second library scene is the stage for one of the film's many notable song-and-dance numbers, "Marian the Librarian." Harold, expecting to find a "sadder but wiser girl" in Marian after listening to the gossip of River City's social women, visits the library to take out "the librarian." As Harold sings, Marian performs many occupational tasks—stamping books, typing, copying from a dictionary, flipping through a card tray, and, of course, uttering the "shush," as does most everyone in this scene. Willson's lyrics include two lines that reinforce the library dictum of silence. During one energetic routine with the boys during this musical number, Marian gleefully tosses away her glasses as they dance around the library.

In a very brief third library scene, Marian stamps a book and utters a "shush," but more importantly, notices a volume of the *Indiana State Educational Journal* for the years 1890–1910. She checks Harold's professed alma mater, Gary (Indiana) Conservatory of Music, in the volume and discovers that the professor could not have been a member of the class of 1905, as the city was not founded until 1906. With these pages the mayor can prove that Harold's academic credentials are fraudulent. As she rushes to give the journal to the mayor, the Wells Fargo wagon arrives in River City with the band instruments. Marian's change of opinion about Harold occurs when Winthrop receives his cornet. Having exhibited antisocial behavior and seldom speaking more than "three words a day" since his father's death two years ago, Winthrop suddenly becomes happy and talkative, a complete change of personality. Marian reacts to her brother's change of behavior by tearing out the incriminating pages; without these pages, the mayor cannot expose Harold as a flimflammer. Marian, by this action, permits the professor, with his enchanting and hypnotic charm, not only to capture her heart but also to energize the imagination of the entire population of River City.

Marian, an attractive young blonde (finger waves; multiple jelly roll buns at crown), lives at home with her mother and younger brother. She dresses colorfully and fashionably in period (circa 1912) clothes throughout the film; she wears wire-rim eyeglasses only in the library, even though she reads sheet music and a newspaper

The Music Man (1962). Professor Harold Hill (Robert Preston) and Marian Paroo (Shirley Jones) perform the "Marian the Librarian" song-and-dance sequence in the River City Public Library. Note the eyeglasses and bun.

in other scenes. As the only librarian in the film, her use of eyeglasses in the library is one visual characteristic that reinforces the stereotypical image. As previous female librarians, she demonstrates a keen intellect and displays the ability to best Harold.

One of Francis Ford Coppola's earliest directorial efforts, *You're A Big Boy Now* (1966), follows the adventures of innocent 19-year-old Bernard Chanticleer (Peter Kastner[10]), who is struggling to reach manhood and to attain freedom from his parents in New York City in the 1960s. Bernard works at the New York Public Library (NYPL) roller skating the closed stacks to retrieve books that are requested. His ineptitude and difficulties at work and with women provide many comedic scenes. Bernard and two other major male characters—I. H. Chanticleer (Rip Torn[11]), Bernard's father and NYPL's curator of incunabula, and Raef del Grado (Tony Bill[12]), Bernard's friend and fellow library assistant—provide unflattering images of male librarians.

The film features one female library assistant, Amy Partlett (Karen Black[13]), who is interested in Bernard, but he is enamored with Barbara Darling (Elizabeth

Hartman), a streetwise young lady who zestfully pulls, pushes, and plucks Bernard's heartstrings—a thoroughly enjoyable encounter for her. For example, she invites Bernard to move into her apartment, becomes infuriated with his behavior, kicks him out the same night, and then begs him to return as he trudges off, dragging his clothes down the street. As he endures this painful yo-yo relationship with Barbara, he fails to discern the true affection that Amy offers.

Library scenes are interspersed among Bernard's various adventures and are primarily comedic in nature. When Bernard's overbearing mother, Margery (Geraldine Page), visits NYPL to talk with her husband about their son, Chanticleer pulls out a mirror and trims his mustache while his wife assists Bernard with a new pair of contact lenses. The curator demonstrates similar vain behavior later in the film when he pulls out the mirror and combs his hair. Chanticleer is just as meticulous in the care of his highly prized acquisition, a Gutenberg Bible, which is placed on a dictionary stand in his office, a few feet from his desk, as he is with his own personal appearance. He is constantly lamenting about the "lint" that falls on the open Bible and is preoccupied with tenderly brushing the pages of the Bible to remove the airborne down.

Miss Nora Thing (Julie Harris), Bernard's landlady, visits the curator to discuss Bernard's aberrant behavior—staying out all night. She enters the rare book vault where Chanticleer is working and closes the door, locking the two in the vault. The sexually repressed Miss Thing is appalled at the artwork contained in the vault; she considers NYPL's prized incunabula to be obscene and promptly begins tossing items indiscriminately around the vault. When the time lock triggers, the vault door opens and Miss Thing immediately rushes out. Chanticleer, however, after spending several minutes attempting to save the collection from the rampaging Miss Thing, exits the vault a very harried, beleaguered librarian.

The resolution of Bernard's erring behavior is reminiscent of a Keystone Kops caper. All of the film's major characters are assembled in Chanticleer's office attempting to pull all of the loose ends of the story together (an impossibility) when a disgruntled Bernard suddenly grabs the Gutenberg Bible and runs out of the office with everybody in quick pursuit. What follows is a chase through the NYPL, out onto the city's streets, through a parading marching band, and into a department store with a maze of merchandise aisles. The chase in the maze finally ends when Barbara cold-cocks Bernard with the leg of a mannequin. The film concludes as Amy bails Bernard out of jail, and the two of them, with Bernard's Old English Sheepdog, go happily skipping and running through the busy streets of New York City to the music of the Lovin' Spoonful.

Chanticleer as curator of incunabula is the supervisor of library assistants, indicating the possibility of nepotism in NYPL's hiring of Bernard. In his first office scene with his wife and son, Chanticleer establishes the film's story line. The curator indicates disappointment with Bernard's progress, stating, "You've been here a month and aside from developing unnatural skills on roller skates, you've been a complete failure. If your father wasn't what your father is, you'd been fired your first week here. Now, here it is, Big Boy. Straight and to the point. Grow up." As Bernard's mother insists he is "too young," Chanticleer informs Bernard that he is "going to live in

You're a Big Boy Now (1966). Bernard Chanticleer (Peter Kastner) and Amy Partlett (Karen Black) at the New York Public Library.

your own apartment in the city paid for with your own money. What do you say to that?" "Terrific," responds Bernard, as his mother continues to weep, knowing that she is about to lose control of her little boy.

Chanticleer is an "only 38" librarian, receding hairline with some light graying around the temples, who wears appropriate formal business dress—suits, ties, and vests. The curator is very concerned about his appearance, and one rationale for Chanticleer's narcissistic behavior comes into focus when the curator requests Raef to ask Amy to assist him with some work in the vault. Amy is not available, and Raef responds, "She do?" and nods toward a nearby young female library assistant (uncredited[14])—an overly plump brunette, with a large white bow in her hair, who chews gum with her mouth open. Chanticleer glances at her and decides that he can manage alone. This is not the first time that the curator has asked for Amy to assist him. While Chanticleer was asking Raef for Amy, she was in the snack area informing Bernard that his father "made a pass" at her and "it was terrible." Bernard blurts out in response, "My poor Mother!" Margery, unaware of Bernard's involvement with Barbara, blames Amy for her son's behavior and demands that Chanticleer fire Amy, but the curator is reluctant to do so, which suggests that some inappropriate behavior may have occurred between the two.

Although Chanticleer is not an exemplary supervisor of personnel, he displays a zealous, if not fanatical, concern for the documents under his jurisdiction. Few reel librarians communicate the interest and responsibility of librarians to protect and care for library materials. In the majority of films, the focus of brief library scenes with reel librarians, whether in major or in supporting roles, is the interpersonal conflicts among the film's characters; the maintenance of the integrity of library materials is seldom mentioned or shown.

Raef and Bernard dress casually, slacks and shirt; Raef wears a tie while Bernard occasionally dons one. Amy, a brunette (full bang; top and sides pulled back; curls at nape) wears modest casual clothing. Most other librarians who are visible in the various library scenes appear in casual clothes similar to those worn by Bernard and Raef, if men, or by Amy, if women. Other than pulling books off shelves and answering telephones, Raef, Bernard, and Amy are rarely engaged in library tasks. Other librarians are shown filing and typing.

Goodbye, Columbus (1969), an adaptation of Philip Roth's novella of the same title, is a romantic comedy with an unconventional dramatic ending. The picture features Richard Benjamin[15] as Neil Klugman, a poor Bronx librarian, and Ali MacGraw as Brenda Patimkin, a Radcliffe College student spending her free summer months at home with her wealthy parents in Westchester. The couple engages in a whirlwind summertime romantic romp, but their differences are too great to sustain the relationship. Brenda's mother, recently achieving nouveau riche status—a house in Westchester—desires a man of higher financial and social stature than Neil for her daughter. When Brenda's mother displays initial concern about Neil, her father remarks, "Leave her alone. She'll get tired of him."

The film's first library scene highlights some of Neil's occupational skills and talents. As Neil enters the library, supervisor Mr. Scapelle (Delos V. Smith, Jr.[16]) asks him to work at the main desk because a staff member is absent. Neil joins Gloria (uncredited[17]) behind the desk and toys with a date stamp to ensure that it has the correct date. A young boy soon appears at the desk asking for books. Unable to understand the category of books for which the youngster is asking, Neil requests the youth to spell the word for him; "a-r-t," the youth replies. Neil identifies the location of the art collection, and the youngster heads for the books. As Neil and the young patron are concluding their discussion, librarian John McKee (Bill Derringer[18]) descends the stairway behind the desk and confronts Neil, "Why did you let him in for?" "It's a public library," Neil responds. John informs Neil that the youngster looked at art nudes on the previous morning and "of course, I threw him out." Neil and John discuss the behavior of young boys who look at nudes in art books:

> John: You know what those boys do up there?
> Neil: Oh, John. I don't think they do it right there.
> John: They do so. I've seen them. Not out in the open, of course, but you can tell what they're doing.
> Neil: Johnny, why don't you let him alone.

John rejects Neil's suggestion and hustles up the stairs to see Scapelle about evicting the youngster. Neil follows, stating he will get the boy. John is adamant about removing

GC-105-13A

Goodbye, Columbus (1969). Anthony McGowan as the young boy who enjoys art books and Richard Benjamin as librarian Neil Klugman.

the boy, "It's disgusting what they do up here." Neil responds, "Don't worry about it, Johnny. They're the ones that are going to get warts all over their dirty little hands." Neil then goes to find the boy in art room. The youngster is in the balcony, sitting at the edge of the walkway railing and dangling his legs over the balcony. Neil climbs a ladder to be near the boy, and the two discuss some of Gauguin's paintings that intrigue the boy. Looking at one of the paintings, the boy remarks, "Hey, look at this one. Man, ain't that the life," as the scene fades into Neil arriving at the Patimkins' Westchester house in his convertible.

In the second library scene, Neil is flipping through a card tray at the desk when an elderly bespectacled gentleman approaches him with the Gauguin book. Neil asks if he wants to check out the book. The patron is hearing impaired and replies loudly, "What?" Neil, recognizing the book, looks at a notebook and loudly informs the gentleman that he cannot check out the book because there is a hold on it. Again, the loud response, "What?" Neil's increasingly loud explanations are all greeted with a loud "What?" Scapelle walks down the rear stairway as Neil shouts at the patron, and other patrons working quietly in the reading area voice their disapproval of the vociferous exchange by uttering "shush" and "quiet." Scapelle asks, "Any problem?" Neil responds with a loud "What? Huh? No!" The supervisor inquires, "You're going on a vacation tomorrow, aren't you?" Neil replies affirmatively, and Scapelle remarks, "You need it." Neil grabs the Gauguin book and dashes off to the art room. The youth is in the balcony, and Neil asks the boy to come down and talk with him. Attempting to prevent further problems the boy might have with John, Neil offers the youngster the opportunity to check out the book. When he asks the youngster if he has a library card, the boy immediately assumes a defensive stance, "No, sir. I haven't done anything wrong." Neil explains that a card will permit him to take the book home, but the boy remains defensive, "Why don't you want me around here?" Neil, becoming attuned to the youngster's interpretation of his questions, states, "I didn't say I didn't want you around here." "I like it here" is the boy's response. Neil tackles the problem from a different angle: "Someday, somebody is going to want to take this book out of here sometime. Aren't you worried about that?" The boy's response is to the point: "Why should I be worried? Nobody's done it yet." Neil smiles at the boy's response, and the scene fades.

The cast of *Goodbye, Columbus* includes five librarians—three men and two women; only the male librarians have dialogue. Neil, John, and Scapelle appear in business dress; both John and Scapelle wear eyeglasses. Gloria, an "only 38" librarian with gray hair (bun at crown), wears a gray, long-sleeve dress with a white puritan collar and a black bow. Natasha (uncredited[19]), a blonde (braided bun at crown) works at the desk and wears a dark blue sleeveless dress with a bateau neckline, and eyeglasses.

Scapelle, an "only 38" individual, presents the image of a worried and frustrated library supervisor. After asking Neil to work at the desk for an absent employee, Scapelle complains, "There's always something, always." Scapelle carries an "egg and pepper sandwich" in a brown paper bag around the library, occasionally taking a bite; his actions resembling those of an alcoholic who carries his bottle in a brown paper bag. When John rushes to speak with Scapelle about evicting the boy, Neil asks John if he wants to give Scapelle an ulcer so soon after his sandwich, indicating such problems upset Scapelle's equilibrium. Eating in public areas of libraries is universally prohibited, but the supervisor apparently does it regularly. Scapelle is not reticent about breaking into Neil's discussion with the hearing impaired patron nor telling Neil that he needs a vacation, implying that Neil is becoming too edgy with patrons.

As a public librarian, John exhibits an elitist attitude toward library clientele that is contrary to the majority of working public librarians, who envision public libraries as inclusive, rather than exclusive, institutions. John is determined to have the young boy removed immediately. He either is very judgmental about the reasons young patrons look at the nudes in art books and their resulting behavior or spends a great deal of time spying on these young patrons; neither behavior is encouraged, promoted, or condoned by working librarians. John's consternation about the thought of something sexual occurring in the library indicates he is, to some extent, a sexually dysfunctional adult. The young patron is a Black American, but there are no verbal or visual indications in the film that race was instrumental in John's decision to have the youngster evicted.

Of the three male librarians, Neil projects the most decent image of a librarian. Neil's interaction with the young boy demonstrates an earnest endeavor to assist; his concern for the youngster is admirable, even though he is unable to disarm the youth's apprehension about the sincerity of his intentions. The young boy fails to realize that he is shielded from eviction only as long as Neil is there to protect him. Neil's suggestion to check out the book is interpreted by the youngster as a way to get him out of the library, the apparent underlying purpose of the library staff. Neil's intent is to get the boy and the book of Gauguin prints together; however, one unstated and important corollary, of which Neil is undoubtedly cognizant, is that by checking out the book the youngster would not have to visit the library daily and become a target of eviction. The young boy, however, lacks knowledge of John's prejudices and that they pose a threat to him. Neil's mediation, perhaps admirable, achieves nothing because the youngster likes the library and maintains his innocence. Neil's encounter with the hearing impaired adult, however, inadvertently becomes a shouting match before he realizes the situation is out of control.

My Side of the Mountain (1969), adapted from Jean Craighead George's juvenile novel of the same title, follows the solo adventures of 12-year-old Samuel Gribley (Ted Eccles) in Quebec's Laurentian mountains. When Sam's father breaks a promise to take him camping, Sam leaves home, informing his parents in a note that he has to "go out and live by myself, all alone off the land, like Thoreau." Sam's mountain home—a trunk of an old large tree which he hollows and burns out—is near the village of Knowlton. When Sam becomes interested in capturing a young peregrine falcon, he visits the Knowlton Public Library. He goes directly to the librarian's desk and asks for books on falcons. The librarian, Miss Turner (Tudi Wiggins[20]), "an old bird watcher from away back" as she later identifies herself, goes to the shelves with Sam and offers some interesting historical tidbits as they walk: "Peregrine falcons were famous in England, I do believe. As a matter of fact, they were known as hunters for kings, if my memory serves me right, and it usually does." Turner climbs a small ladder, takes two books from a top shelf, and hands them to Sam, remarking that they cannot be taken from the library. Returning to her desk, she gives Sam a pencil that he needs for notes; Turner then removes her glasses, introduces herself, and asks Sam for his name. They chat briefly and Sam goes into a nearby reading room to study the two books. After locating the information he needs, he returns to Turner's desk, stating, "Those birds sure are interesting. If I could only catch me one." Turner again removes her glasses while listening to Sam and demonstrates a wide range of knowledge about birds by quoting Proverbs 1:17 (KJV), "Surely, in vain the net is spread in the sight of any bird." As he starts to leave, Turner offers some very useful advice, "Sam, you'll need a leather glove."

Turner also appears in two nonlibrary scenes. In the first scene, she meets Sam in the mountains on one of her bird-watching excursions. They immediately recognize one another, and she asks if he has been observing peregrine falcons, as she has "found another very good book on them." Sam has caught a young falcon and asks if she would like to see it. She responds affirmatively, and Sam grabs her by the wrist and the two run to his falcon. The two watch the falcon soar through the mountain sky, and when the falcon returns, Turner suggests, "C'mon down and take a look at

My Side of the Mountain (1969). Tudi Wiggins as Miss Turner, librarian at the Knowlton Public Library. Eyeglasses, of course.

the new book I found." Sam seldom visits Knowlton, commenting that he likes to be alone. Turner extends an invitation to Sam, "If you ever want to, come and see me. Please." This time she quotes Cicero, "We are never less alone than when completely alone." They part, but without a firm commitment from Sam to accept her invitation to visit the Knowlton Library. Turner reveals a sincere interest in Sam's welfare during this chance meeting.

In her second nonlibrary scene, Turner accompanies Bando (Theodore Bikel), a vagabond mountaineer, to Sam's tree home. When Bando appears in Knowlton, he visits "the library lady" whom Sam had mentioned to him. After a big winter storm passes through the Laurentian mountains, Turner and Bando are concerned about Sam's welfare and decide that they must visit him. They find his tree home covered with several feet of snow, and Bando digs him out. Turner had the foresight to pack a large picnic basket, and as the three eat and sing around some burning logs, she remarks, "This is the best Christmas dinner I ever had!" Sam decides to end his sojourn with nature, and with Bando shouting, "Let's go, Thoreau!" Sam joins his two friends for the walk back to Knowlton.

Turner appears in only three scenes, but presents a very worthy, meritorious image of librarians. An attractive brunette (front and sides pulled back with headband; shoulder length flip), she wears colorful, fashionable attire and is a friendly, soft-spoken, competent librarian. She quotes from the Bible and Cicero, demonstrating that she is a widely read and intelligent individual. More importantly, she displays a very humane concern for a young teenager who wants to live alone with nature in the Laurentian mountains. Turner is so concerned about Sam's personal safety that she accompanies Bando to find the youngster. Turner's enthusiasm is unique, even to the point of proclaiming that picnicking with Sam and Bando in the open mountain air by a campfire is her "best Christmas dinner." *My Side of the Mountain* presents a commendable image of a public librarian in a small village.

The foregoing five films continue a cinematic dichotomy between men (ineptitude) and women (competence) librarians that first appeared during the silent era. Marian and Turner display visual characteristics of the stereotype, but they also project bright, polished images of independent women. The degree of competency portrayed on screen by women reel librarians is a quality that cannot be projected by a visual image, which results in any vestige of the visual characteristics of the stereotype to persist. The bizarre behavior of male reel librarians presents a detrimental image of librarians, but the cinematic depiction of male librarians in this manner is commonplace and firmly entrenched in the psyche of filmmakers. The dichotomy of male ineptitude and female competence continues throughout the twentieth century.

The large number of supporting actors portraying reel librarians during the 1960s reinforced the stereotypical image, primarily by utilizing the established visual characteristics of the stereotype.

A reel librarian appears briefly in *Bluebeard's Ten Honeymoons* (1960; b/w) and in *This Rebel Breed* (1960; b/w), and both films present the librarians as competent but station the camera so that filmgoers see very little of them. In *Bluebeard's Ten Honeymoons*, a British production, actor Milo Sperber[21] is a librarian assisting Landru (George Sanders), who visits the library to read some old newspapers. As in earlier British productions, the camera is placed behind the librarian, permitting full facial views of the patrons but only a brief glimpse of the librarian's right profile. The librarian exchanges pleasantries with patrons in a cheerful manner and competently handles their requests for service. Although appearing on-screen for less than 30 seconds, he assists three patrons. An "only 38" librarian with a full complement of black hair, he wears eyeglasses and a conservative business suit. The visual characteristics and occupational tasks identify the cast member as a librarian, indicating that, as the 1960s begin, the stereotypical image remains an important device for filmmakers.

An uncredited actress[22] portrays the librarian in *This Rebel Breed* (1960; b/w), a film dealing with teenage drug, gang, and racial problems among Black, Hispanic, and White students in a Los Angeles high school. Lola (Rita Moreno), a Hispanic student, visits the public library to find information for a debate in a social science class. She asks for the location of the "sociology section," and the librarian directs her to the proper area of the library. The camera is stationed to the left of the librarian and slightly behind her, permitting full facial shots of library patrons but permitting only the left profile of the librarian to appear on-screen. Visible for about 10 seconds, the "only 38" librarian, a brunette (braided sides pulled back; twisted bun at nape), is a conservative dresser—dark skirt with a matching jacket over a light blouse. In these few seconds, she is able to demonstrate a high level of competency with routine occupational tasks.

A second British film of 1960 with a librarian (uncredited; Sheila Hancock[23]) is *Doctor in Love* (1960), an entry in the comedy series about medical students at St. Swithins Hospital. As the film begins, Dr. Richard Hare (Michael Craig) becomes ill and is confined to a hospital bed, where the hospital librarian attempts to provide him with a "nice book." Unsuccessful, she announces, "I'll push in again tomorrow and see if I can tempt you," while raising her eyebrows several times in comedic fashion. This 25-second scene demonstrates how difficult it is for a patient to simply relax in a hospital, even when the patient is a physician on the hospital's staff. Although this scene with the librarian is played for laughs—she annoys Hare, the librarian is service oriented. For humor, she diligently attempts to provide Hare with service that he obviously does not want; her efforts are more nuisance and annoyance than helpful. A brunette (bob; angel wing bang), the librarian dresses very fashionably—a gray suit over a light blouse with a V-neckline. Visually, she does not match the image of many preceding reel librarians, but occupational tasks identify her as a librarian.

A third British film of 1960 with a reel librarian, *Peeping Tom*, is director Michael Powell's horror film dealing with scoptophilia. Helen Stephens (Anna Massey[24]), the film's leading woman character, is an attractive young redhead (angel wing bang; bouffant) who wears fashionable, colorful clothes. In one scene, she identifies her occupation: "I work in a public library, in the children's section." In her spare time, she writes short stories for children and her first book will be published "in the spring." In a later scene, she is seen leaving the grounds of a public library. The film contains no other personal or occupational hints to indicate that Helen is a librarian. Helen's occupation is irrelevant to the story line, her writing is instrumental in developing a relationship with Mark Lewis (Karlheinz Bohm), the film's Peeping Tom. Working in a library presupposes an interest in books; therefore, Helen's writing of short stories and books is believable, more so than if she were working in a pedestrian occupation.

One of the twentieth century's most popular screen characters, Holly Golightly, debuted on American screens in October 1961 in the romantic comedy *Breakfast at Tiffany's*. Audrey Hepburn is the charming Holly, and George Peppard portrays writer Paul Varjak. The film's brief library scene occurs when Paul and Holly decide to go for a walk to celebrate the sale of one of his stories. Holly suggests that they "spend the whole day doing things we've never done before. We'll take turns." After Holly takes Paul to Tiffany's, Paul takes Holly to the New York Public Library. Holly, surrounded by card catalog cabinets, asks "What is this place, anyway?" When Paul states it is the public library, she responds, "I don't see any books." Paul walks her to the reading room so that she can see some books. He then takes her to the card catalog, letter V, and briefly explains the catalog's purposes. She finds the card for Varjak, Paul, and they take the card drawer to the "slips desk" to request the book. Handling requests at this desk is a male librarian (uncredited[25]), wearing a brown suit, white shirt, and tie. When the book arrives in the reading room, Holly approaches the librarian (Elvia Allman[26]) and loudly announces "57, please. *Nine Lives* by Varjak, Paul." Holly receives an immediate "shush" from the librarian. Holly, intent upon engaging the librarian in a conversation, asks the librarian if she has read Varjak's book. As Holly is extremely talkative, the librarian responds, "Would you kindly lower your voice, Miss?" Holly is not easily discouraged and continues talking, eliciting another request for silence from the librarian. Holly then encourages Paul to autograph the book. As he autographs the book, he draws the ire of the librarian, "What are you doing?" She continues in a loud voice, "Stop that," only to receive a "shush" from Paul. In a softer voice, the librarian complains, "You deface public property." Holly, sensing that it is time to leave, remarks to the librarian, "Well, all right, if that's the way you feel."

The scene elicits a smile when the librarian is shushed by Paul, one of the few times a librarian is the recipient of a shush. Taking Paul's arm and ushering him away from the librarian, Holly concludes, "I don't think this place is half as nice as Tiffany's." The librarian is a redhead (bob; soft curls) and wears a multicolored pattern suit with large lapels. The occupation of this cast member is obvious—"only 38," demanding silence with a "shush," and demonstrating outrage when Paul autographs the book. The scene uses many of the usual visual characteristics and occupational tasks, reinforcing the image of the stereotype.

Shortly after Holly Golightly delighted filmgoers, the first of four British-produced Miss Marple films appeared in American theaters. The four films appeared during a three-year span, 1962–1964. Margaret Rutherford stars as Agatha Christie's amateur detective, Miss Jane Marple, and in a supporting role, Stringer Davis[27] (Rutherford's real-life husband) as librarian Mr. Stringer. The antics of Rutherford's Marple and Davis' Stringer give these films a decidedly humorous overtone. Mr. Stringer is not a character created by Agatha Christie, but he evidently was written into the series to accommodate the couple, as Rutherford and Davis appeared together in more than 20 films.

In the first film, *Murder She Said* (1961; b/w),[28] Marple witnesses a murder while on a train journey and reports it to officials. Inspector Craddock (Charles Tingwell) believes that she saw a couple embracing, as no body was found on the train or along the trackway. Marple, upset over Craddock's insinuation that she is a doty old woman, rushes to the public library to discuss the matter with Stringer, a close confidant. At the library, Stringer is busily apologizing to a library patron, Mrs. Hilda Stainton (Barbara Hicks), an avid mystery reader, for not having a new mystery in the library. "Plain inefficiency," she remarks, adding, "Anyway, I want to know the minute it comes in." "Of course, of course, Mrs. Stainton," he replies in a self-humbling manner. Marple enters the library at this point, and Stringer immediately looks past Stainton to greet his friend, "Good morning, Miss Marple!" As Stainton walks away from the desk, Stringer reaches under the desk for a book—the one Stainton requested—and places it on the desk for Marple, saying, "I've been keeping it for you." She pulls him by the arm into the book stacks, where she convinces him to assist her in her attempt to solve the murder. Stainton returns to the desk, notices the book she wants, and exclaims, "So it has come in!" Stringer, walking back to the desk with Marple, manages to respond, "Ah, ah, has it?" Marple tells Stainton that "the mother did it, of course," and then extends an invitation to Stringer as she leaves, "Hot buttered crumpets for tea, Mr. Stringer, if you care to join me." "Indeed I would, Miss Marple," he responds and then stamps the book for Stainton.

Stringer, an elderly man with gray hair and receding hairline, dresses conservatively—dark suit, white shirt, and dark tie, and wears wire-rimmed eyeglasses. The librarian, easily led by Marple, is, in essence, her sidekick; he performs the necessary leg work and research when required, as well as accompanying Marple whenever necessary. Stringer also provides the obligatory comedic antics of a sidekick. Occupational tasks are abundant—Stringer stands behind a desk, discusses books with patrons, and stamps books. In addition, he demonstrates a lack of self-confidence in his discussions with Stainton and Marple. When talking with Stainton, Stringer's mannerisms and responses exude the "plain inefficiency" of public service employees that she criticizes. He is a devious public servant, as he deliberately withholds a book from Stainton in order to give it to his friend. He is a classic image of a mild-mannered, meek librarian who struggles to keep local library patrons happy. He is the embodiment of the stereotype.

During Marple's investigation, Stringer is quick to assist but is concerned about her safety. When Craddock suggests that Marple may be in danger, Stringer encourages her to follow Craddock's advice and stop her investigation. A sidekick always lacks courage and advocates safety.

As the second entry, *Murder at the Gallop* (1963; b/w),[29] begins, Stringer is helping Marple solicit contributions for the Reformed Criminals Assistance League. They stroll to the edge of the village to the Enderby residence, and Marple insists they enter, but Stringer is hesitant, "I really must be getting back to the library.... It's a very worthy cause no doubt, but my employers...." Marple interrupts, insisting that he is "entitled" to his tea, and after this visit, she will prepare "a very special tea to reward us for our labors." Stringer, always a step or two behind Marple, both physically and mentally, accompanies her to the door reluctantly and is ready to leave when no one answers immediately. Marple, however, walks into the house with Stringer on her heels and sees Old Enderby at the top of the stairs grabbing at his chest and then falling down the staircase. Enderby is dead; Craddock calls it "heart failure;" Marple calls it "murder." The inspector refuses to investigate, leaving Marple to pursue her own investigation.

Marple immediately enlists Stringer to assist her, and they are soon scampering up a wall, despite Stringer's objection, to overhear the reading of Old Enderby's will.

Stringer is always unwilling to engage in any activity that poses the remotest possibility of danger; he serves as the anchor for Marple's runaway investigative ideas, but she ignores his suggestions. When Stringer reappears later in the film, Marple sends him to London to get appraisals for a painting that several of the beneficiaries desire. As he obtains his instructions from Marple, Hector Enderby (Robert Morley), the son of Old Enderby, interrupts their conversation. Stringer departs and Marple identifies him as the "custodian of the local library." Although there are no library scenes in this film, Stringer continues to dress as he did in the first film—very modestly and conservatively; on one occasion, he wears knickers, suspenders over a white shirt, tie, and belted sport coat. There are two references to Stringer's occupation as a librarian—his comment about "my employers at the library" and Marple's remark that he works at the local library.

In the third film, *Murder Most Foul* (1964; b/w),[30] and fourth film, *Murder Ahoy* (1964; b/w)[31], Stringer continues his sidekick duties—running errands, locating information, and, ever vigilant, urging caution. Neither film contains a library scene nor includes a reference to Stringer's occupation.

In the first film of this series, Stringer is working in a library and is clearly identifiable as a librarian. In the second film, he is identified as a librarian by Marple. However, in these last two films, Stringer does not participate in any activity that establishes or identifies his occupation nor do any screen characters refer to his occupation. Stringer projects the stereotypical image of reel librarians throughout the series. Filmgoers, however, must be familiar with the first two films to know his occupation; otherwise, Stringer appears to be Marple's elderly sidekick who, without economical or occupational restrictions, can travel at will to accompany her.

Two family comedies released by Walt Disney in the early 1960s contain brief library scenes. *Bon Voyage!* (1962), a Disney version of the typical American family's long-awaited vacation to Paris, stars Fred MacMurray as Harry Willard, the family's patriarch. Crossing the Atlantic, Harry's daughter meets a young man whom she likes, but Harry does not. When Harry visits the ship's library to find a mystery book, the librarian (James Millhollin[32]) eagerly offers to assist, "We have any number of stimulating items in that category. I rather lean toward the intellectual type crime, myself. Now, if you will allow me to suggest...." Harry interrupts the librarian, preferring to find a mystery without his glib assistance. The librarian retreats to his desk, remarking, "Well, just as you say, sir. Oh, and good hunting." Observing his daughter in the library, Harry stops to chat with her about the young man. Harry's communication skills are suspect, as he fails to understand, but easily misunderstands, his daughter's problems with the opposite sex. Upset with her father, she runs out of the library. The librarian reappears, asking, "Did you find your mystery, sir?" Harry rejoins, "Yes. It's called 'The Case of the Puzzled Parent Who Can't Understand Why His Children Keep Saying He Doesn't Understand.'" He then exits the library, leaving the librarian with a disturbed and deeply puzzled look on his face. After several seconds of pensive thought, the librarian utters, "Hum," and then remarks to himself, "Oddish title." The librarian is an "only 38" individual and appears in the uniform of the ship's crew. He is knowledgeable about the contents of the ship's small collection, but just too helpful and too talkative. The librarian's insistence upon assisting is similar to the efforts of the librarian at St. Swithins Hospital in *Doctor in Love*. Instead of smiling at the title of Harry's real-life mystery, as undoubtedly were all filmgoers, the librarian endeavors futilely to recall such a title. This librarian, as others in preceding films, is not part of the humor; he is the humor. Filmgoers are laughing at, not with, him.

The second Disney film containing a library scene is *The Misadventures of Merlin Jones* (1964), which features Tommy Kirk and Annette Funicello as Midvale College students Merlin Jones and Jennifer, his girlfriend. When an experiment on brain waves goes awry, Merlin receives an electric shock, which permits him to hear the thoughts of other people. When Merlin enters the library, he tiptoes and whispers his request to the librarian (uncredited[33]), who maintains a very quiet college library and has a large QUIET sign on her desk. In the library, Merlin finds it impossible to study as he hears the various thoughts of all the students. Merlin, frustrated by listening to these random thoughts, jumps up and shouts, "Quiet!" The librarian rushes to him, uttering, "Shush!" Merlin notices Norman (Norman Grabowski), one of Midvale's star football players in the library, who is thinking that Merlin is a creep. Hearing the jock's thoughts, Merlin confronts the football star and the two engage in a brief shoving match. Merlin manages to push Norman into a book stack that tips over, creating a domino effect and knocking over three ranges. Norman, attempting to stop the ripple effect, falls to the floor amidst the books. The librarian, aghast at the turmoil and shambles, rushes to Norman, who is prone on the floor, declaring that "Rowdiness will not be tolerated in this library. You will pick up every one of those books and return it to its proper place!" The bespectacled, redheaded (multi-pincurl bang; bun at crown) librarian is an "only 38" individual and wears a gray striped suit over a yellow blouse with a plain collar. This librarian enforces the silence of a traditional library; the students are accustomed to this type of environment and make no effort to challenge the authoritative rules of the library. The actress portrays this librarian in stereotypical fashion and as a comic figure.

Rome Adventure (1962) stars attractive Suzanne Pleshette playing opposite Troy Donahue, a major Hollywood movie and television heartthrob of the late 1950s and early 1960s. As the film opens, Prudence Bell (Pleshette[34]), assistant librarian at Briarcroft College for Women, is appearing before the faculty board to explain why she permitted a senior student to read *Lovers Must Learn* by Irving Fineman,[35] a book considered "too adult" for the students of Briarcroft. Prudence defends her decision to give the book to the young student and delivers "a lecture on love" to the five elderly women who compose the board. Sensing the futility of her situation, she resigns, informing board members, "Perhaps I should thank you for making me realize that I should take the book's advice myself.... I'm going to where they really know what love's about. To Italy." Prudence walks away, but stops at the doorway to exclaim, "Arrivederci, Briarcroft!"

Prudence unhesitatingly leaves Briarcroft in search of romance. In Rome, she meets and falls in love with Don Porter (Troy Donahue), who is trying to extricate himself from an affair with Lydia (Angie Dickinson), resulting in numerous familiar soap opera situations. Loving Don but believing he loves Lydia, Prudence, with tears and a broken heart, returns home. Don, however, loves Prudence and takes a flight home to meet Prudence when her oceanliner docks. Filmgoers, for a brief two minutes at the beginning of the film, recognize Prudence as a librarian. She is identified as a librarian and is adept at defending her rationale for giving and encouraging a student to read Fineman's novel. A brunette (full bang; bouffant brushed back behind ears), Prudence dresses colorfully but conservatively. Prudence's activities during the remainder of the film belie her professed occupation. As many preceding reel librarians, she never looks back. She leaves Briarcroft and her occupation to search for love in Rome.

A Doris Day and Cary Grant romantic comedy, *That Touch of Mink* (1962), contains one comedy sketch in a motel room involving a librarian on her honeymoon. Carrying out a plan to elicit a commitment from boyfriend Philip Shayne (Grant), Cathy Timberlake (Day) accompanies a nondescript lothario to Al's Motel. Philip, upon being told of Cathy's tryst, becomes enraged and jealous, and hastily races to the motel. At the motel, Philip asks the desk clerk if "a couple just registered here from New York, a blonde about so high?" as he illustrates the height with his hand. The clerk identifies the couple as Mr. and Mrs. Smith, "They're in the bridal suite, Number 9." Mr. and Mrs. Smith, of course, are not Cathy and her lothario. This mistaken identity is the foundation for the ensuing humor. Smith (John Fiedler) is in robe and pajamas, chilling champagne, when Philip pounds on the motel door. Smith opens the door, and Philip demands, "All right, where is she?" "Changing," the bridegroom remarks, as he motions toward a room door. Philip rushes to the door, bangs on it, and comments to Smith, "At least I had the decency to take her to a hotel, not a rabbit hutch." Smith, bewildered and befuddled, responds, "She went to a hotel with you?" Philip, exasperated at waiting, opens the door and goes into the room, only to come out seconds later. "Congratulations, my friend," he states as he grabs and shakes Smith's hand, "You've got a great little girl there." As Philip hurriedly exits Number 9, Mrs. Smith (Barbara Collentine[36]) enters the room, asking, "Who was that man?" Smith, now wondering about his wife's past, replies with a very disapproving facial expression, "You librarians really live it up pretty good!" Philip then meets Cathy in the motel parking lot, throws her over his shoulder and as they drive away Philip's assistant, Roger (Gig Young), arrives at the motel. Roger, unaware that he has just passed his boss and Cathy, rushes into the motel office, playing essentially the same scene as Philip with the desk clerk, while in Room 9, Smith, with his bride in his lap, utters, "But what was I to think when...." She puts her hand on his lips, saying, "You do believe I never cared for another man till you walked into the library?" "Of course," he answers. She stands up, promising, "I won't be long," and blows a kiss to her husband as she retreats into the other room. His doubts erased, Smith goes to answer the bang on the door and is greeted with Roger's outburst, "All right, where is she?" Smith points to the door, and Roger remarks, "You're even more repulsive than she said. No wonder she begged me to come here with her." He rushes to the door, knocks, and goes in. The telephone rings, and Smith answers, "Hello. Mother? You were right about women. Yes, Momma, I'll wait outside. Come and get me." Smith, with a resigned, forlorn expression on his face, hangs up the telephone as the scene ends.

In Mrs. Smith's first motel room sequence, "you librarians" is used to identify her as a librarian, and in the second sequence, she makes an oblique reference to working in a library. An attractive "only 38" blonde, she displays the appropriate librarian's hairstyle—a bun at her nape. In her brief two screen appearances, Mrs. Smith displays several visual characteristics of the stereotype, and Mr. Smith is the perfect doubting Thomas husband for such a librarian. The humor of both sequences depends upon Smith believing the statements of Philip and Roger. Mrs. Smith convinces her husband that Philip's statements are false, but Roger's statements, following just minutes after Philip's, convince Smith that his wife is a wanton woman, necessitating that he wait outside for his "momma." In addition, he is short and balding, finds solace and wisdom in his mother's advice, and has a very distinctive voice that projects a total lack of self-esteem and self-confidence, perhaps just the type of man for a mild-mannered librarian. The depiction of Mrs. Smith as a librarian is instrumental to the success of these comedy sequences, as filmgoers know that she is a librarian and that the staid lifestyle associated with stereotypical librarians is being bombarded by accusations that are blatantly false.

France Nuyen[37] appears as Tamiko, a Japanese woman who works as librarian of the Foreign Press Club and whose wealthy family is steeped in Japan's traditional culture and values, in *A Girl Named Tamiko* (1962). The film's star, Lawrence Harvey, portrays Ivan Kalin, a Chinese citizen (mother, Chinese; father, Russian) in Tokyo who has waited 12 years for a visa to America. A photographer, Kalin finds Tokyo, with its traditional culture, a difficult city in which to gain recognition and financial success with his camera. Martha Hyer is cast as Fay Wilson, a wealthy American woman who works at the American Embassy, wants Ivan, and can expedite his visa. Ivan manipulates both women for his own economic and romantic purposes. On the day he and Fay are to leave for America, he cannot sign the final visa papers; instead, he gives up America and Fay, and rushes to find Tamiko.

There are two scenes in the Press Club's small library. In both scenes, Tamiko wears the same colorful two-piece suit with turned back cuffs and her black hair is in a bun at her nape, accessorized with a black bow. Tamiko demonstrates minimal basic library skills—she shelves books, locates and pulls a book from the collection for Ivan, and delivers library materials to members in the club's bar and restaurant. The film's second library scene utilizes one occupational clue—standing on a ladder. Tamiko's occupation, however, is not pertinent to the story line.

Another British production of the early 1960s that includes a librarian in the cast is *That Kind of Girl* (1963; b/w). The film deals with venereal disease among English twenty-somethings. Two men, Max (Frank Jarvis[38]) and Ted (Charles Houston[39]), are identified as librarians, but there are no library scenes to corroborate their occupation. In one scene, however, Max smugly informs a physician that he is not worried about venereal disease because, "I work at a library. I looked it up in a medical dictionary." The physician quickly corrects Max's misconceptions about venereal disease. Max and Ted's occupation is not relevant to the story line of this film. Although reel librarians are seldom cast as young twenty-somethings, as in this film, the fact is that librarians are not immune to problems relating to sexual activity. A working librarian would have known that looking something up in a medical dictionary is only the first step in research, not the definitive answer. Max's reference talents, at best, are highly suspect.

George Pal's *7 Faces of Dr. Lao* (1964), a fantasy film showcasing the talents of Tony Randall in multiple roles, is set in the early part of the twentieth century (circa 1920). Co-starring and providing the story's romantic interest are Barbara Eden[40] as Angela Benedict, librarian of the Abalone (Arizona) Public Library, and John Ericson as Ed Cunningham, editor of the city's newspaper. Angela, a widow rearing a 6-year-old son and living with her mother-in-law, rejects Ed's overtures; her mother-in-law, however, touts Ed's worthiness—a situation remarkably similar to that which appeared two years earlier in *The Music Man.*

When Ed enters the library early in the film, Angela is at her desk wearing pince-nez attached to a fabric lanyard. He immediately begins speaking in a loud voice, eliciting a "shush" from her as she points to the SILENCE sign on her desk. Angela, pointing with her pencil, informs him that materials "on courtesy and good manners" are located "right over there." Ed, however, needs a book on China. Angela happily remarks, "Ah, when do you leave?" Ed retorts, "As soon as you marry me. I thought it would be a nice place for a honeymoon." He then leans across the desk and kisses her. Appalled by his boldness, she screams, "Ed Cunningham!" only to receive a "shush" from the editor. Angela identifies the appropriate location for Ed to obtain a book on China, "Section on Asia, third shelf from the top." He suggests that she assist him, but Angela refuses, remarking that "it's called *The History of China* by D. Boulger."[41] Ed then asks, "I don't suppose you would like to have dinner with me tonight?" She maintains that she is not interested in him, she's too busy—"I have a little boy and mother-in-law to take care of.... So please stop asking." Ed, although speaking humorously to this point, becomes serious, maintaining that she is afraid "of falling in love, of being a woman...." Disturbed by his bluntness, Angela jumps up from her desk and rushes off to another part of the library, and Ed goes searching for *The History of China* as the scene ends.

Angela, a young, attractive woman with auburn hair (half bang; bouffant; bun at nape), wears colorful period clothing—a floor-length blue dress, high collar with black piping, and full-length sleeves. Angela continues to wear similar colorful and conservative clothes throughout the film. This library scene is a typical cinematic depiction of initial encounters involving men and women librarians who eventually fall in love. The verbal exchanges are humorous; even the library patrons gawk at the boisterous couple, creating more visual humor.

There are two town meeting scenes in the library, which is housed in City Hall, but they do not pertain to library situations or business. In the first town meeting, however, Angela asks businessman Clinton Stark (Arthur O'Connell) why he desires to buy the city of Abalone, if it is as worthless as he maintains. He responds, "You're a teacher, a librarian, and as such you can take a dull boy and make him into a smart boy. In a manner of speaking, you can turn a profit.... I'm a businessman, and as such, I feel I can do this, well, without taking a loss." This comparison of librarian to businessman acknowledges the importance of the librarian in the education of youth—a smart boy is the librarian's profit. Although Angela projects the visual characteristics and occupational tasks of the stereotype, *7 Faces of Dr. Lao* also manages to espouse the value of librarians in this brief verbal exchange.

The critically acclaimed release *The Spy Who Came in from the Cold* (1965; b/w) stars Richard Burton[42] as Alec Leamus, an ostensibly retired British spy who is referred by the labor exchange to a psychical research institute where he seeks employment as a librarian. Miss Crail (Anne Blake[43]), librarian at the institute, briefly interviews Alec before giving him a position. She poses several questions, and his responses indicate his lack of enthusiasm:

> CRAIL: You used a card index?
> LEAMUS: Now and then.
> CRAIL: Is your handwriting legible?
> LEAMUS: Except at weekends.

Crail explains the principles of cross-referencing, using examples which he understands, and the need for preparing a subject index for the collection. She asks if he comprehends, and Alec replies, "They told me the job pays £11.10 a week." Working in the library, Alec meets Nan Perry (Claire Bloom[44]); she is talkative, but Alec, initially, is unsociable. She offers to share her lunch with him, but he prefers to go to a pub. After several days at the library, Alec presents a respectable image. He dresses professionally, suit and tie. He reveals a sense of humor at the library with Nan when he asks about the subject heading for a book on werewolves. She pulls the book for him; he looks at the circulation page, remarking, "It seems popular." She replies that one patron checks it out monthly, and he theorizes, "Full moon." They both smile and giggle at his remark. As soon as the interaction between the two improves, Nan invites him to her apartment for dinner, beginning a romance that ends disastrously. Alec, always a British spy, utilizes the library and his library job to establish his pseudo-identity for an elaborate British espionage plot. When he is incarcerated for beating a shopkeeper, Alec loses his library job; after his release, Alec leaves Great Britain, seemingly defecting to the Communists.

Crail, the librarian-in-charge, resembles the stereotype—"only 38," blonde (angel wing bang; bun at crown), and dresses modestly but businesslike—dark suit jacket over a collarless, front button, light-colored blouse. She apparently spends a great deal of time conversing with her "MaMa" on the telephone; she cut short a conversation with her to interview Alec and is interrupted by "MaMa" during the interview. Crail is very understanding of Nan's request to take a vacation to Germany. When Nan mentions she has comrades, not friends, in Germany, Crail notes she has "never held this [political activities] against you, Miss Perry. This is a free country." When informed that Nan will be visiting Leipzig, Crail remarks that she will tell her superior that Nan will be visiting "Germany, not East. He doesn't hold with the Russians." The communications between Crail and Nan are friendly and straightforward; they are very formal—it is always Miss Crail and Miss Perry. Although engaged in a minimal number of library tasks, such as interviewing Alec and placing magazines on a rack, Crail's interaction with Nan indicates that she is a competent supervisor, and one who has an interest in her subordinates, regardless of their political leanings.

Nan, a young, attractive brunette (full bang; A-line cut), performs various library tasks: she brings in the morning mail, carries books, shelves books, pushes a book-truck, and works in card files. She dresses modestly throughout the film; most often appearing in sweaters and skirts; at the tribunal proceeding in East Germany, she appears in a tweed suit. At this tribunal hearing, Nan's finances are disclosed—salary, £11; rent, £3.10; and savings, a few pounds. These are indicative of unpretentious living on a salary that is, as Nan states, "pretty small." Such a humble environment, however, does not prohibit Nan from becoming a principled young woman who believes in peace and works as a member of the British Communist Party to achieve such a goal. During the tribunal hearing, which is Nan's first real experience with truth and deception in the Cold War, Alec, in an attempt to convince tribunal members that Nan is not a participant in the British espionage plot, decides to reveal his role in the operation. To shelter Nan from involvement, Alec summarizes his evaluation of her principles, "As for the girl, she is nothing but a frustrated little thing from a crackpot library. She's no good to you. Send her home."

Nan, as many previous single women reel librarians, enjoys male companionship; she makes the first overture to Alec, inviting him to dinner at her apartment. Nan, although it is difficult to understand from Alec's personae, is captivated by his aloofness from worldly ideals and his belief in nothing. Nan develops a strong bond to Alec, meeting him with a kiss and hug at the prison gate after he completes his sentence for battering a shopkeeper. His commitment to her, however, is questionable but revealed at the end of the film.

The fourth librarian in the film is Mr. Lofthouse (Michael Ripper[45]), Alec's replacement at the library, who appears on screen for less than 20 seconds. Lofthouse is a mustachioed "only 38" man, graying at the temples, who dresses in a conservative dark suit and tie. When Nan compliments him on his work—"You're at the J's already. You are settling down quickly."—he responds, "I was so very happy the job fell vacant." The two display a friendly relationship in this brief library scene. It is evident that Lofthouse's personality is in harmony with the library, quite a marked difference from Alec's personality.

The importance of the occupation of Alec, Nan, Crail, and Lofthouse, however, is incidental to the development of the story line. Alec, Crail, and Lofthouse project visual characteristics of the stereotypical image; Nan, however, uses many occupational clues to confirm her status as a librarian.

Jerry Gross wrote, directed, and produced *Teenage Mother* (1968), a film that deals with teenage pregnancy and the introduction of sex education into the curriculum of a high school. Julie Ange is Erika Petersen, the high school's new health education teacher who has just arrived from Sweden. At the principal's request, she begins developing a sex education program for her classes. Although the principal believes in developing such progressive programs, there is not unanimous support throughout the school. After a student informs Petersen that a book, *Male and Female*,[46] is not available at the school library, the teacher tries to find out why. When she asks the librarian, Miss Fowler[47] (uncredited[48]), about the book, the librarian, a foul-mannered character in this scene, responds emphatically, "Most certainly not!" Petersen maintains the book is a standard on the subject, but the librarian asserts, "It's a filthy book." The librarian, after Petersen questions her assertion, continues to degrade the work, "Filthy. I wouldn't allow one of our students to even leaf through it. The illustrations are positively vulgar." The two engage in a bitter dialogue about the value of the book, and as the conversation concludes, the librarian again expresses her opposition,

Teenage Mother (1968). Librarian Miss Fowler (left; uncredited; not identified; note glasses and bun) and health education teacher Erika Petersen (Julie Ange, right) discuss the lack of sex education materials in the school library.

"That book has never appeared in this library and never will as long as I'm here." Petersen's rebuttal is: "Let's hope that's not too long." During this discussion, Petersen argues for the freedom of teenagers to read such materials, but the librarian is adamant in her opposition—"Teenage children are not meant to see such things" as male and female bodies. The librarian's reading eyeglasses convey the impression that she is looking down her nose at Petersen during the discussion. Fowler is the stereotype—an "only 38" brunette (half bang; French twist; demi-beehive), spectacles on a bead lanyard, and modest clothes. She resumes working in a card file when Petersen leaves.

Teenage Mother is one of the few films that confronts the topic of sex education materials in secondary schools. Although the principal of the school is progressive, the librarian scorns the value of sex education. Without the support of the librarian, whose responsibility includes obtaining the appropriate learning materials to support instruction and student research, the program's success is problematical. The film depicts the librarian as the high school's misguided moral watchdog who uses her power to censor library materials.

The Prime of Miss Jean Brodie (1969) stars Maggie Smith as Jean Brodie, a teacher of history at the Marcia Blaine School for Girls in Edinburgh in 1932. The film includes a scene in the school library with Isla Cameron[49] as librarian Miss McKenzie. Two of "Brodie's girls," as the students are called, are composing a letter of fancy from their teacher to Gordon Lowther, one of Brodie's paramours. The girls, giggling excessively as they create their masterpiece, attract the attention of McKenzie, who is busy checking out books to students. McKenzie, frustrated at their behavior, goes to investigate the problem. Approaching the library table where the girls are seated, the librarian asks, "What are you two girls up to?" The girls hurriedly shove the unfinished letter into one of the books on the table, and McKenzie continues, "Now gather your things together and leave at once. This is a library, not a funfair." McKenzie gathers the books on the table and returns to her desk. As librarian, McKenzie supervises the school library according to a strict code of silence and decorum; she reacts promptly to the unruly behavior of the two girls, instructing them to leave immediately. McKenzie is an "only 38" brunette (front-to-back center part with circular bun over each ear[50]) who dresses modestly (as do most other faculty members) in a dark green skirt and long sleeve sweater.

Hayley Mills,[51] who achieved success as a child actor, stars as librarian Susan Harper in *Twisted Nerve* (1968), a British production released in the United States in early 1969. The film contains two library scenes in which Harper and Mr. Groom (Timothy Bateson[52]), the library supervisor, appear. The focus of the film, however, is Martin Durnley (Hywel Bennett), a young man with a psychopathic personality who cleverly assumes a second identity, Georgie Clifford, who is supposedly mentally retarded but capable of functioning in society. Susan and Georgie meet when they are detained for shoplifting by department store officials who erroneously believe they are a team. Susan volunteers to pay for the item that Georgie attempted to steal and they are released. Georgie becomes infatuated with Susan and follows her to the library the next day.

As the first library scene opens, Susan, whose youth and attractiveness is emphasized by miniskirts, is on a tall ladder retrieving a book for two young boys who enjoy ogling her legs. She informs the boys that Lady Jane Grey is in the book, but they would rather have something with Lady Chatterly. As she stamps the book for the boys, Georgie enters; he states that he came to repay her for yesterday. As they talk, he pulls the front of his shirt apart, and Susan approaches him and begins straightening the shirt and buttoning it for him. Mr. Groom is disturbed by the actions of the pair. He grabs several books and takes them to Susan, remarking, "Take these, Miss Harper. Look, I don't know whether you're dressing or undressing your friend, but I do wish you wouldn't do it in the public library." Georgie then asks for a book about animals and she gets *The Jungle Book*. He does not have a card, but Susan agrees to put it on her card so that he can take the book.

In the film's second library scene, Groom is turning out the lights in the rear of the library and Georgie is reading a book while leaning against a book stack near Susan's desk. Returning to the front of the library, Groom informs Georgie that the library is closed. "I know," Georgie responds. Groom, seeing that Georgie is not moving toward the door, replies, "Well then?" Georgie simply retorts, "Rat face," and

Groom, as if he did not understand or hear the comment, quizzes, "What was that?" Georgie, not in an accommodating mood, replies, "Get lost." Susan enters the scene at this point, saying, "Good night, Mr. Groom." As she and Georgie leave, Susan states, "I think he's taking a liking to you." As they walk out of the library, a young man in a convertible sports car picks up Susan, leaving Georgie standing alone on the sidewalk. Groom soon exits the library and remarks, "What did I understand you to say to me in there?" The young man, again revealing his antagonism toward Groom, answers, "I said get stuffed." Groom is taken aback by this statement, and Georgie walks away.

The dichotomy between Susan, a young attractive blonde (ponytail), and Groom, the stereotypical image—"only 38," eyeglasses, and dark suit—is most often displayed by two women. The visual contrast between Susan and Mr. Groom demonstrates that the beauty of a young starlet is considerably enhanced when a male librarian, rather than a female librarian, assumes the role of the stereotype. Susan's occupation is not an integral part of the story line of this film.

The films of the 1970s provided few roles for reel librarians. Those with a reel librarian in a supporting role offer little more than a brief library scene and a cast member who projects the stereotypical image to establish the character's status as a librarian. Two films of the late 1970s, however, sustain focus on the librarian throughout and contain several library scenes. The more popular of these two films is *Foul Play* (1978); the other, certainly not comparable to *Foul Play* in either stature or box office success, is *The Attic* (1979).

American International Pictures (AIP) released three films in the 1970s with reel librarians. The first, *The Dunwich Horror* (1970), focuses on Wilbur Whateley (Dean Stockwell) and his attempt to bring back "the old ones, princes of darkness" so that they can "repossess the Earth." To do this, he needs a book, *Necronomicon*, and a young virgin. He visits a nearby university for the book and also finds librarian Nancy Wagner (Sandra Dee[53]), the perfect young woman for his work. As the film opens, students Nancy and Elizabeth Hamilton (Donna Baccala[54]) are returning the *Necronomicon* to the university library where they work. They meet Wilbur, who asks to use the book. Elizabeth rejects his request, "That's impossible." She is adamant about refusing Wilbur access to the book and buttresses her decision by declaring, "The library is closing." Nancy, however, permits him to take the book into a nearby reading room. As the two students discuss the pros and cons of permitting Wilbur to use the book, Nancy remarks, "Did you notice his eyes? He's really got great eyes." Elizabeth, worrying about Nancy's decision to give the priceless book "to the first kook who comes along," is rebuffed by Nancy, "I trust him." Dr. Henry Armitage (Ed Begley) soon returns and takes the book from Wilbur, and after a brief discussion with Wilbur, he tells the two students, "It's easy to see why you two girls were effectively charmed." The four leave the library for an enjoyable dinner, and Nancy drives Wilbur back to his home in Dunwich, where she falls under his spell. Nancy is rescued during the closing minutes of the film.

Both students are young and attractive—Nancy, a blonde (bouffant; ponytail at nape), wears a black turtleneck sweater and pleated camel skirt; Elizabeth, a brunette (front and sides pulled up into ponytail at crown; back hangs in page), has on a white blouse with an open convertible collar and a dark pleated skirt. The only library-related task they undertake is putting the *Necronomicon* back into its glass-enclosed case, which they immediately reopen to give to Wilbur. This brief scene permits filmgoers to easily identify the two students as librarians.

The second AIP film, also a horror genre release, *Scream, Blacula, Scream!* (1973), a sequel to its 1972 blaxploitation film *Blacula* (1972),[55] stars William Marshall as the eighteenth century African prince Mamuwalde/Blacula. Investigating several recent murders, Justin (Don Mitchell) believes that the evidence supports the possibility that a vampire may be the murderer. To further research his idea, he visits a library to read some books about vampires. A librarian (Sybil Scotford[56]) locates the subject area for him, "This is it. The whole shelf. Black arts, the occult. That should keep you busy for awhile." She removes her eyeglasses immediately after completing her lines and walks out of the scene; she is on-screen for less than 15 seconds.

The bespectacled librarian, an attractive brunette (full bang; ponytail at nape), wears a multicolor pattern blouse with an open large, high collar, a brown vest and a matching skirt. The library received little budgetary consideration; less than 15 feet of shelving is visible, and the only furniture available to Justin are two chairs—each a green plastic seat and back with wood arms. They are located at the end of the aisle under a small cork bulletin board. The librarian walks in front of the shelves with Justin as she points to the materials for which he is looking, validating the set as a library and the supporting actress as a librarian.

AIP's third film, a departure from the horror genre, is *Dragonfly* (1976), a modest drama that follows Jesse Arlington (Beau Bridges) after his release from a mental institution in which he had been a patient since the age of 13. Jesse attempts to locate his family by going back to Danbury, his family's home before he was institutionalized. Visiting the neighborhood street of his youth, Jesse quickly discovers that the area has changed and his family has moved. He then goes to the Danbury Public Library for information and encounters an "only 38" librarian (Mimi Obler[57]). Although she has worked 30 years in the library, including service at the "old" library, she does not remember the Arlington family. Jesse raises his voice in disappointment, and she shushes him immediately. He continues to press her about remembering his family, but she insists she does not recall them, shakes her head negatively, and apologizes, "I'm sorry." In this 20-second scene, the librarian, a brunette with advanced graying hair (top pinned back at side with barrettes; collar length page), wears a blue pullover blouse with a wide collar, epaulets and a single patch pocket. The librarian, even without eyeglasses and a bun, projects the basic visual characteristics of the stereotype.

The first highly successful box office movie with a reel librarian in the 1970s is *Love Story* (1970), a sentimental tear-jerker starring Ryan O'Neal as Harvard University student Oliver Barrett IV and Ali MacGraw[58] as Radcliffe College student Jenny Cavalleri. Oliver, in a constant struggle with his father, desires to make it on his own without the family name and wealth; Jenny, without family wealth, works at the Radcliffe library. The romantic attraction between the two is obvious during the opening minutes of the film. Jenny, behind a library desk, gives Oliver an extremely difficult time when he asks for a book. She calls him "preppie," maintaining that he looks

Love Story (1970). Ali MacGraw as Jenny Cavalleri, a poor Radcliffe College student who works in the library, and Ryan O'Neal as Oliver Barrett IV, a wealthy Harvard University student.

"stupid and rich." Oliver rejects her assumption, stating that he is "smart and poor," which begins the following brief conversation:

> JENNY: I'm smart and poor.
> OLIVER: What makes you so smart?
> JENNY: I wouldn't go for coffee with you.
> OLIVER: Yeah, I wouldn't ask you.
> JENNY: Well, that's what makes you stupid.

This verbal interplay in the library is representative of the sharp and smart repartee between the two throughout the film. Jenny is capable of holding her own with Oliver, if not besting him in many of the barbs they exchange.

Jenny appears in the library only in this opening scene. A young, vibrant, and attractive brunette (center part, straight shoulder blade length), she wears a black turtleneck sweater, red tartan scarf, and large black plastic frame eyeglasses. The glasses are donned in the library, for playing the piano, and while directing a youth choir rehearsal; Jenny does not require or need them for reading, driving, or any other activity. The poor college girl versus rich college boy relationship is similar to that of the Connie Lane–Tommy Marlowe pairing in *Good News* (1947). The poor college girl works in the library, indicating the absence of wealth, while the rich college boy engages in athletics—Tommy was a football star; Oliver, a hockey star. Jenny is very much a girl of the late 1960s; she has few inhibitions, she does not adhere rigidly to the tenets of Roman Catholicism, and she shamelessly pursues Oliver, who is easily caught. The library provides Jenny with temporary employment and is a most convenient place for a young poor college girl to meet a young rich college boy.

The librarian in director Curtis Harrington's murder thriller, *The Killing Kind* (1973), never appears in a library scene. The film is about a psychopathic young man, Terry Lambert (John Savage), who served two years in prison for his participation in a gang rape. Upon release, he returns to live with his mother, Thelma (Ann Sothern), in her boardinghouse.

Terry, lounging by the swimming pool one evening, is approached by next-door neighbor Louise (Luana Anders[59]), an inebriated, sexually repressed, single librarian who has been watching him from her second story bedroom window. She begins talking, revealing how bored she is with her life: "I work in a library, and I hate it!" She speaks of her "hallucinations, they're so real, about burning all the books." They laugh, and she leaps into the patio swing next to him, takes off her eyeglasses, and remarks, "It must be wonderful." Terry is unable to put the remark into any context until she adds, "Being raped!" She moves her glasses up and down his inner thigh, uttering, "I wouldn't have told on you." He bounces off the swing and stands by the edge of the pool. She immediately follows him, challenging him to guess her age. He blurts out, "35," which is correct. She looks at him, responds in a hopeless voice, "Too old?" and runs away.

Louise returns to poolside the next day to apologize for her "childish" behavior. "I was drunk. I hope you don't think I was actually intending to se-, se-, seduce you." Louise's difficulty in saying "seduce" is indicative of her sexual problems. Terry rebukes the apology, "The next time you're stoned lady ... and you don't actually know that you're horny ... why don't you just hop into a goddamn cold shower." Louise's anger is visibly apparent as he rebuffs her; as soon as Terry quiets down, she turns and leaves but immediately comes back to further frustrate him. She thoroughly enjoys tormenting the young man; she speaks softly in a seductive bedroom voice. He attempts to ignore her until she remarks, "That thing [guitar] that you hold so close to you, like a woman. You can't even play it." Terry jumps to his feet and raises the guitar as if he is going to strike her. Fear engulfs her face, but he bashes the guitar on the edge of the pool and runs into the house. Louise's face of fear is slowly replaced by a self-satisfying smile, and in only seconds, her face beams with smugness, indicating that she enjoyed every moment of torment that she inflicted upon Terry.

Louise, an attractive, mature brunette (full bang; bun at nape) appears in other scenes, always maintaining her image as a librarian. She professes to be a librarian and exhibits the visual characteristics throughout the film. Louise dresses colorfully but conservatively and wears eyeglasses in every scene. She is dissatisfied with her occupation, professing her desire to burn the library's books, the very same utterance that

Lulu Smith spat out in *Forbidden* (1932). She is bored with life, just as Connie Randall in *No Man of Her Own* (1932) unhesitatingly exclaimed about the boredom of Glendale. In addition, she resides at home and cares for an invalid father—a staid home life for librarians. At one point, her father comments about her excessive reading, "You read too much. It's bad for your eyes." Reading is the type of home activity that filmgoers would expect of librarians. Although she never appears in a library, filmgoers easily identify her as a librarian.

The Paper Chase (1973) focuses on the difficulties that confront first-year law students. The film contains several library scenes, and a librarian (uncredited[60]) appears in two of these. The librarian has some dialogue in her second scene; after greeting a student by name, she continues working until interrupted by student James G. Hart (Timothy Bottoms) who asks for a specific volume from the *Pacific Reporter, 2d Series*. The librarian answers that if the volume is not on the shelf, it is out. James then asks about the items located at the top of the stairs; the librarian responds that it is a secure area and houses the memoranda of professors and that access is prohibited without special authorization or the approval of the professor whose work is being examined. This "only 38" brunette (collar length; sides and back held at nape with barrette) wears a white blouse with a large open collar, under a dark shift dress. She engages in several occupational tasks.

Two couples en route to an Aspen vacation in a 32-foot motor home in *Race With the Devil* (1975) become involved in a tale of horror when the husbands, Roger March (Peter Fonda) and Frank Stewart (Warren Oates) witness a satanic ritual in which a girl is murdered. Chased by members of the group, they escape in their motor home and report the incident to local police. The wives, Kelly March (Lara Parker) and Alice Stewart (Loretta Swit), find a document, unintentionally dropped by one of the men who chased them, when they clean the motor home. Believing the document is a witchcraft message, the two women visit the local public library to find information. They find several pertinent books and take them to the librarian (uncredited[61]) who informs them the books cannot be taken from the library. Alice hands the books to Kelly, telling her to return them. While Alice engages the librarian in a conversation, Kelly simply walks into the shelving area, puts the books in her large bag, and returns. As they hustle out of the building and into the street with the books, Alice remarks to Kelly, "We'll mail them back when we're finished."

The bespectacled "only 38" librarian displays a friendly and courteous service policy, even though she does not move from her desk, where she is filing in a card tray. A redhead (sides and front pulled into bun at crown; back hangs loose to waist), the librarian wears a multicolor pattern dress with a modest V-neckline and a white, narrow collar. She displays the visual characteristics of the stereotypical image.

Two young *Washington Post* reporters—Bob Woodward (Robert Redford) and Carl Bernstein (Dustin Hoffman)—struggle to uncover the facts of the break-in of the headquarters of the National Democratic Committee in *All The President's Men* (1976). As the journalists uncover leads in their search for the truth about this break-in, they find it necessary to contact several librarians. When Carl telephones a librarian at the White House Library about materials that Howard Hunt may have checked out, the librarian states that Hunt checked out some materials. She puts him on hold while she verifies her statement. When the librarian resumes the conversation, however, she maintains that her previous statement was incorrect and that she doesn't know Hunt and hangs up. The two reporters then visit a librarian (James Murtaugh[62]) at the Library of Congress to obtain information about White House transactions. He is evidently a librarian in a mid-level management position with some degree of authority, as he quickly impedes their search by stating that "all White House transactions are confidential. Thank you very much, gentlemen." This librarian projects the image of an "only 38" male—thinning, receding hairline, and dressed in suit and tie. To solidify his image, he has a personal office, a further indication of his administrative position.

To circumvent the rejection of this librarian, the two ingenious reporters go to another office in the library and ask another librarian (Jaye Stewart[63]) for White House transaction records. This bespectacled librarian sports an Afro hairstyle and wears a long-sleeve, tan shirt with a necktie. Seated at a work station surrounded by book shelving, this librarian, definitely farther down the organizational chart than the previous librarian, informs the reporters, "I'm not sure you want 'em, but I got 'em." He then gives them hundreds of completed request forms which they filter through in the reading room.

In this specific case, library policy regarding the confidentiality of White House records is well understood and adhered to by supervisory personnel but not by the working librarians on the lower end of the organizational chart. The failure of all librarians to act in a consistent manner indicates that vertical communication (that is, administrators to middle managers to working librarians) within the organization is inadequate. The ease of obtaining library records from reel librarians, whether fiction, as in *The Seventh Victim* (1943), or fact, as in this film, jeopardizes the trust that filmgoers expect of their local libraries. Working librarians must be vigilant to ensure that policies relating to the confidentiality of patron records, which reel librarians seemingly ignore at will, are understood and uniformly observed.

A *Washington Post* librarian (Jamie Smith-Jackson[64]) appears briefly on-screen, informing Woodward that she could not find any information in the clipping files on an individual whom he is attempting to locate. She did find, however, a picture of the individual and gives it to Woodward. A young, attractive blonde (eyeglasses hold back the top and sides of shoulder blade length hair), the librarian wears an A-line black skirt with pink flowers and a long-sleeve ash blouse. As the camera is stationed behind the librarian, filmgoers only see her back when she delivers her lines. The actress' right profile is visible momentarily when she turns and walks away from Woodward's desk.

Movie Movie (1978; b/w and color) reaches back to the halcyon days of double features for its inspiration; it offers filmgoers two 50-minute stories—"Dynamite Hands," a black and white boxing feature, and "Baxter's Beauties of 1933," a color musical feature.[65] "Dynamite Hands" is a rags-to-riches yarn about delivery boy Joey Popchik (Harry Hamlin) who wants to go to law school but becomes a fighter because his sister needs $25,000 for an operation. Joey's girlfriend is Betsy McGuire (Trish Van Devere[66]), a librarian at the New York Public Library. Betsy displays many of the visual characteristics of reel librarians. A brunette (collar length page), she wears eyeglasses and dresses modestly and conservatively, departing only from her modest attire to attend a nightclub with Joey. When she walks out of her apartment building in one scene, she resembles Donna Reed's character, Mary Bailey, the old maid librarian, in *It's A Wonderful Life* (1946), the quintessential stereotypical reel librarian. When Joey falls into the clutches of a shady promoter, he also falls in love with siren Troubles Moran (Ann Reinking). Finally realizing his mistakes, Joey rushes back to Betsy, waiting for her at a side door of the New York Public Library.

As there are no scenes in the library, an exterior door with a library name is undoubtedly the least expensive means of suggesting a library. Betsy is the third reel librarian to fall in love with a boxer, following in the sentimental tradition of Betty Grant in *The Spirit of Youth* (1929), whose boxer boyfriend also came back to her in defeat, and Susan Merrill in *Gentlemen Are Born* (1934), whose heartthrob was a miserable boxer unable to cope with life's severe challenges.

Goldie Hawn[67] is librarian Gloria Mundy in *Foul Play* (1978), a romantic comedy abounding with murder, mystery, and suspense. Gloria, the major female role, works in a branch of the San Francisco Public Library. She is an attractive, young blonde (center part; shoulder length hanging in soft curls) divorcée who lives a quiet lifestyle—watching a little television while knitting and occasionally attending a retrospective film showing.

Gloria's nondescript lifestyle is revealed in the first few minutes of the film. While attending a party, Gloria is corralled by long-time friend and hostess Sally (Barbara Sammeth), who demands to know how she is coping with life. "Ever since the divorce," she informs Gloria, "you lock yourself in that library and hide behind those glasses." According to Sally, Gloria is no longer an animated, energized young woman. The hostess continues, "You used to be a cheerleader, you used to show some cleavage," and suggests that Gloria mingle and connect with someone at the party. Sally also recommends that she reveal "some skin, shake your booty, take some chances." Gloria, dressed in a smart brown dress with a low V-neckline, is showing as much cleavage as possible without actually revealing her breasts. Tony Carlson (Chevy Chase), overhearing Gloria and Sally's conversation, makes a pass at Gloria as she prepares to leave. They earlier exchanged glances on the patio, but Tony's propensity for physical ineptitude, knocking everything over on the portable bar, quickly dissipated her interest. Now, he demonstrates his linguistic ineptitude, ending his pitch line with "Would you like to take a shower?" She quickly retorts, "I don't pick up strange men." "That's your problem," he responds with a smile. "So why don't you try it?" she rejoins as she brushes him aside.

Driving back to San Francisco, Gloria ponders Sally's advice, and when she sees a young man standing alongside a broken-down car, she picks him up. They agree to meet at a retrospective film showing later that evening. Gloria does not know that the young man, Scotty (Bruce Solomon), is an undercover policeman being pursued by gangsters—the Albino and the Dwarf—who plan to assassinate the Pope during a performance of *The Mikado*. When Scotty fails to appear at the theater, Gloria goes in. Moments later, he lumbers into the seat next to her and begins telling her things. Unaware that he has been shot, Gloria assumes Scotty is talking about the movie, until he dies and slumps onto her. The Albino and the Dwarf assume that Scotty passed microfilm containing details of the assassination plot to Gloria; they now pursue Gloria.

The next morning at the library, Stella (Marilyn Sokol[68]), busily picking up books from library tables, stops at the desk to ask Gloria about lunch. Gloria, taking off her glasses to respond, remarks that she has a lot to tell her. A brunette (soft curled Afro), Stella mirrors 1970s fashion—brown patterned skirt and a light-color cowl-neck sweater with a wide waist belt. At lunch on a park bench, Stella, a decidedly 1970s feminist, admonishes Gloria for picking up Scotty, but when Gloria protests that he did not appear to be after sex, Stella informs her that "rape is not an act of sex; rape is an act of violence." Discovering that Gloria has only an umbrella for defense, Stella brandishes her weapons. The first item is a "Screamer," which generates a high shrill sound; to demonstrate its effectiveness, Stella pulls the switch and watches with glee as dogs bark and children cover their ears. The second item is a can of mace, a spray substance that temporarily blinds an attacker. The third and last item is brass knuckles, for "infighting." Stella, ready for any masher, summarizes her philosophy: "Nobody's gonna mess with Stella, unless Stella wants to be messed!" She advises Gloria to "get them before they get you." This insightful scene reflects attitudes of women during the 1970s toward personal safety and the types of items that provided a sense of personal security.

At library closing time, Mrs. Monk (Irene Tedrow[69]), obviously a supervisor, is leaving with an armful of books. "Taking your work home again?" Gloria asks. Monk comments that she is "on a fascinating sleuth," and finds it "so exciting." As Monk begins to walk away from Gloria, she states that "a nice, little man, you know, a dwarf" was in the library looking for her. With an armload of books to shelve as she makes her way toward the rear exit, Gloria slowly strolls the aisles shelving the books and turning out lights. As the library darkens, the suspense builds. When Gloria bends down to shelve a book on a lower shelf, she sees a face staring at her through the stacks, startling her so much that she falls backwards onto the floor. Albino, whom she doesn't know, appears at the end of the aisle, towering above her. "Oh, you frightened me, I thought you were a dwarf." She scrambles up, telling him that he can "go out the back" with her. As she speaks, the Albino pours ether on cotton gauze and then grabs her arm. She reacts immediately, clubbing him with her umbrella and running for the exit. Outside the library, she manages to run into a nearby bar, where she approaches Stanley Tibbets (Dudley Moore), a customer sitting alone at a table. Instead of telling him what is happening, she utters statements that are loaded with sexual innuendoes. "Take me home," she demands. Surprised that such an attractive woman would be so direct, Stanley is elated but cautious, "What?" "Take me home please," she answers. "My place or yours?" he asks. "Which is closer?" she quizzes. "I have a little pad just around the corner," he offers, and she immediately accepts, "Perfect!" Stanley is overwhelmed by his good fortune.

At Stanley's apartment, the miscommunication continues in outlandish proportions. Both are interpreting the conversation on different levels. Gloria interprets their conversation literally, while Stanley believes that she is desperate to find a man for the evening and interprets her responses as very sexually suggestive, intimating that she is in the same mood as he. Taking a sip from a drink laced with Spanish Fly,

Gloria comments, "Tastes like Tabasco." When Stanley tells her it's Spanish Fly, she remarks innocently and nonchalantly, "I've never had it before." He plays along with her innocence, "I know a few people ... in Spain." The stereo, blasting loudly with a disco number, and a revolving mirror ball create a discotheque ambiance. Stanley begins preparing the room, exposing many of his sexual playthings and activities; for example, binocular watching of pornographic films, full-sized inflated women, and a Murphy bed with overhead lights and mirror. Gloria is unaware of his machinations, as she is preoccupied looking out the window, with binoculars, for her attacker. Stanley strips off his clothes and is wearing only boxer shorts, with his trousers at his knees, when Gloria turns around. Shocked by the extravaganza, she mutters, "Oh, my God!" and Stanley replies inquisitively, "What's the matter, baby?" "What is this? What are you doing? Why are you undressed?" she wants to know. Gloria is bewildered by the "diversity" of the gadgets and playthings, but her curiosity compels her to ask about them as Stanley frantically attempts to put them away. This is one of the funniest scenes in 1970s films and relies upon Gloria's innocent responses to Stanley's questions for the situation to develop from its sane beginning to its absurd ending. Not surprisingly, the woman initiating and perpetuating the action is a young blonde librarian. Gloria's naïveté appears natural, but few women could have sustained such innocence for so long.

Shortly after Gloria arrives at her apartment from Stanley's place, an intruder assaults her in an effort to obtain the microfilm. While defending herself, she manages to wound the assailant and call the police but then faints when she sees the Albino outside her kitchen window. Tony is one of the police officers responding to her call, but they find her story difficult to believe because there is nothing in the apartment to substantiate her statement that a struggle occurred. Stella, the next morning at the library, reiterates the salient points of her previous lecture about men and personal safety. At the conclusion of her warnings, Stella reaches into her handbag and gives Gloria the arsenal of weapons, adding, "Without them you are a walking light bulb, waiting to be screwed!" Gloria scoops up the weapons, and within minutes of leaving the library, she is drugged and kidnapped by the Albino.

Gloria uses Stella's arsenal to escape, and when Tony discovers that an undercover officer called "Scotty" was murdered and that Rupert Stiltskin—the Dwarf—is in town to assassinate someone, the story line accelerates, with numerous comedic interludes that illustrate Gloria's propensity for ineptitude. While Tony attempts to uncover some leads about the assassination plot, Gloria telephones Stella, requesting that Monk look for information on the "Tax the Churches League," the only slim lead that has been found. Stella later appears at the police station and gives the research materials to Tony; a picture in the file immediately gives Tony the key to what is happening and who is planning the assassination. During the ensuing action, Tony and Gloria are recklessly driving and crashing vehicles up and down the hills of San Francisco in order to reach the opera in time to save the Pope.

Gloria and Stella do not portray the stereotypical image of reel librarians; in fact, they faintly remind one of the "girls in research" in *Desk Set* (1957). Gloria displays one visual characteristic in the library—eyeglasses. Their clothes reflect 1970s fashions, and they dress modestly for library work. In non-library scenes, Gloria does not reveal the amount of cleavage suggested by Sally at all times, but she reveals more than enough to disqualify her as a modestly attired stereotypical librarian. Both librarians perform occupational tasks—picking up books from library tables, shelving books, and turning out lights. There is little interaction with library patrons; in one instance, Stella holds up her right index finger to two women who appear at the desk, indicating that she will be with them in just a moment. Gloria and Stella portray competent librarians. Stella's role, to some degree, is equivalent to the role of a comic sidekick. Although she doesn't accompany Gloria on her adventures throughout the film, Stella is a comedienne when she is on-screen.

Monk, on the other hand, is very much the stereotypical image of reel librarians. Even her name, Monk, implies restrained living, a corollary of the image. In her first library appearance, she displays the visual characteristics—dark blue high-neck dress and coat, matching hat with feather, eyeglasses, and a bun at her crown. In her last library scene, Monk reaffirms this image; although dressing in lighter colors, her dress is high-neck, long sleeves, with a modest bow. Monk, friendly with Gloria and Stella, does not appear to maintain more than a supervisor-employee relationship with either of them. Hawn (the established star) as Gloria and Tedrow (the elderly supporting actress) as Monk illustrate the continuing dichotomy between leading roles and supporting roles. Since *Desk Set* exposed the fallacy that the stereotype is an absolute corollary of the occupation, the stereotype is no longer necessary to validate a cast member as a librarian. Filmmakers, however, appear to retreat to the stereotype because it is so easy to fashion, thereby requiring a minimal creative effort, and so easy for filmgoers to recognize.

Foul Play contains a variety of comedic situations; many of them initiated and carried out by Gloria. In these scenes, she repeatedly demonstrates that her intellectual capability is frequently absent or extremely lackadaisical. This type of behavior suggests that she is a blonde with minimal intellect, resembling the perennial stereotype against which women struggle. This is not the behavior expected from a librarian; consequently, it is difficult to visualize Gloria becoming a Mrs. Monk. Stella frequently harangues her with personal safety lectures, undoubtedly forcing Gloria to seriously consider the inherent evil in men. The library provides Gloria with employment she enjoys. She is content with her lifestyle. She also enjoys and likes Tony's companionship, but there is no mention of leaving the library for love.

Library scenes occur throughout the film, continually reinforcing Gloria's occupation as a librarian. Her lifestyle, however, is suspect; for Gloria to be young and living in San Francisco during the 1970s and to be unfamiliar with or unaware of Spanish Fly defies explanation. She is, as Sally inferred, way out of the loop of San Francisco activities. The only plausible inference is that only a librarian could be so totally uninformed about the San Francisco scene. For Gloria, the library serves as an envelope of isolation.

Carrie Snodgress[70] stars as librarian Louise Elmore in *The Attic* (1979), a drama with minor trappings of suspense and horror genres. The film centers on Louise and her invalid (wheelchair-bound) and oppressive father, Wendell (Ray Milland). The relationship and personalities of Louise and Wendell are remarkably similar to those of Louise and her father, also confined to a wheelchair, who appeared in *The Killing Kind*

(1973). Screenwriters Tony Crechales and George Edwards penned both scripts; reusing similar characters with the same names is evidently a deliberate attempt to evoke the mood of their earlier film, perhaps intensifying the aura of *The Attic* for the filmgoers who saw and remembered *The Killing Kind*.

One library scene early in the film begins with a patron at the main desk asking Louise about her bandaged wrists. The result of an "accident," she responds, but they are bandaged because of a recent bungled suicide attempt, prompted by her inability to overcome the despondency resulting from the disappearance of her boyfriend on their wedding day 19 years ago. Louise has failed to move past 1960. At a nearby card catalog, Emily Perkins (Ruth Cox[71]), who will soon replace Louise as head librarian, is entangled in a conversation with a gossipy library patron who wants to know if she likes the library. "I like it here. Beats being a college librarian." The patron then shifts the topic and eventually remarks, "It's sad they're retiring her." The apparent reason for Louise's forced retirement is a library fire, which, according to the patron, "They say she deliberately set." When Emily states that it was an accident, the patron comments, "Of course, it had to be, I mean, in her intoxicated condition." The card catalog is in close proximity to the main desk, permitting Louise to overhear the discussion. Before listening, however, she bends down to pour herself a drink, which she thoroughly enjoys, from a hidden liquor flask she keeps behind some items on an interior bottom shelf of the main desk. The patron also tells Emily about the fire that destroyed Wendell's store; Louise's father jumped from the second floor to escape, but the fall resulted in his present paralytic condition. During this scene, Louise and Emily engage in various tasks—assisting patrons, stamping books, carrying books, using the card catalog, and shelving books. When the patrons leave at closing time, Louise comments, "Nineteen years I've been here. I guess they do need new blood." Emily, attempting to mollify the situation, responds, "People can be very unfair. Besides, being a head librarian is not exactly my idea of a lifetime career." This prompts Louise to remark, "How I wish I thought the way you did. I wish I had the courage to..." but fails to complete her thought. Louise hustles Emily out of the library and begins organizing the main desk, closing stamp pads and placing date stamps on the pads, indicating the attention to detail that she observes as head librarian.

In the second library scene, Emily, glancing at photographs in an oversized book, asks, "Did you know that the snake is probably the longest surviving species of reptile on Earth today?" Louise replies, "Not true. My father is." Although the two librarians smile at her comment, the statement reflects Louise's deep dislike of her father. Throughout the film, Louise fantasizes about killing her overbearing and demanding father (for example, poisoning him or tossing an electrical heater into his bath). Every one of her actions is calculated to infuriate him; she never bypasses an opportunity to offend him. In addition, she appears as a kook to several local residents. She telephones the Bureau of Missing Persons regularly to see if there is any new information about her boyfriend's disappearance; she visits a travel agency for information about summer vacations which she never takes. She, however, maintains a normal friendship with Emily, who suffers from a domineering mother. Louise empathizes with Emily's position because it resembles the relationship she has with her father; she displays no reservations in advising Emily to leave. When Louise dines at Emily's,

Mrs. Perkins (Rosemary Murphy) remarks that she would like Emily to find a stable job, as the library is her fourth position since college. Louise chimes in, "I wish that I'd had the good sense to try some other jobs when I was young. I may not have been a librarian." "It's a perfectly respectable job," responds Mrs. Perkins. Louise counters, "Respectable. Yes. And often boring." Later, during coffee in the living room, Emily's young brother David (Patrick Brennan) spills chocolate on his coat, and exclaims, "Aw, shit!" Mrs. Perkins disciplines her son similar in manner to Wendell's harangues against Louise. In response to Mrs. Perkins' action, Louise immediately drops an expensive porcelain collectible, breaking it. Acting surprised by her own clumsiness, Louise exclaims, "Aw, shit!" and apologizes profusely. Louise, realizing her own life has been destroyed by such a parent, strikes back in defense of David, who is too young to rebel against his mother, and Emily, who is too timorous.

The day after dining at Emily's, the library closes briefly near the end of the day to celebrate Louise's retirement. Joining Louise are Emily, an unnamed librarian (Frances Bay[72]), and Donald (Terry Troutt[73]). A large table loaded with food and champagne is in the middle of the library. While laughing and talking about the previous evening, Louise comments to Emily that "emasculation is some mothers' primary instinct. And some fathers, too." Emily, not having suffered as long as Louise, is resigned: "You can't fight it." Louise's immediate response is, "The hell you can't." Louise then walks around the library and addresses the books, "Goodbye, all you bastards. If I never see you again, it'll be too soon."

Several days later, Louise receives a severance and unpaid vacation check ($631) and sends $500 to Emily. She advises Emily to rush to her boyfriend in California, emphasizing that "everyone deserves the right to lead their own life." Louise is very instrumental in ensuring that Emily escapes the type of parent-child relationship that she has endured for years. The same day she sends the money to Emily, Louise discovers that her pet monkey, whom her father hates, has disappeared. The following day, a delusional Louise believes the youngster hired to mow the lawn is her missing boyfriend and rushes to him; Wendell denigrates and admonishes her, insisting that he is the "only one" she has. When Louise takes her father to the park for his Sunday excursion, the wheelchair overturns, and he falls on the ground, only to immediately stand up and brush off his trousers—his paralysis was a sham. Louise, in a raging fervor, struggles with her father; he slips and falls down a hill. Louise rushes home and finds her father's key to the forbidden attic, where she discovers the truth of the past.

Of the four librarians, three—Louise, Donald, and the female librarian (unnamed character)—project the "only 38" image. Although only 33, Snodgress, by adding a few gray streaks and pulling her hair into a French twist with bun at her crown and sporting a half bang, projects the image of an older woman in the library. Adding gray to a hairstyle to attain an older appearance is the same technique that Lois Wilson used 56 years earlier in *Only 38* (1923). Emily is a brunette (blonde streaks; shoulder length page with half bang), as is the other librarian (collar length soft curls, brushed back). Donald wears eyeglasses, and Emily occasionally does. The three women dress in modest and colorful 1970s clothes, while Donald dresses complacently, appearing in patterned short sleeve shirts and a narrow, square hem necktie.

Louise dresses sharply, but her father, whose only objective is to maintain his dominance over her, quips in one scene, "Look at you. Look at the clothes you wear. You're a mouse. That's what you are." Louise, berated relentlessly throughout this film by her father, exhibits little self-confidence and little desire to continue living. When she attends a movie, meets a sailor, and goes to a hotel with him, Louise informs the sailor that his "name is Robert [her boyfriend's name]. It is 1960, and we're in love." Although an attractive "only 38" woman who displays the visual characteristics of the stereotypical image, Louise displays behavior contrary to that expected of a staid librarian, a result of her mental instability. She wants to keep her library position but is not hesitant about calling the job "boring" and the books "bastards." Over the years, she accepts her fate, corralling the fortitude only to fantasize about her father and to support Emily.

Emily is blunt about library positions—she believes that working in a public library "beats" working in a college library. She is not enamored with library work, although her mother calls it a "respectable job." In addition, Emily is not an advocate of the occupation, maintaining that being a "head librarian" is not her ideal "lifetime career." The library offers Emily a respectable job, but she leaves at her earliest opportunity, the same afternoon that she receives Louise's gift in the mail. Emily, as previous reel librarians, could not resist the expectation of a happier life with her boyfriend.

Conclusion

Reel librarians during the 1960s and 1970s, with few exceptions, continued to demonstrate the visual characteristics and occupational tasks of the stereotypical image. In retrospect, John Lewis, whom Peter Sellers so adroitly invigorated with life in *Only Two Can Play*, is the preeminent male reel librarian of these two decades. Lewis, whose cinematic lineage as an inept librarian goes back to 1919—LeRoy Sylvester (*A Very Good Young Man*), solidifies the image of the maladroit and bungling male reel librarian for the remainder of the twentieth century. Lewis' leers, mishaps, and embarrassments—all in response to and the result of his pressing "creative urges"—provide filmgoers with innumerable grins, chuckles, and guffaws. Few male librarians, if any, will attain the image of a successful, devil-may-care paramour. Bernard Chanticleer suffered a yo-yo relationship with Barbara Darling in *You're A Big Boy Now* (1966), further supporting the inept legacy. In *Goodbye, Columbus*, however, Neil Klugman scores with Brenda Patimkin, a young college student from a nouveau riche family; Neil envisions a meaningful relationship, but their affair is only a wisp of summertime fun for Brenda. Male reel librarians continued to be perplexed by the opposite sex, a destiny that irreparably denigrates the image of male librarians.

The stereotypical image of reel librarians abounded in small roles for supporting actors. The majority of supporting roles were straightforward; actors simply displayed the necessary occupational tasks to ensure their status as a reel librarian. Actors in these roles occasionally are uncredited; for example, the librarian in *The Paper Chase* and the librarian in *Teenage Mother*. Also evident is the lack of a name for the screen character portraying a reel librarian; when an actor receives credit, the role may be identified simply as "Librarian."

Marian Paroo (Shirley Jones) is the preeminent reel librarian, not just of the 1960s, but of the twentieth century. New stage productions of Willson's *The Music Man* will continue to keep "Marian the Librarian" in the limelight for decades and future generations. The 1962 film and other productions of *The Music Man* will continue her legacy. Tudi Wiggins' portrayal of Miss Turner, a supporting role in *My Side of the Mountain*, is praiseworthy. Miss Turner is one reel librarian whose performance should be emulated by actors and filmmakers. Although Wiggins displays several of the visual characteristics and occupational tasks for reel librarians, she portrays Miss Turner with dignity, a characteristic conspicuously absent in most representations.

Reel librarians in supporting roles continued unhesitatingly to demand adherence to library rules of silence; for example, the college librarian in *The Misadventures of Merlin Jones* and Miss McKenzie in *The Prime of Miss Jean Brodie*. Mr. Stringer in the Miss Marple series of films continued to keep alive the comic sidekick role.

4

A Plethora of Librarians, 1980–1999

The trend of renovating theaters to accommodate more than one screen that began during the late 1960s and early 1970s intensified during the last two decades of the century. By the end of the century, theaters with one screen were the anomaly; the movie palaces of grandeur were gone, and filmgoers were attending new theaters with multiple screens—the multiplex theaters. The number of seats in the smaller screen theaters varied; many were capable of seating no more than 250, a dramatic change from the palaces of only four decades earlier. The number of screens in a building appeared to be limited only by the imagination of the architect. Only the smallest venues retained one-screen theaters. The increase in the number of screens also increased the demand for motion pictures, and films released during the 1980s and 1990s contain more scenes in libraries and with librarians than those of previous decades. This is indicative of the growing emphasis, importance, and demand for information in American society during the last two decades of the twentieth century. Many of these scenes, however, are only seconds in length; inattentive filmgoers may miss the entire scene.

A great number of reel librarians projected the stereotypical image during the 1980s and 1990s, reinforcing its dominance and indicating that the image remained the choice of filmmakers. One film released in the 1990s chided the stereotypical image, doing so with humor and warmth and presenting the occupation as not only very worthwhile but also requiring academic preparation. By the 1980s, most films were listing every actor appearing on-screen, with or without dialogue, in the cast credits. Supporting actors portraying librarians in brief scenes were most frequently cited as "Librarian," even though the supporting actor, on occasion, may have a character name that was used in the film. The detailing of cast members helps a viewer identify many of the supporting actors appearing as librarians.

The 1980s

The films of the first five years of the 1980s contained few outstanding reel librarians. A librarian (Noreen Walker[1]) in *Somewhere in Time* (1980) is reluctant and hesitant to assist Richard Collier (Christopher Reeve), a playwright who visits a library to find information about Elise McKenna (Jane Seymour), an actress of the early twentieth century. When Richard asks the librarian if there are theatrical biographies in closed areas that he may use, she responds that the items are in the back and she would have to find them. She sighs and looks at her wristwatch, suggesting that this is an imposition and that she does not have the time for such a request. Before she can respond negatively to his request, however, Richard inquires, "Could you do that for me? Please." He flashes a smile; the librarian accedes to his request. She reappears shortly with an armload of periodicals, depositing them on the table where he is working. The librarian's obvious reluctance to assist Richard projects a public service commitment that is inimical to the image of librarians. Although the librarian helps Richard, filmgoers may be more inclined to remember her initial response to his request. Whether overworked or fearful that her break or lunch period is in jeopardy, the librarian is not enthusiastic about the work of her occupation. The bespectacled librarian, a Black American with a short Afro hairstyle, engages in several occupational tasks and wears a pink blouse with a shawl collar under a dark cardigan; she projects the stereotypical image.

Two years later, *Sophie's Choice* (1982) presents a bespectacled male librarian (John Rothman[2]) whose reference skills are severely deficient and whose attitude is decidedly hostile toward library patrons. The year is 1947, and Holocaust survivor Sophie Zawistowska (Meryl Streep) is taking a language class to become fluent in English. After the instructor reads several passages from Emily Dickinson during class, Sophie visits a library to obtain some of the poet's works. The library is imposing—it has extremely high ceilings, ornate floor-to-ceiling marble columns, a marble floor, and a library desk that is elevated so that patrons must look up to the librarian. Sophie in her broken English and lack of self-assurance manages to ask the librarian where she can find entries in the catalog for Emil Dickens. The librarian doesn't deign to either look at or take any observable interest in Sophie; he continues to work in a card file while she asks for assistance. He tells her where the catalog is located but that she will not "find any such listing." Sophie, confused by his statement, asks why, and the librarian, with a smug countenance, replies, "Charles Dickens is an English writer. There is no American poet by the name of Dickens." Sophie insists that she is correct about the poet being an American and begins to spell the name for the librarian; he interrupts Sophie, stating in a rancorous tone, "Listen ... I told you. There's no such person. You want me to draw you a picture?" Sophie mutters, "No," as the librarian continues, "I'm telling you. You hear me." Sophie, overwhelmed by the hostility of the librarian, recognizes the futility of continuing. She offers a mild response, "All right," as she turns away from the desk.

Although Rothman is 33, he displays the visual characteristics of the stereotype—eyeglasses, receding hairline, and conservative clothing (white shirt, black and white polka-dot bow tie, dark cardigan sweater)—which result in promoting the image of an "only 38" individual. The fact that the desk and the librarian are elevated above floor level physically positions patrons in a subservient role. The librarian purposely flaunts his intellect and his personal disregard for Sophie's quest for assistance, creating an overbearing atmosphere which places Sophie at great disadvantage. For this librarian to be acceptable to filmgoers, however, his personality and behavior must reflect, at least minimally, the type of service and treatment that filmgoers could envision receiving from working librarians. Reel librarians are occasionally exasperated by a patron (for example, Ellen Shavley in *Wonder Man*, 1945), but none demonstrates, as this librarian in *Sophie's Choice*, total antipathy and disregard for a patron.

A 1981 Italian production, *The House by the Cemetery*, released in the United States in 1984, contains a quirky librarian, Daniel Douglas (Gianpaolo Saccarola[3]). Daniel is eager to assist Norman Boyle (Paolo Malco), who is on a six-month research sabbatical in New Whitby, Massachusetts. Daniel exhibits several irritating personality features—clearing his throat and mild laughter, always accompanied with a ubiquitous smile; they are integral parts of his speech pattern. His mannerisms suggest a lack of self-confidence, giving him the aura of a meek, mild librarian. In addition, Daniel has a fascination with the details of a previous researcher's suicide in the library; he remarks to Norman, "You know where he hanged himself?" as he points to a railing above a nearby bookshelf. One film critic commented that Daniel is "an unctuous librarian who is the sole truly entertaining character in the picture." [4]

Several actresses in the early 1980s displayed visual characteristics of the stereotypical image: Dorothy Scott,[5] librarian in *My Bodyguard* (1980), is an "only 38" brunette wearing eyeglasses; Jan Burrell[6] in *Christine* (1983) is an "only 38" brunette (full bang; short cut) with eyeglasses on a lanyard; and Helena Stevens[7] in *The Lords of Discipline* (1983) is a silver-haired "only 38" librarian. Scott and Stevens appear on-screen for only seconds and are in the background; inattentive filmgoers may actually miss their brief appearances.

In *Wacko* (1981), a spoof of teenage slasher films, supporting actress Jacqulin Cole[8] is a librarian at Alfred Hitchcock High School. A brunette (bun on crown), Cole appears in a brief, designed-for-comedy library scene with Mary Graves (Julia Duffy), who suffers from nightmares of lawnmowers and the lawnmower killer. Mary is seated in the library as the scene opens, and the librarian is dressed and acting like a flight attendant as she passes out pillows to students. Mary rejects a pillow but quickly falls asleep; having a nightmare, she suddenly screams, waking all the students and prompting the librarian (now in modern clothing—blazer and skirt) to ask, "Another lawnmower nightmare, Miss Graves?" Mary meekly responds with an affirmative nod of her head. The librarian then grabs Mary by the collar of her blouse, stating that she needs to get over "this silly lawnmower phobia." Mary agrees, and the librarian remarks that Mary will "be screwed up by the terrible images ... the rest of your life." The librarian then proceeds to the matter at hand and comments, "If one can't sleep in the library without being disturbed, where can one sleep? I think you owe the entire library an apology." Mary turns around, faces the students, and utters, "I'm sorry." In this frivolous film, the librarian demands silence for sleeping, not studying.

Three teenage sex farce films, *The Last American Virgin* (1982), *Getting It On* (1983), and *Screwballs* (1983), contain high school library scenes. Blanche Rubin,[9] a bespectacled "only 38" brunette (full bang; collar length layered cut), is the librarian in *The Last American Virgin*. She attempts to stop a fight among students in the library by shouting, "Stop it. I will not have that in here." She finally yells at one student, demanding that he leave or she will call the principal. In the other two films, the emphasis is humor. Fran Taylor[10] is librarian Mrs. Hatfield in *Getting It On*. After shelving several books, Hatfield, a blonde (Dorothy Hamill wedge) with eyeglasses who dresses smartly but conservatively, asks a student in the library, Alex (Martin Yost), to preview a videotape of the faculty-student basketball game for her. Alex, a peeping tom who secretly tapes the sexual activities of some of the high school girls, and three of his friends go to the media area, but instead of previewing the basketball video, they watch one of Alex's videotapes of girl students. When Hatfield returns and hustles them off to a convocation, Alex manages to remove his videotape from the VCR before taking the machine to the auditorium for the convocation. Hatfield, however, picks up Alex's videotape, carries it to the convocation, and puts it in the VCR. When it is time to watch the basketball video, the students are treated to a sexual romp and are in stitches as they enjoy the change in programming, much to the chagrin and consternation of Hatfield and the faculty.

Screwballs features the antics of students at Taft and Adams (T&A) High School. Supporting actress Carolyn Tweedle[11] portrays a librarian in stereotypical fashion in a comedy sketch. The scene begins with the librarian attempting to maintain silence. As soon as she walks by two girls at a table with a large QUIET! sign, they begin whispering. The librarian immediately returns to the table, uttering "Shush. No talking." As she continues walking, the librarian hears a young student humming while reading a paperback; the librarian grabs the book from the student and shoves it into his mouth. She next passes two students using sign language to communicate; the librarian slams her notebooks on the table, grabs their hands, and screams, "I said no talking!" A loud announcement then comes over the school's public address system; the librarian snarls at the speaker, and the message is repeated in a very low whisper. The librarian then smiles and returns to her desk where she relishes looking at a magazine containing photographs of nude young men with red stickers placed on specific parts of their anatomy. At a nearby table, four boys are looking at oversized books, all with adult magazines inside the open books. The students become visibly excited while looking at the magazines, causing the librarian to scream, "Quiet!" Silence returns momentarily, but the boys continue looking at the magazines. The librarian reacts by walking toward the table and announcing, "That's it. This table out!" The four boys stand up and carry the table out of the library.

Tweedle's makeup and dress project the stereotypical image. A bespectacled blonde (French braid on both sides, pulled into a braided bun at nape), Tweedle wears a long, pleated black skirt and a pink short-sleeve blouse (plain collar) under a gray cardigan sweater, with an extremely large white handkerchief hanging out of the sweater's right pocket. She repeatedly juts her chin out and up or pulls her chin in and down, both expressions of disapproval. A mustache line, undoubtedly penciled in, is faintly visible on her upper lip. Because the librarian enjoys adult magazines and does not wear a wedding ring or band, she is evidently a single "only 38" woman.

The sole purpose of this reel librarian is to provide comedy, and by caricaturing the visual characteristics and occupational tasks of librarians, Tweedle and director Rafal Zielinski successfully create a reel librarian at whom filmgoers can laugh.

A comedy horror film of 1983, *Hysterical*, stars the Hudson brothers—Bill, Mark, and Brett—and uses a library and librarian for comedic purposes in two scenes. Mark is Dr. Paul Batton and Brett is Fritz; they are two itinerant, incompetent adventurers who are hired to solve a problem confronting the residents of Cape Hellview. A zombie captain who died one hundred years ago after a fall from the local lighthouse suddenly reappears, killing local residents who immediately become white-faced zombies. To research this mystery, Paul and Fritz visit the public library, and at closing time, librarian Leroy (Franklyn Ajaye[12]) approaches them and says, "It's closing time, gentlemen." They complain, but Leroy, a Black American, apologetically responds, "I'm sorry, all white people have to leave." They show Leroy a card that says, "Official Card/ Allowed to Stay in the Library Past Closing Time."

Leroy remarks, "Oh well, that's different.... I'll lock up and you all let me know when you finish. I'll let you out." They respond with a loud "Thank you," to which Leroy rejoins, "Shush!" Before leaving the pair of adventurers, he points toward the materials scattered over the table and remarks, "And you all clean this up." Several minutes later, the zombie captain suddenly appears in the library, and Leroy, seeing the captain, screams, "Aw, shit!" The same phrase was used by librarian Louise Elmore only four years earlier in *The Attic* (1979); reel librarians seldom engage in verbal obscenity, and this phrase is mild when compared to mainstream obscenity in the films of the 1980s and 1990s. Leroy is killed by the zombie captain, and as the captain closes in on Paul and Fritz, they manage to escape by pushing over a book stack which, in domino effect, knocks over all of the book stacks.

Later in the film, the mayor and medical examiner visit the library to find Paul and Fritz, who are missing—they are trapped under the book stacks. Even though it is Sunday and the library is closed, Leroy opens the door for them. Leroy, now a zombie, is in whiteface and greets them, "Hey, you know. What difference does it make?" Leroy follows them around the library, repeating the zombies' favorite phrase, "What difference does it make?" Leroy, bearded and bespectacled, dresses very casually— open collar madras shirt under a gold cardigan sweater, which projects, when coupled with his white socks, an "only 38" image. These visual characteristics and his many occupational tasks—reading at his desk, maintaining silence, and enforcing the library's closing time—buttress the stereotypical image.

Two films during the early 1980s include cast members who are identified as librarians but do not appear in a library scene. In *Ragtime* (1981), a film set in the 1910s, Herman Meckler[13] is Vernon Elliott, Curator of the Morgan Library. Several Black Americans have taken possession of the Morgan Library, and the police are considering options for evicting them. Vernon appears at the standoff and insists that the police do not destroy any materials in the library, emphasizing that the library "is a national treasure." Vernon maintains that he will "go to the president" if the police continue "this climate of violence." Commissioner of Police Rheinlander Waldo (James Cagney) puts the curator on the spot by suggesting that he go into the library and explain its value to the dissidents. Vernon refuses the invitation, and Waldo informs him that as long as the library is occupied by this group, he is "not the curator of anything." Vernon displays the visual characteristics of reel librarians—"only 38," a homburg hat atop his gray hair, a dark top coat over a dark suit, and a high, stiff white collar with tie, all indicative of the time period.

The second reel librarian who doesn't appear in a library is Kit Conger (Marilu Henner[14]), who assists writer-detective Samuel Dashiell Hammett (Frederic Forrest) in *Hammett* (1982). Hammett introduces her as a "librarian downtown" and remarks on another occasion that he can trust "only two people" and that one of them "is a librarian with a smart mouth." Kit, a redhead (half bang; shoulder length hanging in waves) does not establish credentials as a reel librarian. In the film's only library scene, Hammett meets and chats briefly with an attractive brunette (Liz Roberson[15]) while in a stack area. Roberson is identified in the cast credits as Lady in the Library; however, she is shelving a book, an occupational task of librarians, and she displays visual characteristics of reel librarians—a bun at her crown, eyeglasses, and conservative clothes (a light blouse, sailor collar, under a brown sweater jacket). Filmgoers are compelled by the circumstances to conclude that she is a librarian.

In Walt Disney Pictures' 1983 release *Something Wicked This Way Comes*, Jason Robards[16] portrays Ray Bradbury's librarian Charles Halloway in a captivating manner. Charles is not only the stereotypical image, elderly, eyeglasses, gray hair and balding, and a conservative dresser, but also a very caring, humane individual who must battle Mr. Dark (Jonathan Pryce) and his Pandemonium Carnival, the Autumn people, to save his young son. The film centers on the attempts of Charles' 12-year-old son, Will (Vidal Peterson), and his friend, Jim Nightshade (Shawn Carson), to elude the evil Mr. Dark. Charles is librarian of the Green Town Public Library, which features two lions (very small) in front of its entrance, a concept undoubtedly borrowed from the New York Public Library. A library of its size—multiple floor levels and spiral stairs—is unbelievable for a city like Green Town in the 1930s. The size of the library is quite apropos, however, for the suspenseful action that occurs late in the film when Mr. Dark confronts Charles in the library and offers him the opportunity to be young again. Charles refuses and is disabled by Mr. Dark's supernatural powers. Mr. Dark then begins searching for Will and Jim, who are hiding in the shelves among the books. Charles, an older parent, strives to maintain a compassionate and responsive relationship with his son. He suffers psychologically not only because of the age differential, but also because of his inability eight years earlier to rescue Will from drowning. Charles did not learn to swim as a young boy because his father, a preacher, did not believe in swimming; consequently, Jim's father rescued Will. This continually haunts Charles, underscoring his failure as a father and a man. The bond which he has nurtured with Will, however, is too powerful for Mr. Dark to weaken. The film ends in the destruction, not the triumph, of Mr. Dark. Charles is an admirable father and projects a commendable image of librarians.

Ghostbusters (1984), an enormously successful film, has two librarians in the cast. Alice Drummond[17] is librarian Alice and John Rothman[18] is administrator Roger Delacorte. The film opens with Alice, a brunette (half bang; collar length pageboy), pushing a booktruck in the Reading Room of the New York Public Library, picking up books. She takes an armload of books to a closed stack area for shelving, and as she walks down an aisle in this nonpublic area, books begin to float from the shelving on one side of the aisle to the shelving on the opposite side. As she walks past a card catalog, the trays open and the cards begin flying out. She screams and runs, unable to easily find her way out of the shelving maze. She turns down one aisle, stops, and screams as an enormous gust of wind rushes over her. Ghostbusters are called in to investigate this occurrence. Dr. Peter Venkman (Bill Murray) questions Alice, wanting to know if any family members were "schizophrenic, mentally incompetent." Alice responds that her uncle believed he was St. Jerome.[19] Venkman replies, "I'd call that a big yes." Rothman, who was cast as the obnoxious librarian in Sophie's Choice, portrays Roger as a competent supervisor. As is often the case, the male librarian holds a higher (management) position than the female.

Two other films released in 1984 present librarians in the leading female roles. Cal, a British production, deals with murder and romance amid the Protestant-Catholic violence in Belfast. Helen Mirren[20] stars as Marcella, a Catholic and librarian whose husband, a Protestant and police officer, is murdered by the IRA, a shooting in which Cal (John Lynch) participated. The film focuses on Cal, riddled with mental anxieties as a result of the shooting, and his love for Marcella, whom he notices in the library after the assassination. Cal, as filmgoers anticipate, does not inform Marcella about his participation in the murder of her husband, although he makes a futile attempt to do so at the end of the film. Also at play in their budding relationship is the fact that Marcella was not overwhelmingly enthusiastic about her husband and marriage. An elderly man (J. J. Murphy) in the library responds to Cal's question about the librarian by remarking, "No luck with a mixed marriage. She's one of ours, you know." Although an unlikely couple—a youth in his late teens and a widow twice his age, Cal and Marcella eventually get together; Cal is more completely infatuated and in love with Marcella than a tentative Marcella is with him. Marcella is one of the few reel librarians to appear nude, indubitably more a sign of the growing acceptance of nudity in films rather than an insight into the character of librarians. Marcella's occupation as a librarian is insignificant to the film's story. Because Marcella works in a library, however, Cal can freely enter the building and discreetly ogle her. If Marcella were employed in any other type of business establishment, this type of self-indulgence would be decidedly more difficult for Cal.

Three library scenes occur before Cal and Marcella become romantically involved. Marcella is the only on-screen librarian in these three scenes. In the first and second, she works at the circulation desk competently checking items in and out for library patrons. In the third scene, she is in the stack area shelving books. When she notices Cal staring at her through a bookshelf, she greets him, "Oh, hello!" and walks to the end of the aisle to speak with him. "Have I seen you here before?" Cal, extremely nervous, can barely get out an audible "Yes." "Do you read much? It's part of our job, you know, to encourage the public." They engage in some friendly conversation about books and reading, with Marcella remarking, "I wish I was like you. I could start all over again." At this moment in the conversation, a siren of a passing police vehicle can be heard, prompting Cal to utter, "They're playing our tune." The scene abruptly ends when Marcella is called away from her shelving duties.

Marcella briefly interrupts her shelving responsibility to talk with Cal, a patron whom she believes is looking for materials. She manages to get Cal to reveal that he does not like fiction, but she is unable to further assist him because she is summoned away. Marcella's encounter with Cal demonstrates that she is friendly with patrons and willing to assist them in their search for materials. In the first two library scenes, Marcella, a brunette, has a half-bang, collar length flip hairstyle, and wears the same outfit—pullover sweater, boat neckline, and brown skirt. In the third library scene, she sports a full bang and a bun at her crown, and wears a front-button white blouse (stand-up open collar, peasant sleeves) and a circular plaid skirt. She wears some costume jewelry—earrings and a single strand necklace with a cross pendant. Marcella is an attractive "only 38" librarian who dresses modestly and engages in several occupational tasks of librarians.

The second film of 1984 to feature a librarian in the female leading role is *Racing With the Moon*, Richard Benjamin's second directorial effort. The film recounts the experiences of two high school teenagers—Henry Nash (Sean Penn) and Nicky (Nicholas Cage)—as they waste away their school days while awaiting induction into the Marines on February 12, 1943. During this waiting period, Henry meets and dates Caddie Winger (Elizabeth McGovern[21]), who attends a different high school than Henry and works in the public library. In the first of two library scenes, Caddie, while shelving books, notices and informs the library supervisor, Mrs. Spangler (Patricia Allison[22]), that one range of shelving is not securely anchored and rocks—"Religion is a little shaky." As she continues putting books on the shelves, Henry, who has a crush on her, enters the library, grabs the nearest book, and engages her in frivolous conversation. Caddie responds to his overtures, "I don't go out with strangers." When he asks about the flowers he sent to her, she replies, "So you're the one. Well, at least you're harmless." Henry, puzzled by her remark, asks her to explain, "What makes you think I'm so harmless?" As she talks to him, he looks at the title of the book he picked up, *When a Girl Grows Up*, remarking, "What the hell is this?" He leans back onto the Religion shelving to examine the book, but the shelving is unable to support his weight and immediately topples over. Caddie exclaims, "Oh, I take it back. You are definitely not harmless."

In the second library scene, Henry, going directly to the library after a school emergency drill, is dressed in feigned blood and bandages and surprises Caddie in the stack area as she collects books for a hospital visit. She is not impressed with Henry's little joke and says, "It's not funny." She tells him to get "cleaned up and meet me outside." Caddie takes Henry on her hospital round where he meets young men who have been injured and dismembered by the war. Confronted with real injuries, especially after his blood-and-bandages "joke" in the library, he expresses anger toward Caddie after they leave the hospital. "If you think I needed you to teach me some kind of lesson today, you're wrong," he says. Although Henry is only weeks away from becoming a Marine and being sent to a combat zone, he never talks about the war. Caddie apologizes for putting Henry in an uncomfortable situation, but she could not understand why he avoids discussing the war—one topic on the mind and in the discussion of every American adult.

Spangler and Caddie dress remarkably similar in the first library scene—light blue blouses under light blue front-button sweaters. Spangler, an "only 38" brunette (bun at nape), assists patrons at the main desk, while Caddie, a very young, attractive brunette (half bang; sides held back with barrettes; collar length with curls in back), shelves and retrieves books in both library scenes. Caddie's library duties also include visiting hospitalized GIs who are recovering from battle wounds. Caddie enjoys these hospital visits, joking and laughing with the GIs; such visits, however, require courage and perseverance on the part of Caddie, as well as all librarians who extend this type of service to hospitalized GIs during periods of armed conflicts. Caddie demonstrates that she possesses the fortitude to confront the horrors of battle wounds, while Henry remains aloof from the GIs, preferring war in the abstract. As most young, attractive reel librarians, Caddie functions primarily as a love interest; she is a recreational channel for Henry while he waits to join the Marines.

Three films released during 1985–1989—*Maxie* (1985), *Off Beat* (1986), and *Shadows in the Storm* (1988)—feature librarians in major roles. *Maxie* is a fantasy romantic comedy starring Glenn Close and Mandy Patinkin[23] as Jan and Nick Chaney, a San Francisco thirty-something couple. While redecorating their new apartment, Jan and Nick find, under countless layers of wallpaper, a message written on March 3, 1927, by Maxie Malone, a young flapper whose limited acting experience—one bit part in the silent film *Flapper Melodies*—showed promise of an outstanding movie career. Maxie, however, was killed in an automobile accident on her way to screen test for a D. W. Griffith picture before *Flapper Melodies* was released. Nick rents the film, and shortly after viewing the film, an apparition of Maxie appears and talks to him. Maxie has the ability to appear from time to time, inhabiting Jan's body and creating innumerable problems for Nick. He is never certain whether Jan or Maxie occupies Jan's body. In addition to this identity problem, Nick[24] is hotly pursued by his library supervisor, Miss Ophelia Sheffer (Valerie Curtin[25]), whose aggressive behavior reveals that sexual misconduct occurs even in such public service institutions as staid libraries.

Nick appears in three library scenes. The first occurs during the opening credits and establishes Nick as a rare books librarian; he works in an impressive, large study room, providing service from his desk which is topped with books and office supplies. Only one patron is doing research at the large, round study desk; Nick announces closing time and then assists the patron to gather up his materials, then Nick gives his daily patron a ride home. The patron suggests that he may complete his research "tomorrow," prompting Nick to reply, "You've been saying maybe tomorrow for almost two years." The second library scene begins with Nick in the book stacks standing on a rolling metal ladder with a single handrail; he is perusing the pages of a book on silent films. Miss Sheffer sashays toward Nick, stating she is surprised that Nick is a movie buff. Nick remarks to her, "A book scout came in with some incunabula which I think will fit into our special collection." She interrupts, informing him that "it's important we get to know each other as people." She suggests they use first names and begins climbing up the ladder. Noticing Nick's wedding band, she asks if he is married, and as Nick answers, Ophelia continues her ascent until only millimeters separate them. Nick, in all seriousness, asks, "Have you had a chance to read my Mylar cover proposal?" Ophelia responds, "You have wonderful eyes, Nick. You should open them." Nick then begins some contortive moves under and between the handrails to elude Ophelia, but is unable to free his

Maxie (1985). Mandy Patinkin as Nick Chaney and Valerie Curtin as his library supervisor, Miss Ophelia Sheffer. Note Chaney's eyeglasses in his hand.

left leg. Ophelia leans on Nick's leg and remarks, "Most women avoid married men, I improve them!" Nick finally manages to free himself from the ladder and Ophelia. When she questions him about attending the library's fundraiser, Nick responds that he will be attending—with Jan. Nick's frustration is evident when Ophelia remarks that she's "looking forward to meeting the lucky woman," and he promptly replies, "Me, too."

As Nick and Jan enter the black-tie fundraiser, Nick fails to discern that Jan's behavioral changes are the result of Maxie taking over Jan's body. Ophelia quickly whisks Nick to the dance floor, assuring him that "I wasn't just fooling around with you, I was very serious." Maxie/Jan has several drinks and goes to find Nick on the dance floor. Ophelia and Maxie/Jan battle over Nick, with Maxie/Jan becoming so enraged that she pours a drink down the front of Ophelia's evening dress. Ophelia immediately leaves to change clothes and Nick runs after her, managing to stop her car before she pulls away from the building. Ophelia, rather than firing Nick immediately, states she will keep him on the library staff, providing that "the woman is gone by the time I get back; second, make this up to me." Nick, failing to comprehend the implication of Ophelia's demand, mumbles, "I'll pay for the dry cleaning bill." Ophelia, with a petulant smile and smart retort—"Keep thinking!"—drives away. Inside, Maxie/Jan entertains the attendees with a 1920s rendition of "Bye, Bye, Blackbird," receiving an enthusiastic blast of applause from a rather subdued group before Nick hustles her out of the building. Driving home, Nick finally discovers that it is Maxie, not Jan, a switch of personalities that begins to occur too frequently for Nick.

In the third library scene, Nick receives a telephone call for assistance from Jan. As he leaves the library, Ophelia reminds him that "there's a staff meeting in ten minutes" and if he leaves, he will be fired. Nick, demonstrating for the first time that he is not Ophelia's plaything, bounces back with, "Fire me. I'm not a towel boy in a country club. I'm an expert in rare books. I'm a professional. I'm paid to service the public's needs, not yours." He leaves Ophelia standing and weaving in the lobby, disbelieving that Nick could demonstrate such courage.

Nick, in the tradition of LeRoy Sylvester in *A Very Good Young Man* (1919) and John Lewis in *Only Two Can Play* (1962), displays his bumbling ways and ineptitude on numerous occasions. For example, when the leading man in a commercial starring Maxie/Jan fails to appear at the filming site, Nick agrees to take over the part, believing that he can "ride a stupid horse and look like a stupid hero." Tied up and lying on railroad tracks in the path of an oncoming steam locomotive, Maxie/Jan waits anxiously for Nick to ride to her rescue. The intrepid Nick, dressed as a flashy B-western cowboy movie star of the 1930s–1940s, flounders in the saddle as his horse gallops across the tracks and around the company's equipment. When the horse doubles back and crosses the tracks again, Nick falls out of the saddle, entangling his left foot in the stirrup. Fortunately, as Nick hangs from the saddle, his basset hound, Al, demonstrating the heroic exploits and rescues of early cinema canine stars, races to Maxie/Jan and unties her. The commercial is reshot with Maxie/Jan as heroine and Al as hero.

In the first and third library scenes, Nick's library attire is a long-sleeve shirt, necktie, and coat; in the second library scene, Nick wears a long-sleeve sweater over a shirt and necktie. He wears eyeglasses in the first scene; he takes them off when Ophelia approaches him in the second scene; and he is without them in the third scene. Nick wears his glasses in only one other scene—in a restaurant while holding a menu. Ophelia is a brunette (full bang; shoulder length shag); she dresses colorfully and fashionably, complementing her outfits with large earrings and necklaces. She wears eyeglasses on a lanyard, but never puts them on in the second scene; she has them on momentarily in the third scene, taking them off as soon as she begins to speak. The possession of eyeglasses, whether or not they are worn, is a critical visual characteristic of male and female reel librarians.

Off Beat, a 1986 romantic comedy, follows the humorous struggles of Joe Gower (Judge Reinhold[26]), a young staff member at New York Public Library who spends his working hours roller skating about and around aisles, retrieving books in closed stack areas for patrons. The work is neither high profile nor especially rewarding but provides Joe with a livelihood and library patrons with access to the library's extensive collections.

Bicycling to the library one morning, Joe spots his close friend, police officer Abe Washington (Cleavant Derricks), walking with a man and stops to chat with them, asking if they are on a stakeout. Unfortunately for Abe, the police are in the midst of a drug arrest and his companion is not a policeman, but the target of the bust. After Abe's intense gesturing for him to leave, Joe pedals away, oblivious to the fact that he has just disrupted a police operation. Joe is totally unaware that this brief stop to chat with Abe will change dramatically his commonplace existence.

When Joe arrives at the library, his supervisor, Neil Pepper (John Turturro[27]), informs him that the promotion he wanted was given to another employee. To make the day even more dreary for Joe as he walks away from the Reading Room desk area, Neil loudly asks Mary Ellen Gruenwald (Amy Wright[28]), Joe's girlfriend, "Did you tell him?" She stands quietly, shaking her head, and whispers an almost audible answer, "No." Neil unhesitatingly adds, "By the way, Gower, Mary Ellen will be moving in with me this evening." Neil enjoys informing Joe of his two losses; his face emits a degree of smugness and self-gratification as he delivers this distressing news to Joe. Mary Ellen, now Joe's former girlfriend, is an attractive young brunette (half bang; chin length page). She is a very mild, shy, unassertive woman and conservative dresser; for this scene she wears a multicolored dress with a large white collar, and a single strand of beads. Even after receiving such depressing news, Joe manages to continue, without enthusiasm, his job of roller-skating and retrieving books.

As a consequence of the drug bust fiasco, Abe's precinct sergeant volunteers Abe to try out for the police department's modern dance performance in the city's annual civic event at Lincoln Center. Abe immediately scampers to the library, interrupts Joe's roller skating and demands that Joe take his place at the dance tryout; he maintains that Joe owes him because of the drug bust fiasco. Abe's advice is simple, "Just keep your mouth shut and fall down a lot. Couple hours you'll be out, I'll be off the hook." Abe assures Joe that no one will ever discover the switch. Unfortunately for Abe, the evening does not go as planned. Before tryouts start, the dance instructor excuses all officers who do not wish to participate, just the invitation that Joe and many officers were waiting to hear. As he walks off the stage with others—all very happy to get out, Rachel Wareham (Meg Tilly), an attractive young police officer, calls him "chicken shit." Joe is surprised by this affront to his masculinity. He turns around and whispers to himself, "On second thought, maybe I'll stick around," and begins the audition. For Joe, romance begins; for Abe, trouble starts.

Just as women reel librarians use employment at the library for comfort and security until the right individual appears, Joe uses the library for a similar purpose. He continues to work at the library, finally exhibiting the courage to quit his position

Off Beat (1986). Joe Gower (Judge Reinhold) and Mary Ellen Gruenwald (Amy Wright), Joe's mild-mannered on-again, off-again girlfriend. Note Gruenwald's large white collar.

only after his romance with Rachel blossoms. Mary Ellen reappears during Joe's relationship with Rachel, asking Joe on one occasion to go on a Sunday bike ride with her, but Joe is past Mary Ellen. She, however, is not past Joe. When she appears again, the timing and place could not be more disastrous for Joe. After an evening dance practice, Joe takes Rachel to his apartment to disclose his participation in Abe's misguided masquerade and to confess that he is not a member of the New York Police Department (NYPD). When they walk into the apartment, Mary Ellen is standing nude in the kitchen. Joe, bewildered and surprised, simply asks, "What are you doing here?" "I'm back, Joey, for good!" she responds, and Rachel copies back to Joe, "She's back, Joey, for good." Joe, still shocked, exclaims, "She's naked!" and Mary Ellen reaffirms, "I'm naked." Rachel reacts, "Yea, I couldn't help noticing that." Rachel then hurries out of the apartment with Joe in pursuit, pleading with her to come back. When he returns to the apartment without Rachel, Joe listens to Mary Ellen's explanation for this sudden visit. She reveals not only that Neil flunked his bar exam and is in a terrible mood but also that she misses having fun and sex with Joe. For Joe, however, Rachel is now paramount; Mary Ellen is no longer a viable partner. He attempts to describe his present state of mind to her, confiding that "three weeks ago if you'd have showed up naked in my apartment ... I would have felt just the opposite of what I do now.... I feel just a tad hostile, just a teensy bit contemptuous." Mary Ellen learns a valuable lesson in relationships; when you unceremoniously dump a partner, you risk losing that individual forever.

Neil, Joe's supervisor, is arrogant and patronizing, just the type of supervisor that subordinates love to hate. In two scenes with Neil in the closed stack area, Joe demonstrates his dislike for Neil. In the first scene, Joe is skating up and down the aisles with a revolver; he appears to be playing Cowboys and Indians, a popular children's outdoor game during the heyday of low-budget western films, but his antics are really an attempt to learn the techniques of handling a revolver. Joe is unaware that Neil is in the next aisle observing his bizarre behavior. At the end of a shelving range, Neil steps out of hiding and taps him on the shoulder, surprising Joe and causing him to fall. Neil, looking down on Joe, demands to know, "What the hell is going on up here?" Joe points the revolver at Neil, "Bang, bang, you're neutered, Neil!" Telling his supervisor the weapon is not loaded, Joe pulls the trigger, resulting in the click of an empty chamber. After a few verbal exchanges, Neil remarks, "We pay you to work, not to play," and retreats to the elevator. As the door closes, Joe pulls the trigger again; this time, however, the chamber is not empty. The clock near the elevator door is blasted off the wall, and the recoil knocks Joe off his skates and onto the floor.

The second scene opens with pneumatic tubes arriving at Joe's desk and falling out of an already filled basket onto the floor, returning book boxes falling off a crowded book lift conveyor belt, and Neil marching out of the elevator to confront Joe about the delay in service. Joe is on the telephone attempting to speak with Rachel, but she refuses to take his calls. "In the name of God, what is going on up here?" Neil asks. "Don't bother me now, Pepper," Joe replies and keeps talking on the telephone. "Let's get our ass in gear here, Gower!" Neil orders. After some heated verbal exchanges, Neil remarks that he "should report" Joe to a higher administrator. "Don't bother, I quit!" Joe interjects as he takes off his roller skates and slams them on the desk. Neil, responding as if he did not hear or understand, "You what?" Joe begins changing clothes and tells Neil "it's payday" and to get his paycheck ready because he is leaving. Minutes later in the Reading Room, a long line of angry patrons are demanding their books, and Neil, apologizing in his best public relations style, tries to pacify the group with an old, trite management stock line, "We'll have your orders down here in just a jiffy." Dressed in Abe's police uniform, Joe goes to the front of the line, receives his check, and dances down the center aisle of the Reading Room on his way out of the library, telling the library staff to be at Lincoln Center at 8 o'clock. He leaves the library in a very happy mood for a new life. Neil watches Joe's dancing exit with a disapproving frown, knowing that Joe created the present patron problem.

When Joe, still in Abe's uniform, stops at a bank to cash his paycheck, two holdup men appear and everyone in the bank is held hostage. As the two robbers negotiate a getaway deal with the NYPD, Joe manages to disarm the not-too-bright men. The police commissioner is ecstatic that one of his officers disrupted the robbery attempt and apprehended the two men, until, of course, he discovers that Joe is not a member of the NYPD.

Joe summarizes his own existence at the end of the film; he confesses his identity to Rachel at the beginning of the big dance number at Lincoln Center: "I'm just a twenty-eight-year-old guy that's never done anything with his life until today." For Joe Gower, "today" is the day he quit his library position and achieved momentary fame by foiling a bank robbery as he attempted to cash his paycheck.

Three other library employees interact with Joe on several occasions. Pud, a security officer, converses with Joe about regularity and bran in his diet. Norman, a young delivery man, loves only two things, "the Dewey Decimal System and demolition pyrotechnics," and is going to send books loaded with explosives to television networks to protest the cancellation of *Family Feud*. Alvin (Jack Fletcher[29]), an elderly librarian, works in the Reading Room with Mary Ellen and Neil. Alvin is a natty dresser, always in a suit, tie, and eyeglasses; he is the male stereotype. Alvin lives quietly and uneventfully, as disclosed in a conversation with Joe one morning as they enter the library. "Have a nice night, Joseph?" Joe replies, "No, you?" Alvin answers, "No, not particularly," and then Joe offers a concise commentary on their lackluster night and, by extension, their lives, "That's good."

Off Beat portrays librarians as inept individuals, both in and away from the library, as workers having problems with their supervisors, as supervisors with little compassion, and as individuals living rather mundane lives. Joe's disruption of the bank robbery attempt is more the result of happenstance than gallantry.

Shadows in the Storm (1988), a mystery thriller, stars Ned Beatty[30] as Thelonious Pitt, librarian at Begonia Research. Visual characteristics and occupational tasks identify Thelo as a librarian, and the film continues the cinematic trend of presenting male librarians in a leading role as inept. Thelo's wife, Elizabeth (Donna Mitchell), wakes him in the morning; at breakfast, he reads the poetry of John Donne while she talks at him. As he pulls into the boss' parking space at work, he fails to stop before running into and knocking over the reserved parking sign. At his desk in the library, the wannabe poet works diligently on composing verse; unfortunately, Thelo is also an on-the-job drinker, an addiction that other employees use to extract favors. One fellow employee demands that Thelo leave the library for 15 minutes so that he can engage in sexual intercourse with a female employee, informing Thelo, "You'll never be missed." As Thelo stands outside the library in the hallway, his boss, Bob Birkenstock (Joe Dorsey), strolls by and stops to chat. Thelo begins talking about downloading a file when his boss hears the rumblings and moans from the couple in the library. Thelo loses his job, and as he and Bob walk out of the building, Bob informs the librarian that he "sabotaged" himself and recommends that he take a vacation, using an old company vehicle. Elizabeth believes that Bob is sending her husband on a fishing trip, and when she asks, "Thelo, where can you fish in Death Valley?" he responds, "Fishing in Death Valley makes this country what it is, Elizabeth." Thelo does not tell her about losing his job or cleaning out his bank account. He drives north into redwood country and finds a cabin where he can relax, read Donne, and write poetry. Unfortunately, he overhears a man beating a woman (Mia Sara as Melanie) in a nearby cabin. Thelo begins to ask questions about the incident, initiating an odyssey of deception that he does not comprehend; his only touch with reality is his love for Melanie and her professed love for him. In the maze of deceit, Melanie appears to murder the man who beat her and Thelo assists Melanie by disposing of the body. Now, Thelo believes he is an accessory to murder. Melanie, however, is a partner in this deceptive façade to exploit Thelo's fears of wrongdoing and to fleece Thelo of his cash. Thelo believes the events are as they appear but displays enough common sense to send his money back home to Elizabeth, frustrating the plan of the swindlers.

Shadows in the Storm continues to manifest male reel librarians in most unflattering images. Thelo's actions and decisions at home, at work, and during his odyssey with Melanie fail to display the intellectual acumen expected of a librarian with a Ph.D. Melanie, a young twenty-something, becomes the master of deception, in part because of her plausible answers to his questions and in part because Thelo wants to believe her. Thelo—balding, bespectacled, pudgy, and "only 38"—as Melanie's primary love interest is too incredible for any filmgoer to accept.

Some interesting facts about Thelo's finances as a librarian are revealed during the film. In the cabin, he tells Melanie that he's "got a little money saved." As they drive away from the cabin, Thelo reveals a secret to her—he "put $100 a week in a savings account for twenty years." As filmgoers undoubtedly anticipated, Melanie immediately rejoins, "Well, where is it?" Back home, when Elizabeth realizes that Thelo is missing, she visits Bob, who informs her that Thelo was dismissed. She is visibly upset and responds emotionally, "How could you? After all these years. He's a damned good librarian. We've lived off my parents all these years because of the measly salary you paid him. He was loyal to you. He hated being poor, but he kept it all inside." In the cinematic tradition of reel librarians, Thelo's salary is marginal. How he managed to save $100 a week, with or without Elizabeth's knowledge, is not disclosed.

When Thelo finally goes to the police to confess his participation in the murder, he discovers there is nothing to substantiate his story about the murder. One officer remarks to Thelo, "I don't know where you've been all your life, you know, but I think you've been taken for a ride." Moments later, the officer adds that Thelo is "no murderer" but "ain't no genius, neither." As he leaves the police station, Thelo unwittingly steps out onto the street and into the path of an oncoming vehicle; he awakens in a hospital, bandaged from head to foot. Elizabeth enters the hospital room and informs Thelo that he was struck by a bookmobile. She then proclaims her love for her errant husband, explaining that "everybody deserves a taste of romance now and then."

Two actors appearing as librarians in brief supporting roles in films released during the last half of the 1980s, Victor Desy[31] in *Agnes of God* (1985) and William Duff-Griffin[32] in *The House on Carroll Street* (1988), resemble the stereotypical image; they are "only 38" individuals and dress conservatively. Desy and Duff-Griffin wear eyeglasses, and Duff-Griffin has thinning gray hair. In *Agnes of God*, Desy portrays a librarian who locates a building plan of a convent for Dr. Martha Livingston (Jane Fonda). The librarian finds the correct folder in the first drawer he opens. He remarks that the convent's layout, including underground passages, "has everything." The film is set in France, and the librarian and Martha speak in both French and English during their conversation. In *The House on Carroll Street*, Duff-Griffin appears as Wentworth, an FBI librarian (circa 1951). Wentworth operates an opaque projector while agent Mike Cochran (Jeff Daniels) scrutinizes the projected photographic images for Nazi war criminals, attempting to identify Nazis who are posing as Jewish immigrants and being aided by the United States government. The scene ends when Wentworth answers the telephone and informs Mike, "Your boss wants you."

Approximately twice as many women librarians as men librarians appeared in films during 1985–1989; all of the women project one or more visual characteristics or occupational tasks of the stereotypical image. In three films, *Defense of the Realm* (1985), *Lamb* (1986[33]), and *Baby Boom* (1987), the librarians[34] are uncredited and appear on-screen for less than 10 seconds in each film. In *Lamb* and *Baby Boom*, the librarians wear eyeglasses, and in *Lamb*, the librarian sports a bun hairstyle. In *Lamb*, a British production, the camera is located slightly behind and to the right of the librarian so that only her profile appears on-screen while the lead actor, Liam Neeson, is in full view. The minimization of the on-screen presence of this reel librarian is typical of British filmmakers; the authors first noted this visual de-emphasis of reel librarians in *The Good Companions*, a 1933 British film.

Actresses receiving credit for their supporting roles as librarians display various visual characteristics and occupational tasks; each actress unmistakably projects the stereotypical image. In *The Empty Beach* (1985), Deborah Kennedy[35] is a newspaper librarian who works in a confidential library where access is limited to authorized personnel. After reading through several newspapers on microfilm, private detective Cliff Hardy (Bryan Brown) wants to examine a file folder on an individual in a restricted area; he goes to a library door, opens it, and sticks his head into the room, requesting "S for Singer." The librarian, a brunette (Dutch-boy; bouffant), responds, "I can't hear you, I can't see you, along the right hand wall and you've got 20 seconds." Cliff and the librarian apparently know one another, judging from the tone and brevity of their conversation. In a 30-second library scene in *Slamdance* (1987), C. C. Drood (Tom Hulce) visits a library to locate information about a murder and is bent over a table reading newspapers when the librarian (Lin Shage[36]) calls, "Mr.

Drood. There's just the two." Drood goes to the information desk where the librarian lays the papers out so that he can read them. Although youthful and attractive, the librarian wears conservative colors—black blouse (plain neckline) and gray skirt. Rocky Parker[37] appears as an academic librarian in two very brief library scenes in *Happy Together* (1989). In the first scene, a bespectacled Parker wears a pink jumper over a white blouse and utters a "shush"; in her second scene, Parker, with eyeglasses again, is turning out lights on library tables.

Ironweed (1987[38]), a drama starring Meryl Streep as Helen Archer in the leading female role, contains one library scene. Helen is a destitute, often drunken, vagrant in 1938 Albany, New York, and on one occasion, she visits a public library to enjoy the library's warmth and comfortable furniture. After Helen falls asleep in a leather chair by the fireplace, the "only 38" librarian (Bethel Leslie[39]), a graying brunette (side finger waves; bun at nape), puts a magazine in her lap, which awakens Helen. The librarian informs Helen that she can stay in the library and read but cannot sleep in the building. Helen insists that she is just waiting for "the fire ... to die." After the librarian leaves, one of Helen's past friends recognizes her and begins a conversation. When the friend mentions that she saw Helen's brother in church, Helen reacts violently and loudly, proclaiming that "he and my mother, they stole all the money my father left me." The librarian rushes to the couple, utters several "shushes," and ushers Helen out the door, maintaining that she must leave because she is "making too much noise." The librarian demonstrates a degree of empathy toward Helen by giving her a magazine, thereby permitting Helen to remain in the warmth and comfort of the library. This seeming act of compassion is tempered because the librarian's primary concern appears to be enforcing library rules, as she quickly evicts Helen because of her verbal outburst.

A second film of 1987, *Harry and the Hendersons*, contains one of the most insensitive, degrading visual introductions to a librarian in twentieth century cinema. Shortly before the library scene, George Henderson (John Lithgow) and his father are in their sporting goods store talking, and during the conversation, they mention an extremely large stuffed bear which towers over them. As they continue to talk, the camera goes to the head of the stuffed bear for a close-up; the shot of the bear's head is then replaced with a head shot of a librarian (Peggy Platt[40]), a brunette with a full bang and exaggerated shag. The blatant humor of this transition undoubtedly elicited laughter from many filmgoers, as did the ensuing library scene. George enters the library, approaches the librarian, but is reluctant to speak very loudly to her, as he is embarrassed about asking for information on Bigfoot. She also speaks softly until clearly understanding that he is asking about Bigfoot; at this juncture, she points to her left and blurts out loudly so that everyone can hear, "Fantasy, Folklore, Myths and Legends. Basement Floor. Take the stairs." As George leaves the desk, she adds, in a voice just as loud as her previous directions, "Could also try children's books." The librarian is helpful but displays little enthusiasm. She wears an orange sweater over a blue turtleneck blouse and eyeglasses on the end of her nose. A second librarian (uncredited[41]) at the desk is assisting a patron; she appears briefly on-screen and also projects the stereotypical image—an "only 38" individual, eyeglasses, and conservative clothes—a dark skirt and gray coat.

In *Criminal Law* (1988) Irene Kessler[42] appears as Peggy, a librarian who is on-screen for less than ten seconds. Peggy is taking books out of a box and carrying them to a professor who is shelving them. One of the professor's former students arrives to discuss some legal items, and the professor asks the student to help him so that Peggy can return to her other library duties. Peggy, as she leaves the two, remarks that the professor is "a hard master." An "only 38" brunette (collar length; flip), Peggy dresses modestly—a pumpkin-color shift dress under an open long-sleeve black cardigan sweater.

Another actress appearing in a film released in 1988, *Running on Empty*, and conforming to the stereotypical image is Justine Johnston.[43] This drama focuses on the problems of a fugitive middle-aged couple, Arthur (Judd Hirsh) and Annie (Christine Lahti) Pope, and their oldest son, a teenager who needs to break away from his parents and younger brother in order to pursue his own life. Two decades earlier, Arthur and Annie engaged in anti-war protests and bombed a military research laboratory at the University of Massachusetts. Since then, they have moved frequently to evade the grasp of federal law enforcement officials who are pursuing them. At one city in which they stop, Arthur goes to the library to glance at obituaries in the local newspapers. He conceals his primary reason for using the library, informing the librarian that he is looking for information on "the MacArthur feud with Truman." The librarian doubts the local newspaper covered the story and suggests that Arthur use the national newspapers. Arthur, however, maintains that he is researching local reaction to the incident, which prompts the librarian to remark, "we just put our back issues on microfilm." She finds the roll of microfilm in a cabinet behind the desk, points to the microfilm readers and says, "Sit right over there." An "only 38" brunette (bouffant; collar length flip), the librarian dresses modestly. She displays a very pleasant and friendly personality while providing quality reference service. It is a spartan library set, as there are no visible shelving ranges, tables and chairs, or reading area. The librarian stands behind a counter-height desk, and located several feet in front of it are two steel office desks covered with books and file trays. When Arthur uses the microfilm reader, the camera focuses on the screen of the reader, thereby preventing a glimpse of the interior of the library. The set is not easily recognizable as a library until Arthur asks for information.

In *How I Got into College* (1989), a high school comedy, Marlene Warfield[44] appears briefly as a stereotypical librarian—"only 38" and eyeglasses—at Roosevelt High School in Detroit. A recruiter from Ramsey College visits the school to speak with some athletes; she also spots a young female student studying in the library and approaches the librarian to ask about the girl. The camera is behind the librarian as the recruiter approaches the library desk, but soon changes to a front shot of the librarian. The librarian is helpful, finally suggesting that the recruiter speak directly with the student. The librarian holds her eyeglasses while conversing with the college recruiter, putting them on when the recruiter goes to talk to the student. At this time, a student walks through the library with music blasting from his large boom box. The librarian makes no effort to rebuff the student, as other students in the library yell at him to turn it off. For high school students to accept the responsibility of censuring one another for misconduct in the library is indicative that the librarian has developed a good rapport with the students. Warfield, a Black American, sports a bouffant hairstyle (front and sides combed back) and wears, in contrast to dark conservative clothes expected of librarians, a bright yellow blouse with horizontal front pleats.

Laurel Lyle[45] projects the stereotypical image in *Old Gringo* (1989). Within the first ten minutes, Harriet Winslow (Jane Fonda) visits a library in Washington, D.C., to obtain some books to assist her in learning Spanish. The librarian greets Harriet in a friendly and sociable manner, asking about her classes and her mother. When Harriet asks for books on the Spanish language, the librarian responds, "Spanish? Well, we must have something. Let me see." As the librarian walks away to locate some books, she mutters, "Spanish. How interesting." The librarian locates some materials and returns shortly. A brunette (multi-pincurl bang; bun at nape), the librarian wears eyeglasses and dresses in period (circa 1913) clothes.

Two additional films released in 1989, *UHF* and *Chances Are*, contain library scenes that are designed for comedy and laughter. *UHF* features a brief 40-second sketch with Conan the Librarian (Roger Callard[46]), a cute spoof of Conan the Barbarian. A library patron asks Conan about the location of books, and Conan lifts him about three feet off the floor, intimidating the patron with this question: "Don't you know the Dewey Decimal System?" At the "Return Books Here" desk, a young boy apologizes for returning his books late: "I'm sorry. These books are a little overdue." Conan snarls, lifts his enormous sword over his head and swipes it down toward the youngster. Although filmgoers undoubtedly found this brief sketch entertaining, many of them, providing they had the misfortune of encountering the ire of an overbearing librarian, may have considered Conan the Librarian an accurate portrayal.

In *Chances Are*, Kathleen Freeman[47] provides some entertaining moments as academic librarian Mrs. Handy. The scene opens with Alex Finch (Robert Downey, Jr.[48]) pushing and riding a booktruck to the library's main desk, where Mrs. Handy is delivering a stern lecture on overdue books to law student Miranda Jeffries (Mary Stuart Masterson), commenting, "So you just assumed that nobody at Yale University or Yale Law School had any interest in checking out these six books in the last three months." When informed that the overdue fine is $87.25, Miranda responds, "Can I put that on a credit card?" Handy informs the young student that the library "isn't a boutique. Cash only or we'll have to hold up your grades." Alex, standing off to the side listening to the discussion, rushes to Handy, whispering, "The Rare Books Room. The Shakespeare folios." When Handy quizzes him about the folios, he states, "They're fooling with the folios." Handy becomes agitated upon hearing this troubling news, and Alex further incites her to action by commenting, "and they're fiddling too. Go ... I'll take over here." Handy hastily hustles off to save the folios, with Miranda asking Alex, "Is she always that awful?" Alex responds, "Mom? No." After a few keyboard strokes on the computer, he informs Miranda that the "books were never legally checked out"; consequently, there is no overdue fine. Alex announces, "You beat the system." After exchanging several embarrassing verbal niceties with Alex, Miranda leaves, but returns in a few seconds, stating, "That wasn't really your mother, right?"

Handy, an "only 38" brunette (full bang; bouffant curls), wears a white blouse with a notched shawl collar and V-neckline under a long lab jacket. As she rushes off to save the folios, moviegoers see that she is wearing white pedal pushers and white sneakers. Handy believes in rules, as evidenced by her insistence that Miranda owes $87.25, and in the safety of the library materials, as evidenced by her quick exit from the main desk to stop the presumed "fooling" and "fiddling" of the Shakespeare folios in the Rare Books Room. Handy and Miranda demonstrate the generational gap between librarians and library patrons, an age differential that promotes the "only 38" visual characteristic. Handy and Alex demonstrate the generational gap between older librarians and younger librarians and their approach to public service. When Alex assumes the responsibility of the main desk after Handy rushes off, he displays an understanding of Miranda's overdue fines and resolves the problem in a matter of seconds. In this instance, the younger librarian achieves a meaningful dialogue with a patron because he can, as a student, empathize with Miranda and, perhaps most importantly, he realizes that he can bypass the rules at will. Handy, however, is the stereotype, and, as such, she is the unheralded enforcer of library regulations and rules.

Two British films of the late 1980s, *Wetherby* (1985) and *Prick Up Your Ears* (1987), received numerous nominations and won several awards. Vanessa Redgrave's performance as Jean Travers dominates *Wetherby*, and in a supporting role for which she received a British Academy of Film and Television Arts Award nomination, Judi Dench[49] portrays Jean's best friend, Marcia Pilborough, a librarian. The focal point of the drama is the suicide of a young man, John Morgan (Tim McInnerny), in Jean's home and the subsequent reaction of Jean and her friends to the incident and their attempts to understand the young man's motivation. The scenes are presented non-linearly, and various flashback scenes, including a series of Jean's youthful romance with a young serviceman, further enhance this lack of chronological order. The only library scene occurs prior to the suicide, but after the suicide scene in the film. John enters the library, walks through long lines of card catalog cabinets, and finds an organizational chart of the library posted on a wall; the chart identifies Marcia as a deputy librarian. He then visually scans the arrangement of desks in the area, observing Marcia at her desk. John goes to her desk, stating that he has "a list of books" he wants to borrow. When Marcia informs him that the library does not lend books, John remarks, "It's the British Library, Lending Division." Marcia responds that they lend books only "under special circumstances." John has a letter from his professor, but Marcia retorts the letter "won't be nearly special enough." He wonders if he can look at the books, and Marcia acknowledges that is permissible, providing he is a registered user, which requires authorization. He implies that he will obtain authorization and return later.

This scene occurs at Marcia's office desk, and she continues to work at her desktop computer as she talks, glancing up occasionally to look at him. She does not indicate even a slight interest in his quest for books; in addition, her responses are delivered sternly and in rote memory fashion, explaining Marcia's ability to pay more attention to her computer work than to John. Marcia is an "only 38" blonde (full bang; Sassoon cut) librarian and dresses colorfully and fashionably—a pink long sleeve cowlneck blouse under a pink and gray plaid three-quarter sleeve dress jacket. Marcia's stereotypical reel librarian image is reinforced by occupational clues. She recites the restrictions on lending and use in a cavalier delivery and offers neither suggestions nor avenues for John to pursue to obtain the books he requires. Marcia responds only to John's inquiries; the continuance of the conversation depends entirely upon John. As soon as Marcia responds, she quietly returns to working at her computer, completely ignoring John while he stands near her desk and develops another question. Assisting walk-in patrons is not a high priority at the Lending Division.

Within the first five minutes of the film, Marcia, while dining with Jean and friends, describes "a new girl at work at the library" as "vacant." She observes that the girl attracts men and is pliable—"she doesn't really have a personality, she just has a way of suggesting to them that she'll be whatever they want her to be." The other diners suggest that this is "youth," an attribute that should not be severely criticized. Although the conversation reveals that the young girl has done nothing to elicit criticism, other than the offense of being young, Marcia remarks that the girl simply "exists," eventually will "get married, have children, get a mortgage." The girl's lack of ambition, motivation, and spirit is incomprehensible to Marcia, who views the girl's banal existence more a rebuff of evolution than a result of youth. Marcia's observation is very insightful, perhaps pertinent not only to this single young girl but also to all young female reel librarians. Directors, writers, and actors frequently portray young librarians as waiting for Mr. Right to rescue them from the library—their self-imposed cocoon of tedium and apathy.

Prick Up Your Ears[50] (1987) stars Gary Oldham as playwright Joe Orton and Alfred Molina as Kenneth Halliwell. Joe and Kenneth go to the Islington Public Library for some books, and as soon as they check out their selections, they leave. Librarians Miss Battersby (Selina Cadell[51]), a blonde (angel wing bang; short layered cut), and Mr. Cunliffe (Charles McKeown[52]), however, discreetly follow the pair out of the library and observe the two as they walk away. Cunliffe remarks to Battersby that she failed to tell him that one of the men (Halliwell) was a homosexual. Cunliffe, who dislikes the two men, comments, "This calls for a little detective work," as he and Battersby go back into the library.

The two librarians work diligently to discover that some of the books returned by either Joe or Kenneth have phrases and statements typed on the book jackets; both librarians consider the phrases and statements to be obscene. Cunliffe then checks the street on which Joe and Kenneth live and finds near their address an old dilapidated automobile. He ascertains that the automobile is licensed to them. Battersby types a letter, dictated by Cunliffe, to Joe and Kenneth, informing them they must remove the car or the authorities will be notified. Incensed upon receiving the letter, they promptly respond. When Cunliffe receives their letter, he checks the type on the letter against the type on the book jackets. The two librarians are very smug when they realize that they have incontrovertible evidence that Joe and Kenneth are the culprits defacing library books. In the next scene, Joe and Kenneth are in court, and for defacing *Clouds of Witness* by Dorothy L. Sayers by typing offensive passages on the book jacket, each receives a six-month prison term.

In the last year of the decade, Rene Russo[53] appears as librarian Lynn Wells[54] in a baseball comedy, *Major League* (1989). Russo, a brunette (long curly hair; loose braid in back), imbues her character with spunk, a spirit similar to that demonstrated by Carole Lombard more than a half century earlier in *No Man of Her Own* (1932). Although she appears in a minimal number of scenes, Lynn is one of the more captivating reel librarians of the 1980s. She demonstrates the ability to match wit and words with Jake Taylor (Tom Berenger), a previous boyfriend who wants to revive their romantic passion of the past. The banter between the two is entertaining but underlying their exchange of words is the pain suffered by Lynn during their stint together. Even though Lynn is engaged to an attorney and insists she is no longer interested in Jake, every filmgoer recognizes the scenario—the more she objects to Jake, the more she loves him, regardless of past disappointments.

Jake, a down-and-out, over-the-hill baseball catcher with bad knees, gets one more chance to play in the major leagues with the Cleveland Indians. The owner of the Indians, however, is intent upon fielding a losing team so that she can move the team to Miami, a more promising, lucrative location. Jake is just one member of an assemblage of baseball's old has-beens and young wannabes, a team of decidedly marginal talent—just the right combination to ensure a losing season for the owner. Jake left major league baseball and Lynn three years earlier, retreating to Mexico and enduring a situation of which he "wasn't exactly proud." Jake now considers the past to be the past and is intent upon rekindling the heart of Lynn. Tom (Richard Pickren), her fiancé, will provide Lynn with a secure future and a stable relationship, two basic elements that were absent during her relationship with Jake.

Upon his return to Cleveland, Jake first sees Lynn, with Tom, in a restaurant and manages to obtain her telephone number despite her reluctance. When he attempts to call her later, however, he discovers that the telephone number belongs to a sheet metal company; Lynn purposely gave him an incorrect number. Jake then visits the library and follows Lynn throughout the building on the way to her office, attempting to convince her that he has changed. "Still sore I never read *Moby Dick?*" he asks as they walk up and down the book aisles. When Jake quizzes Lynn about the attraction of her fiancé, she replies that "he's stable, intelligent, and I never found him in bed with a stewardess." Jake refuses to give up, even when Lynn announces, "Tom and I are getting married in the fall." As they trek through the library, Jake jogs her memory about their three nights in Vera Cruz, but Lynn suggests he explain "the nights you had in Detroit with Miss Fuel Injection." Jake's answer typifies the kind of beau he was when they were together: "She bet me 50 bucks that she had a better body than you and I had to defend your honor." The response upsets Lynn, and she screams, "Oh, what a bunch of bullshit! I have a much better body than she does!" They quiet down, suddenly aware that they are screaming, and as they look around, everybody in the library is now rising from their chairs to watch and listen to them. Jake acknowledges the truth of Lynn's statement by announcing to their audience, "She's right!" Lynn continues walking, with Jake tagging along and pleading, "Don't make me do time for things that happened years ago." Lynn stops in front of an office door and informs him that he will "always be the little boy who wouldn't grow up." She goes into the office and closes the door, leaving Jake in the hallway.

Lynn's negativity in the library toward rekindling their relationship, however, fails to deter the persistent Jake. After this rebuff, he follows Lynn as she leaves the library,

Major League (1989). Librarian Lynn Wells (Rene Russo, in glasses) listens while Jake Taylor (Tom Berenger), an over-the-hill baseball player, attempts to convince her that he is a changed man.

and mistakenly believing that Lynn is at her apartment, Jake dashes into the apartment, only to discover she is visiting Tom, who politely welcomes Jake to have a drink with his invited guests, two other couples. The discussion quickly turns to baseball. When asked about the large salaries of baseball players, Jake states the salary depends upon the ability of the player. They ask Jake about his salary, and he admits that he makes the "league minimum." Lynn immediately and quite unexpectedly comes to his aid, volunteering that "he was one of the best in baseball before he had problems with his knees." When asked what he will do in retirement, Jake remarks he always wanted to live in Hawaii and "have a couple of kids who grow up to be Olympic champions." The group laughs, and when asked "What event?" Jake responds unhesitatingly, "Swimming. The two hundred meter individual medley. I figure it ought to be real big by then." This, of course, intrigues them, prompting them to ask about the girl he might choose. Jake states he selected one but that he "wasn't smart enough to hold onto her." The conversation turns to Lynn when one member of the group remembers that Lynn was an athlete. When asked about the event in which she competed, Lynn responds, "Two hundred meter individual medley." The group becomes quiet, and Jake blurts out, "Alternate on the '80 Olympic Team." Silence prevails again, as everyone is aware of the uneasy situation among Tom, Jake, and Lynn. When the discussion is obviously dead, Jake stands and remarks, "Well, I'd better be going." Lynn maintains her poise during this informal cocktail occasion, but her quick defense of Jake's "league minimum" salary reveals that her engagement to Tom may be in jeopardy.

Lynn attends a baseball game, and after the game, Jake spots her in the stands. Still in his baseball uniform and driving the Indians' baseball cap bullpen car, he follows her. This time it is her apartment, and the excitement between the two is obvious as they talk. "What's all this?" Jake inquires, as he looks around her apartment, which is in disarray. "I'm moving in with Tom." "Uptown?" he retorts. Lynn just wants a normal life, while he likes, as Lynn maintains, "hanging with the boys, living in hotels, having girls send you their underwear in the mail." To illustrate her point, she asks if he remembers when he failed to show up for his surprise birthday party. She replays her embarrassment: "The doorbell rang once, and we all got real quiet and hid behind the furniture. It was a guy to serve you with a paternity suit." Jake pleads his case, but Lynn insists, "I can't afford to believe you anymore." The "last hurrah" is upon them, and as Jake begins to mope out of the apartment, Lynn asks, "Did you ever read *Moby Dick?*" "Cover to cover, babe," he responds walking back to her. In only a few seconds they are in a passionate embrace, with Jake asking about the wedding, and Lynn asking, "Who saved Ishmael at the inn?" Jake had the right answer, as he had been reading the Classic Comics edition of *Moby Dick* on roadtrips. Jake asks if he is invited to the wedding at the same time he remarks that the zipper on her skirt is stuck. Lynn replies, "Use your imagination," and Jake lifts his foot, catches her skirt with his spikes, and rips the skirt off her. As he pulls her into the bedroom, she insists, "You know, this doesn't change anything, we were always good at this." Lynn appears to have spoken the truth. Jake awakens in the morning to find Lynn gone. When Jake returns after a roadtrip, he finds the apartment empty; Lynn moved out. At the deciding game of the season, Jake gets the winning hit in the bottom of the 9th inning. As the celebration begins, he sees Lynn in the stands; she holds up her left hand, revealing the absence of a wedding ring. Jake rushes to her, carrying her out of the stands and onto the field as the team and fans continue their celebration.

Lynn continues the thread of reel librarians who either attract athletes or are attracted to athletes—Betty Grant in *The Spirit of Youth* (1926), Susan Merrill in *Gentlemen Are Born* (1934), Connie Lane in *Good News* (1947), Jenny Cavalleri in *Love Story* (1970), and Betsy McGuire in *Movie Movie* (1978). Unfortunately, she also continues the practice of many previous reel librarians of selecting a less than top-notch partner; although the library provides stability and security, reel librarians appear to be more reckless in their personal lives, often selecting mates who cannot provide these amenities. Such luxuries are evidently not essential to a librarian in love.

Lynn is very comfortable in her occupation; during her encounter with Jake in the library, she emphasizes her competency by declaring that "books are my life now ... in two years I put together one of the best special collection departments in the country." Five other librarians are on-screen for only seconds, four of whom project the stereotypical image. The one visual characteristic that Lynn displays prominently, and which solidifies her image as a librarian, is large tortoise-shell plastic frame eyeglasses; this is the only scene in which Lynn wears glasses, indicating the importance of eyeglasses to project the image when clothes, age, and hairstyle do not.

As the twentieth century progressed, eyeglasses became one of the most important prop items for reel librarians. An actor does not have to wear them throughout the film; in library scenes, an actor's possession of glasses, whether worn or held, verified the screen character's status as a librarian. This is evident in *Major League* (1989), as demonstrated by Russo's character. In director Hal Hartley's comedy drama *Trust* (1990), there is one verbal exchange between the film's two principal characters that illustrates the relationship between eyeglasses and librarians. Maria Coughlin (Adrienne Shelly), a pregnant high school dropout, accepts a helping hand from Matthew Slaughter (Martin Donovan), a high school graduate who cannot keep a job. The two develop a friendship, and on one occasion, Matthew notices a problem with Maria's vision. Maria admits that she is nearsighted; Matthew asks the obvious question, "Why don't you wear your glasses?" Maria dislikes wearing them, as they make her "look stupid." Matthew, puzzled by the response, inquires about its meaning. "You know," Maria begins, "brainy, like a librarian." Matthew's retort is "I like librarians." Maria then puts on her plastic tortoise-shell frame glasses. As Judith Chase Churchill articulated in 1946,[55] more than four decades earlier, brainy women and librarians are the least likely to obtain husbands. Matthew's fondness for librarians, however, removes the basis for Maria's objection to glasses.

One of the last motion pictures of the 1980s with male librarians, *Transylvania Twist* (1989), is a lighthearted comedy about vampires. The film, a horror spoof, is pure verbal and visual comedy, belonging to and resembling the type of comedy showcased in *Airplane!* and the many films that attempted to emulate its success. The story begins in Arkham, Massachusetts, as librarian Dexter Ward (Steve Altman[56]) attends the funeral of his Uncle Ephram (Jay Robinson[57]), head librarian of the Arkham Public Library. As Dexter views the body, his uncle rises up from the casket and grabs his nephew's tie, insisting that Dexter must find *The Book of Ulthar*. Ephram climbs out of the casket, berating the physician who pronounced him dead and the mortician who failed to embalm him. The next scene is the film's only library scene. As Ephram and his nephew walk through the nonpublic book stack area, Ephram explains the importance of *The Book of Ulthar* and urges Dexter to locate Lord Byron Orlock (Robert Vaughn) and recover the book that he checked out two decades ago. As they walk through the book stacks, Ephram and Dexter engage in the following type of verbal banter that permeates the film:

> EPHRAM: Ulthar was a sorcerer at a time before history when all the world was in darkness and chaos prevailed.
>
> DEXTER: Oh yeah, I remember, the Reagan administration.

The film's treatment of Ephram and Dexter as librarians is inconsequential, as all characters are subjugated to the film's overall purpose of comedy. Ephram, however, decidedly approximates the stereotypical image—elderly, receding hairline, and dressed in dark slacks, red sportscoat, white shirt, and neckwear that resembles an ascot scarf. Dexter wears stonewashed jeans and a blue long-sleeve T-shirt. Both librarians wear white athletic shoes.

Dexter's pilgrimage to Transylvania is successful; *The Book of Ulthar* is recovered. The filmmakers attempt to be cute with this film, from its opening scene through its closing credits, as evidenced by the last two lines of the credits:

> "The Book of Ulthar"
> Available soon in paperback

The 1990s

The first film of the 1990s with a librarian in a leading role to become modestly successful at the box office is an amusing comedy, *Joe Versus the Volcano* (1990). Tom Hanks[58] stars as Joe Banks, a hypochondriacal advertising librarian for a medical supply company, who suffers from a physician-diagnosed "brain cloud" and has six months to live. Tom quits his terrible $300-a-week job and accepts a "live like a king, die like a man" offer to leap into an active volcano on a tropical island. The film includes two references to Joe as a librarian. When Joe's supervisor at American Panascope—the "Home of the Rectal Probe," with "712,766" gratified customers and still counting—comments that he put Joe "in charge of the entire advertising library," Joe responds, "You mean this room?" The room is sparse. It contains Joe's desk, a four-drawer metal file cabinet, and metal shelving—free standing along the walls—that are partially filled with cardboard storage boxes. The second reference occurs later in the film during Joe's journey to the tropical island. Angelica Graynamore (Meg Ryan) asks about his occupation, and Joe answers that he "was an advertising librarian for a medical supply company." Angelica bounces back with, "Oh, I have no response to that." Many discerning filmgoers, in all probability, failed to notice or react to this undoubtedly intended-for-humor statement. This utterance reveals the lack of esteem accorded to librarians by many films during the twentieth century. "Oh, I have no response to that," is one of the most understated and subtle put-downs of the occupation in film.

Supporting actresses appearing as reel librarians during 1990–94 relied to a great degree on the visual characteristics of the stereotypical image. Dortha Duckworth[59] in the first library scene of *Stanley & Iris* (1990), a romantic drama about illiteracy, resembles the reel librarians of the 1930s; she is an "only 38" individual with gray hair set in a bun at her crown. She wears a dark skirt and white Bishop sleeve blouse with an enormously large, black bow collar. In the second library scene, two "shushes" are heard shortly before Duckworth enters the scene to reprimand Stanley Everett Cox (Robert De Niro) for reading aloud in the library. Demanding silence, she informs Stanley that "this is a library." In a subdued tone, he happily replies, "I know it's a library, lady. It's my library!" The visual characteristics and occupational tasks of Duckworth's character vividly reaffirm that the image developed in the 1930s is just as viable for films of the 1990s as it was for the films produced six decades earlier.

Mary MacLeod[60] appears as a librarian in *Hear My Song* (1991), a romantic comedy starring Ned Beatty as Irish tenor Josef Locke. When a concert is hurriedly scheduled for Locke, Micky O'Neill (Adrian Dunbar) and girlfriend Nancy Doyle (Tara Fitzgerald) go to a library to obtain musical compositions for the evening's performance. The librarian informs the couple that they are "in luck" as the arrangements "are registered." However, they are to complete the requisite forms and "can collect these [arrangements] in, oh, ten days." As Micky and Nancy must procure the compositions within the hour, they must convince the librarian to retrieve them immediately. Nancy begins their strategy, "We were born in peace time." Micky chips in with, "We haven't been where you've been." Then Nancy adds, "We haven't seen what you've seen." The librarian is very impressed with this reasoning and is sympathetic to their immediate need for the scores. In a matter of minutes, Micky and Nancy are rushing down the library's main aisle with the compositions. MacLeod, a redhead (center part, rolled sides; French twist in back), dresses conservatively and holds eyeglasses, but never wears them.

Another "only 38" librarian, Susan Philpot,[61] appears briefly in *Straight Talk* (1992), a Dolly Parton comedy. Parton's character, Shirlee Kenyon, arrives in Chicago and goes job hunting. Seeing an advertisement for a library position, she visits the library. Shirlee's high heels create a great deal of noise as she walks across the library's marble floor, eliciting a "shush" from a male patron. Shirlee is dressed in a short skirt, attracting the attention of every male patron in the library. When she arrives at the main desk, Shirlee inquires about the job; the librarian, pausing between each word and slightly moving her head in a negative motion, replies, "I ... don't ... think ... so." Philpot, a brunette (full bang; layered cut), wears eyeglasses.

Other "only 38" women librarians appear in *Lorenzo's Oil* (1992), *Rudy* (1993), *City Slickers II: The Legend of Curly's Gold* (1994), *Clean, Shaven* (1994), *With Honors* (1994), and *Monkey Trouble* (1994).

Although several librarians are visible in the library scenes of *Lorenzo's Oil*, only one (Mary Pat Gleason[62]) assists Augusto and Michaela Odone (Nick Nolte and Susan Sarandon) in their untiring research to save their young son who suffers from ALD (adrenoleukodystrophy), a fatal disease of the nerves that affects young boys. Gleason's character is helpful; when Augusto becomes agitated about getting information, she manages to calm him so that she can determine exactly what type of information he needs. When she returns with the materials, Augusto apologizes for creating a noisy scene. The librarian sympathizes with his anxieties, patting him on the shoulder and remarking, "Well, you're Italian." In a succeeding scene, she brings him some materials and he thanks her in Italian and she responds back in Italian. She is friendly and personable. Gleason is a portly brunette (full bang; naturally curly hair pulled into ponytail at crown) who wears colorful, fashionable clothing. The other reel librarians appear only briefly on-screen, primarily in the background and out of focus; they are engaged in various occupational tasks behind the desk. Two of these librarians are "only 38" women wearing eyeglasses.

Rudy is an inspirational story about Rudy (Sean Astin), a wannabe Notre Dame football player who is not tall enough, heavy enough, or strong enough to fulfill that dream. In addition, he is not smart enough to get into Notre Dame. Rudy overcomes his intellectual deficiencies, gets admitted, and gets to dress and play in the last game of his senior year. Rudy spends a great deal of time in the library, often with his tutor and often sleeping. Marie Anspaugh[63] portrays an academic librarian in one scene. When turning off the lights in the library, she approaches Rudy, who is sleeping in a comfortable chair, shakes him, and announces that it is "12 o'clock." Rudy awakens, responding "Thanks, Miss McKenzie." "You're welcome," she replies. Judging from the exchange between the two, this wake-up procedure appears to be a regular occurrence. McKenzie, an "only 38" individual, dresses modestly and sports a bun hairstyle.

June Kelly,[64] a strawberry blonde (full bang; side and top pulled into ponytail at crown; back hangs loose), appears as a librarian in *Clean, Shaven*, a film focusing on the ordeals of a schizophrenic young man named Peter Winter (Peter Greene). When released from institutional care, Peter begins a search for his daughter who was given up for adoption during his institutionalization. Peter visits a library several times, always looking at pictures of young children in an attempt to find a picture that matches a photograph of his daughter. In Kelly's first scene as librarian, she informs Peter that it is closing time. When she arrives for work the next day, Peter is waiting in his car for the library to open. In a later scene, a police officer attempting to locate Peter interviews the librarian about him. She informs the officer that she was afraid of him, that he did not do anything to harm her, but that "he made me think that he was going to do something bad to me." She asks the officer, "So, are you going to protect us? Are you going to be here?" He assures her that he will be around "for quite a while." She is very concerned about the possible threat that Peter may pose and wants assurance from the officer that they will be safe. Kelly's portrayal of a librarian in fear, whether imagined or real, mirrors a real problem. Many working librarians who are beset by unruly patrons have felt the very apprehension that this librarian displays because of Peter's presence.

In *City Slickers II: The Legend of Curly's Gold*, Helen Siff[65] portrays an "only 38" stereotypical image by pushing a booktruck and by uttering a "shush" at Mitch Robbins (Billy Crystal) and Phil Berquist (Daniel Stern), who are talking loudly. A brunette (full bang; short layered cut) with eyeglasses on a lanyard, Siff appears on-screen for only a few seconds.

Patricia B. Butcher[66] portrays an academic librarian in the comedy drama *With Honors*. Harvard student Monty Kessler (Brendan Fraser) loses his honors thesis which is found by a bum, Simon Wilder (Joe Pesci), who lives in the basement of Widener Library. There are several library scenes in the film, and on one occasion, Simon accompanies Monty into the library where they sit across from one another at a table. A librarian (Butcher), in a decidedly disapproving manner with respect to Simon's presence in the library, approaches Simon, "Sir, sir, you can't stay here." Monty speaks up immediately, "It's okay, he's with me. He's, uh, part of my research project." The librarian responds, "Oh, I beg your pardon." She retreats, leaving the two at the table. This scene with the librarian is about 20 seconds in length, and Butcher adequately projects the stereotypical image. An "only 38" blonde (short Hamill cut), Butcher wears reading glasses and dresses conservatively—gray suit, white blouse, ruffled collar and cuffs. In addition, she holds a book in her left hand during her conversation with Simon and Monty.

In the comedy *Monkey Trouble*, Julie Payne[67] appears as a public librarian. A young elementary school student, Eva Boylan (Thora Birch), is having a difficult time at home until she befriends a monkey (capuchin) in a park. The monkey is running away from its owner, Shorty Kohn (Harvey Keitel), a Gypsy who not only mistreats but also uses the monkey, appropriately named Fingers, to steal from park visitors. Eva goes to a public library with the monkey, whom she has named Dodger, and tells the librarian, "My teacher sent me. I need all the books you have on monkeys." The librarian responds appropriately, "All monkeys or a specific species?" Eva, a little unsure about Dodger, responds, "I think I need a cappuccino." The librarian sees only humor in Eva's statement, "Oh, sweetheart, I need one too." She states that the library does not "have a cappuccino machine," and as Eva bends down and takes Dodger out of her backpack, the librarian continues, "Do children drink that stuff?" The librarian yawns but suddenly jumps back and out of her chair when she sees Dodger. "This specific species," Eva maintains, continuing, "The names sounds like cappuccino." The librarian resumes her position at the desk and begins pounding away on a computer keyboard, finally bringing up a computer screen with four types of monkeys and stating, "Capuchin—that sounds like cappuccino, no doubt about it, huh?" Eva asks where the books are, but the librarian volunteers to get them and make copies "for both of you so you won't even have to come back." This scene, although Eva obtains the information she is seeking, is designed for laughs. The librarian, reading when Eva enters the library, approaches Eva's request for information with competency. She quickly, however, adds humor to the situation with her remark about cappuccino and then yawning at the desk. The presence of Dodger not only creates fear and apprehension in the librarian's demeanor but also accelerates the pace of her reference service. The librarian only feels the urgency to hustle when Dodger appears. Payne, a brunette (collar length layered cut), wears reading glasses on a lanyard and a modest pink print dress under a white blazer.

Supporting actresses who do not adhere to the stereotypical image appear as librarians in *Forever Young* (1992), *Public Access* (1993), and *I Love Trouble* (1994).

Amanda Foreman[68] is librarian Debbie in *Forever Young*, a romantic adventure film starring Mel Gibson as Capt. Daniel McCormick. In 1939, Daniel volunteers for a cryogenic experiment and the military misplaces the capsule in which he is sealed. In 1992, two youngsters playing in a warehouse accidentally open the capsule that houses Daniel. In an attempt to contact the people with whom he was working in 1939, Daniel goes to the public library where he is assisted by Debbie, a young, attractive brunette (shoulder length page). He is trying to locate the man who was in charge of the project, and Debbie informs Daniel that he is "gonna want to write the National Personnel Record Center.... They got a form, takes like six weeks." Appalled by the length of time, he grasps her hand, stating, "This is urgent. I need to find this man today. It's a matter of life and death for me. Please." She is suspect about Daniel holding her hand but believes that he is interested in her. She agrees to help, remarking, "1939? That'd make him pretty damn old, huh?" Debbie then states that she has a friend working for a locator service who may be able to find something in a couple of days; Daniel finds this acceptable. Debbie now appears to be interested in Daniel, since he made the first overture—holding her hand. She writes the library's telephone number on a note, telling him to call tomorrow after 12 o'clock, and "if Susan answers, ask for me, Debbie." She also writes her home telephone number on the note, "Just in case." Debbie's demeanor indicates that she is interested in Daniel and would not be reluctant to go out with him. Reel librarians, since silent films, often meet young male admirers at the library. Daniel, however, is interested only in locating the project director; he telephones Debbie the next day but she has not received any information for him. "Couldn't you rush it?" he quips, adding that he will telephone again.

In a most unusual thriller, *Public Access*, Dina Brooks[69] is cast as Rachel, the librarian in Brewster, a quiet, peaceful, and, apparently, happy small community until Whiley Pritcher (Ron Marquette) walks into town. Ostensibly a wanderer with a traveling bag in each hand, he rents a room by the week and purchases four one-hour programs at a local cable television company for a talk-TV program, *Our Town*. Whiley visits the public library, gleaning information—historical and current—on Brewster, requisite knowledge so that he can speak with an authoritative voice about Brewster and its townspeople. Rachel points out the location of the microfilm readers for Whiley, and as he works, she can be seen pushing a booktruck and reading a paperback at the circulation desk. At closing time, she suggests he leave the materials on the desk and walks him to the door. Rachel is talkative and inquisitive about the purpose of his research; he remarks that he has a hobby and she should "watch Sunday, channel 8 at 7." As he turns to leave the library, he stops, turns back and offers a compliment, "Beautiful hat." As soon as he turns his back, she takes off the dark gray cloche and throws it on the floor, believing his remark to be more jest than compliment.

On the first program, Whiley poses the question that begins to tear apart the underlying social framework of Brewster: "What's wrong with Brewster?" Rachel telephones the show, offering her opinion, "The town is full of ignorant people who punish others for their own insecurities." When pressed by Whiley about her statement, Rachel mentions her concern is about a man in town but refuses to give other details. The next evening Rachel telephones Whiley, telling him what she believes is wrong with Brewster; after a brief discussion, they agree to meet for a pizza—in the library. Their friendship becomes a relationship; Rachel is talkative, about herself, her ambitions, but she gleans nothing about Whiley—his past, present, or future. Whiley's motives remain as mysterious and unknown as his past. The next Sunday, Rachel asks Whiley to meet her in the library before *Our Town*. She is upset about the murder of a teacher whom she admired. The teacher, dismissed because he was gay, recently disrupted Brewster's annual Founder's Day Celebration, accusing the mayor of fraud and lying. At the library, Whiley calms a distraught Rachel, and she reveals that she has found papers belonging to her former teacher behind some library book shelves. Whiley reads the papers, remarking, "The fucker was right. I can't believe it. The fucker was telling the truth!" Rachel responds, "Wha, what are you talking about?" Whiley comments that he had a conversation with the teacher the day before but did not believe him. As Rachel probes for more information, Whiley remarks that he talked with the teacher "last night, in his apartment." Rachel, now suspicious, asks, "What are you talking about?" Whiley replies calmly, "Uh-oh, damn it!" The scene immediately shifts to Whiley walking to the television station; *Our Town* goes on the air as usual. As Whiley and the mayor talk, there are occasional flashes of the depressed and deteriorating shops and streets of Brewster, of Whiley and Rachel struggling in the library, and of Rachel lying dead on the floor of the library. After the program, Whiley with a traveling bag in each hand is on the highway, walking away from Brewster.

A young, attractive redhead (naturally curly; braided at nape), Rachel dresses modestly but fashionably during the film; she most often wears three-quarter sleeve colorful print dresses with scoop necklines. She performs a minimal number of occupational tasks—sitting behind a circulation desk, assisting patrons, and pushing a booktruck. She uses the library after its closing hours for meetings with Whiley, evidently an acceptable activity for Rachel, which suggests that she is Brewster's only librarian. Rachel's choice of Whiley as a friend and lover is understandable—his clean-cut appearance is striking and his on-the-air personality is charming. In addition, Rachel desperately wants to leave Brewster, and Whiley is the outside catalyst revealing the "wrongs" of her hometown. Rachel, as all of the townspeople, is lulled by Whiley's facade; as he becomes an integral part of the community, there is no discernable reason to seriously question his motives, his past. Previous reel librarians often misjudged the character of their lovers but such errors of judgment seldom resulted in the forfeiture of life, as in the case of Rachel.

In *I Love Trouble*, a young actress, Annie Meyers-Shyer,[70] appears in a library scene and is credited as Student Librarian. When Peter Brackett (Nick Nolte) and Sabrina Peterson (Julia Roberts), reporters for rival Chicago newspapers, join forces to work on a train wreck story, they visit a library to research their story. As they read aloud at a library table, the librarian, pushing a booktruck behind the two reporters, remarks "Ma'am. Shush!" Meyers-Shyer is a blonde (shoulder length; top and sides combed back) who wears a long sleeve horizontally striped blouse and light slacks. She appears on-screen for about five seconds. In the background of this scene, an "only 38" blonde librarian (uncredited[71]) with eyeglasses is assisting patrons at the circulation desk.

Filmmakers relied heavily upon the stereotypical image for their female reel librarians during the early 1990s. An "only 38" appearance is essentially a prerequisite; most supporting cast members appear to be in their 50s and 60s. In one instance, *Stanley & Iris*, supporting actress Dortha Duckworth was 85. In *I Love Trouble*, one of the few films with a very young librarian, the actress was the daughter of the director and the producer of the film. The director and producer—the authors of the script—identify their daughter's character as a student librarian in the cast of characters, suggesting a character who is learning the occupational tasks of librarians.

Young male librarians are in *Scent of a Woman* (1992) and *The Seventh Coin* (1993). In *Scent of a Woman*, Chris O'Donnell[72] is Charlie Simms, a poor prep school student who works in the school library. When a student asks Charlie for permission to check out a reserve book overnight, Charlie reiterates the library's policy regarding reserve books—they cannot be checked out. The student insists he must have the book to pass a test and promises to bring it back by 7:30 the next morning. Charlie permits the student to take the book but reminds him that the book must be returned on time or "it's going to be my ass." Charlie, as was Alex Finch in *Chances Are*, is sympathetic to the needs of fellow students and is willing to circumvent policy and rules to accommodate a student. Both Charlie and Alex know policy and rules, but they evaluate the circumstances of each situation to determine their course of action. "Only 38" librarians adhere to library policy and rules and, undoubtedly, would not have acquiesced to the student's request to check out a book on an instructor's reserved list.

Mark Nelson[73] appears briefly as a librarian in *The Seventh Coin*, which is set and filmed in Jerusalem. Lisa (Ally Walker), the niece of a local police captain, is at a microfilm reader glancing through newspapers for information about a murder involving ancient gold coins. The librarian is seated next to Lisa as they read the newspapers and talk. Lisa finally concludes that one of the men in the newspaper article must be "the key" to solving the crime. She then asks, "Now, how do we find this man?" A long silence follows with the camera on Lisa's face; her blank facial expression indicates that she has no idea how to proceed. The librarian, now off-screen, is silent, but finally responds in a very tentative voice, "How ... how about a phone book?" This is a weak response by this librarian; he appears to be asking a question rather than answering Lisa's question. As telephone directories are one of the first sources that working librarians often suggest, the librarian's response, had he stated it in a more declarative manner, would have demonstrated the efficiency of his reference skills. In this scene, however, his response appears more humorous than definitive. The librarian dresses casually and wears eyeglasses.

Ron Gural[74] appears briefly as an "only 38" librarian in *Storyville* (1992). The librarian works in a non-circulating collection of a governmental agency. When he assists Cray Fowler (James Spader) in a search for records from 1939 and 1940, he is helpful and talkative, remarking that the collection was too low on the priority list to be computerized. He indicates that the records are rarely used and that he "could drop dead in here. They wouldn't find me for a month." The records are not on the shelf, and the librarian explains that "they may as well have fallen into the Bermuda Triangle." The implication is that because these records do not circulate to patrons they should be on the shelf; if records are misplaced or erroneously shelved in another area of the collection, they might not be found for years, perhaps decades. The librarian is sociable, but his interest in Clay's research is significantly curtailed when the records are not found. As they continue talking, he engages in some occupational tasks—gathering volumes from a table and shelving them in their appropriate location. Gural displays several visual characteristics of the stereotypical image: "only 38," eyeglasses, receding hairline and graying beard, and modest business dress (gray suit, white shirt, bow tie).

Two films released in 1993, *Joey Breaker* and *Philadelphia*, deal with AIDS and contain "only 38" supporting actors as librarians in the cast. *Joey Breaker*, a low-budget film, features Richard Edson as Joey Breaker, a workaholic agent who represents performers and writers. Joey falls in love with Cyann Worthington (Cedella Marley), a young Jamaican nursing student who plans to return home when she graduates. As Joey manages his hectic workload, he occasionally visits Alfred Moore (Fred Fondren[75]), a librarian suffering from AIDS. Joey first meets Alfred when he accompanies another agent, Esther Trigliani (Mary Joy), whose volunteering efforts include delivering meals to Alfred. Joey is apprehensive during the visit; noticing Alfred's large collection of books, he remarks, "I see you're quite a reader." Alfred informs Joey that "most librarians are." As Esther and Alfred eat lunch, Joey is visibly troubled by being in the presence of Alfred. When they leave, Esther gives Alfred a buss on the check, for which she receives a lecture from Joey. Esther and Joey plan to visit Alfred again, but Esther has an emergency, and Joey must go alone. While Alfred dines, they discuss misconceptions about AIDS, and when they discuss films, Joey forgets his apprehensions and the two have a meaningful conversation about films. Joey later remarks to Esther, "I had a good time with Alfred. I ... I like Alfred." On Joey's third visit, the librarian is "having a bad day" and confined to bed, requiring Joey to spoon-feed him. During this discussion, Alfred speaks about his dreams and regrets. He wanted to write, but was afraid of critics, of not being a good writer. Now bedridden, he remarks,

"I lay here wondering why I was so afraid, and the funny thing is, I can't remember." The message brings Joey's life into sharper focus, as he is laboring with his love for Cyann, who will soon return to Jamaica, and his career. Alfred succumbs to AIDS several days later. He continually confronted his nemesis with dignity, with courage even though death was inevitable. Alfred's final words to Joey are instrumental in effecting a change in the agent's life—they propel Joey to quit the agency and to follow Cyann to Jamaica, events that may not have occurred without Alfred's insight. Alfred, an "only 38" individual, displays no other visual characteristic associated with the stereotypical image. His discussions with Joey and Esther establish his occupation as a librarian. As a librarian suffering from AIDS, Alfred is a sympathetic character.

In *Philadelphia*, Tracey Walter[76] portrays an insensitive and repugnant librarian, quite similar in manner and tone to the librarian whom John Rothman portrayed in *Sophie's Choice*. AIDS-afflicted Andrew Beckett (Tom Hanks), recently fired by a prestigious law firm, believes that he was fired because of AIDS rather than incompetence as the law firm alleges. He initiates a wrongful dismissal suit against his former employer, and while researching his case in a law library, the librarian approaches Andrew with a book, announcing, "This is the supplement," and lays the volume on the table next to Andrew. Taking off his eyeglasses, the librarian remarks, "You're right. There is a section of HIV-related discrimination." Andrew opens the supplement and thanks the librarian, who remains standing near Andrew, commenting that "a private research room is available." Andrew responds the table is suitable. The librarian, however, remains at the table; his actions indicate that he is mulling over something. Finally Andrew looks up at him, and the librarian asks, "Wouldn't you be more comfortable in a research room?" Andrew now realizes that AIDS is the librarian's problem; as he pauses and looks around the library, it is evident that everyone in the library is aware of the librarian's desire to get him out of the reading room and into a private room. Andrew coughs, then responds, "No. Would it make you more comfortable?" Andrew and the librarian are at an impasse; another attorney, Joe Miller (Denzel Washington), who is working at a nearby table, comes to greet and assist Andrew. The librarian maintains his position at the table as the two attorneys talk; Joe gives the librarian a nod with his head, indicating everything is all right. "Whatever, sir," the librarian remarks as he departs. As soon as the librarian leaves to resume his other tasks, a patron, seated at the same table as Andrew, gathers his materials and leaves.

Although the librarian assists Andrew, he is portrayed in an unfavorable manner; he is anxious about Andrew's presence in the reading room and adamant that Andrew move to a private room. Offering Andrew a private research room in a library is equivalent to segregating AIDS-afflicted individuals from the general public; this is the type of prejudice, ignorance, and behavior that Andrew is contesting in his lawsuit. The librarian backs down from his stance only after Joe, who does not approve of Andrew's lifestyle but is not offended by his presence in the reading room, offers unspoken assurance that Andrew may remain in the reading room. Whether the librarian's offer of a private room was taken on his own initiative or prompted by other library patrons is not revealed. Walter's librarian wallows in fear and prejudice, projecting a most unfavorable image of male librarians.

Walter, an "only 38" individual with a receding hairline, wears eyeglasses but removes them when he puts the supplement on the desk; he does not put them on during the remainder of the scene. Walter's character projects the stereotypical image and provides an exceedingly cogent example of public service gone awry.

Another film during 1990–1994 with a supporting actor is *The Neverending Story III* (1994[77]). Freddie Jones[78] is Mr. Coreander, a school librarian who reflects the stereotypical image—"only 38," receding hairline, reading glasses on a lanyard, and conservative clothes. When chased by a group of boys, student Bastian Bux (Jason James Richter) ducks into the library to hide. The librarian, busy working in the book stacks, hears Bastian enter the library and begins to describe the arrangement of books. Bastian utters a loud "Shush," hoping to quiet the librarian. Coreander is standing on a ladder and out of sight; he peers around the corner of a book stack, exclaiming, "Shush!" Descending the ladder, he unhesitantly informs Bastian that he will "do the shushing around here"; walking toward Bastian, he announces, "Shushing is the job of a librarian." Filmgoers have recognized this truism since the 1940s.

Two films in the early 1990s with women librarians in major roles, *Salmonberries* (1991[79]) and *The Gun in Betty Lou's Handbag* (1992), were poor box-office performers but presented interesting librarians. *Salmonberries* focuses on the lives of two women, Roswitha (Rosel Zech[80]), a librarian, and Kotzebue (k.d. lang), whom everyone believes is a male mine worker, in a small isolated Alaska outpost. Roswitha and her husband, Karl, a violinist, made a dash to cross the border from East Germany 21 years earlier, but Karl was shot and killed by guards. Roswitha then made her way to Kotzebue, Alaska, an outpost discovered by Otto von Kotzebue, and became its librarian. Kotzebue the person, on the other hand, knows nothing about herself, other than she was found in a box with the word *kotzebue* on it when she was an infant and, consequently, was given the name Kotzebue. The two women, Roswitha with a haunting past and Kotzebue with a past unknown, develop a tenuous relationship through which their issues of the past are resolved. As the film begins, a bespectacled Roswitha is hustling patrons out of the library at closing time when she notices Kotzebue, who is reluctant to leave. Kotzebue asks for a book, and Roswitha gets it for her. Kotzebue, however, grabs and crumbles the pages of the book, flipping through the pages as if she wants to destroy the book. Kotzebue then throws several books across the library and runs out of the library while Roswitha telephones for assistance.

When she later returns to the library, Kotzebue meets Noayak (Jane Lind[81]) who also works in the library. When Kotzebue asks about Roswitha, Noayak comments, "You don't have a crush on her, do you?" As soon as Roswitha arrives, Noayak leaves, and Roswitha attempts to open a conversation with Kotzebue, who seldom speaks. Kotzebue shows her displeasure with the conversation by shoving a book off a table, which infuriates Roswitha: "I hate your kind of jokes, boy." Kotzebue turns her back to Roswitha, who continues, "This time you won't get far. This time the sheriff will come. And then the handcuffs will say 'click,' and the books will be safe again from you and your kind, young man." Kotzebue, in response to Roswitha's outburst, goes to the far end of the library and into a stack aisle where she undresses and then steps out into the main aisle to show Roswitha that she is a girl. Noayak returns to the library, and Kotzebue leaves; Noayak then remarks, "I see your admirer is still here.

Did you both have fun throwing books again?" Only Roswitha knows that Kotzebue is a woman; Kotzebue frequently visits the library, always with the intent of gaining information about her past, about her parents, about who she is. After being informed by Roswitha that many people are ignorant of their lineage, Kotzebue brings a large fish to Roswitha at her home. During this visit and discussion, their relationship begins to change in tone and manner; during the remainder of the film, the overriding emphasis becomes sexual, with Kotzebue initiating the overtures and Roswitha rejecting them.

When the Berlin wall is torn down, Kotzebue steals money from Bingo Chuck (Chuck Connors), the city's lone Anglo and operator of the city's only entertainment, a bingo parlor, and purchases airline tickets to Berlin so that she and Roswitha can reconstruct and resolve the questions surrounding Karl's death during the attempt to escape. As Roswitha always feared, her brother had informed the authorities of the couple's escape plans, and when they find Karl Scheinhardt's grave, Roswitha's personal conflict with the past is resolved. Kotzebue attempts a physical relationship with Roswitha, but she objects, "Stop, Stop ... you have to stop now, please, please ... that's not me."

Back in Alaska, they discover that Bingo Chuck, who has been promising to marry Noayak for 20 years, is Kotzebue's father. Chuck confesses to having had many sexual escapades with Eskimo women two decades earlier, but blames the socio-cultural milieu at the time for his shortcomings. Noayak, frustrated by Chuck's admission of self-gratification at the expense of her people, leaves him.

Although Roswitha projects the stereotypical image—an "only 38" blonde (half bang; pulled back into French twist) who wears eyeglasses only in the library, she is one of the more complex librarians in twentieth century cinema. She lives in Alaska, a self-imposed snowy sanctuary, to hide from her past; she travels to Berlin to confront her fears; she vacillates about a lesbian relationship; and she assists Kotzebue in her search for the past, deducing that Bingo Chuck is her father. Noayak's waist length black hair (half bang) hangs loose in library scenes, but in her last nonlibrary scene, she exemplifies the stereotypical image—a bun at her crown. She engages in various occupational tasks: pushing a makeshift booktruck (a shopping cart), working at the desk, carrying and shelving books. Noayak, as previous single reel librarians, makes a decidedly poor choice for a mate—Bingo Chuck. She permits Chuck to drag on their relationship without marriage for 20 years. His promises were never filled nor did he plan to fulfill them. Every filmgoer undoubtedly realized that Chuck was a loser; he was not the type of man on which young women pin their hopes and future.

Penelope Ann Miller[82] stars as librarian Betty Lou Perkins in *The Gun in Betty Lou's Handbag* (1992), a mixture of comedy and murder mystery. Betty Lou, a redhead (ponytail at crown; back hangs loose), is an enthusiastic children's librarian whose storyhours produce moments of fun, laughter, noise for youngsters, but too much noise for the head librarian, Margaret Armstrong (Marian Seldes[83]). Margaret prefers a quiet library and interrupts the fun and noise of Betty Lou's storyhour with a "shush." She announces that "libraries are for reading" and gives each child a book even though, as Betty Lou informs her, "they can't read!" Discussing books as they leave the children's room, Betty Lou quotes (almost verbatim) Thomas Carlyle, "The best effect of any book is to excite the reader to self-activity." Margaret immediately stops Betty Lou, stating, "That man clearly never ran a library.... The best effect of any book is that it be returned unmutilated to its shelf." Looking at Betty Lou's display of new books for the library's fundraiser, Margaret expresses her disapproval. She then reads the publicity brochure that Betty Lou designed for the fundraiser, stating that it is not necessary, as the library has "a solid guest list." Margaret adds, "If we have twenty or thirty people, I say success." Betty Lou responds, "Imagine if we could get a hundred." Margaret's one-word answer: "Terrifying." It is a Margaret-induced bad day at the library for Betty Lou, but the day becomes an outright disaster when her husband, Alex (Eric Thal), a police detective, skips the anniversary dinner that she had so painstakingly prepared. The next morning Alex, down to his last clean shirt, expresses his displeasure with Betty Lou: "You know, something completely irrelevant you remember it for life, but something relevant to our lives, like my having a clean shirt to wear for work...." Betty Lou attempts to explain that she had to stay late at the library, but Alex insists that she learn to say no. "It's not that difficult." Alex skips breakfast, informs her that he will probably be living at the station for the next several days, and when Betty Lou mentions the library fundraiser, he responds with some z's. "Maybe we can make it fun this time," Betty Lou suggests, but Alex counters, "Yeah, we can, by not going."

Betty Lou is a mousy librarian whose home life mirrors that of her occupation—staid, never changing (Margaret's dictum), and uneventful. While walking her dog, Betty Lou finds a gun by a riverbed. The gun was used to murder a former member of the "Cajun Mafia" the previous day. She telephones the police station to inform Alex that she found a gun, but he is too busy to talk with her. She is insistent, however, and Alex blurts out, "Look, I said I'll call you back. Now, I'll call you back," and hangs up the phone, without giving Betty Lou an opportunity to tell him about her discovery of the gun. An angry Betty Lou goes into a department store and discharges the gun in the restroom; she is taken to the police station where Alex maintains that the gun cannot possibly belong to her. When the police discussion turns to possible lovers, Alex vigorously asserts, "There is no way on earth that Betty Lou had a lover." Betty Lou, overhearing Alex's remarks, discards her mousy character and states, "I'm guilty. Can I please go to jail, now." The police, anticipating some time in jail would convince Betty Lou to repudiate her confession, fail to realize that Betty Lou is admired by the other inmates. Absorbing the information the women tell her about their troubles with the police, Betty Lou becomes confident that she can play the role of a murderer. Betty Lou goes to court with a new hairstyle (half bang; Sassoon cut), a suggestive black fishnet minidress and black stockings; her appearance prompts the judge to exclaim, "Hell, I don't go to the library enough!" Betty Lou continues her charade and becomes the citywide topic of gossip; Alex is off the case and off the police force. Released on her own recognizance, Betty Lou attends the library's fundraiser, which attracts everybody, or, as Margaret observes, "It's a mob scene." Alex is now following Betty Lou, as are federal agents and members of the Cajun Mafia. The ensuing action includes numerous comic antics, misadventures, mistaken identities—all demonstrating that Betty Lou is no longer a mousy librarian but a brave and courageous woman.

Margaret typifies the image of libraries. She adores the silence, a vestige of library rules from previous decades. She is reluctant to change, preferring the continuance of a library steeped in traditional silence rather than energizing the library with creative programming and greater public awareness. A brunette (full bang; French twist), the head librarian dresses conservatively but smartly and with color; she wears eyeglasses on a lanyard, which always dangle from her neck because she never uses them. Betty Lou is undoubtedly a novice, as she is not attuned to Margaret's idiosyncrasies. Although much younger than Margaret and bubbling with program ideas to enrich the library, Betty Lou, as the film begins, exhibits personality traits that are associated with librarians—mousy, lack of self-confidence, accepting without questioning, working to please others, and a denial of self-gratification. By film's end, Betty Lou has changed, but she still must work with Margaret, who has not.

Reel librarians projecting the stereotypical image peppered the screens of movie theaters during the last five years of the 1990s. Two actresses portraying stereotypical librarians, Pamela Glen[84] in *The Last Supper* (1995) and Sharon Collar,[85] in *Mad Love* (1995), appear very briefly. Glen's character is listed as Illiterate Librarian in the cast credits; she appears in a one-minute scene. Five graduate students, all politically liberal, are inviting right-wing ideologues, one by one, to dinner at their house where they summarily murder each ideologue. One individual invited to dine with them is a librarian. During a discussion, the librarian remarks that "*Catcher in the Rye* is just mean spirited garbage littered with the 'f' word." She has difficulty talking about "the 'f' word"; she can barely say the phrase, rolling her eyes as she does. The students laugh at her comment and pour her a drink of deadly wine, the preferred method of extinguishing their guests. A teetotaler, the librarian rejects the wine; the students then go to their second option—a knife in the back. The librarian, a youthful "only 38" brunette (bun at crown), dresses conservatively.

In *Mad Love,* Collar is a secondary school librarian who appears briefly in two scenes. In her first scene, Collar is busy scrutinizing a student in the school library. In her second scene, she is pushing a booktruck outside a building and observes student Casey Roberts (Drew Barrymore) breaking a fire alarm box and pulling the switch. As students exit the building, the librarian waves her arms and yells at the teacher who soon announces that it is a false alarm. As the students trudge back into their classrooms, the librarian identifies Casey, "There she is ... that little blonde, there...." Collar wears reading glasses in the library but is without them when outside. A brunette (half bang; collar length page), she wears dark clothes in both scenes.

Three school librarians appear in three films released during 1996—*Big Bully, High School High,* and *The Substitute.* Norma MacMillan,[86] a 75-year-old supporting actress, portrays librarian Mrs. Rumpert in a brief comedy scene with David Leary (Rick Moranis) in *Big Bully.* David returns to teach creative writing at the middle school he attended as a youngster. On his first day, he walks into the library and informs Mrs. Rumpert that the school library had "a big impact" on his life. David smiles proudly as he comments that the library "was the first place that taught me the importance of reading, of books." The librarian responds quickly in a solemn tone, "*Green Eggs and Ham.*" Impressed with Mrs. Rumpert's memory, David remarks, "That was my favorite book. How did you remember that?" She cites a fact that he has long forgotten—the book is "8,862 days overdue."[87] David, who can hardly believe what the librarian is saying, exclaims, "You're serious!" Mrs. Rumpert, before stamping a book, replies, "That's what I live for, dear!" This scene, not essential to the story, is for comedy purposes only. The librarian, an obviously dyed redhead (bouffant; petal curls), is way over "only 38" and uses reading glasses. She embodies the spirit of the stereotypical image that filmgoers expect in short comedy scenes.

In *High School High*, a librarian (uncredited[88]) appears in two nonlibrary scenes. Jon Lovitz stars as Richard Clark, an idealistic and oblivious but nonetheless effective high school teacher who accepts a position at Marion Barry High School, a prime example of an urban secondary school fiasco. The exterior and interior of the school more closely resemble a burned-out neighborhood ravaged by riots and armed conflict than a tax-supported public school. At the opening day assembly, Richard gives a brief talk, concluding, "I see in you, the future of America." At this point, someone in the audience yells, "You suck!" The shouter, an adult, stands and gives Richard the bird with both hands. The principal's administrative assistant informs Richard that the shouter is "the school librarian." Later in the film, the principal announces that Richard's students achieved the "lowest scores in the country" and dismisses Richard. Leaving the school in disgrace, Richard is pushed out of the building by a security guard and is jeered loudly by students and teachers as he leaves the schoolground; the librarian, in top shouting form, reaffirms her earlier evaluation, "You suck!" The librarian, a brunette (half bang; bouffant, probable bun), dresses modestly in both scenes and, in the second scene, wears eyeglasses on a bead lanyard. In both scenes, she has a pencil stuck in her hair. These visual characteristics, along with the administrative assistant's statement, establish her identity as a librarian.

Supporting actress Peggy Pope[89] is Hannah Dillion, an "only 38" redhead (bouffant; Sassoon cut) librarian in *The Substitute*. She first appears on-screen in the teachers' lounge, taking a quick nap. Hannah appears exhausted; with head tilted back, resting on her shoulder and arm, she has propped her feet upon a nearby chair. As she and teacher Darrell Sherman (Glenn Plummer) exchange quips about the coffee, Shale (Tom Berenger), who is posing as substitute teacher Jim Smith, enters the lounge and engages the two faculty members in a discussion about the school's problems. Darrell identifies the "Kings of Destruction" as "the top gang in school." Hannah corrects Darrell, "Posse, please. You're so unhip." Very perceptive about the situation, the librarian blames the principal; Darrell defends the administrator, and as she picks up her books and glasses from the table, Hannah remarks, "That's right Darrell, you keep the faith."

She appears in a library scene, which occurs after school hours and is the setting for an extended fight scene between Shale and members of the Kings of Destruction and school security officers who are aligned with the principal and Kings of Destruction. Shale surprises the group and has Hannah take their weapons into her office, telling her to call the police in 15 minutes. A fight follows, and Hannah watches the free-for-all from her office; Shale tosses three members of the group through one of the library's windows (the library is on the second floor). When Shale is temporarily stopped, one of the gang members goes to Hannah's office and points a pistol at her. She picks up and aims one of the pistols at him, but she is shaking so much that had she pulled the trigger she would have undoubtedly missed the troublemaker. Shale, back up and in action, grabs the gang member from behind and hustles him to and out of the second story window. When he returns to Hannah's office, Shale apologizes, "I'm sorry about those windows." Hannah, revealing that she knows and can use the language of the school's hallways, responds, "Hey, fuck it!"

Hannah projects the visual characteristics of the stereotypical image. She displays a resigned attitude about the school problems, as challenging the status quo results in physical attacks on faculty members. When threatened in the library, Hannah defends herself with a pistol, a courageous feat totally unexpected from a school librarian. Hannah is one of the few reel librarians confronted with extreme violence in a library; basically timid and passive, Hannah shows that courage is a personality trait that even "only 38" librarians can manifest when necessary.

Public librarians, as the foregoing school librarians, were portrayed in stereotypical fashion in 1995, 1996, and 1997. *The Young Poisoner's Handbook* (1995), a fictional account of a British murderer, begins in the early 1960s when 14-year-old Graham Young (Hugh O'Conor) becomes interested in chemistry and experiments. Graham needs some books from the library, but the books are restricted. One female librarian (uncredited[90]) at the circulation desk is in the process of stamping the books for Graham, when a male librarian (uncredited[91]) interrupts her, stating that the books "are considered unsuitable for readers under 18 years of age." Graham offers a blatant lie to the librarians, maintaining that he is doing research for his father who is a general practitioner. The male librarian rebuffs Graham's statement and informs the 14-year-old patron that his father is a "machine setter," not a GP, and that his mother is an accordion player. Although Graham insists that he needs the books, the librarian is resolute about the teenager using "the appropriate section," which is the "Children's Library, through the swing doors on your way out."

Going through the swinging doors, Graham sees attractive Sue Butler (Samantha Edmonds[92]), a young blonde (full bang; ponytail at crown; back hangs loose) librarian whom he met earlier in the book stacks. "Hey, in here," she whispers, as she motions for him with her head. As he approaches, she asks, "Are these what you wanted?" Sue gives the restricted books to him and stamps his wrist and laughs. She definitely enjoys the company of young men and displays more than a casual interest in Graham. As the film progresses, Graham discovers that Sue likes to stamp not only the wrists of young men but also other parts of their anatomy.

The librarians at the circulation desk are models of the stereotype. The female librarian is a plump bespectacled "only 38" brunette (bun at crown), who dresses modestly and maintains a frown on her face during the scene. The male librarian, mustachioed and "only 38," wears a brown business suit and tie; judging by his enforcement of library rules, he is undoubtedly the on-duty library supervisor. Sue, however, disregards the circulation policies and gives the books to Graham. This action by Sue continues the scenario of stereotypical librarians adhering strictly to policies and rules while younger librarians assist the same patron by circumventing them. Younger librarians display a degree of empathy with patrons their own age who are stifled by stereotypical librarians, and since young librarians have the knowledge and expertise to get around the library's established procedures, they do so without any apparent fear of supervisory reprimand.

Jean Speegle Howard[93] is librarian Miss Phelps in director Danny DeVito's family fantasy comedy *Matilda* (1996). At four years of age, Matilda (Sara Magdalin) loves to read and treks daily to the library to enjoy its many books. Upon entering the library on her first visit, Matilda is greeted at the information desk by Miss Phelps, who directs her to the children's department. Matilda declines Miss Phelps' offer to find a book with pictures for her. Moments later, Miss Phelps, this time wearing eyeglasses, displays a puzzled look as she listens to Matilda giggling while she reads. In her third appearance, Miss Phelps walks down a book stack aisle with Matilda, informing the youngster that with a library card, she could take books home and avoid daily excursions to the library. Following Miss Phelps' advice, Matilda loads her little wagon with books and pulls it home.

Scenes at the information desk are shot from little Matilda's vantage point, which makes the desk appear to be an enormously imposing, tall structure. Viewing the librarian from that angle also reinforces her "only 38" appearance, as does her snowy white hair (half bang; layered with soft curls). When one is four years old and must bend the head back to look up and talk with a librarian, the librarian, irrespective of actual age, is perceived to be old. The high ceilings and imposing chandeliers emphasize the diminutive size of Matilda in the house of books. For a four-year-old to venture into such a library alone is an adventure, but Matilda is confident that she "can manage," a statement of patron self-assurance that working librarians seldom hear from adults. Miss Phelps' discussions with Matilda indicate that the librarian is friendly and competent.

Actress Beverly Cooper[94] appears in *Summer of the Monkeys* (1998), a family comedy drama set in the early twentieth century (circa 1910) and focusing on John Lee (Michael Ontkean), a young teenager determined to earn the reward for capturing several monkeys that escaped during a train wreck. John visits the Ridgewell Library to read about monkeys. The library is very quiet when John enters; as soon as he reaches the librarian's desk, he blurts out, "Howdy Miss," and the bespectacled librarian gives him a very sedate "shush," right index finger over lips, and motions for him to be quiet. John whispers that he wants "all the books" on monkeys; this request for "all the books" is one of the most popular catchphrases of patrons seeking information on a specific topic. To provide John with the information he needs, the librarian responds, "Could you be more specific?" John informs her that he wants "to trap a bunch of 'em" that escaped from the train wreck. He is in the library because "My grandpa thought that if I read up on 'em, it'd help me out." She asks him to sit at one of the tables while she locates some materials for him. She soon arrives at the table with an armload of books, stating, "This should get you started." At closing time, the librarian rings the bell, and everybody begins leaving except John, who is unaware of the significance of the bell. She informs him that the library is closing, and as he shuffles his reading materials, the librarian states, "You can leave the books where they are." As John makes his way to the exit, the librarian reminds him to "Come back again." John, who appears to have enjoyed his time in the library, replies, "I believe I will." The librarian smiles, evidently because she elicited just the response she wanted from John, and begins picking up the books on the table.

A friendly "only 38" librarian with graying blonde hair (half bang; bun at back of head), she wears wire-rimmed glasses that she removes when talking. The librarian not only engages in several occupational tasks but also provides very capable assistance. Cooper presents a very effective stereotypical image of reel librarians.

In *Keep the Aspidistra Flying* (1997),[95] Joan Blackham[96] appears as an "only 38" librarian in a brief library scene. Gordon Comstock (Richard E. Grant), upon learning that his girlfriend is pregnant, goes to a library for books on pregnancy. He is basically penniless, dirty and grungy, and has not bathed in weeks. When Gordon asks for books on pregnancy, the librarian responds, "Not for the general public." He explains that he is an expectant father, and she asks him to be seated while she retrieves material for him. She takes an oversized volume to Gordon, reminding him "to sign for it before you leave." As Gordon reads the volume, the camera shifts to the librarian who is stamping books and keeping an eye on Gordon and the oversized volume, as she does not consider Gordon a trustworthy individual, judging by his clothes and odor. The librarian has graying hair (half bang; fingerwaves; bun at nape) and wears dark plastic frame eyeglasses and conservative clothes. The librarian provides adequate assistance, but she monitors Gordon, fearful that he may purloin the library's book. This librarian mirrors, to some degree, the same philosophy—the best place for a book is on the shelf where it cannot be damaged—espoused by library supervisor Margaret Armstrong in *The Gun in Betty Lou's Handbag* (1992).

Lois Chiles[97] appears in a supporting role as librarian Eva in *Bliss* (1997), a film about sex for adults. Baltazar Vincenza (Terence Stamp), a sex therapist, stops by a library to obtain a book that he had previously requested. Eva soon appears with the book and remarks that the book has "been out of print since 1932." Baltazar obviously admires the librarian: "You have yet to let me down, Eva. I find the combination of charm and intelligence a rare union these days." They gaze at one another until Baltazar turns away and leaves the library; filmgoers readily discern the spark of mutual attraction between the pair. Eva is a stunningly attractive "only 38" redhead (French braid at crown) with eyeglasses on a lanyard dangling from her neck. Eva reappears near the end of film when a patient of Baltazar's enters his house and begins shouting the therapist's name when he finds the living room empty. Eva comes out of Baltazar's bedroom hurriedly putting on her clothes and remarks, "Are you here for a violin lesson?" Baltazar soon exits from the bedroom in a robe, and Eva rushes to embrace and kiss him. "Good bye, love," she exclaims, adding, "I'll see you Friday, unless you want to drop by the library." After Eva leaves, Baltazar utters rhetorically, "Isn't she glorious?" Baltazar's client is inquisitive, "You don't have to heal her?" Baltazar, in response to his client's question, concedes he has not informed Eva that he is a sex therapist. Judging from her initial question to Baltazar's client about a violin lesson, the therapist appears to have purposely misled Eva about his occupation. Although Eva displays the visual characteristics of the stereotypical image, she is a vivacious, self-assured, and extremely attractive mature woman.

Three films released during the last five years of the 1990s with librarians in the leading female role—*Party Girl* (1995), *A Simple Plan* (1998), and *The Mummy* (1999)—present significantly different images of librarians. *Party Girl*, as *Desk Set* forty years earlier, has many library scenes and portrays the occupation of librarians as a worthy endeavor. *A Simple Plan* has a limited number of library scenes, but the librarian confronts a very basic ethical issue; her decision and actions are reminiscent of the manner in which librarian Elsie Braden in *Violent Saturday* (1955) handled a similar dilemma and with the same final result. In the most successful box office film of the three, *The Mummy*, filmmakers use its one library scene for comedy, giving filmgoers one of the funniest library ladder scenes in twentieth century cinema.

Released in June 1995, *Party Girl* provides its filmgoers with a rollicking 98-minute view of the New York City scene in the early 1990s; for working librarians, *Party Girl* is one of the must-see motion pictures of the twentieth century about librarians and their occupation. *Party Girl* presents a librarian, Mary (Parker Posey[98]), whose life is not just different from all previous librarians in twentieth century films, but the complete reverse. Mary is the epitome of mod; in most films, women librarians leave the occupation in order to attain just a slight degree of what Mary embodies.

Mary is the consummate twenty-something party girl—college graduate without a profession or career, no means of support or income, and extravagant party-goer and party-giver, with an occasional overnight stay in jail for such misbehavior as selling liquor without a license and possessing controlled substances. Mary best illustrates and summarizes her situation when responding to questions raised by Judy Lindendorf (Sasha von Scherler[99]), her godmother and a librarian, about possible options for meeting her financial needs: "I'm freelancing." "I am not a waitress." "Do you realize how broke I am? What do you want me to do, huh? I don't have a job. I'm a loser! Shoot me!" With this admission and realization, Mary begins a long, arduous journey that results in her choice of a career—"I want to be a librarian."

The transformation of Mary begins when Judy challenges her goddaughter to get a job. Judy informs Mary that she cannot be a librarian because she does not have a master's degree in library science and cannot be a library clerk because her mother had "no common sense," implying that Mary also has none. Mary, insisting that Judy suspects she is not smart enough to work in the library, tauntingly responds, "You're ashamed of me, Judy. You're my only family, and you're ashamed of me." Judy accepts the challenge and asks Wanda (C. Francis Blackchild[100]) to put her to work. Wanda's first question is: "I assume you're familiar with the Dewey Decimal System?" Mary's face goes into sudden shock and disbelief. The camera cuts to a large Dewey Decimal Classification poster on the library wall, and then back to Mary holding a "New York Public Library" placard in front of her chest in a simulated mug shot. Mary knows nothing about the system.

Mary continues her lifestyle, dressing mod, and demonstrates little respect for the library. Mary's progress with library work and the system is slow; a more accurate evaluation is that she demonstrates a total lack of progress. Judy, perplexed and exhausted with Mary's inability to learn, confronts her with the truth: "It amazes me how you can come here every day and absorb no knowledge of the system. A trained monkey learns this system on PBS in a matter of hours." Later in a bar, Mary laments her predicament. She decides to go back to the library; with liquor bottle in hand, she opens and climbs through a window, sits on a desktop, lights up a weed, and begins reading *DDC20* (Dewey Decimal Classification, 20th edition). To impress Judy and reassure herself, Mary begins the task of learning the intricacies of the system. She spends the night at the library studying the system, shelving books while dancing on library tables, doing cartwheels, and riding book carts down the hallways.

Working at the public service desk the next day, Mary becomes irate when she catches a patron shelving a book: "I guess you didn't know we have a system for putting books away here.... Why are we wasting our time with the Dewey Decimal System when your system is so much easier ... we'll just put the books in any damned place we choose." By this time she is shouting at the patron, and librarian Howard (L. B. Williams[101]) rushes to the desk, interrupts her outburst, and suggests that it is time for a break. The system has worked its way into the fabric of Mary's being.

In a succeeding library scene, Mary assists a patron at the circulation desk, having located some information on twins that the patron needs. Although Mary impresses staff members with her substantial progress and newly acquired talents, Judy removes her from the desk, much to the dismay of Mary and the disbelief of other library staff members. In a discussion about the reasons for removing Mary from the desk, Judy remarks, "It's so busy, and you're such a speedy little shelver." Mary stresses that she is doing a good job but that Judy does not understand and appreciate the progress of her goddaughter. Mary is developing an appreciation for and understanding of the Dewey Decimal System as well as improving her reference skills, but Judy has not yet observed these behavioral changes. Mary's commitment to reform appears genuine. The following night, however, she is responsible for closing the library and a disaster occurs. Mustafa (Omar Townsend), an immigrant falafel street vendor who was a teacher in his homeland, wants to obtain teaching certification and enters the library at closing time. Mary becomes so engrossed with Mustafa, whom she knows because of her frequent purchases of sandwiches, that she forgets to close the windows; consequently, rain spews into the library while she and Mustafa have sex on the library floor. The next morning, Judy is sitting in the midst of rain-soaked books when Mary appears; outraged at Mary's failure to close the windows, Judy cannot quietly accept Mary's disregard for the occupation and for the loss of books. She shouts at Mary, "Get out. I won't have you working here."

In discussing her sudden state of unemployment with Mustafa, Mary observes that she deserved to be fired, adding, "Keith Richards would make a better librarian than me." Self-analyzing her talents, her future, her desire to do something, Mary concludes that she is "not good at anything" and is "just like my mother" and, consequently, throws a big party.

The next morning Mary, resolutely determined to prove her worth to Judy, marches into the library, grabs Judy by the arm, and demands that they have a meeting—8 o'clock at Mary's place. Mary then walks to the shelves, pulls out several books on library science, and when Wanda walks near her, Mary grabs her turtleneck sweater at the throat and pushes her up against the shelves exclaiming, "You're going to help me, bitch!" Mary, with several library staff members, discusses where she should go to graduate school and the field of library work she should enter. Howard decries status degrees, advocating "the best program for the least money in the shortest amount of time." Ann (Becky Mode[102]) responds that Howard went to Columbia University, adding, "Do you think you would be working here if you went to some dinky small town program?" Wanda recommends the University of Michigan, where she had so much fun as an undergraduate. Mary resolves the geographical problem; she refuses to leave New York. With that issue resolved, a friendly but caustic exchange ensues between Howard and Ann about the types of libraries. Howard praises public library service while Ann upholds the dignity of academic library work.

When Mary returns to her apartment to prepare for her meeting with Judy, she is dressed very conservatively—gray miniskirt and black box jacket over a black turtle-neck sweater. She wears plastic tortoise-shell frame eyeglasses and sports a French twist. At twenty-something, Mary mimics the stereotype. Unfortunately, her friends have planned a surprise birthday party, and the activities are just getting started when Judy arrives. Mary quiets the group and pleads for Judy's support. Testimonials from Mary's friends whom she helped while working at the library convince Judy that her goddaughter really wants to be a librarian. Impressed by Mary's library skills, of which she was unaware, Judy proudly agrees to help her. The party resumes.

Party Girl gently plays with the stereotypical image of librarians. The film includes the mandatory visual characteristics and occupational tasks of librarians. Judy, the library's supervisor, is the obligatory "only 38" individual and, with the exception of Mary, wears the most colorful outfits. Wanda, the youngest individual on the staff, appears several times with eyeglasses on a lanyard dangling from her neck, but she never puts them on. Bun hairstyles do not appear in this film, but ponytails appear frequently and Ann's hair is pulled into Afro curls at her crown. Howard, a Black American, sports a clean-shaven head, which exceeds the natural receding hairline or baldness associated with male librarians. Mary, the wannabe librarian, is the only cast member who closely resembles the stereotype and this occurs in the film's last scene. In other films, young women in libraries stampede away from this image to find love and happiness, to become a party girl. Mary wants more from life; she has the desire "to do something," having realized early in the film that she does not want to be Sisyphus even though she may be "an existentialist."

Judy is a consummate professional; she provides excellent public service and defends and advocates the tenets and principles of library work. On Mary's first visit to the library, Judy rebukes her for flippantly referring to a complaining library patron as "a dick." Judy corrects Mary's vocabulary by stating, "He's not a dick, he's a patron." In one scene, Judy observes Mary misinterpreting a mumbling patron's request for *Origin of Species* as "oranges and peaches" and quickly intervenes, asking Howard to find Darwin's book for the patron. On another occasion when talking with Mary, Judy interrupts their discussion to inform a patron leaving the library that "I've got you on the waiting list for the new Danielle Steel."

Admonishing Mary for leaving the windows open and having sex in the library, Judy laments Mary's vision, "When I look at you, a smart, powerful woman, and see you acting like the town idiot, it makes me sick." When Mary attempts to explain, Judy comments, "When most women are struggling to demonstrate their intelligence, their complexity, here you are, trying to prove just how stupid you can be." Showing Mary a handwritten catalog card, Judy begins a loud emotional outburst on the plight of librarians and their profession:

> See that handwriting! Look at the flowering script! That's what young lady librarians were taught. Penmanship. Melvil Dewey hired women as librarians because he believed the job didn't require any intelligence. It was a woman's job.... That means it's underpaid and undervalued. This country has more

illiteracy than some of the most underdeveloped nations. Even Americans who can read, don't. They watch movies. They watch television. They watch movies on the television.

As she lectures Mary, Judy becomes so incensed and outraged at Mary's behavior, insensitivity, and affront to the library occupation that she fires Mary and orders her out of the library.

The film's second library scene focuses on the orderly, precise, and minutia-related demands of the Dewey Decimal System. Mary, still suffering from the effects of a party the previous night, stands between Wanda and Judy as they discuss the new technological advances in library work while stamping cards (a continuous loud thumping noise) and using a book charger (an incessantly loud clacking noise as date due cards are notched and stamped). Wanda looks at Mary's filing and matter of factly remarks that the "last time I checked, 016 point 301677 [016.301677] came before 016 point 301682 [016.301682]." Mary, wearing eyeglasses on this occasion, looks at the catalog cards, all of which are visually too fuzzy for her to arrange in any order. Underlying the broad-brush humor of this scene is the conviction that librarians, as individuals, are not minutia-oriented; they follow a system of rules as other professionals—architects, certified public accountants, engineers, and statisticians. Indiscriminate variations from principles destroy the integrity of the entire occupation. In the case of libraries, the library's collection of materials is sacrosanct—the library's raison d'être.

The visual characteristics and occupational tasks of reel librarians are evident in every library scene, and although the visual images of librarians in this film are similar to the visual images of librarians in other films, *Party Girl* presents a favorable image of librarians. They are portrayed in a radically different manner: they are competent and well-educated, and they neither condone nor rationalize the substandard work and inappropriate behavior of Mary, a member of their own staff. They assist and tutor Mary as she works toward improving her skills; as Mary's mastery of the Dewey Decimal System improves, the overall quality of the library staff increases. Mary must meet the demands, the criteria of the occupation if she is to become a librarian, and very importantly, they offer Mary advice and guidance about academic institutions that offer library education programs and the types of career choices that are available. Most working librarians are very conscientious about tutoring and advising young staff members who desire to work toward a graduate degree in library science. One pithy synopsis of *Party Girl* concludes, "Despite a lack of training, she becomes a librarian with the New York Public Library. The Old Lady will never be the same again."[103]

A Simple Plan (1998) presents a scenario that filmgoers realize cannot possibly be accomplished. The Mitchell brothers, Hank (Bill Paxton) and Jacob (Billy Bob Thornton), and a friend, Lou Chambers (Brent Briscoe), discover an airplane that crashed in a snowy countryside. In the airplane, they find a bag containing $4.4 million. Hank is a college graduate with a mediocre job in a feed store; his pregnant wife, Sarah (Bridget Fonda[104]), a redhead (full bang; hair hangs loose to middle of back), is a librarian. Jacob is not too bright but functions marginally in society; he comprehends the distinction between right and wrong, but is barely surviving financially. Lou is unemployed; he and his wife are continually at odds about money and his alcoholic lifestyle. The three agree that Hank will keep the money until they can safely spend it; the plan unravels quickly as both Jacob and Lou make demands upon Hank for their share of the money.

When informing Sarah about the money, Hank maintains that they should keep it, suggesting that it is a crime only "if someone gets hurt." Sarah believes they have enough money but is swayed by his arguments and agrees that they should keep the money. She convinces Hank that he should return $500,000 to the airplane, reasoning that authorities would believe that if someone found the money, they would never leave such a sum in the airplane. With this suggestion, Sarah becomes an integral participant in the scheme; she may believe that it is wrong to keep the money, but she wants it. She stresses the need to be careful, telling Hank, "That's what we have to be from now on. We have to be careful. We have to be thinking ahead all of the time."

Visiting Sarah in the library, Hank reads some articles that Sarah obtained about a kidnapping. The child's parents paid a $4.4 million ransom to the abductors. Hank insists that because they now know from whom they are stealing, the situation is changed. Sarah objects: "Hank, it's always been stealing. We just didn't know who were we stealing from." Hank is uneasy about the money, but Sarah persuades him that because the money is not counterfeit, everything will be satisfactory.

While in the hospital for the birth of her daughter, Sarah devises a scheme for Hank to tape-record Lou confessing that he killed one of the local townspeople, a murder actually committed by Hank to protect the money. Using the scheme designed by Sarah, Hank manages to record Lou confessing to the murder. Shortly after Hank reveals that he recorded the confession, Lou becomes incensed about Hank's deceptive ploy to obtain his confession on tape. Lou grabs a shotgun and demands the tape. In the ensuing argument, Lou is shot by Jacob and Lou's wife is shot by Hank. The brothers, primarily Hank, prepare a story to give to the authorities, making the shootings appear as if it were a husband-wife conflict that ended tragically. The police accept their account of the incident, but Jacob is troubled with his part in the scheme.

Shortly after the funerals, an FBI agent arrives and wants the two brothers and sheriff to assist in locating the downed airplane. Sarah suspects the agent is not from the FBI, but one of the two men involved in the kidnapping—the pilot's accomplice. Hank, frustrated about the involvement of the FBI, decides to take the money back to the airplane. Sarah makes an impassioned plea for Hank to keep it, stressing that Hank needs the money, their daughter needs the money, and she needs the money. "What about me?" she asks Hank, continuing, "Spending the rest of my life, eight hours a day, with a fake smile plastered on my face. Checking out books." She continues on, complaining about living on a meager income, "Only going out to restaurants for special occasions ... having to watch what we order, skipping the appetizer, coming home for dessert. You think that's going to make me happy?" She then mentions the fate of his brother, "It's back to the welfare office for Jacob. The occasional odd job.... Just himself and his dog all alone in that filthy apartment. How long do you give him, Hank?"

Sarah's argument to keep the money prevails. She rationalizes that their economic

A Simple Plan (1998). Librarian Sarah Mitchell (Bridget Fonda) appears hopelessly imprisoned as she peers through book stacks.

situation demands it. Knowing that the money will provide a better life for them is justification for Sarah. Having committed murder to protect the money, Hank vacillates between keeping and returning it. Sarah fails to understand Hank's dilemma; she unabashedly demands they keep the money.

The next morning, Sarah telephones the FBI and discovers the man posing as an FBI agent is an imposter; he is one of the kidnappers. She informs Hank, who is able to obtain a revolver in the sheriff's office before driving out to the crash area. At the crash site, the imposter shoots the sheriff and Hank shoots the imposter. Jacob, however, cannot go on with the subterfuge and requests that Hank shoot him, making it look as if the imposter did it. Hank shoots his brother and fabricates a story to account for the shootings and death of the three men.

While interviewing Hank, the authorities mention that they will recover the missing money; they have the serial numbers of about 1 in 10 of the bills. They just have to wait until some of the bills begin to circulate, because individuals remember who give them $100 bills. The authorities believe Hank's version of the incident, permitting him to leave. At home, he burns the money in the fireplace, fighting with a desperate Sarah who wants to keep it and move away. In the film's next and ending scenes, Sarah, with a depressive, somber face, is shelving books in the library, while Hank dishearteningly works in the feed store.

Sarah continues the long line of reel librarians who are dissatisfied with their financial position. Initially believing they had "enough money," Sarah envisions a lifestyle without overriding monetary problems. She, as Elsie Braden in *Violent Saturday* (1955), is tempted by and easily succumbs to the opportunity to obtain money. The right or wrong associated with taking such money is an ethical issue that is quickly brushed aside by both women. Both need money; consequently, they use a Machiavellian approach—obtaining something you desperately need cannot be wrong. For Sarah, however, the price of retaining the money is the murder of five individuals— four by Hank and one by Jacob. Her brother-in-law Jacob could not intellectually rationalize his participation in these deaths, requesting that he be shot rather than live with such an ethical burden. Sarah is unaffected by these events, failing to realize their significance in her quest for money. She is willing to accept a 1-in-10 chance of being apprehended and struggles with Hank over the burning of the money. Hank and Sarah commit a number of felonies during this film and walk away free as it closes. They end where they began, poor and hardworking, but with bitter memories of what might have been and the loss of friends and a family member.

In the film's library scenes, the camera is located on one side of a book stack, taking shots of Sarah through vacant slots of standing books on the shelves. Sarah appears to be imprisoned; the books remaining on the shelves appear as bars as the camera follows Sarah moving in the next aisle. These camera shots are reminiscent of the shots of an imprisoned John Lewis in the Aberdarcy Public Library in *Only Two Can Play* (1962).

Rachel Weisz[105] stars as librarian Evelyn Carnahan, in *The Mummy* (1999); the film's location is Egypt during the 1920s. Although Evelyn is the leading female character, her occupation is incidental to the storyline and the film's one library scene is designed for comedy. Reel librarians have appeared frequently on ladders since Sylvia Hayes used a ladder to shelve books in *The Lost Romance* (1921). Since 1932, when Connie Randall and Babe Stewart utilized the library ladder for an amusing and comedic scene in *No Man of Her Own*, filmmakers have developed innumerable scenes involving reel librarians and library ladders for the express purposes of comedy. *The Mummy* provides filmgoers with the funniest library ladder scene of the century.

As the library scene opens, Evelyn is working in the Museum of Antiquities, shelving books atop a very tall ladder between two rows of book stacks. Standing on the 10th rung of a 13-rung ladder, she is shelving an armload of books when she notices that one of the volumes belongs in the shelves behind her. She turns the ladder so that she can lean back and put the book where it belongs. The shift of her weight, however, pulls the ladder away from the stacks; the ladder is now perpendicular to the floor and swaying between the shelving. The ladder is too difficult for her to balance; as Evelyn manages to turn the ladder around, it falls into the stack in which she is shelving books. The impact of the ladder and Evelyn tip the stack over and it falls into the next stack, and in domino fashion, knocks over all 18 free-standing book stacks. The stacks located at the four corners of the room are placed at 45-degree angles, which permits the domino effect to turn corners and circle back to Evelyn. "Oops!" she utters to herself, as she surveys the fallen book stacks; the books and documents, just moments ago shelved in proper order, are now in complete disarray over the floor of the library.

The curator and head of the library, Dr. Terrence Bey (Erick Avari[106]) appears, completely flabbergasted at the shambles of the collection, and concludes that Evelyn is "a catastrophe." He asks why he continues to employ her, and she offers, in her defense, this logical explanation: "Well, well, you put up with me, because, because I can, I can read and write ancient Egyptian, and I can, I can decipher hieroglyphs and hieratic, and, well, well, I am the only person within a thousand miles who knows how to properly code and catalogue this library." The curator, however, cuts to the quick and responds immediately, "I put up with you because your mother and father were our finest patrons." He demands that she "straighten up" the shambles and leaves.

The librarian, hearing an unusual noise from a nearby gallery, goes to investigate and finds her brother Jonathan (John Hannah), slightly inebriated, in the gallery. He shows her an ancient box he allegedly found in Thebes, and upon opening the box, Evelyn finds a map on a sheet of papyrus. They take the map to the curator who shows little interest until Evelyn suggests that it reveals the location of Hamunaptra, a rumored city of the dead where early pharaohs hid their wealth; the city, according to legend, disappeared about four thousand years ago. Bey maintains that Hamunaptra is a myth, and as he examines the map, he leans too close to a candle on his desk and the map catches fire. Evelyn and Jonathan rush to put out the flames but part of the map is destroyed. Bey's deliberate carelessness with the map is explained later in the film; he is a member of a secret society that guards Hamunaptra to ensure that the city remains concealed so that Imhotep, an evil high priest, never returns to destroy mankind.

Jonathan finally admits that he obtained the box from Richard O'Connell (Brendan Fraser), who is in Cairo Prison and sentenced to hang. Evelyn, bargaining with the warden, manages to secure his release. On the boat trip to Hamunaptra, Evelyn wears reading glasses to read a book; the second and last time she wears them in the film. At their base camp at Hamunaptra, Jonathan one evening becomes drunk and passes out while Evelyn and O'Connell, although very inebriated, remain conscious and talk. Evelyn attempts to explain why she came to Hamunaptra, and cites the fact that both of her parents were adventurers. She then remarks, "I may not be an explorer, or an adventurer, or a treasure seeker, or a gunfighter, Mister O'Connell, but I am proud of what I am!" O'Connell, a little puzzled by her statement, wants to know, "And what is that?" "I ..." Evelyn begins and then pauses for several seconds, appearing as if she does not know what to say; she finally finds the right words and announces with some degree of pride, "am a librarian!" From this point, the film centers on the group's efforts to stop Imhotep from being reborn and the action adventure story becomes fantasy.

Evelyn, in the library scene, projects the stereotypical image. In his screenplay, director Stephen Sommers describes Evelyn, a brunette, in this manner: "eye-glasses, hair-in-a-bun, long boring dress, your typical prudish nightmare."[107] Sommers and Weisz achieved this image of Evelyn on-screen. The librarian demonstrates her mastery of ancient languages on occasion, revealing that she is an accomplished linguist. Evelyn provides the intellect; O'Connell provides the muscle; while Jonathan, playing the role of bumbling sidekick, provides comedy and miscues.

Conclusion

The occupational tasks of reel librarians changed very little during the twentieth century. Although libraries and librarians began converting card catalogs to online catalogs, which necessitated the replacement of card catalog cabinets with computer stations during the 1980s, only a few films of the 1990s (for example, *Monkey Trouble*, 1994, and *City of Angels*, 1998) showcase librarians demonstrating their expertise with computers. This technological advance changed many of the occupational tasks of working librarians that have yet to be reflected extensively in motion pictures. As a great number of libraries no longer have card catalog cabinets in public areas, filmmakers in the twenty-first century should encounter minimal difficulties accommodating this change in occupational tasks. The observable, staple occupational tasks of working librarians, such as shelving books and pushing booktrucks, undoubtedly will continue to be used frequently by filmmakers.

Afterword

The image of librarians in motion pictures during the twentieth century remained relatively stable; changes that occurred were infinitesimal and insignificant. On the whole, libraries and working librarians, as their image in films, changed very little during the twentieth century. From a casual perspective, there were few meaningful visual modifications in libraries until the widespread use of computer applications revolutionized cataloging, public service, and reference functions. Libraries and librarians began converting to online catalogs, replacing cabinets with computer stations during the 1980s, but few films reflected this change.

Any filmgoer of any generation of the twentieth century would immediately recognize a librarian in any motion picture released during any year of the century. The visual characteristics associated with the stereotypical image—age, eyeglasses, hairstyle (bun or baldness), and clothes—which began to appear in 1917 were displayed unabatedly in films released throughout the remainder of the century. The most apparent change during the century was in clothing, which was affected most dramatically by the introduction and widespread use of color, primarily Technicolor and DeLuxe Color. Clothes prior to the use of color appeared on-screen as black, white, or a shade of gray; for reel librarians, already dressed in nondescript clothes, black and white enhanced the drab personality of their screen characters. Color provided a slight degree of relief to prosaic costumes, but many supporting actors portraying reel librarians were often dressed in darker hues, negating the effect of color. The majority of reel librarians who are or appear to be middle-aged or older dress conservatively, adhering to a real-life cliche that these individuals dress more conservatively than their younger counterparts.

The percentages of reel librarians displaying the visual characteristics of eyeglasses, receding hairline or baldness (in the case of males) or bun (in the case of females), and age, are shown in Table 1, Visual Characteristics of Male Reel Librarians, and Table 2, Visual Characteristics of Female Reel Librarians. The clothing characteristic is not included in the tabulation. The data for these tables is compiled from

TABLE 1. VISUAL CHARACTERISTICS OF MALE REEL LIBRARIANS

Decades	Glasses	Receding/ Bald	Ages									TOTAL
			Teens	20s	30s	40s	50s	60s	70s	80s		
Silent		1			1	1	1					3
1930s	4	2		1			2	2	1			6
1940s	4	3			1	2	2	1				6
1950s	2	2		1	3	2	1	2				9
1960s	7	3		4	5	7	2	3				21
1970s	2	1		1		1	1	1				4
1980s	11	4		5	4	2	3	5				19
1990s	6	7		5	6	2	8	1				22
TOTALS	36	23		17	20	17	20	15				90
	40%	26%		19%	22%	19%	22%	17%	1%			

Filmography A; one film, *UHF* (1989), which features Conan the Librarian, however, is not included in the data. Of the 326 total librarians, 236 (or 72 percent) are women, and 90 (or 28 percent) are men. The three formative films of 1932 (*Forbidden, Young Bride,* and *No Man of Her Own*) had a combined total of 10 librarians; 8 were women, a percentage that closely approximates the percentage for the entire century. The occupation is predominantly female, and this is reflected in motion pictures.

The percentages relating to visual characteristics for men and women reel librarians are remarkably similar. Thirty-four percent of women and 40 percent of men wear or hold eyeglasses, while 28 percent of women sport a bun and 26 percent of men display a receding hairline or baldness. Three percent of women, but no men, are or appear to be younger than 20; 53 percent of women and 41 percent of men are between the ages of 20 and 40; 42 percent of women and 58 percent of men are between the ages of 40 and 70; and 2 percent of women and 1 percent of men are over the age of 70. Throughout the century, 59 percent of the men are 40 or older, while only 43 percent of the women are over 40.

The fact that 57 percent of women reel librarians are or appear to be younger than 40 has not impacted the elderly characteristic of the stereotypical image. This may be attributable to the size of the differential; 14 percent (32 reel librarians) may be significant statistically, but the data covers more than an 80-year time span and is based on only 236 screen characters. The numbers, quite frankly, are too insignificant to effect any change of the image. In the silent era and in every decade through the 1980s, the greatest number of women librarians are or appear to be younger than 40; in the 1990s, however, this trend changed. During this last decade of the twentieth century, 54 percent of the women librarians are 40 or older. Whether the percentage of women librarians over 40 will continue to increase is unclear.

TABLE 2. VISUAL CHARACTERISTICS OF FEMALE REEL LIBRARIANS

Decades	Glasses	Bun	Teens	20s	30s	40s	50s	60s	70s	80s	TOTAL
Silent	1	3		5	2	3	1				11
1930s	7	7	2	6	3	3	3				17
1940s	6	11	1	11	5	9	3	1		1	31
1950s	4	7	1	6	8	6	3	2			26
1960s	6	10	1	9	5	2	5	1			23
1970s	11	6		8	8	1	4	1	1		23
1980s	19	9	1	6	17	8	7	3	1		43
1990s	26	13	1	14	14	10	10	11	1	1	62
TOTALS	80	66	7	65	62	42	36	19	3	2	236
	34%	28%	3%	28%	26%	18%	15%	8%	1%	1%	

The stereotypical image of librarians is embedded deeply in the psyche of American popular culture, and librarians, on the whole, display some degree of concern about this image. Although many working librarians have expressed displeasure with the universally recognized stereotype over the decades, this aversion to the image has not effected one whit of change. Members of the occupation have acquiesced to the entertaining but ineffectual activity of talking among themselves about the stereotype; they have reached, in effect, a tenuous accommodation with the image. Librarians, however, need to embrace the stereotype, as have filmgoers and the general public. Acknowledging the validity of the century-old stereotypical image is essential to revolutionizing the image. Librarians laboring in concert, and with assiduity, have the intellectual capacity to modernize this image in the twenty-first century, provided they have the desire. The twentieth-century salutation and, by extension, epitaph for librarians, "Old Lady Foureyes," will continue indefinitely until librarians accept the challenge to modernize the stereotypical image for the benefit of their cultural, social, and economic welfare. This occupational task must become the "manifest destiny" of librarians and their local, state, and national organizations and associations. Without such dedication on the part of librarians, the stereotypical image will persevere not only in films but in all media.

Filmography A: Films Considered for Inclusion in the Narrative

The motion pictures in the following filmography were considered for inclusion in the narrative, and many were; the authors have not, however, chosen to discuss every motion picture meeting the basic inclusion criteria.

The following abbreviations are used:

B	Bun
Dir	Director
E	Eyeglasses
LC	Library cast
NCN	No character name
[NV]	Not viewed
R	Receding hairline, balding, or bald

Adventure   (Metro-Goldwyn-Mayer, 1945) Dir: Victor Fleming
    LC: Greer Garson (41) as Emily Sears E

Agnes of God   (Columbia Pictures, 1985) Dir: Norman Jewison
    LC: Victor Desy (50s)—NCN E

All the President's Men   (Warner Bros., 1976) Dir: Alan J. Pakula
    LC: James Murtaugh (50s)—NCN R; Jaye Stewart (20s)—NCN E; Jamie Smith-Jackson (20s)—NCN E

Angel's Dance   (York Entertainment, 1999) Dir: David L. Corley
    LC: Caroline Alexander (30s)—NCN B

Apartment for Peggy   (20th Century–Fox, 1948) Dir: George Seaton
    LC: Jeanne Crain (23) as Peggy

As Young As You Feel   (20th Century–Fox, 1951) Dir: Harmon Jones
    LC: Carol Savage (20s)—NCN

The Attic   (Atlantic, 1979) Dir: George Edwards
   LC: Carrie Snodgress (33) as Louise Elmore B; Ruth Cox (20s) as Emily Perkins E;
   Frances Bay (61)—NCN; Terry Troutt (40s) as Donald E

Baby Boom   (United Artists, 1987) Dir: Charles Shyer
   LC: Uncredited (20s)—female NCN E

Bed of Roses   (New Line Cinema, 1996) Dir: Michael Goldenberg
   LC: Mary Alice (55) as Alice

Big Bully   (Warner Bros., 1996) Dir: Steve Miner
   LC: Norma MacMillan (75) as Mrs. Rumpert E

The Big Sleep   (Warner Bros., 1946) Dir: Howard Hawks
   LC: Carole Douglas (20s)—NCN B, E; Uncredited (30s)—female NCN B

Black Mask   [Hap Hak] (Artisan Entertainment, 1996; Hong Kong) Dir: Daniel Lee
   LC: Jet Li (33) as Michael/Simon/Tsui Chik/Black Mask; Karen Mok (26) as Tracy Lee;
   Uncredited (50s)—male NCN E; Uncredited (30s)—male NCN E; Uncredited (30s)—
   male NCN

Bliss   (Triumph Releasing Co., 1997) Dir: Lance Young
   LC: Lois Chiles (50) as Eva E

The Blot   (Lois Weber Productions, 1921) Dir: Phillips Smalley/Lois Weber
   LC: Claire Windsor (29) as Amelia Griggs; Uncredited (40s)—female NCN

Bluebeard's Ten Honeymoons   (Allied Artists, 1960; UK) Dir: W. Lee Wilder
   LC: Milo Sperber (49)—NCN E

Bon Voyage!   (Buena Vista, 1962) Dir: James Neilson
   LC: James Millhollin (47)—NCN

Breakfast at Tiffany's   (Paramount Pictures, 1961) Dir: Blake Edwards
   LC: Elvia Allman (57)—NCN; Uncredited (40s)—male NCN

The Broken Gate   (J.L. Frotheringham Productions, 1920) [NV] Dir: Paul Scardon
   LC: Evelyn Selbie (49) as Julia Delafield

The Broken Gate   (Tiffany Productions, 1927) [NV] Dir: James C. McKay
   LC: Florence Turner (42) as Julia Fisher

Buried on Sunday aka **Northern Extremes**   (Salter Street Films International, 1992;
      Canada) Dir: Paul Donovan
   LC: Jean Gregson (60s)—NCN B, E

Cain and Mabel   (Cosmopolitan/Warner Bros., 1936) Dir: Lloyd Bacon
   LC: Lillian Lawrence (50s)—NCN B, E; Harry C. Bradley (67)—NCN R, E

Cal   (Warner Bros./Goldcrest, 1984; UK/Ireland) Dir: Pat O'Connor
   LC: Helen Mirren (39) as Marcella B

The Captain Hates the Sea   (Columbia, 1934) Dir: Lewis Milestone
   LC: Helen Vinson (27) as Janet Grayson

Celine and Julie Go Boating [Celine et Julie Vent en Bateau]   (Action Films/Les Films
      Christian Fachner, 1974; France) Dir: Jacques Rivette
   LC: Dominique Labourier (31) as Julie; Ann Zamire (20s) as Lil

Chances Are   (TriStar Pictures, 1989) Dir: Emile Ardolino
  LC: Kathleen Freeman (70) as Mrs. Handy; Robert Downey, Jr. (24) as Alex Finch

Christine   (Columbia, 1983) Dir: John Carpenter
  LC: Jan Burrell (50s)—NCN E

Citizen Kane   (Mercury/RKO, 1941) Dir: Orson Welles
  LC: Georgia Backus (41) as Miss Anderson E

City of Angels   (Warner Borthers, 1998) Dir: Brad Silberling
  LC: Sid Hillman (30)—NCN R, E

City Slickers II: The Legend of Curly's Gold   (Castle Rock–Columbia, 1994) Dir: Paul
    Weiland
  LC: Helen Siff (50s)—NCN E; Uncredited (20s)—male NCN

Clean, Shaven   (Strand Releasing, 1994) Dir: Lloyd Kerrigan
  LC: June Kelly (60s)—NCN

Commandments   (Gramercy Pictures, 1997) Dir: Daniel Taplitz
  LC: Uncredited (40s)—female NCN

Confessions of a Nazi Spy   (Warner Bros., 1939) Dir: Anatole Litvak
  LC: Uncredited (20s)—male NCN

The Convent [O Convento]   (Strand Releasing, 1995; Portugal/France) Dir: Manoel de
    Oliveira
  LC: Leonor Silveira (25) as Piedade

Cop-Out aka **Stranger in the House**   (Cinerama Releasing Corp., 1967; UK) Dir: Pierre
    Rouve
  LC: Pippa Steel (19) as Sue Phillips; Melinda Mays (30s)—NCN

Criminal Law   (Hemdale Film Corporation, 1988) Dir: Martin Campbell
  LC: Irene Kessler (50s) as Peggy

The Crimson Kimono   (Columbia, 1959) Dir: Samuel Fuller
  LC: Stafford Repp (41)—NCN R; Neyle Morrow (30s) as Paul Sand

Curse of the Demon aka **Night of the Demon**   (Columbia, 1957; UK) Dir: Jacques
    Tournear
  LC: John Salew (60)—NCN R

Dangerous Minds   (Hollywood Pictures–Buena Vista, 1995) Dir: John N. Smith
  LC: Jeff Feringa (50s)—NCN; Sarah Marshall (62)—NCN B

December   (IRS Releasing, 1991) Dir: Gabe Torres
  LC: Ann Hartfield (40s) as Mrs. Langley

Defense of the Realm   (Hemdale Film Corporation, 1985; UK) Dir: David Drury
  LC: Uncredited (30s)—female NCN

Desk Set   (Fox, 1957) Dir: Walter Lang
  LC: Katharine Hepburn (50) as Bunny Watson B; Joan Blondell (51) as Peg Costello;
    Dina Merrill (32) as Sylvia Blair; Sue Randall (22) as Ruthie Saylor

Destiny   (Universal, 1944) Dir: Julien Duvivier and Reginald Le Borg
  LC: Grace McDonald (26) as Betty

Doctor in Love   (Governor Films, 1960; UK) Dir: Ralph Thomas
    LC: Sheila Hancock (27)—NCN

Dragonfly aka *One Summer Love*   (American International Pictures, 1976) Dir: Gilbert
        Cates
    LC: Mimi Obler (56)—NCN

Dream with the Fishes   (Sony Pictures Classics, 1997) Dir: Finn Taylor
    LC: Beth Daly (20s)—NCN E; Uncredited (40s)—female NCN

The Dunwich Horror   (American International Pictures, 1970) Dir: Daniel Haller
    LC: Sandra Dee (26) as Nancy Wagner; Donna Baccala (25) as Elizabeth Hamilton

Empty Beach   (Jethro Film Productions, 1985; Australia) Dir: Chris Thomson
    LC: Deborah Kennedy (30s)—NCN

The FBI Story   (Warner Bros., 1959) Dir: Mervyn LeRoy
    LC: Vera Miles (30) as Lucy Ballard B; Uncredited (40s)—female NCN B, E

Fighting Trouble   (Allied Artists, 1956) Dir: George Blair
    LC: Uncredited (20s)—female NCN B

Flesh and Fantasy   (Universal, 1943) Dir: Julien Duvivier
    LC: Ian Wolfe (47)—NCN E

Flight of the Intruder   (Paramount Pictures,1990) Dir: John Milius
    LC: Adam Biesk (20s)—NCN

Forbidden   (Columbia, 1932) Dir: Frank Capra
    LC: Barbara Stanwyck (25) as Lulu Smith E; Thomas Jefferson (76) as Mr. Wilkinson E;
    Uncredited (50s) as Phil

Forever Young   (Warner Bros., 1992) Dir: Steve Miner
    LC: Amanda Foreman (26) as Debbie

Foul Play   (Paramount, 1978) Dir: Colin Higgins
    LC: Goldie Hawn (33) as Gloria Mundy E; Marilyn Sokol (30s) as Stella; Irene Tedrow
    (71) as Mrs. Monk B, E

The Freeze Out   (Universal Film Manufacturing Company, 1921) [NV] Dir: John Ford
    LC: J. Farrell MacDonald (46) as Bobtail McGuire

Gentlemen Are Born   (First National–Warner Brothers, 1934) Dir: Alfred E. Green
    LC: Ann Dvorak (32) as Susan Merrill; Virginia Howell (50s) as Miss Graham B, E

Getting It On   (Comworld Pictures, Inc., 1983) Dir: William Olsen
    LC: Fran Taylor (30s) as Mrs. Hatfield E

Ghostbusters   (Columbia Pictures, 1984) Dir: Ivan Reitman
    LC: Alice Drummond (55) as Alice; John Rothman (35) as Roger Delacorte

A Girl Named Tamiko   (Paramount Pictures, 1962) Dir: John Sturges
    LC: France Nuyen (23) as Tamiko B

The Girl Rush   (Paramount, 1955) Dir: Robert Pirosh
    LC: Rosalind Russell (48) as Kim Halliday

Gods and Monsters   (Lions Gate Films, 1998; UK) Dir: Bill Condon
    LC: Lisa Vastine (20s)—NCN B

The Good Companions   (Gaumont/Fox, 1933; UK) Dir: Victor Saville
  LC: Hugh E. Wright (55)—NCN E

Good News   (Metro-Goldwyn-Mayer, 1947) Dir: Charles Walters
  LC: June Allyson (30) as Connie Lane; Uncredited (50s)—female NCN

Goodbye, Columbus   (Paramount Pictures, 1969) Dir: Larry Peerce
  LC: Richard Benjamin (31) as Neil Klugman; Delos V. Smith, Jr. (63) as Mr. Scapelle E;
  Bill Derringer (30s) as John McKee E; Uncredited (50s) as Gloria B; Uncredited (30s) as
  Natasha B, E

The Gun in Betty Lou's Handbag   (Touchstone Pictures, 1992) Dir: Allan Moyle
  LC: Penelope Ann Miller (28) as Mrs. Elizabeth Louise "Betty Lou" Perkins; Marian Seldes
  (64) as Margaret Armstrong B, E

Hammett   (Zoetrope Studios, 1982) Dir: Wim Wenders
  LC: Marilu Henner (30) as Kit Conger; Liz Roberson (20s)—female NCN B, E

Happy Together   (Apollo, 1989) Dir: Mel Damski
  LC: Rocky Parker (50)—NCN E

Hard Boiled [Lashou Shentan]   (Rim, 1992; Hong Kong) Dir: John Woo
  LC: Hoi-Shan Lai (20s)—NCN E

Harry and the Hendersons   (Universal Pictures, 1987) Dir: William Dear
  LC: Peggy Platt (20s)—NCN E; Uncredited (30s)—female NCN E

Has Anybody Seen My Gal?   (Universal, 1952) Dir: Douglas Sirk
  LC: Uncredited (40s)—male NCN; Uncredited (60s)—female NCN B, E

Hear My Song   (Miramax Films, 1991; US/UK) Dir: Peter Chelsom
  LC: Mary MacLeod (60s)—NCN E

Henry Fool   (Sony Pictures Classics, 1997) Dir: Hal Hartley
  LC: Uncredited (50s)—female NCN E

High School High   (TriStar Pictures, 1996) Dir: Hart Bochner
  LC: Uncredited (40s)—female NCN B, E

Homicide   (Triumph Releasing Corporation, 1991) Dir: David Mamet
  LC: Steven Goldstein (28)—NCN; Charlotte Potok (60s)—NCN

Hot Spell   (Paramount, 1958) Dir: Daniel Mann and George Cukor
  LC: Clint Kimbrough (26) as Billy; Elsie Weller (50s)—NCN B

The House by the Cemetery [Quella Villa Accanto al Cimitero]   (Almi Pictures, 1981;
    Italy) Dir: Lucio Fulci
  LC: Gianpaolo Saccarola (20s) as Daniel Douglas E

The House on Carroll Street   (Orion Pictures, 1988) Dir: Peter Yates
  LC: William Duff-Griffin (48) as Wentworth R, E

How I Got into College   (20th Century–Fox, 1989) Dir: Savage Steve Holland
  LC: Marlene Warfield (49)—NCN E

The Human Comedy   (Universal, 1943) Dir: Clarence Brown
  LC: Adeline De Walt Reynolds (81)—NCN B

Hysterical   (Embassy, 1983) Dir: Chris Bearde
  LC: Franklyn Ajaye (34) as Leroy **E**

I Love Trouble   (Touchstone–Buena Vista Pictures, 1994) Dir: Charles Shyer
  LC: Annie Meyers-Shyer (teens)—NCN; Uncredited (40s)—female NCN **E**

I Love You to Death   (TriStar Pictures, 1990) Dir: Lawrence Kasdan
  LC: Audrey Rapoport (30s)—NCN

I Was a Shoplifter   (Universal, 1950) Dir: Charles Lamont
  LC: Mona Freeman (24) as Faye Burton

Indiana Jones and the Last Crusade   (Paramount, 1989) Dir: Steven Spielberg
  LC: Uncredited (60s)—male NCN **E**

Interlude   (Universal, 1957) Dir: Douglas Sirk
  LC: June Allyson (40) as Helen Banning; Frances Bergen (32) as Gertrude Kirk

Invasion of the Bee Girls   (Centaur, 1973) Dir: Denis Sanders
  LC: Victoria Vetri (29) as Julie Zorn **B, E**

Irezumi: Spirit of Tattoo [Sekka Tomurai Zaski]   (Daiei Films, 1982; Japan) Dir: Yoichi
  Takabayashi
  LC: Masayo Utsunomiya (20s) as Akane; Yuhsuke Takita (40s) as Fujieda

Ironweed   (TriStar Pictures, 1987) Dir: Hector Bobenco
  LC: Bethel Leslie (58)—NCN

It's a Wonderful Life   (Liberty Films/RKO, 1946) Dir: Frank Capra
  LC: Donna Reed (25) as Mary **B, E**

Joe Versus the Volcano   (Warner Bros., 1990) Dir: John Patrick Shanley
  LC: Tom Hanks (34) as Joe Banks

Joey Breaker   (Skouras Pictures, 1993) Dir: Steven Starr
  LC: Fred Fondren (46) as Alfred Moore

Katie Did It   (Universal, 1951) Dir: Frederick De Cordova
  LC: Ann Blyth (23) as Katherine Standish; Uncredited (60s)—male NCN **E**

Keep the Aspidistra Flying   (Overseas Film Group, 1997; UK) Dir: Robert Bierman
  LC: Joan Blackham (50s)—NCN **B, E**; Uncredited (30s)—female NCN

Kes   (United Artists, 1969; UK) Dir: Ken Loach
  LC: Zoe Sutherland (20s)—NCN

The Killing Kind   (Media Cinema, 1973) Dir: Curtis Harrington
  LC: Luana Anders (35) as Louise **B, E**

Lady in the Dark   (Paramount, 1944) Dir: Mitchell Leisen
  LC: Mary MacLaren (48) as Ms. Black

Lamb   (Capitol Films, 1986; UK) Dir: Colin Gregg
  LC: Uncredited (40s)—female NCN **B, E**

The Last American Virgin   (Cannon, 1982) Dir: Boaz Davidson
  LC: Blanche Rubin (62)—NCN **E**

The Last Supper   (Sony Pictures Entertainment, 1995) Dir: Stacy Title
  LC: Pamela Glen (38)—NCN **B**

The Likely Lads   (EMI, 1976; UK) Dir: Michael Tuchner
LC: Brigit Forsyth (30s) as Thelma; Uncredited (50s)—female NCN

Lily of the Dust   (Famous Players–Lasky, 1924) [NV] Dir: Dimitri Buchowetski
LC: Pola Negri (30) as Lily Czapanek

Lola   (United Artists Classics, 1981; West Germany) Dir: Rainer Werner Fassbinder
LC: Andrea Heuer (30s)—NCN B, E

The Lords of Discipline   (Paramount Pictures, 1983) Dir: Franc Roddam
LC: Helena Stevens (60s)—NCN E

Lorenzo's Oil   (Universal Pictures, 1992) Dir: George Miller
LC: Mary Pat Gleason (40s)—NCN; Uncredited (60s)—female NCN; Uncredited (30s)—female NCN E; Uncredited (40s)—female NCN E

The Lost Romance   (Famous Players–Lasky, 1921) [NV] Dir: William C. DeMille
LC: Lois Wilson (27) as Sylvia Hayes B; Mayme Kelso (54)—NCN B, E

Love Story   (Paramount, 1970) Dir: Arthur Hiller
LC: Ali McGraw (32) as Jenny Cavalleri E

Mad Love   (Touchstone–Buena Vista, 1995) Dir: Antonia Bird
LC: Sharon Collar (40s)—NCN E

The Magician   (Metro-Goldwyn-Mayer Pictures, 1926) Dir: Rex Ingram
LC: Uncredited (50s)—male NCN R; Uncredited (40s)—female NCN

Maisie Was a Lady   (Loew's/Metro-Goldwyn-Mayer, 1941) Dir: Edwin L. Marin
LC: None

Major League   (Paramount Pictures, 1989) Dir: David S. Ward
LC: Rene Russo (35) as Lynn Wells E; Uncredited (60s)—male NCN E; Uncredited (60s)—female NCN; Uncredited (50s)—male NCN; Uncredited (40s)—female NCN; Uncredited (20s)—male NCN E

A Man Betrayed aka **Wheel of Fortune**   (Republic, 1941) Dir: John H. Auer
LC: Minerva Urecal (47)—NCN B, E

The Man Who Never Was   (Sumar/Fox, 1956) Dir: Ronald Neame
LC: Gloria Grahame (33) as Lucy Sherwood E; Uncredited (60s)—female NCN

Margie   (20th Century–Fox, 1946) Dir: Henry King
LC: Lynn Bari (33) as Miss Isabelle Palmer

Matilda   (TriStar Pictures, 1996) Dir: Danny DeVito
LC: Jean Speegle Howard (69) as Miss Phelps E

Maxie   (Orion Pictures, 1985) Dir: Paul Aaron
LC: Mandy Patinkin (33) as Nick Chaney E; Valerie Curtin (40) as Miss Ophelia Sheffer E

Mercury Rising   (Universal Pictures, 1998) Dir: Harold Becker
LC: Barbara Alexander (40s)—NCN E

The Misadventures of Merlin Jones   (Walt Disney, 1964) Dir: Robert Stevenson
LC: Uncredited (50s)—female NCN E

Mr. Belvedere Rings the Bell   (20th Century–Fox, 1951) Dir: Henry Koster
LC: Dorothy Neumann (37)—NCN B

Mr. Moto in Danger Island   (20th Century–Fox, 1939) Dir: Herbert I. Leeds
LC: Renie Riano (40)—NCN **B**

Mr. Sycamore   (Capricorn/Film Venture, Inc., 1975) Dir: Pancho Kohner
LC: Jean Simmons (46) as Estelle Benbow **E**

Monkey Trouble   (New Line Cinema, 1994) Dir: France Amurri
LC: Julie Payne (54)—NCN **E**

Movie Movie   (Warner Bros., 1978) Dir: Stanley Donen
LC: Trish Van Devere (35) as Betsy McGuire **E**

The Mummy   (Universal, 1999) Dir: Stephen Sommers
LC: Rachel Weisz (28) as Evelyn Carnahan **B,E**; Erick Avari (47) as Dr. Terrence R. Bey

Murder Ahoy   (Metro-Goldwyn-Mayer, 1964; UK) Dir: George Pollock
LC: None

Murder at the Gallop   (Metro-Goldwyn-Mayer, 1963; UK) Dir: George Pollock
LC: Stringer Davis (67) as Mr. Stringer **R, E**

Murder Most Foul   (Metro-Goldwyn-Mayer, 1964; UK) Dir: George Pollock
LC: None

Murder She Said   (Metro-Goldwyn-Mayer, 1961; UK) Dir: George Pollock
LC: Stringer Davis (65) as Mr. Stringer **R, E**

The Music Man   (Warner Bros. Pictures, 1962) Dir: Morton DaCosta
LC: Shirley Jones (28) as Marian Paroo **B, E**

My Bodyguard   (20th Century–Fox, 1980) Dir: Tony Bill
LC: Dorothy Scott (40s)—NCN **E**

My Science Project   (Buena Vista, 1985) Dir: Jonathan Butuel
LC: Linda Hoy (30s)—NCN; Raphael Sbarge (21) as Sherman **E**

My Side of the Mountain   (Paramount Pictures, 1969) Dir: James B. Clark
LC: Tudi Wiggins (30s) as Miss Turner **E**

Mystery Broadcast   (Republic, 1943) Dir: George Sherman
LC: Frances Pierlot (68) as Mr. Crunch **R, E**

Navy Blues   (Republic, 1937) Dir: Ralph Staub
LC: Mary Brian (31) as Doris Kimbell **B, E**

The Neverending Story III   (Miramax Films, 1994) Dir: Peter MacDonald
LC: Freddie Jones (67) as Mr. Coreander

No Man of Her Own   (Paramount, 1932) Dir: Wesley Ruggles
LC: Carole Lombard (24) as Connie Randall; Lillian Harmer (49) as Mattie **B**

Off Beat   (Touchstone Films, 1986) Dir: Michael Dinner
LC: Judge Reinhold (29) as Joe Gower; John Turturro (29) as Neil Pepper; Amy Wright (36) as Mary Ellen Gruenwald; Jack Fletcher (65) as Alvin **E**

Old Gringo   (Columbia Pictures, 1989) Dir: Luis Puenzo
LC: Laurel Lyle (30s)—NCN **B, E**

The Old Lady Who Walked in the Sea [La Vielle Qui Marchait Dans la Mer]
(Cinepix Film Properties, Inc., 1991; France) Dir: Laurent Heynemann
LC: Lara Guirao (20s)—NCN

One Eight Seven aka *187*   (Warner Bros., 1997) Dir: Kevin Reynolds
LC: Harri James (30s)—NCN

Only 38   (Famous Players–Lasky, 1923) [NV] Dir: William C. DeMille
LC: Lois Wilson (29) as Mrs. Stanley **B**

Only Two Can Play   (Kinsley International Pictures, Columbia Pictures, 1962; UK) Dir:
Sidney Gilliat
LC: Peter Sellers (37) as John Lewis; Kenneth Griffith (41) as Ieuan Jenkins; David
Davies (56) as Mr. Beynon; Uncredited (20s) as Miss Jones; Uncredited (40s) as
Kennedy

Ordeal by Innocence   (London-Cannon Films, 1984; UK) Dir: Desmond Davis
LC: Uncredited (30s)—female NCN **B**

The Pagemaster   (20th Century–Fox, 1994) Dir: Maurice Hunt and Joe Johnston
LC: Christopher Lloyd (56) as Mr. Dewey **R**

The Paper Chase   (Paramount, 1973) Dir: James Bridges
LC: Uncredited (50s)—female NCN **B**

Paperback Romance aka *Lucky Break*   (Metro-Goldwyn-Mayer, 1994; Australia) Dir:
Ben Lewin
LC: Lynda Gibson (30s) as Carol **B, E**

Party Girl   (First Look, 1995) Dir: Daisy von Scherler Mayer
LC: Parker Posey (27) as Mary **E**; Sasha von Scherler (61) as Judy Lindendorf; C. Francis
Blackchild (30s) as Wanda **E**; L. B. Williams (30s) as Howard **R**; Becky Mode (30s) as Ann

Peeping Tom aka *Face of Fear*; *Fotographer of Panic*   (Astor Pictures, 1960; UK)
Dir: Michael Powell
LC: Anna Massey (23) as Helen Stephens

Peggy   (Universal, 1950) [NV] Dir: Frederick De Cordova
LC: Ellen Corby (39) as Mrs. Privet

The Phantom   (Paramount, 1996) Dir: Simon Wincer
LC: Alan Zitner (50s) as Dr. Fleming **R, E**

Philadelphia   (TriStar Pictures, 1993) Dir: Jonathan Demme
LC: Tracey Walter (51)—NCN **R, E**

The Philadelphia Story   (Metro-Goldwyn-Mayer, 1940) Dir: George Cukor
LC: Hilda Plowright (50)—NCN **B**

Pickup on South Street   (20th Century–Fox, 1953) Dir: Samuel Fuller
LC: Uncredited (50s)—male NCN **E**; Uncredited (30s)—male NCN; Jaye Loftin (30s)—
NCN

The Pit aka *Teddy*   (New World Pictures, 1981; Canada) Dir: Lew Lehman
LC: Laura Hollingsworth (30s) as Marg Livingstone **B, E**; Cindy Auten (teens)—NCN

Playroom   (Smart Egg Pictures, 1990) Dir: Manny Coto
LC: Olivera Viktorovic (27)—NCN

Prick Up Your Ears   (Samuel Goldwyn Company, 1987; UK) Dir: Stephen Frears
LC: Selina Cadell (40s) as Miss Battersby; Charles McKeown (50s) as Mr. Cunliffe;
Uncredited (30s)—female NCN

The Prime of Miss Jean Brodie   (20th Century–Fox, 1969) Dir: Ronald Neame
LC: Isla Cameron (40s) as Miss McKenzie **B**

Public Access   (Triboro Entertainment Group, 1993) Dir: Bryan Singer
LC: Dina Brooks (20s) as Rachel

Quiet Please, Murder   (20th Century–Fox, 1942) Dir: John Larkin
LC: Fern Emmett (46) as Miss Philbert **B, E**; Lynne Roberts (23) as Kay Ryan; Byron
Foulgar (43) as Edmund Walpole **R, E**; Margaret Brayton (40s) as Miss Oval; Mae Marsh
(47) as Miss Hartwig

Race with the Devil   (20th Century–Fox, 1975) Dir: Jack Starrett
LC: Uncredited (40s)—female NCN **B, E**

Racing with the Moon   (Paramount Pictures, 1984) Dir: Richard Benjamin
LC: Elizabeth McGovern (23) as Caddie Winger; Patricia Allison (40s) as Mrs. Spangler

Ragtime   (Paramount Pictures, 1981) Dir: Milos Forman
LC: Herman Meckler (60s) as Vernon Elliott

Rome Adventure   (Warner Bros., 1962) Dir: Delmer Daves
LC: Suzanne Pleshette (25) as Prudence Bell

The Rosary Murders   (New Line Cinema, 1987) Dir: Fred Walton
LC: Sandy Broad (30s)—NCN **B**

Rudy   (TriStar Pictures, 1993) Dir: David Anspaugh
LC: Marie Anspaugh (60s) as Miss McKenzie **B**

Running on Empty   (Warner Bros., 1988) Dir: Sidney Lumet
LC: Justine Johnston (50s)—NCN **B**

Salmonberries   (Roxie Releasing, 1991; Germany) Dir: Percy Adlon
LC: Rosel Zech (49) as Roswitha; Jane Lind (35) as Noayak

Scandal Street   (Paramount, 1938) Dir: James P. Hogan
LC: Louise Campbell (27) as Nora Langdon **E**

Scent of a Woman   (Universal Pictures, 1992) Dir: Martin Brest
LC: Chris O'Donnell (22) as Charlie Simms

Scream, Blacula, Scream!   (American International, 1973) Dir: Bob Kelljan
LC: Sybil Scotford (20s)—NCN **E**

Screwballs   (New World Pictures, 1983) Dir: Rafal Zielinski
LC: Carolyn Tweedle (40s)—NCN **E**

Sea Devils   (RKO, 1937) Dir: Benjamin Stoloff
LC: Ida Lupino (19) as Doris Malone; Fern Emmett (41) as Miss McGonigle **B, E**

7 Faces of Dr. Lao   (Metro-Goldwyn-Mayer, 1964) Dir: Kevin Reynolds
LC: Barbara Eden (30) as Angela Benedict **B, E**

The Seventh Coin   (Hemdale Film Corporation, 1993) Dir: Dror Soref
LC: Mark Nelson (20s)—NCN **E**

The Seventh Victim (RKO, 1943) Dir: Mark Robson
LC: Sarah Selby (38) as Miss Gottschalk

Shadow of a Doubt (Universal, 1943) Dir: Alfred Hitchcock
LC: Eily Malyon (64) as Miss Cochran **B**

Shadows in the Storm (TriMark Pictures, 1988) Dir: Terrell Tannen
LC: Ned Beatty (51) as Thelonious Pitt **R, E**

A Simple Plan (Paramount Pictures, 1998) Dir: Sam Raimi
LC: Bridget Fonda (34) as Sarah Mitchell

Slamdance (Island Pictures, 1987) Dir: Wayne Wang
LC: Lin Shage (20s)—NCN

Sleeping with the Enemy (20th Century–Fox, 1991) Dir: Joseph Ruben
LC: Julia Roberts (24) as Sara Waters/Laura Burney

The Snapper (Miramax, 1993; UK) Dir: Stephen Frears
LC: Uncredited (40s)—female NCN; Uncredited (20s)—female NCN **E**

So Well Remembered (Alliance/RKO, 1947; UK) Dir: Edward Dmytryk
LC: Martha Scott (33) as Olivia Channing; Roddy Hughes (56) as Mr. Teasdale **R**

Something Wicked This Way Comes (Walt Disney Pictures, 1983) Dir: Jack Clayton
LC: Jason Robards (61) as Charles Halloway **R, E**

Somewhere in Time (Universal Pictures, 1980) Dir: Jeannot Szwarc
LC: Noreen Walker (30s)—NCN **E**

Sophie's Choice (Universal Pictures, 1982) Dir: Alan J. Pakula
LC: John Rothman (33)—NCN **R, E**

Special Agent (Paramount, 1949) Dir: William C. Thomas
LC: Uncredited (50s) as Miss Tannahill **B**

Spencer's Mountain (Warner Bros., 1963) Dir: Delmer Daves
LC: James MacArthur (26) as Clayboy Spencer

The Spirit of Youth (Tiffany-Stahl Productions, 1929) [NV] Dir: Walter Lang
LC: Dorothy Sebastian (26) as Betty Grant

The Spy Who Came in from the Cold (Paramount Pictures, 1965) Dir: Martin Ritt
LC: Richard Burton (40) as Alec Leamus; Anne Blake (50s) as Miss Crail **B**; Claire Bloom (34) as Nan Perry; Michael Ripper (52) as Mr. Lofthouse

Stanley & Iris (Metro-Goldwyn-Mayer, 1990) Dir: Martin Ritt
LC: Dortha Duckworth (85)—NCN **B**

Start Cheering (Columbia, 1938) Dir: Albert S. Rogell
LC: Arthur Hoyt (64)—NCN **R, E**

Storm Center (Columbia, 1956) Dir: Daniel Taradash
LC: Bette Davis (48) as Alicia Hull; Kim Hunter (34) as Martha Lockridge; Alice Smith (20s) as Susie

Storyville (20th Century–Fox, 1992) Dir: Mark Frost
LC: Ron Gural (50s)—NCN **R, E**

Straight Talk   (Hollywood Pictures, 1992) Dir: Barnet Kellman
   LC: Susan Philpot (50s)—NCN **E**

Strike Up the Band   (Metro-Goldwyn-Mayer, 1940) Dir: Busby Berkeley
   LC: Judy Garland (18) as Mary Holden

The Substitute   (Orion, 1996) Dir: Robert Mandel
   LC: Peggy Pope (67) as Hannah Dillion **E**

Summer of the Monkeys   (Edge Production, 1998; Canada) Dir: Michael Anderson
   LC: Beverly Cooper (30s)—NCN **B, E**

Teenage Mother   (Arrow, 1968) Dir: Jerry Gross
   LC: Uncredited (60s) as Miss Fowler **B, E**

That Kind of Girl   (Tekli, 1963; UK) Dir: Gerry O'Hara
   LC: Frank Jarvis (20s) as Max; Charles Houston (30s) as Ted

That Touch of Mink   (Universal-International, 1962) Dir: Delbert Mann
   LC: Barbara Collentine (40s) as Mrs. Smith **B**

They Might Be Giants   (Universal, 1971) Dir: Anthony Harvey
   LC: Jack Gilford (60s) as William Peabody

This Rebel Breed aka *The Black Rebels*   (Warner Bros., 1960) Dir: Richard L. Bare
   and William Rowland
   LC: Uncredited (50s)—female NCN **B**

This Was Paris aka *So This Was Paris*   (First National Pictures/Warner Bros., 1942)
   Dir: John Harlow
   LC: Miles Malleson (54) as Watson **E**

Threesome   (TriStar Pictures, 1994) Dir: Andrew Fleming
   LC: Anna Marie O'Donnell (60s)—NCN

Transylvania Twist   (Concorde, 1989) Dir: Jim Wynorski
   LC: Steve Altman (20s) as Dexter Ward; Jay Robinson (59) as Uncle Ephram **R**

A Tree Grows in Brooklyn   (20th Century–Fox, 1945) Dir: Elia Kazan
   LC: Lillian Bronson (43)—NCN

The Trespasser   (Republic, 1947) Dir: George Blair
   LC: Janet Martin (20s) as Stevie Carson; Adele Mara (24) as Dee Dee; Warren Douglas
   (36) as Danny Butler

Trust   (Fine Line Features, 1990) Dir: Hal Hartley
   LC: None

Twisted Nerve   (Charter/NG, 1968; UK) Dir: Ray Boulting
   LC: Hayley Mills (22) as Susan Harper; Timothy Bateson (42) as Mr. Groom **E**

UHF   (Orion Pictures, 1989) Dir: Jay Levey
   LC: Roger Callard (40s) as Conan the Librarian

A Very Good Young Man   (Famous Players–Lasky Corporation, 1919) [NV] Dir: Donald
   Crisp
   LC: Bryant Washburn (30) as LeRoy Sylvester

Violent Saturday (20th Century–Fox, 1955) Dir: Richard Fleischer
LC: Sylvia Sidney (44) as Elsie Braden; Joyce Newhard (40s) as Dorothy

Wacko (Jensen Farley, 1981) Dir: Greydon Clark
LC: Jacqulin Cole (30s)—NCN

The War of the Worlds (Paramount, 1953) Dir: Byron Haskin
LC: Ann Robinson (18) as Sylvia Van Buren **B**

The Web (Universal, 1947) Dir: Michael Gordon
LC: Robin Raymond (25)—NCN

Web of Evidence (Georgefield Productions/Allied Artists, 1959; UK) [NV] Dir: Jack Cardiff
LC: Vera Miles (30) as Lena Anderson

Weird Woman (Universal, 1944) Dir: Reginald Le Borg
LC: Evelyn Ankers (26) as Ilona Carr **B**

Wetherby (MGM/UA Entertainment Co., 1985; UK) Dir: David Hare
LC: Judi Dench (51) as Marcia Pilborough

Whispering Footsteps (Republic, 1943) Dir: Howard Bretherton
LC: Marie Blake (48) as Sally Lukens; Uncredited (20s)—female NCN **B**

A Wife on Trial (Universal Film Manufacturing Company, 1917) [NV] Dir: Ruth Ann Baldwin
LC: Mignon Anderson (25) as Phyllis Narcissa Braithwaite

Wishing Ring Man (Vitagraph Company of America, 1919) [NV] Dir: David Smith
LC: Dorothy Hagan (30s) as Phyllis Harrington

With Honors (Warner Bros., 1994) Dir: Alek Keshishian
LC: Patricia B. Butcher (50s)—NCN **E**

Wonder Man (Goldwyn/RKO, 1945) Dir: H. Bruce Humberstone
LC: Virginia Mayo (25) as Ellen Shavley

Young Bride (RKO, 1932) Dir: William A Seiter
LC: Helen Twelvetrees (24) as Allie Smith; Blanche Frederici (54) as Margaret Gordon; Polly Walters (19) as Daisy; Uncredited (20s)—female NCN **B, E**; Uncredited (30s)—female NCN

Young Poisoner's Handbook (CFP Distribution, 1995; UK/Germany/France) Dir: Benjamin Ross
LC: Samantha Edmonds (20s) as Sue Butler; Uncredited (50s)—male NCN; Uncredited (50s)—female NCN **B, E**

You're a Big Boy Now (Seven Arts Pictures, 1966) Dir: Francis Ford Coppola
LC: Peter Kastner (22) as Bernard Chanticleer **E**; Rip Torn (35) as I. H. Chanticleer **R**; Tony Bill (26) as Raef del Grado; Karen Black (27) as Amy Partlett; Uncredited (20s)—female NCN

Filmography B: Films Not Considered for Inclusion in the Narrative

The motion pictures listed in this filmography have been identified by various writers and published lists as having librarians in the cast of characters or containing library scenes. These films were not considered for inclusion in the narrative for various reasons. The following abbreviations identify these reasons:

E	Erotica
H	Historical (not set in 20th century)
NL	Unable to discern librarian; film viewed, unless marked NV
NV	Not viewed
P	Prison film
PHL	The library is a personal home library
S	Film less than feature length
SF	Science fiction/fantasy
TV	Film made for television
V	Film released on video in United States

The Accountant. 1999 S/NV

Age to Age. 1998 SF/NV

Agent Trouble. 1987 NL

Air Hostess. 1949 NV

All the King's Men. 1949 NL

American Hot Wax. 1978 NL

Amityville II: The Possession. 1982 NL

An Angel at My Table. 1990 NL

The Asphalt Jungle. 1950 NL

Awakenings. 1990 NL

Bachelor. 1999 NL

Ball of Fire. 1941 NL

Beyond the Valley of the Dolls. 1970 NL

Blade. 1998 SF

The Blue Kite. 1993 NL

Brazil. 1985 SF

The Breakfast Club. 1985 NL

The Browning Version. 1994 NL

Burglar. 1987 NL

Cape Fear. 1962 NL

The Capetown Affair. 1967 NL

Carrie. 1976 NL

Carry on, Columbus. 1992 H

The Catman of Paris. 1946 H

The Census Taker. 1998 S/NV

Chilly Scenes of Winter aka Head Over Heels. 1979 NL

Chinatown. 1974 NL

The Claydon Treasure Mystery. 1938 NV

Cleopatra. 1963 H

Clue. 1985 NL

The Cobweb. 1955 NL

The Comfort of Strangers. 1990 NL

The Cook, the Thief, His Wife and Her Lover. 1989 NL

Debbie Does Dallas. 1978 E/NV

Deceived. 1991 NL

The Deep. 1997 NL

Delivery Boys. 1984 NL

Demolition Man. 1993 SF

Desperate Measures. 1998 NL

Down with America. 1997 S/NV

Dream Trap. 1990 NL

The Drivetime. 1995 NV

Educating Julie. 1984 NV

Entertaining Mr. Sloan. 1970 NL

Ernest Rides Again. 1993 NL

Escape from Alcatraz. 1979 P

Evil Has a Face. 1996 TV

The Eyes of Julia Deep. 1918 NL

Fast and Loose. 1939 PHL

Father Makes Good. 1950 NV

Field of Dreams. 1989 NL

Final Analysis. 1992 NL

Fletch. 1985 NL

Footloose. 1984 NL

Forbrydelsens Element aka The Element of Crime. 1984 NV

Frenchman's Farm. 1987 V

A Friend of Dorothy. 1994 S/NV

Fun. 1994 NV

The Garden. 1994 NV

Genghis Cohn. 1993 NV

Georgia. 1988 V

Get That Venus. 1933 NV

Getting In aka Student Body. 1994 V

The Gospel According to Vic aka Heavenly Pursuits. 1986 NL

The Green Cloak. 1915 NV

Half Baked. 1998 NL

The Handmaid's Tale. 1990 SF

Harvey Middleman, Fireman. 1965 NV

Heading Home. 1991 TV/NV

Heart and Souls. 1993 NL

Heaven Help Us. 1985 NL

Hidden City. 1988 V

High. 1969 NV

His Master's Voice. 1925 NV

Horror of Dracula. 1958 H

Ice Storm. 1997 NL

Imitation of Life. 1934 NL

Imitation of Life. 1959 NL

In the Name of the Father. 1993 P

Information Received. 1962 NV

Invisible Stripes. 1939 NL

It Happened Tomorrow. 1944 H

Jailbreak. 1936 P

Jenatsch. 1987 NV

Judicial Consent. 1994 V

A Kiss Before Dying. 1991 NL

La Totale!. 1991 NV

Les Cousins. 1959 NL

Letter from an Unknown Woman. 1948 NL

Letter to My Killer. 1996 TV

Little Secrets. 1991 NV

Little Witches. 1996 NL

Logan's Run. 1976 SF

Love and Money. 1982 NV

Love Lies Bleeding. 1993 TV

Love on the Run. 1980 NL

Lucky Jim. 1957 NL

The Mad Doctor. 1941 NV

Magic Town. 1947 NL

Main Street. 1923 NL/NV

Making It. 1971 NV

The Man in Blue. 1937 NV

The Man in Grey. 1943 H

The Man in the White Suit. 1951 NL

Martha, Ruth and Edie. 1988 NV

The Mechanic. 1973 NL

Meeting Mr. Subian. 1996 NL

Mindkiller. 1987 SF

The Misadventures of Margaret. 1998 V

Most Wanted. 1997 NL

Mutiny in the Big House. 1939 P

Naked Gun 2½: The Smell of Fear. 1991 NL

NEA. 1976 NV

Necronomicon, Book of the Dead aka Necronomicon. 1994 V/NV

Out of Sight. 1998 NL

Paid. 1930 NL

Passport to Pimlico. 1949 NL

Picture Perfect. 1997 NL

Plain Clothes. 1988 NL

Pleasantville. 1998 NL

The Prodigal. 1983 NL

Putting It Over. 1922 NV

Quatermass and the Pit. 1967 SF

Quiz Show. 1994 NL

The Racket. 1951 NL

Raiders of the Living Dead. 1986 V

The Real Howard Spitz. 1998 V

Red Hot. 1993 NL

Rehearsals for War. 1998 NV

The Remake. 1977 NV

Return to Peyton Place. 1961 NL

Rollerball. 1975 SF

Savage Messiah. 1972 NV

Se7en. 1995 NL

The Shawshank Redemption. 1994 P

Sidewalk Stories. 1989 S/NV

Sitting Pretty. 1948 NL

Slaughter of the Innocents. 1994 V

Sleepless in Seattle. 1993 NL

Slightly Dangerous. 1943 NL

Small Faces. 1996 NL

Soylent Green. 1973 SF

Spanking the Monkey. 1994 NL

Spellbound. 1945 NL

Stanley's Dragon. 1994 NV

Star Trek: Insurrection. 1998 SF

Stepping Out. 1991 NL

The Strangler aka East of Picadilly. 1941 NL

Summer School. 1987 NL

Summertime. 1955 NL

The Sure Thing. 1985 NL

Tale of a Vampire. 1992 V

The Tell-Tale Heart aka The Hidden Room of 1,000 Horrors. 1960 H

The Thief. 1952 NL

This Happy Breed. 1944 NL

The Time Machine. 1962 SF

To Love, Honor, and Deceive. 1997 TV

Trading Favors aka Do Me a Favor. 1997 V

Traps. 1986 NV

Traxx. 1988 V

True Colors. 1991 NL

The Truman Show. 1998 NL

Twelve Monkeys. 1995 SF

The Two Jakes. 1990 NL

The Two Lives of Mattia Pascal. 1985 NV

Unnamable II: The Statement of Rudolph Carter. 1993 V

Vera. 1987 NV

Wag the Dog. 1997 NL

Welcome to Sarajevo. 1997 NL

What's New, Pussycat?. 1965 NL

The Whisperers. 1966 NL

The Wicker Man. 1973 NL

Wimps. 1986 V

Wings of Desire. 1987 NL

A Winter's Tale. 1992 NV

Within the Law. 1939 P

You Can't Get Away with Murder. 1939 NV

You Must Be Joking!. 1965 NV

Young Cassidy. 1965 NL

Z.P.G. (Zero Population Growth). 1972 SF

Zardoz. 1974 SF

Chapter Notes

Chapter 1. Reel Librarians in Silent Films, 1917–1928

1. Film presumed lost.

2. Anderson was 25 in 1917. The age of an actor is determined by subtracting the year in which the actor was born from the year in which the film was released.

3. Robert C. McElravy, review of *A Wife on Trial*, *The Moving Picture World*, August 18, 1917, 1084.

4. D. Burton Howard in an adaptation of the screenplay *Moving Picture Stories*, August 3, 1917, 22, and review of *A Wife on Trial*, *The Moving Picture World*, August 4, 1917, 847. In the novel, children refer to Phyllis primarily as the "Liberry Teacher;" Margaret Widdemer, *The Rose-Garden Husband* (New York: Grosset & Dunlap, 1915), 8.

5. Although the film is presumed lost, one still from the film reveals an attractive, well-dressed Phyllis sitting at a dinner table with Allan and the de Guenthers, in Robert C. McElravy, review of *A Wife on Trial*, *The Moving Picture World*, August 18, 1917, 1084.

6. Film presumed lost.

7. Margaret Widdemer, *The Wishing-Ring Man* (New York: A. L. Burt Company, 1917). Harrington's first name is Allen in this film, rather than Allan as in the novel; the preceding film, *A Wife on Trial*; and Widdemer's novel, *The Rose-Garden Husband*.

8. Birth year not cited. The character of Phyllis Harrington is in her 30s; the authors, therefore, assume that Hagan in this film would also appear to be in her 30s.

9. There are several references in the novel to Phyllis' occupation as librarian but probably none in the film. Bessie Love was the leading actress, and as the Harringtons were in supporting roles, focusing on Phyllis' past as a librarian would not have contributed to the storyline of the film.

10. Film presumed lost.

11. Washburn was 30 in 1919.

12. Several names of characters were changed for the film production. For instance, in the film the leading character is LeRoy Sylvester and his girlfriend is Ruth Douglas, while in the play his name is LeRoy Gumph and her name is Pearl Hannigan.

13. Review of *A Very Good Young Man*, August 8, 1919, *Variety's Film Reviews, 1907–1920*, Vol. 1 (New York: R. R. Bowker, 1983).

14. "Special Service Section on Bryant Washburn in *A Very Good Young Man*," *Motion Picture News*, July 5, 1919, 365.

15. The reverse—librarian to other occupation—also occurs; for example, Carol Milford is a librarian in Sinclair Lewis' novel *Main Street*, but in the film *Main Street* (Warner Bros., 1923), which was adapted from Lewis' novel, she is not a librarian.

16. Both films presumed lost.

17. Selbie was 49 in 1920.

18. Turner was 42 in 1927.

19. In the novel, Julia's surname is Delafield.

20. December 26, 1920, 17.

21. March 30, 1927, *Variety's Film Reviews*,

1926–1929, Vol. 3 (New York: R. R. Bowker, 1983). The reviewer also wrote that "One could no more swallow a village milliner being mobbed because she was seen to kiss a young man ... than one could observe the poor widow, her equally poor son and a humble friend depart in one of those $6,000 automobiles when all the troubles had been cleared away."

22. Virginia Morris, adaptation of the screenplay; *Moving Picture Stories*, April 19, 1927, 15.

23. Film presumed lost. The authors were unable to determine the precise time setting of this motion picture, but one reviewer wrote "before prohibition evidently"; Fritz Tidden, review of *The Freeze-Out*, *Moving Picture World*, April 19, 1921, 628.

24. MacDonald was 46 in 1921.

25. April 29, 1921, *Variety Film Reviews, 1921–1925*, Vol. 2 (New York: R. R. Bowker, 1983).

26. For example, in director George Marshall's *Destry Rides Again* (Universal Pictures, 1939), the town drunk is appointed sheriff.

27. Film presumed lost.

28. Wilson was 27 in 1921.

29. Discussion of this scene is based on the scenario of *The Lost Romance*, General Script Collection (No. 972), Cinema-Television Library, Doheny Memorial Library, University of Southern California.

30. Kelso was 54 in 1921.

31. Anthony Slide, *Early Women Directors* (South Brunswick and New York: A. S. Barnes and Company, 1977), 34.

32. One criticism about Weber's work on this film was that she "is inclined to over-emphasize details, and there is just a little too much repetition"; *Wid's Daily*, August 21, 1921, 2.

33. Windsor was 29 in 1921.

34. Working in a female-dominated occupation, librarians have always confronted the challenge of low-paying positions.

35. This actress appears to be in her 40s. When an actor's age cannot be determined, the "appears to be" age is based upon the appearance of the screen character. Ages are categorized within ten-year ranges—teens, 20s, 30s, 40s, 50s, 60s, 70s, and 80s.

36. The *American Film Institute Catalog* (*Feature Films, 1921–30*, 70) entry for this film states that "Amelia and Phil become engaged," and *Wid's Daily*, August 21, 1921, 2, states that "Amelia decides to marry Phil."

37. Film presumed lost.

38. Wilson was 29 in 1923.

39. A. E. Thomas, *Only 38* (New York: Samuel French, 1922). Discussion of this film is based on the scenario *Only 38*, William DeMille Collection, Box 1:12, Cinema-Television Library, Doheny Memorial Library, University of Southern California.

40. Lewis F. Levenson, review of *Only 38*, *Movie Weekly*, July 14, 1923, 15, 28. Levenson praises DeMille's talent as a director in this review. Regarding 29-year-old Wilson, he comments, "Imagine ... a charming young actress, such as Lois Wilson, powdering her hair to make it appear gray, and etching wrinkles into her fair skin with a pencil." Such details "do not make 'Only 38' a wonderful picture, but they make it a good picture." May McAvoy, a personal friend of Wilson's, was only five years younger than Wilson but played the role of her daughter; William M. Drew, *Speaking of Silents; First Ladies of the Screen* (Vestal, New York: The Vestal Press, Ltd., 1989), 260.

41. In DeMille's *The Lost Romance*, Wilson stood atop a three-step ladder.

42. Negri was 30 in 1924.

43. Film presumed lost. The film is based on Hermann Sundermann's novel *The Song of Songs: A Love Story*, and on Edward Sheldon's Broadway play *The Song of Songs*.

44. Review of *Lily of the Dust*, August 25, 1924, 16:2, *The New York Times Film Reviews*, Vol. 1, 1913–31 (New York: New York Times, 1970), 208–209.

45. This actor appears to be in his 50s.

46. This actress appears to be in her 40s.

47. Film presumed lost.

48. Sebastian was 26 in 1929. She can be seen in a supporting role in *Our Dancing Daughters* (Metro-Goldwyn-Mayer, 1928), a readily available silent film starring Joan Crawford.

Chapter 2. The Stereotypical Image, 1932–1959

1. This film opened in the New York City area with the title *Love Starved*.

2. Stanwyck was 25 in 1932.

3. In Arthur Housman's novelization of Capra's screen story, one of Lulu's coworkers at the library who is not in the film tells her that she will "have to change a lot.... No man in the world would go for a get-up like that." Lulu exclaims in response, "I'm not interested in men!" The coworker then adds, "You don't have to look quite like forty, you know." *Forbidden* (New York: Grosset & Dunlap, 1932), 9.

4. Jefferson was 76 when *Forbidden* was released in January; he died in April 1932.

5. Lulu's bank balance indicates that she lived a very frugal lifestyle, as she would have had to save about $10 a month during her eight-year employment to accumulate such a sum.

6. This actor appears to be in his 50s.

7. Twelvetrees was 24 in 1932.

8. Frederici was 54 in 1932.

9. Walters was 19 in 1932.

10. Lombard was 24 in 1932.

11. Harmer was 49 in 1932.

12. The play has a tragic ending; Charlie leaves Allie, taking her savings, and Allie commits suicide. Burns Mantle, ed., *The Best Plays of 1929-30 and the Year Book of the Drama in America* (New York: Dodd, Mead and Company, 1930), 441. One reviewer states, "The characters are recognizable as hundreds and thousands of young New Yorkers, and the tawdry settings of lower middle class amusements are not exaggerated." This reviewer found Hollywood's happy ending "a fairly plausible one." October 17, 1933; *Variety Film Reviews*, v. 4, 1930-1933.

13. This actress appears to be in her 20s.

14. Wright was 55 in 1934.

15. The is the first use of "shush" by a reel librarian that the authors detected in films of the early 1930s.

16. Dvorak was 32 in 1934.

17. Birth year not cited. Howell appears to be in her 50s.

18. Vinson was 27 in 1934.

19. Birth year not cited. Lawrence appears to be in her 50s.

20. Bradley was 67 in 1936.

21. Lupino was 19 in 1937.

22. Emmett was 41 in 1937.

23. Brian was 31 in 1937.

24. Len D. Martin, *The Republic Pictures Checklist; Features, Serials, Cartoons, Short Subjects and Training Films of Republic Pictures Corporation, 1935-1959* (Jefferson, N.C.: McFarland & Co., Inc., 1998), 286–287.

25. May 12, 1927, *Variety Film Reviews, 1934-1937*, v. 5.

26. Campbell was 27 in 1938.

27. There is nothing in the film that verifies this statement. She works in a public library, further confusing the meaning of her statement. When Nora speaks about her work, she comments that she stamps out cards and puts dates in books, and in the film's one library scene, she assists a patron with a reference question. These activities are inconsistent with the responsibilities of "organizing another state library."

28. This storyline resembles *The Cowboy Star*, a 1936 "B" western released by the same company, Columbia Pictures. In *The Cowboy Star*, Starrett is a Hollywood cowboy star who quits Hollywood to go work on a ranch as a cowboy, hiding the fact that he is a movie cowboy.

29. Hoyt was 64 in 1938.

30. This actor appears to be in his 20s.

31. Riano was 40 in 1939.

32. Garland was 18 in 1940.

33. Plowright was 50 in 1940.

34. Urecal was 47 in 1941.

35. Backus was 41 in 1941.

36. Herman J. Mankiewicz and Orson Welles, screenplay, "Citizen Kane," in *Best American Screenplays 2: Complete Screenplays*, ed. Sam Thomas (New York: Crown Publishers, Inc., 1990), 20–21.

37. Malleson was 54 in 1942.

38. Bosley Crowther, review of *Quiet Please, Murder*, December 22, 1942, *The New York Times Film Reviews*, Vol. 3, 1909.

39. Blandy, a rare books, autographs, and manuscripts dealer, sold the forgery to Cleaver despite Fleg's warning not to deal with him. She told Fleg the copy sold for $7,500; giving $1,500 to the antique dealer who handled the transaction (and who is subsequently murdered by one of Cleaver's henchmen for his transgression), keeping $1,000 for her commission, and giving Fleg his profit of $5,000. The selling price was actually $20,000; she pocketed the remaining $12,500.

40. Emmett was 46 in 1942. This is Emmett's second supporting role as a librarian; she portrayed Miss McGonigle in *Sea Devils* (1937).

41. Roberts was 23 in 1942.

42. Foulger was 43 in 1942.

43. Birth year not cited. Brayton appears to be in her 40s.

44. Marsh was 47 in 1942.

45. Malyon was 64 in 1943.

46. Reynolds was 81 in 1943.

47. Bosley Crowther, review of *The Seventh Victim*, *The New York Times*, September 18, 1943, 11:3, in *The New York Times Film Reviews*, v. 3, 1958.

48. Selby was 38 in 1943.

49. Wolfe was 47 in 1943.

50. Blake was 48 in 1943.

51. This actress appears to be in her 20s.

52. Pierlot was 68 in 1943.

53. MacLaren was 48 in 1944.

54. Ankers was 26 in 1944.

55. McDonald was 26 in 1944.

56. Bronson was 43 in 1945.

57. Mayo was 25 in 1945.

58. Garson was 41 in 1945.

59. Birth year not cited. Douglas appears to be in her 20s.

60. This actress appears to be in her 30s.

61. Reed was 25 in 1946.

62. Judith Chase Churchill's "Your Chances of Getting Married" appeared in *Good Housekeeping* (October 1946, 38ff) only months before *It's A Wonderful Life* opened in New York City in December 1946. Churchill begins her article by identifying marriage as "not only woman's No. 1 career but her favorite topic of conversation, and the object of most of her daydreaming." She maintains that men "don't go for brainy wives"–those in the fields of law, medicine, and science. The chances for marriage for "brainy" women are better than for schoolteachers who "are out-old-maided by only women librarians, who get fewer proposals than women in any other profession. If you want to get yourself married ... above all, stay out of the library." The truth of Churchill's statement was seemingly buttressed by the unidentified writer of "Morgues of Culture," an article which appeared in *Magazine Digest*, August 1949, 69–72), who wrote that "of 32,346 librarians listed in the 1940 census, 29,000 were females, 78 per cent of whom were spinsters" (p. 71).

63. Dale Thomajan, *From Cyd Charisse to Psycho* (New York: Walker and Company, 1992), 58–63, and "The Best High School Movie," *Film Comment* 28:4 (July-August 1992): 79. According to Thomajan, "There are two major categories of filmgoers who, given the opportunity, are likely to fall in love with Margie [Jeanne Crain] and *Margie*: (1) any American woman able to recall her adolescence with at least mixed if not positive emotions, and (2) anybody and everybody else."

64. Bari was 33 in 1946.

65. Birth year not cited. Martin appears to be in her 20s.

66. Mara was 24 in 1947.

67. Douglas was 36 in 1947.

68. Allyson was 30 in 1947.

69. This actress appears to be in her 50s.

70. Scott was 33 in 1947.

71. Hughes was 56 in 1947.

72. Raymond was 25 in 1947.

73. Crain was 23 in 1948.

74. The librarian's name sounds like "Tannahill" in the film. This character's name is subject to correction.

75. This actress appears to be in her 50s. She resembles, and may be, Mary Field, who was 40 in 1949. Field, a very busy supporting actress, appeared, credited and uncredited, in at least 50 films during 1945–1949.

76. "Morons Can Be Millionaires," *Magazine Digest*, August 1949, 62–65.

77. "Morgues of Culture," *Magazine Digest*, August 1949, 69–72.

78. Sass was librarian, General Electric Company, Pittsfield Works, Pittsfield, Massachusetts.

79. "Definition of 'Librarian' Too Loosely Applied," *Library Journal* 74 (September 1949): 1126.

80. Freeman was 24 in 1948.

81. Corby was 39 in 1950.

82. *Variety Film Reviews*, v.8, 1949–1953, June 10, 1950.

83. Blyth was 23 in 1951.

84. This actor appears to be in his 60s.

85. Birth year not cited. Savage appears to be in her 20s.

86. Neumann was 37 in 1951.

87. This actor appears to be in his 40s.

88. This actress appears to be in her 60s.

89. This actor appears to be in his 50s.

90. This actor appears to be in his 30s.

91. Birth year not cited. Loftin appears to be in his 30s.

92. Robinson was 18 in 1953.

93. Sylvia mentions that she holds a master's degree, but she appears to be an extremely young university faculty member. In the film, Sylvia asks Clayton for a light for a cigarette, but as a non-smoker, he does not have a match or lighter, and Sylvia puts the cigarette back into her purse. This may have been a simple ruse to give Robinson an additional touch of maturity. Although never stated explicitly in the film, one assumes USC refers to the University of Southern California, which had a graduate program in library science that was accredited by the American Library Association in 1953.

94. Russell was 48 in 1955.

95. Sidney was 44 in 1955.

96. In William L. Heath's novel *Violent Saturday* (New York: Harper & Brothers, Publishers, 1955), Elsie's last name is Cotter. Heath writes that Elsie "was on her way home from the library ... thinking of the fifty dollars she'd found in a coin purse two days before, at the doorway of Rayburn's grocery store" (p. 43). The novel does not indicate that Elsie is a librarian nor does the novel portray Elsie as a thief. Elsie needs the money, as her checking account is overdrawn; her dilemma is whether to search

actively for the owner or to wait until the owner asks her for its return. When Elsie discovers the identify of the owner of the coin purse, she rationalizes that she needs the money more than the owner and decides to keep the $50.

97. Birth year not cited. Newhard appears to be in her 40s.

98. A theft is a misdemeanor or felony, depending upon the value of the stolen item. The amount of money in the purse is unknown.

99. This actress appears to be in her 20s.

100. Grahame was 33 in 1956.

101. *Variety*, February 15, 1956; *Variety Film Reviews, 1907–1980*, vol. 9 (New York: Garland Publishing, Inc., 1983).

102. The Nazi agent reasoned that if he were arrested within the hour, it would prove that the British were waiting for him, indicating that Martin was a deliberate attempt by the British to confuse the Germans. If he were not arrested, it would prove that Martin was genuine.

103. This actress appears to be in her 60s.

104. The film appears to be loosely based on a 1950 incident that occurred at the Bartlesville [Oklahoma] Public Library—the firing of city librarian Ruth W. Brown by the city commission. For a brief contemporary account of the Brown firing, see Darlene Anderson Essary, letter to the editor, *Saturday Review*, 30 September 1950, 24. For a detailed discussion of this incident and *Storm Center*, see Louise S. Robbins' two articles—"Racism and Censorship in Cold War Oklahoma: The Case of Ruth W. Brown and the Bartlesville Public Library," *Southwestern Historical Quarterly* 100 (1996): 18–46, and "Fighting McCarthyism through Film; A Library Censorship Case Becomes a *Storm Center*," *Journal of Education for Library and Information Science* 39 (1998):291–311.

105. Davis was 48 in 1956.

106. The authors were unable to verify this title; for obvious reasons, it is undoubtedly a fictitious title.

107. Hunter was 34 in 1956.

108. Birth year not cited. Smith appears to be in her 20s.

109. Allyson was 40 in 1957.

110. Bergen was 32 in 1957.

111. This film is based on William Marchant's Broadway play of the same title, which opened on October 24, 1955, and starred Shirley Booth in the Bunny Watson role. Booth was 57 in 1955.

112. Hepburn was 50 in 1957.

113. Blondell was 51 in 1957.

114. Merrill was 32 in 1957.

115. Randall was 22 in 1957.

116. Salew was 60 in 1957.

117. Kimbrough was 26 in 1958.

118. Birth year not cited. Weller appears to be in her 50s.

119. This uncredited actor mirrors the stereotypical image of a reel librarian—elderly, receding hairline, bespectacled, conservatively dressed—and is holding a book. He may be, however, a patron upset about the loud talking.

120. Miles was 30 in 1959. A very attractive woman, Miles was "Miss Kansas" in 1948.

121. This actress appears to be in her 40s.

122. Repp was 41 in 1959.

123. Birth year not cited. Morrow appears to be in his 30s.

Chapter 3. Continuance of the Stereotype, 1960-1979

1. Charles Harpole, ed., *History of the American Cinema*, vol. 9, *Lost Illusions: American Cinema in the Shadow of Watergate and Vietnam, 1970-1979*, by David A. Cook (New York: Charles Scribner's Sons, 2000), 133.

2. In this and the next chapter, films released in black and white are indicated by a b/w after the date of release on first mention in the text.

3. Sellers was 37 in 1962.

4. Griffith was 41 in 1962.

5. This actress appears to be in her 20s.

6. This actor appears to be in his 40s.

7. Davies was 56 in 1962.

8. Jones was 28 in 1962.

9. Glyn achieved instant success as a romance writer with *Three Weeks* (1907). The novel, banned briefly in the United States, catapulted Glyn to fame. She also worked on the script of Clara Bow's 1927 successful film *It*.

10. Kastner was 22 in 1966. An interesting note about Kastner is that he worked in a library during the 1990s; see Peter Kastner to Bill Ott, June 30, 1993, published in Bill Ott, "The Back Page: Librarians on Film," *Booklist* 89, no. 18 (May 1993): 1728.

11. Torn was 35 in 1966.

12. Bill was 26 in 1966.

13. Black was 27 in 1966.

14. This actress appears to be in her 20s.

15. Benjamin was 31 in 1969.

16. Smith was 63 in 1969.

17. This actress appears to be in her 50s.

18. Derringer appears to be his 30s.

19. This actress appears to be in her 30s.

20. Birth year not cited. Wiggins appears to be in her 30s.

21. Sperber was 49 in 1960.

22. This actress appears to be in her 50s.

23. Hancock was 27 in 1960.

24. Massey was 23 in 1960.

25. This actor appears to be in his 40s.

26. Allman was 57 in 1961.

27. Davis was 65 in 1961.

28. Adaptation of Christie's novel *4:50 from Paddington*.

29. Adaptation of Christie's novel *After the Funeral*.

30. Adaptation of Christie's novel *Mrs. McGinty's Dead*.

31. According to the film's credits, this is an "Original screenplay by David Pursall and Jack Seddon, Based on their interpretation of Agatha Christie's 'Miss Marple.'"

32. Millhollin was 47 in 1962.

33. This actress appears to be in her 50s.

34. Pleshette was 25 in 1962.

35. Daves based *Rome Adventure* on this novel.

36. Birth year not cited. Collentine appears to be in her 40s.

37. Nuyen was 23 in 1962.

38. Birth year not cited. Jarvis appears to be in his 20s.

39. Birth year not cited. Houston appears to be in his 30s.

40. Eden was 30 in 1964.

41. Probably Demetrius Charles de Kavanagh Boulger's *The History of China* (2 volumes), published in 1898.

42. Burton was 40 in 1965.

43. Birth year not cited. Blake appears to be in her 50s.

44. Bloom was 34 in 1965.

45. Ripper was 52 in 1965.

46. The authors were unable to verify this title.

47. The librarian's name sounds like "Fowler." This character's name is subject to correction.

48. This actress appears to be in her 60s.

49. Birth year not cited. Cameron appears to be in her 40s.

50. After the release of *Star Wars* (1977), this hairdo became popularized as the Princess Leia hairstyle.

51. Mills was 22 in 1968.

52. Bateson was 42 in 1968.

53. Dee was 26 in 1970.

54. Baccala was 25 in 1970.

55. Robert L. Ottoson, *American International Pictures, A Filmography* (New York: Garland Publishing, Inc., 1985), 221, writes that "from 1972 to 1976 AIP made a number of movies that have been called blaxploitation films, films made by whites primarily for the big city black audiences."

56. Birth year not cited. Scotford appears to be in her 30s.

57. Obler was 56 in 1976.

58. MacGraw was 32 in 1970.

59. Anders was 35 in 1973, the same age mentioned in the film.

60. This actress appears to be in her 40s.

61. This actress appears to be in her 40s.

62. Murtaugh was 34 in 1976.

63. Birth year not cited. Stewart appears to be in his 20s.

64. Birth year not cited. Smith-Jackson appears to be in her 20s.

65. The film has appeared on television and on video with both features in color.

66. Van Devere was 35 in 1978.

67. Hawn was 33 in 1978.

68. Birth year not cited. Sokol appears to be in her 30s.

69. Tedrow was 71 in 1978.

70. Snodgress was 33 in 1979.

71. Birth year not cited. Cox appears to be in her 20s.

72. Bay was 61 in 1979.

73. Birth year not cited. Troutt appears to be in his 40s.

Chapter 4. A Plethora of Librarians, 1980–1999

1. Birth year not cited. Walker appears to be in her 30s.

2. Rothman was 33 in 1982.

3. Birth year not cited. Saccarola appears to be in his 20s.

4. Malcolm L. Johnson, *Hartford Courant*, May 19, 1984.

5. Birth year not cited. Scott appears to be in her 40s.

6. Birth year not cited. Burrell appears to be in her 50s.

7. Birth year not cited. Stevens appears to be in her 60s.

8. Birth year not cited. Cole appears to be in her 30s; she strikingly resembles Ann Gillespe, who played Jackie Taylor in *Beverly Hills 90210*, a popular television program of the 1990s. Cole used the names Jackie Taylor and Jacky Taylor in two 1969 films.

9. Rubin was 62 in 1982.

10. Birth year not cited. Taylor appears to be in her 30s.

11. Birth year not cited. Tweedle appears to be in her 40s; however, she is undoubtedly younger.

12. Ajaye was 34 in 1983.

13. Birth year not cited. Meckler appears to be in his 60s.

14. Henner was 30 in 1982.

15. Birth year not cited. Roberson appears to be in her 20s.

16. Robards was 61 in 1983.

17. Drummond was 55 in 1984.

18. Rothman was 35 in 1984.

19. St. Jerome is one of the patron saints of libraries and librarians.

20. Mirren was 39 in 1984.

21. McGovern was 23 in 1984.

22. Birth year not cited. Allison appears to be in her 40s.

23. Patinkin was 33 in 1985.

24. The film is based on Jack Finney's novel *Marion's Wall* (New York: Simon and Schuster, 1973). Nick's occupation in the novel—a desk job in sales promotion, Crown and Zellerbach—was changed to a librarian for the screen adaptation. Male librarians appear to be especially suited for cinematic roles that require comedic antics and bumbling ineptitude with the opposite sex; the change of a male character's occupation to librarian for a screenplay was first noted in *A Very Good Young Man* (1919).

25. Curtin was 40 in 1985.

26. Reinhold was 29 in 1986.

27. Turturro was 29 in 1986.

28. Wright was 36 in 1986.

29. Fletcher was 65 in 1986.

30. Beatty was 51 in 1988.

31. Birth year not cited. Desy appears to be in his 50s.

32. Duff-Griffin was 48 in 1988.

33. *Lamb* was released in the United States in 1995.

34. In *Defense of the Realm*, the actress appears to be in her 30s; in *Lamb*, the actress appears to be in her 40s; in *Baby Boom*, the actress appears to be in her 20s.

35. Birth year not cited. Shage appears to be in her 20s.

36. Parker was 50 in 1989.

37. Birth year not cited. Kennedy appears to be in her 30s.

38. This film was released in the United States during February 1988.

39. Leslie was 58 in 1987.

40. Birth year not cited. Platt appears to be in her 20s.

41. This actress appears to be in her 30s.

42. Birth year not cited. Kessler appears to be in her 50s.

43. Birth year not cited. Johnston appears to be in her 50s.

44. Warfield was 49 in 1989.

45. Birth year not cited. Lyle appears to be in her 30s.

46. Birth year not cited. Callard appears to be in his 40s.

47. Freeman was 70 in 1969.

48. Downey, Jr. was 24 in 1989.

49. Dench was 51 in 1985.

50. For readers unfamiliar with this biographical film, the title is an allusion to the homosexuality of Joe Orton and Kenneth Halliwell, the main characters. In addition, ears is an anagram for arse.

51. Birth year not cited. Cadell appears to be in her 40s.

52. Birth year not cited. McKeown appears to be in his 50s.

53. Russo was 35 in 1989.

54. Russo's character is listed as Lynn Wells. Jake Taylor on one telephone call, however, seems to ask for her using a surname that sounds like Weslin.

55. Churchill, "Your Chances of Getting Married."

56. Birth year not cited. Altman appears to be in his 20s.

57. Robinson was 59 in 1989.

58. Hanks was 34 in 1990.

59. Duckworth was 85 in 1990.

60. Birth year not cited. MacLeod appears to be in her 60s.

61. Birth year not cited. Philpot appears to be in her 50s.

62. Birth year not cited. Gleason appears to be in her 40s.

63. Birth year not cited. Anspaugh appears to be in her 60s. Anspaugh is the mother of the film's director, David Anspaugh.

64. Birth year not cited. Kelly appears to be in her 60s.

65. Birth year not cited. Siff appears to be in her 50s.

66. Birth year not cited. Butcher appears to be in her 50s.

67. Payne was 54 in 1994.

68. Foreman was 26 in 1992.

69. Birth year not cited. Brooks appears to be in her 20s.

70. Birth year not cited. Meyers-Shyer

appears to be a teenager. Meyers-Shyer is the daughter of the film's director, Charles Shyer, and the film's producer, Nancy Meyers. The director and producer are credited as the film's writers. Meyers-Shyer's younger sister, Hallie, also appears briefly in this film.

71. This actress appears to be in her 40s.

72. O'Donnell was 22 in 1992.

73. Birth year not cited. Nelson appears to be in his 20s.

74. Birth year not cited. Gural appears to be in his 50s.

75. Birth year not cited. Alfred states in the film that he is 46. Fondren died in June 1992, eleven months before the film was released.

76. Walter was 51 in 1993.

77. *The Neverending Story III* was released in the United States in 1996.

78. Jones was 67 in 1994.

79. *Salmonberries* was released in the United States in 1994.

80. Zech was 49 in 1991; Roswitha's age in the film is 45.

81. Birth year not cited. Lind appears to be in her 30s; in the film, Noayak states that she is 35.

82. Miller was 28 in 1992.

83. Seldes was 64 in 1992.

84. Glen was 38 in 1995.

85. Birth year not cited. Collar appears to be in her 40s.

86. MacMillan was 75 in 1996.

87. David jokingly remarks later in the film that *Green Eggs and Ham* will cost him $6,886.10.

88. This actress appears to be in her 40s.

89. Pope was 67 in 1996.

90. This actress appears to be in her 50s.

91. This actor appears to be in his 50s.

92. Birth year not cited. Edmonds appears to be in her 20s.

93. Howard was 69 in 1996.

94. Birth year not cited. Cooper appears to be in her 30s.

95. Released in USA as *A Merry War*.

96. Birth year not cited. Blackham appears to be in her 50s.

97. Chiles was 50 in 1997.

98. Posey was 27 in 1995.

99. Von Scherler was 61 in 1995; she is the mother of the film's director, Susan von Scherler Mayer.

100. Birth year not cited. Blackchild appears to be in her 20s.

101. Birth year not cited. Williams appears to be in his 30s.

102. Birth year not cited. Mode appears to be in her 30s.

103. Robert A. Nowlan and Gwendolyn L. Nowlan, *The Films of the Nineties: A Complete, Qualitative Filmography to over 3000 Feature-Length English Language Films, Theatrical, and Video-Only, Released Between January 1, 1990, and December 31, 1999* (McFarland & Company, Inc., 2001), 419–420.

104. Fonda was 34 in 1998.

105. Weisz was 28 in 1999.

106. Avari was 47 in 1999.

107. Stephen Sommers, "The Mummy," p. 10. http://home.online.no/~bhundlan/scripts/The-Mummy.htm.

Selected Bibliography

Adams, Katherine C. "Loveless Frump as Hip and Sexy Party Girl: A Reevaluation of the Old-Maid Stereotype." *Library Quarterly* 70, no. 3 (2000): 287–301.

American Film Institute. *The American Film Institute Catalog of Motion Pictures Produced in the United States.* 14 vols. Berkeley: University of California Press; New York: R. R. Bowker, 1971–88.

Balio, Tina. *Grand Design: Hollywood as a Modern Business Enterprise, 1930–1939.* Vol. 5, *History of the American Cinema.* New York: Charles Scribner's Sons, 1993.

"Below the Average of Picture Entertainment." Review of *The Broken Gate. Wid's Daily,* 26 December 1920, 17.

Benemann, William E. "Tears and Ivory Towers: California Libraries during the McCarthy Era." *American Libraries* (June 1977): 305–09.

Bennett, Alan. *Prick Up Your Ears: The Screenplay.* London and Boston: Faber and Faber, 1987.

Beranger, Clara. *Only 38.* William DeMille Collection, Box 1: 12, Cinema-Television Library, Doheny Memorial Library, University of Southern California, Los Angeles.

Bloss, Meredith. "A Librarian Writes—How to Tell a Librarian." *ALA Bulletin* 46 (July-August 1952): 221–24.

Boldstroke, Gracie. "Sweetiepies for Sourpusses." *Wilson Library Bulletin* 18 (December 1943): 312–14.

Brooks, Jon. "Reel Librarians Don't Always Wear Buns." *School Library Journal* 34, no. 8 (August 1997): 22.

Brown, Martin. Prompt-book of *A Very Good Young Man.* 1918. New York Public Library for the Performing Arts.

Brown-Syed, Christopher, and Charles Barnard Sands. "Librarians in Fiction; a Discussion." *Education Libraries* 21, no. 1 (1997). Available at http://valinor.purdy.wayne.edu/e13.htm.

Bruce, Margaret Buchan. "Librarian a la Hollywood." *Wilson Library Bulletin* 22 (May 1948): 692–93.

Burgett, Shelley Wood, comp. "Libraries and Librarians in Film: An Annotated Filmography." *Kentucky Libraries* 64, no. 1 (Winter 2000): 3–9.

Cheshire, David. "Librarian at Large." *New Library World* 80 (September 1979): 167–69.

Churchill, Judith Chase. "Your Chances of Getting Married." *Good Housekeeping* (October 1946): 38, 39, 313, 314, 316–19.

Cook, David A. *Lost Illusions: American Cinema in the Shadow of Watergate and Vietnam, 1970–1979*. Vol. 9, *History of the American Cinema*. New York: Charles Scribner's Sons, 2000.

Corson, Richard. *Fashions in Eyeglasses*. Chester Springs, Pa.: Dufour Editions, Inc., 1967.

Crafton, Donald. *The Talkies: America Cinema's Transition to Sound, 1926–1931*. Vol. 4, *History of the American Cinema*. New York: Charles Scribner's Sons, 1997.

Davis, Clyde Brion. *Adventure*. Cleveland: World Publishing Company, 1946.

Davis, Marian L. *Visual Design in Dress*, 2d Edition. Englewood Cliffs, N.J.: Prentice-Hall, Inc., 1987.

"Definition of 'Librarian' Too Loosely Applied." *Library Journal* 74, no. 15 (September 1949): 1126.

Drew, William M. *Speaking of Silents: First Ladies of the Screen*. Vestal, N.Y.: The Vestal Press, Ltd., 1989.

Edgar, Neal L. "The Image of Librarianship in the Media." *A Century of Service: Librarianship in the United States and Canada*. Chicago: American Library Association, 1976.

Engelmeier, Regine, and Peter W. Engelmeier, eds. *Fashion in Film*. Translated by Eileen Martin. Munich and New York: Prestel, 1997.

Essary, Darlene Anderson. Letter to the Editor. *Saturday Review*, 30 September 1950, 24.

Fetrow, Alan G. *Feature Films, 1940–1949: A United States Filmography*. Jefferson, N.C.: McFarland & Company, Inc., 1994.

_____. *Feature Films, 1950–1959: A United States Filmography*. Jefferson, N.C.: McFarland & Company, Inc., 1999.

Finney, Jack. *Marion's Wall*. New York: Simon and Schuster, 1973.

Form, William H. "Popular Images of Librarian." *Library Journal* 71 (15 June 1946): 851–55.

Gifford, Denis. *The British Film Catalog 1895–1970: A Reference Guide*. New York: McGraw-Hill Book Company, 1973.

Hall, Alison. "Batgirl Was a Librarian." *Canadian Library Journal* 49, no. 5 (October 1992): 345–47.

Heath, William L. *Violent Saturday*. New York: Harper & Brothers, Publishers, 1955.

Hough, Emerson. *The Broken Gate*. New York: D. Appleton and Company, 1917.

Housman, Arthur. *Forbidden*. New York: Grosset & Dunlap, 1932.

Howard, D. Burton. Review of *A Wife on Trial*. *Moving Picture Stories*, 3 August 1917, 22.

_____. Review of *A Wife on Trial*. *Moving Picture World*, 4 August 1917, 847.

"Image of Librarians in Popular Culture: Librarians in the Movies." University of California, Los Angeles. Available at http://is.gseis.ucla.edu/impact/f01/Focus/Image/Heather/topic.htm.

The Internet Movie Database. http://www.imdb.com.

Johnson, Malcolm L. "Chaotic Cemetery Is Mess of Blood, Bones, Banality." Review of *The House by the Cemetery*. *Hartford Courant*, May 19, 1984.

King, William H. "The Celluloid Librarian: The Portrayal of Librarians in Motion Pictures." MSLS Thesis, University of North Carolina at Chapel Hill, 1990.

Knobleck, Edward. *Lost Romance*. General Script Collection (no. 972), Cinema-Television Library, Doheny Memorial Library, University of Southern California, Los Angeles.

Laver, James. *Modesty in Dress: An Inquiry into the Fundamentals of Fashion*. Boston: Houghton Mifflin, 1969.

Leigh, Robert D., and Kathryn W. Sewny. "The Popular Image of the Library and The Librarian." *Library Journal* 85 (1 June 1960): 2089–91.

Lentz, Harris M., III. *Feature Films, 1960–1969: A Filmography of English-Language and Major Foreign-Language United States Releases*. Jefferson, N.C.: McFarland & Company, Inc., 2001.

Lev, Peter. *Transforming the Screen, 1950–1959*. Vol. 7, *History of the American Cinema*. New York: Charles Scribner's Sons, 2003.

Levenson, Lewis F. Review of *Only 38*. *Movie Weekly*, 14 July 1923, 15, 28.

"Librarians on Film." *Booklist* 89, no. 18 (1993): 1728.

Liebold, Louise Condak. "Changing the Librarian Stereotype." *Library Imagination Paper* 19, no. 2 (1997): 4.

Lurie, Alison. *The Language of Clothes*. New York: Henry Holt and Company, 1981. Reprint 2000.

Mantle, Burns, ed. *The Best Plays of 1929-30 and the Yearbook of Drama in America*. New York: Dodd, Mead and Company, 1930.

Martin, Len D. *The Republic Pictures Checklist: Features, Serials, Cartoons, Short Subjects and Training Films of Republic Pictures Corporation, 1935-1959*. Jefferson, N.C.: McFarland & Company, Inc., 1998.

Mast, Gerald, and Bruce F. Kawin. *A Short History of the Movies*. 6th ed. Boston: Allyn and Bacon, 1996.

Matthews, Ruth Shallcross. "Married Women Librarians." *Library Journal* 66 (August 1941): 650–51.

McElravy, Robert C. Review of *A Wife on Trial*. *Moving Picture World*, 18 August 1917, 1084.

McReynolds, Rosalee. "A Heritage Dismissed." *Library Journal* 110, no. 18 (1985): 25–31.

Monaco, Paul. *The Sixties: 1960-1969*. Vol. 8, *History of the American Cinema*. New York: Charles Scribner's Sons, 2001.

"Morgues of Culture." *Magazine Digest* (August 1949): 69–72.

"Morons Can Be Millionaires." *Magazine Digest* (August 1949): 62–65.

Morrisey, Locke J., and Donald O. Case. "There Goes My Image: The Perception of Male Librarians by Colleague, Student, and Self." *College & Research Libraries* 49, no. 5 (September 1988): 453–64.

Nash, Jay Robert, and Stanley Ralph Ross. *The Motion Picture Guide*. 26 vols. Chicago: Cinebooks, Inc., 1985–2000.

New York Times Film Reviews. 20 vols. New York: New York Times, 1970–98.

Newmyer, Jody. "The Image Problem of the Librarian: Femininity and Social Control." *Journal of Library History* 11 (January 1976): 44–67.

Nowlan, Robert A., and Gwendolyn Wright Nowlan. *The Films of the Eighties: A Complete, Qualitative Filmography to Over 3,400 Feature-Length English Language Films, Theatrical, and Video-Only, Released Between January 1, 1980, and December 31, 1989*. Jefferson, N.C.: McFarland & Company, Inc., 1991.

____. *The Films of the Nineties: A Complete, Qualitative Filmography to Over 3,000 Feature-Length English Language Films, Theatrical, and Video-Only, Released Between January 1, 1990, and December 31, 1999*. Jefferson, N.C.: McFarland & Company, Inc., 2001.

O'Brien, Ann, and Martin Raish. "The Image of the Librarian in Commercial Motion Pictures: An Annotated Filmography." *Collection Management* 17, no. 3 (1993): 61–84.

Ott, Bill. "The Back Page: Librarians on Film." *Booklist* 89, no. 18 (May 1993): 1728.

Ottoson, Robert L. *American International Films: A Filmography*. New York: Garland Publishing, Inc., 1985.

Pankin, Mary Faith Pusey. "Librarians in Mystery Stories." *West Virginia Libraries* 31 (Winter 1978): 11–18.

Parchesky, Jennifer. "Lois Weber's *The Blot*: Rewriting Melodrama, Reproducing The Middle Class." *Cinema Journal* 39, no. 1 (1999): 23–53.

Peacock, John. *Fashion Accessories: The Complete 20th Century Sourcebook*. New York: Thames & Hudson, 2000.

____. *Fashion Sourcebooks: The 1920s*. New York: Thames and Hudson, Inc., 1997.

____. *Fashion Sourcebooks: The 1930s*. New York: Thames and Hudson, Inc., 1997.

____. *Fashion Sourcebooks: The 1940s*. New York: Thames and Hudson, Inc., 1998.

____. *Fashion Sourcebooks: The 1950s*. New York: Thames and Hudson, Inc., 1997.

_____. *Fashion Sourcebooks: The 1960s*. New York: Thames and Hudson, Inc., 1998.

_____. *Fashion Sourcebooks: The 1970s*. New York: Thames and Hudson, Inc., 1997.

_____. *Fashion Sourcebooks: The 1980s*. New York: Thames and Hudson, Inc., 1998.

Picken, Mary Brooks. *A Dictionary of Costume and Fashion: Historic and Modern*. Mineola, N.Y.: Dover Publications, Inc., 1999. Reprint of *The Fashion Dictionary*. New York: Funk & Wagnalls, 1957.

Plumb, Abigail Leah. "Smarty Girl: Three Librarians on Film." *Bitch* (2001): 31–33, 88.

Prince, Stephen. *A New Pot of Gold: Hollywood Under the Electronic Rainbow, 1980–1989*. Vol. 10, *History of the American Cinema*. New York: Charles Scribner's Sons, 2000.

Radford, Marie L., and Gary P. Radford. "Power, Knowledge, and Fear: Feminism, Foucault, and the Stereotype of the Female Librarian." *Library Quarterly* 67, no. 3 (July 1997): 250–66.

Raish, Martin. "Librarians in the Movies." *Library Mosaics* 9, no. 4 (July-August 1998): 12–15.

_____. "Librarians in the Movies: An Annotated Filmography." Brigham Young University. Available at http://emp.byui.edu/raishm/films/introduction.html.

Raish, Martin, Federic Duda, and George M. Eberhart. "Librarians on Stage and Screen." *The Whole Library Handbook 3*, compiled by George M. Eberhart. Chicago: ALA, 2000, 531–45.

Roantree, Dorothy. "Should Librarians Be Glamour Girls?" *Wilson Library Bulletin* 27, no. 7 (March 1953): 521.

Robbins, Louise S. "Fighting McCarthyism through Film: A Library Censorship Case Becomes a *Storm Center*." *Journal of Education for Library and Information Science* 39, no. 4 (1998): 291–311.

_____. "Racism and Censorship in Cold War Oklahoma: The Case of Ruth W. Brown and the Bartelsville Public Library." *Southwestern Historical Quarterly* 100, no. 1 (1996): 18–46.

Rothman, Mary Yust. "There's Figures in Them Dewey Decimals or, Hi Ho, Silver Screen." *Wilson Library Bulletin* 21 (December 1946): 296, 298.

Schatz, Thomas. *Boom and Bust: The American Cinema in the 1940s*. Vol. 6, *History of the American Cinema*. New York: Charles Scribner's Sons, 1997.

_____. *The Genius of the System: Hollywood Filmmaking in the Studio Era*. New York: Henry Holt and Company, 1988.

Schiffer, Nancy. *Eyeglass Retrospective: Where Fashion Meets Science*. Atglen, Pa.: Schiffer Publishing Ltd., 2000.

Schmidt, Steven J. "The Depiction of Libraries, Librarians and the Book Arts in Film and Television." *Indiana Libraries* 15, no. 2 (1996): 15–56.

_____. "Film Librarian." Indiana University–Purdue University Indianapolis University Library. Available at http://www.FilmLibrarian.info.

Sheldon, Edward. Typescript of *The Song of Songs: A Love Story*. Based upon the novel by Hermann Sudermann. 1914. New York Public Library for the Performing Arts.

Sigoloff, Marc. *The Films of the Seventies: A Filmography of American, British and Canadian Films 1970–1979*. Jefferson, N.C.: McFarland & Company, Inc., 1984.

Simon, Jane. "The Construction of Femininity in Discourses of the Woman Librarian: 1890s to 1940s." *Australian Library Journal* (November 1994): 257–71.

Slide, Anthony. *Early Women Directors*. South Brunswick and New York: A. S. Barnes and Co., 1977.

"Special Service Section on Bryant Washburn in *A Very Good Young Man*." *Motion Picture News*, 5 July 1919, 365.

"Splendid Human Interest in Initial F. B. Warren Release." Review of *The Blot*. *Wid's Daily*, 21 August 1921, 2.

Tanner, Clarabel. "The Model Librarian." *Wilson Library Bulletin* 36 (March 1962): 545–47.

Thomajan, Dale. "The Best High School Movie [*Margie*]." *Film Comment* 28, no. 4 (July-August 1992): 79.

_____. *From Cyd Charisse to Psycho*. New York: Walker and Company, 1992.

Thomas, A. E. *Only 38*. New York: Samuel French, 1922.

Thomas, Sam, ed. *Best American Screenplays 2: Complete Screenplays*. New York: Crown Publishers, Inc., 1990.

Tidden, Fritz. Review of *The Freeze Out. Moving Picture World*, 19 April 1921, 628.

TV Guide. http://www.tvguide.com.

Variety Film Reviews. 16 vols. New York: Garland Publishing, 1983–87.

Variety Film Reviews. 7 vols. New York: R. R. Bowker, 1988–95.

Vaughn, Stephen, "Morality and Entertainment: The Origins of the Motion Picture Production Code." *The Journal of American History* 77 (June 1990): 39–65.

Walker, Stephen, and V. Lonnie Lawson. "The Librarian Stereotype and the Movies." *MC Journal: The Journal of Academic Media Librarianship* 1, no. 1 (Spring 1993): 16–28.

Widdemer, Margaret. *The Rose-Garden Husband*. New York: Grosset & Dunlap, 1915.

____. *The Wishing-Ring Man*. New York: A. L. Burt Company, 1917.

Wiebe, Gerhart. "The Image: Its Definition and Measurement." *Library Journal* 85, no. 11 (June 1960): 2092–97.

Wilson, Pauline. *Stereotype and Status: Librarians in the United States*. Westport, Conn.: Greenwood Press, 1982.

Index

Numbers in **bold italics** represent photographs.